Murals and Tourism

T0304172

Around the world, tourists are drawn to visit murals painted on walls. Whether heritage asset, legacy leftover, or contested art space, the mural is more than a simple tourist attraction or accidental aspect of tourism material culture. They express something about the politics, heritage and identity of the locations being visited, whether a medieval fresco in an Italian church, or modern political art found in Belfast or Tehran.

This interdisciplinary and highly international book explores tourism around murals that are either evolving or have transitioned as instruments of politics, heritage and identity. It explores the diverse messaging of these murals: their production, interpretation, marketing and – in some cases – destruction. It argues that the mural is more than a simple tourist attraction or accidental aspect of tourism material culture.

Murals and Tourism will be valuable reading for those interested in cultural geography, tourism, heritage studies and the visual arts.

Jonathan Skinner is Reader in Social Anthropology in the Department of Life Sciences, University of Roehampton, UK.

Lee Jolliffe is Professor of Hospitality and Tourism in the Faculty of Business at the University of New Brunswick, Canada.

Heritage, Culture and Identity
Series editor: Brian Graham
University of Ulster, UK

This series explores all notions of heritage – including social and cultural heritage, the meanings of place and identity, multiculturalism, management and planning, tourism, conservation and the built environment – at all scales from the global to the local. Although primarily geographical in orientation, it is open to other disciplines such as anthropology, history, cultural studies, planning, tourism, architecture/conservation, and local governance and cultural economics.

For a full list of titles in this series, please visit

www.routledge.com/Heritage-Culture-and-Identity/book-series/
ASHSER-1231

World Heritage Sites and Tourism
Global and Local Relations
*Edited by Laurent Bourdeau, Maria Gravari-Barbas
and Mike Robinson*

Heritage, Conservation and Communities
Engagement, Participation and Capacity Building
Edited by Gill Chitty

The Amusement Park
History, Culture and the Heritage of Pleasure
Edited by Jason Wood

Murals and Tourism
Heritage, Politics and Identity
Edited by Jonathan Skinner and Lee Jolliffe

UNESCO and World Heritage
National Contexts, International Dynamics
Edited by Casper Andersen and Irena Kozymka

Murals and Tourism

Heritage, Politics and Identity

**Edited by Jonathan Skinner
and Lee Jolliffe**

Routledge
Taylor & Francis Group

LONDON AND NEW YORK

First published 2017 by Routledge

2 Park Square, Milton Park, Abingdon, Oxfordshire OX14 4RN
52 Vanderbilt Avenue, New York, NY 10017

Routledge is an imprint of the Taylor & Francis Group, an informa business

First issued in paperback 2018

British Library Cataloguing-in-Publication Data
A catalogue record for this book is available from the British
Library

Library of Congress Cataloging-in-Publication Data
A catalog record for this book has been requested

ISBN: 978-1-4724-6143-8 (hbk)
ISBN: 978-0-367-21894-2 (pbk)

Typeset in Times New Roman
by codeMantra

Contents

Illustrations

Figures

Tables

Contributors

Virginia Santamarina Campos has a degree in Fine Arts from the Universitat Politècnica de València (Spain, 1999) and has been a visiting researcher in Uruguay, Italy and Mexico. She gained her PhD on Conservation and Restoration of the Historic-Artistic Heritage (2003) from UPV. She is the recipient of a National Award by the Ministry of Education, Culture and Sports and is Associate Professor at the UPV, Department of Conservation and Restoration of Cultural Heritage, mural art area. Currently, she is the coordinator of the Research micro-cluster VLC/CAMPUS "Globalization, tourism and heritage". She has conducted international R&D projects and contracts supported by public and private organizations.

Lorenzo Cantoni is full professor at USI, Università della Svizzera Italiana (Lugano–Switzerland), Faculty of Communication Sciences, and Director of the Institute for Communication Technologies and Scientific Director of the laboratories webatelier.net, NewMinE Lab: New Media in Education Lab, and eLab: eLearning Lab. L. Cantoni is chair-holder of the UNESCO Chair in ICT to develop and promote sustainable tourism in World Heritage Sites, established at USI, and President of IFITT – International Federation for Information Technologies in Travel and Tourism. His research interests are where communication, education and new media overlap, ranging from computer-mediated communication to usability, from eLearning to eTourism, and from ICT4D to eGovernment.

Eva Martínez Carazo has a degree in Fine Arts from the University of the Basque Country (Spain, 2009) and a Master's degree in the Conservation and Restoration of the Historic-Artistic Heritage (UPV, 2011). She is developing her PhD at the UPV, Department of Conservation and Restoration of Cultural Heritage, mural art area, with professors Virginia Santamarina and María de Miguel, on the topic 'Cultural Sustainable Tourism. Museum Program of the Uruguayan Muralism of the centuries XX and XXI'. She has been a visiting researcher in Uruguay and Australia.

Siun Carden is currently Research Assistant on 'Plantation to Peace: Derry/ Londonderry as the UK's first City of Culture', a 3-year project funded by the Leverhulme Trust and based in the School of Planning, Architecture and Civil Engineering, Queen's University Belfast. Her PhD research in social anthropology looked at the reinvention of an urban neighbourhood as an Irish-language-themed tourist destination, Belfast's 'Gaeltacht Quarter'. Her research interests include tourism, cities, cultural industries and national identity.

Deborah Che is Lecturer in Tourism in the School of Business and Tourism at Southern Cross University, Australia. Deborah's research interests include arts-based economic diversification strategies, heritage tourism, agritourism, gastronomic tourism, ecotourism and human-wildlife interactions. A common theme in her research involves the interconnection between economic restructuring and shifting land uses towards a greater emphasis on tourism and recreation. In examining how culture and entertainment has been used to foster tourism development and to revitalize cities such as Detroit that are impacted by globalization and depopulation, she has collaborated with Detroit environmental artist Tyree Guyton who created the internationally known, open-air art and community Heidelberg Project as well as researched and published on how techno music, tied to the city's Fordist automotive heritage and post-Fordist deindustrialization and flexible production, has fueled local entrepreneurship, a global industry and a festival that draws international visitors to the genre's Detroit birthplace. She is on the editorial board of *Tourism Geographies* and has served as Chair of the Recreation, Tourism and Sport specialty group of the Association of American Geographers.

Martín M. Checa-Artasu is a full-time research professor in the Department of Sociology at the Autonomous Metropolitan University, Iztapalapa. Recently, he has been editor of the following books: *Sacred Architectures at Contemporary Mexico* (2014); *Landscape and territory: Theoretical and Empirical Linkages* (2014); and *Other Mexican Citie: Urbanization Processes Forgotten* (2014).

D'Arcy Dornan was an invited researcher with the Centro Nacional de Desenvolvimento Cientifico e Technologico, Universidade de São Paulo. He also sits on the Research and Education Council of The International Ecotourism Society and works as the Knowledge Management Director for the World Institute for Action Learning Brazil. Dr. Dornan completed his PhD research while at the University of California, Davis, where he specialized in sustainable tourism planning, development and management. He has research and teaching interests in food, drink, travel and hospitality, sense of place, cultural resource management, and the environmental and sociocultural impacts of tourism. He has conducted research on gastronomic tourism, sociocultural impacts of tourism, tourism policy and development, tourism and hospitality education management, tourism development, and peace and hospitality HR management issues in luxury hotels.

Angela C. Flecha is a full professor of Marketing Tourism and researcher at NUPETUR (The Research and Advanced Studies Tourism Group) and Events Studies Group. She worked and served as Event and Tourism consultant in both private and public sector organizations. She played a part in organizing the mega event Rio'92 (ECO'92) and has in her curricula more than 70 other medium and great events. She has a master's degree and PhD in Production Engineering and has extensive experience in marketing, and as a teacher and researcher. Dr. Flechas's research interests include Tourism Network, Destination Marketing Tourism, Tourist Behaviors and Sustainable Tourism Planning & Development.

Warwick Frost is Associate Professor in Tourism at La Trobe University, Australia. His research interests include sports history and tourism, environmental history, tourism and the media and regional heritage. With Jennifer Laing, he is the co-author of four research books, and he is a convener of the International Tourism and Media biennial conference series.

Gareth E. Hamilton is acting assistant professor in the Department of Anthropology at the University of Latvia in Riga. He completed his PhD at the University of Durham in the UK on the rhetoric of personhood among the self-employed in eastern Germany. His interests lie in economic anthropology, personhood and rhetoric, as well as cat-human relations. In this latter area, as a member of the University of Latvia Centre for Public Anthropology, he recently collaborated with Danish film director Jon Bang-Carlsen on the film 'Cats in Riga', shown at various European documentary film festivals and created as part of European Capital of Culture 2014 project *Force majeure*.

Lee Jolliffe is Professor of Hospitality and Tourism in the Faculty of Business at the University of New Brunswick, Canada. She has interests in heritage tourism, culinary tourism, and heritage management and hospitality. She was a founding member of the editorial board for the *Journal of Heritage Tourism* and is a member of the editorial board of *Annals of Tourism Research* where she is the Resource Editor for museums. She is editor of *Tea and Tourism: Tourists, Traditions, Transformations* (2007) and *Coffee Culture, Destinations and Tourism* (2010), and co-editor of *Mining Heritage and Tourism: A Global Synthesis* (2010).

Cristina Jönsson is a Lecturer in Tourism Management at the University of the West Indies – Cave Hill Campus in Barbados. She has worked and served as a consultant in both private and public sector organizations in different countries. As a polyglot mastering seven languages, Cristina has added richly to international projects and research as well as translation and interpretation. Dr. Jönsson's research interests include Foreign Direct Investment (FDI) in Tourism, Sports Tourism, Medical Tourism, Sustainable Planning & Development and Tourism Motivation.

Pamela Karimi is an Associate Professor of Art History at the University of Massachusetts Dartmouth. She is the author of *Domesticity and Consumer Culture in Iran* (2013) and co-editor of *Images of the Child and Childhood in Modern Muslim Contexts* (2012). Karimi is the cofounder of Aggregate Architectural History Collaborative and serves on the board of the Association of Modern and Contemporary Art of the Arab World, Iran, and Turkey. At present, she is working on a second monograph exploring the spatial dimensions of the 'underground' in Iran.

Jennifer Laing is a Senior Lecturer in Management at La Trobe University, Australia. Her research interests include travel narratives, tourism and the media and regional heritage. With Warwick Frost, she is the co-author of four research books, and she is a convener of the International Tourism and Media biennial conference series.

Paula Larruscahim is a PhD candidate of the Erasmus Mundus Doctorate in Cultural and Global Criminology (DCGC) with an MA in Criminal Sciences from the Pontific Catholic University of Rio Grande do Sul (PUC-RS). Currently, she conducts research that focuses on the relationship between urban visual interventions, criminal control, social policies and socio-spatial segregation. More specifically, she investigates how transgression and resistance are shaped in the particular political and historical context of Latin America by exploring the process that has led to the simultaneous criminalization of Brazilian street-writing subculture "Pixação" and the domestication and commodification of graffiti.

Blanca de Miguel Molina has an economics degree from Universitat de València (1991, Spain), an International MBA from Ford-Anglia Ruskin University-UPV (1996), an MA in Business Administration from Anglia Ruskin University, UK (1998), and a PhD in Business Administration from Universitat Politècnica de València (2003). She is currently Associate Professor at the Management Department, Universitat Politècnica de València. Her main research is on innovation in creative and cultural industries, corporate community involvement, scientometrics.

María de Miguel Molina has a law degree from Universitat de València (1996, Spain) and a PhD in Business Administration from Universitat Politècnica de València (2003). She is currently Associate Professor at the Management Department, Universitat Politècnica de València, where she is Head of Studies at the Management School. Her main research concerns in the public sector, public policies, public management and inclusive policies. She is also Visiting Professor at the Lakehead University, Canada, and University of California, Berkeley, USA.

Plácido Muñoz Morán has recently completed a PhD in Social Anthropology with Visual Media at the University of Manchester, UK. He has a special interest in the study of visuality, social movements, artistic practices and the city with particular reference to participatory and collaborative anthropology research and the use of audio-visual means.

Marta Pucciarelli is a PhD candidate at USI (Università della Svizzera Italiana), Faculty of Communication Sciences and a scientific collaborator at the Laboratory of Visual Culture at SUPSI – Scuola universitaria professionale della Svizzera Italiana in Lugano. She hold a bachelor's degree in Communication and Management of Art and Culture at IULM University in Milan (2005–2008), and a master's degree in Technology-Enhanced Communication for Cultural Heritage (2009–2011) at the USI. She worked as an ethnographer in Douala for the project Mobile Access to Knowledge. Her research interests interweave the role of ICTs with art, education and urban studies in developing countries.

Katy Radford is the Senior Researcher and qualified Mediator and Trainer working at the Institute for Conflict Research, Belfast. She was awarded an MBE in 2011 for her community relations work. She writes on a range of issues relating to social inclusion and has a particular focus on the arts and media. She has been commissioned locally and internationally by statutory service providers, government departments and arms' length bodies to deliver transformation and intervention programmes within segregated communities.

Paul Schweizer studied urban geography at Goethe-University Frankfurt, Universidade do Porto (UP) and Universidade de São Paulo (USP). Currently, he is completing the master's programme in Geographies of Globalization at the Institute for Human Geography at Goethe, University Frankfurt. His research interests include urban policies regulating visual interventions in São Paulo's public space, practices of graffiti and the right to the city, as well as postcolonial perspectives on urban development in Latin America. He is a fellow of the Graffiti Archive at Archive of Youth Cultures e.V., Berlin (http://www.graffitiarchiv.org/).

Maria T. Simone-Charteris is a Lecturer in Travel and Tourism Management at Ulster University, Northern Ireland, where she teaches at undergraduate as well as postgraduate level. Her research interests focus on pilgrimage and religious tourism; dark and political tourism; peace and reconciliation through tourism; food and wine tours and festivals; and slow travel and tourism. Maria is completing a PhD on the potential interconnections between religious and political tourism in Northern Ireland and is an Associate Fellow of the Higher Education Academy (AFHEA).

Jonathan Skinner is Reader in Social Anthropology in the Department of Life Sciences, University of Ropehampton, UK. He has interests in niche tourism, social dancing and arts health and has undertaken research in the Caribbean, US, UK and Northern Ireland. He is author of *Before the Volcano: Reverberations of Identity on Montserrat* (1994), editor of *Writing the Dark Side of Travel* (2012), and co-editor of *Dancing Cultures: Globalization, Tourism and Identity in the Anthropology of Dance* (2012) and *Great Expectations: Imagination, Anticipation, and Enchantment in Tourism* (2011).

Russell Staiff holds a doctorate in art history from the University of Melbourne and is an adjunct fellow in the cultural heritage and tourism program within the School of Social Sciences and Psychology, Western Sydney University, and an adjunct professorial fellow in the architectural heritage and tourism program in the Faculty of Architecture, Silpakorn University, Bangkok. His research interests are two fold: (1) the various intersections between cultural heritage, communities and tourism with a particular emphasis on Southeast Asia; and (2) heritage as a socio-cultural phenomenon. He has recently co-edited a volume on Heritage and Tourism for Routledge, and his monograph, *Re-Imagining Heritage Interpretation: Enchanting the Past/Future*, was published in early 2014. Also in 2014, he co-edited two volumes *Travel and Imagination* and *Travel and Transformation*. Another co-edited volume *Travel and Representation: Past, Present, Future* is in press.

Rebecca Yeo worked in the disability sector for many years, at first in an international development context, later in the UK and more recently focusing on the needs and experiences of disabled asylum seekers in the UK. She is keen to use research methods which respect the value of lived experience and contribute to a process of social change. She believes that murals used as research tools have the potential to meet these criteria. She is currently a doctoral student at the University of Bath, exploring constructions of worth and entitlement in the UK, and particularly looking at the experiences of disabled asylum seekers.

Preface

As editors, our experiences with murals and resultant viewpoints of them are quite different, both personally and academically.

Lee Jolliffe has visited a number of towns in Canada where murals have been used as a means of urban regeneration and economic development through tourism, including Bell Island, Newfoundland; Chemainus in British Columbia; and Sussex in New Brunswick, the latter being quite near to where she lives and teaches today. Lee did a case study of the murals in Bell Island, Newfoundland, looking at the murals as part of a broader study of cultural tourism. The findings of this study were that the murals of the people of Bell Island and its mining heritage were constructed as much to celebrate local heritage and revitalize the spirits of the Bell Islanders living in an economically depressed area as to be a resource for tourism (Jolliffe and Baum, 2001). Prior to this study, she had visited the Chemainus Mural Project, born out of economic aims to regenerate the town, but today, it is promoted as the world's leading example of a murals town and a blueprint for community murals projects globally. In Sussex, New Brunswick, Lee has followed a local mural project, inspired by the success of the Chemainus project, through its establishment and growth to the point where this small town promotes itself as 'The Mural Capital of Atlantic Canada'. There are now a total of 26 murals in this small town with a population of just over 4,000 (see our Introduction for more).

With a background in museum studies and tourism, Lee is interested in how murals projects are developed and managed, becoming the focus for visitation. From a museum perspective, she seeks to understand how the murals can be seen as 'museums without walls' and how they might differ in terms of both management and viewing from murals in traditional indoor institutional settings such as museums and galleries. From a tourism perspective, she is curious about the ways they (re)represent heritage and are being utilized to celebrate local identities and histories and to develop a destinations' unique qualities that differentiate one locale from another. As a Visiting Professor to Queen's University Belfast, she began to investigate the evolution of the Belfast murals and their use for tourism.

Jonathan Skinner also has an active academic and personal interest in murals. He is a social anthropologist who lived and worked in Northern Ireland from 2003 to 2013. His daily commute passed a series of religious exhortations on the sides of barns, and past largely protestant murals expressing allegiance to various paramilitary organizations (see Skinner 2017). At Queen's University Belfast, Jonathan trained students in an anthropological perspective: his anthropology of tourism students toured Belfast's muralscape with local tour guides and looked at the construction of the tourist gaze. At home, his neighbours were involved in post-conflict initiatives to depoliticize and 're-image' (Hill and White 2012) their sectarian activities from murals to bonfires and parades. During his recreational time, he often socialized and danced in nationalist quarters, passing the international wall of murals along the Falls Road and commemorative murals to Bobby Sands and other celebrated figures. His vacations were not without murals, such as those found in the Sardinian hilltown of Orgosolo – murals embedded into the architecture of the town (see our Introduction for more).

Before working in Northern Ireland, Jonathan's fieldsite was the British Overseas Territory Montserrat in the Eastern Caribbean. There, Jonathan examined colonial/postcolonial expressions of identity through the arts, from carnival parades and calypso social commentaries to performance poetry and the organization of local heritage events such as the commemoration of a failed slave insurrection on St Patrick's Day, 1768. Looking back

Figure 0.1 Celebrating 40 years of Carnival on Montserrat.
Source: 2002, J. Skinner, 2005.

to those visits, Montserratians used murals along roads to convey messages from environmental protection to healthcare. They also used these points of view to celebrate their present and to commemorate their past. With few main roads, it was easy to use an artery to circulate a message, reinforcing the words with identifiable images such as traditional carnival figures.

These two authors, with their differing experiences and perspectives of murals, were brought together when Skinner hosted Jolliffe as a Visiting Professor at Queen's University Belfast, Northern Ireland. A shared interest in murals, especially in terms of heritage issues, reflections and expressions, and instruments of communication about places that change over time, and related research work on the Belfast murals resulted in the proposal for the current edited volume. The call for contributions for this volume resulted in submissions across a number of disciplines, with responses from scholars with backgrounds in anthropology, geography, heritage studies, heritage management, history, leisure, museum studies and tourism representing a number of global locations where murals exist and are visited, including of course Northern Ireland and also Europe, Africa, the Middle East, North America and South America. We hope you enjoy reading the resulting dialogue that explores a number of key themes regarding both the creation of and visitation to murals.

References

Hill, Andrew and Andrew White. 2012. 'Painting Peace? Murals and the Northern Ireland Peace Process', *Irish Political Studies* 27(1): 71–88.

Jolliffe, Lee and Tom Baum. 2001. *Directions in Cultural Tourism: The Case of Four North Atlantic Islands*. Charlottetown: Institute of Island Studies.

Skinner, Jonathan. 2017. '"On the Face of It": Wall-to-Wall Home Ethnography', in Molina, María and Virginia SantaMarina (Eds), *Conservation, Tourism and Identity of Contemporary Community Art*. New Jersey: Apple Academic Press, forthcoming.

Acknowledgements

The authors appreciate the support of the University of New Brunswick's Fredrik and Catherine Eaton Visitorship to Queen's University Belfast as well as of Queen's University Belfast for hosting Lee Jolliffe's Visitorship. We are also grateful to the University of Roehampton for its support for this volume with its generous research leave practice. Last but by no means least, we thank the willing and patient group of academic colleagues and contributors, and publication professionals, who have made this volume possible.

Part I

Introduction

1 'Wall-to-wall coverage'

An introduction to murals tourism

Jonathan Skinner and Lee Jolliffe

Art this bold won't stay indoors.
—Chemainus Festival of Murals Society

The quote above could apply to many situations around the world where murals are painted on outdoor walls. While the motivations for painting murals may be different, ranging from personal expressions of the artists, to political messages, to enhancement of a destination's tourist appeal, murals are a form of public art that is accessible to all who walk by them. We suggest, then, in this volume that *murals matter*. They are bold, imaginative, revolutionary, emblematic and visionary; they inspire, inform, confront and overshadow the viewer. Murals have compound meanings, often reflecting upon or communicating aspects of the heritage, politics and/or identity of a place. In this introductory chapter, we review in detail why murals matter and then examine the relation of murals to their three themes of heritage, politics and identity that frame the investigation of visiting murals within this volume. This is followed by an introduction to the organization and contributed contents of the volume. In a final section, we conclude by briefly discussing the contributing chapters in the book.

Why murals matter

Chemainus, noted above as a murals destination, is a small town numbering about 3,000 in population (as of 2011) located on Vancouver Island, British Columbia (Canada). Dependent upon the sawmill industry, the community came together in the early 1980s when their sole industry went into decline with a loss of employment due to mechanization of the mill. To counter the economic downturn and to diversify community dependence, the local community response was to develop an art tourism experience about the town (Barnes and Hayter 1992). They saturated the town with forty-two community history images on the sides of buildings, developing the blank canvas of a side or gable end into an attractive eye-catching feature. This 'al fresco gallery' gained the town some 400,000 annual tourists, sustains over

300 small businesses and points to the town's sobriquet: 'The Little Town That Did'. The international recognition of the unique collection of murals that represent the history of the town is now seen as one of the strengths of the region in terms of the development of art- and culture-related tourism (Community Tourism Foundations Programme 2010). Furthermore, the murals of Chemainus have provided a development model and example of employing nostalgia-related murals' subjects that has been pursued by other small towns across Canada, such as in Sussex, New Brunswick (Canada), that now promotes itself of as 'The Mural Capital of Atlantic Canada' (Sussex Murals, n.d.). The example of the mural on Sharps Drugs in Sussex shows how a contemporary mural superimposed on a historic building and complimentary to the heritage neon sign brings alive the long history and importance of this business to the town (Historic places.ca 2007) (Figure 1.1).

Figure 1.1 Mural on Sharps drugs store, Sussex.
Source: L. Jolliffe, 2016.

Seeing a mural, growing up under its gaze, viewing a piece of outside art, is different from looking at an art in a gallery. Murals are a form of public art that can be viewed at all times and from many different physical viewpoints in the context of the urban environments of towns and cities. Forming 'open air' galleries of art, murals can be viewed without the constraint of visitor fees and gallery hours and therefore have a very large audience. Murals hence have a broad appeal as popular art and are accessible, so it is not a surprise that they have become assets for the development of heritage-related tourism. They can regenerate or reanimate a dead zone created by walls, or soften a boundary wall or divide such as the Berlin Wall. They are also used, deliberately, to create a readable, marketable public space – recall the iconic colour and fonts of 'Drink Coca Cola' campaigns that now fade across the walls of US streets. Where Silberman, Till and Ward (2012, 17) write of the wall as border that fulfils our dehumanizing territorial imperatives, it is the mural that humanizes and lives up to our imagination. It brings colour and sometimes a little chaos to the uniform anonymity and regularity of a brick wall. It adds features and expression to that face, depending upon the nature of the wall (brick, concrete, wood, mud). Its signification can shift too, from revolutionary art to official culture (cf. Coffey 2012, 178) and national acclaim for one's *patria* for Mexican muralism: the great populist and indigenist iconography and revolutionary realism of Diego Rivera in the 1920s repurchased as expression of modern Foucauldian governmental power in the Palacio Nacional de Mexico, Mexico City, for example. The changing networks of signification and reception in the murals of Belfast would be another (see below and Lisle 2006).

Moreover, murals can inform and educate with warnings about HIV/ AIDS across South Africa (Marschall 2004). They can warn of the afterlife such as the sixteenth-century Biblical frescoes on the exterior walls of monasteries in Moldavia, Romania, now UNESCO world heritage sites in their own rights. They can signal ideological commitment, solidarity and social identification from Belfast and Berlin to Tehran, Havana and Managua. David Kunzle's *The Murals of Revolutionary Nicaragua 1979–1992* (1995) proves an excellent starting point with detailed case/ material of Nicaragua's late-twentieth-century mural movement that both provided and showed support for the country's Sandinista popular revolution. The murals became an adjunct to the revolution, a form of visual language: defiant, transformative and internationalist. Though often now deleted, painted over by neo-fascists (Kunzle 1995, 21), defaced, ignored, at their heights – both literal and figurative – these murals exemplified citizens taking power into their own hands. Brigades of artists painted for the movement, with support – mural aid – coming from volunteers from the USA, Europe and other countries in Latin America. A Mural School founded by Italian artist Sergio Michilini institutionalized this development of the plastic arts across the country. Religious and postcolonial symbolic imagery, primitivism, indigeneity and jungle themes, Utopian and 'magical realism', historical and worker iconography and expressionism were all used to reframe contemporary identity debates on the walls of Nicaragua. *The Dream of Bolívar* was 100 metres long, a public mural in the centre of Managua sponsored by the army and painted by Chilean artists Victor Canifrú and Alejandra Acuña. It honoured Bolívar as a leader and the freedom he inspired through hyperreal magnified images. It depicted a nation and a continent gaining independence through political struggle and industriousness. The mural lasted from 1983 to 1990/1991. Kunzle (1995, 51) describes it as 'an epic that situated the revolution as the culmination of a while Latin American history of struggle for freedom, with Simon Bolívar as the pivot'. The murals movement that swept across Nicaragua de-alienated the members of this grassroots democracy; Kunzle (1995, 40) suggests that the voluntaristic nature of this mass participation in the murals made it decidedly 'moral'. Muralists created public art for a purpose, for social commentary and social action. The work captured the zeitgeist moment or set the scene for local and national developments and so was left to dry on the walls, not defaced or graffitied over (Kunzle 1995, 64).

In terms of expressions on walls, Kunzle (1995, 64) suggests that mural painting lies at one end of a continuum with graffiti placed at the other end. Spray-can art falls in-between. This suggests that murals (with their image-based focus) contrast with graffiti (with the name- and character-based focus). The one is legal, acceptable and authorized; the other effectively rebellious, typically subversive and equating with vandalism; in terms of legislation, graffiti is uncommissioned 'nuisance' that many civic ordinances such as in the USA require the property owner to clean up (Mettler 2012, 257). Both are dubious arts, as Norman Foster and his team (Foster *et al.* 2003) found, unearthing and displaying Soviet graffiti on the Nazi Reichtag dating from the end of World War II. And yet, both are forms of 'landscape expression' (Moreau and Alderman 2011).

'Banksy' biographer Will Ellsworth-Jones (2012, 37) writes, however, that graffiti can in fact be a way out of vandalism. It is redemptive in turning actors towards the arts, and their works are no less murals for the materials (from stencil to aerosol) used in their production. This puts Banksy, with his satirical anthropomorphic rats, ironically smiling policemen, and saboutaged signposts and CCTV cameras, into the muralist category despite his sharp stencil designs. His work sits alongside the vivid street art of US graphic activist Shepard Fairey and the progressive stencil posters that change over time by Italians Sten and Lex. An ideological tourist attraction and international political commentary came from Banksy and his team's 2005 visit to Israel and subsequent series of trompe d'œil images 'hacking' the monstrous 425-mile-long barrier that separates Israel from the Palestinian territories (Parry 2005). They imagine gaps and breaks in the wall; a vision of the other side. As such, the images allow us to imagine an alternative social order and possibilities for different political relations.

In a world of walls, imagining a world without them, clearly seeing that kind of world in our imagination may, in some cases, lead us to see it in reality (Murakami 2014). The writer Haruki Murakami paints with the words in his novels but has the same objective as Banksy. Here, murals and novels engage the imagination in the same way. Banksy's concrete canvas in the Middle East – first daubed the 'Window on the West Bank' (Jones 2005) – was extended to Gaza in 2015 with a series of satirical travel advert murals to show sympathy for the 62 children who were killed by Israeli bombardment and destruction of some 18,000 Palestinian homes. Concrete is this artist's canvas whether monolithic block or obliterated chip off the old block. The wall – an impediment and boundary marker establishing territory on either side of it – becomes co-opted in a new expression of territoriality, namely one with verticality to it (cf. Brighenti 2009).

Murals have also very often become symbols of places, as with the murals of Detroit, USA, or of Northern Ireland or Orgosolo, Sardinia. Although the historic murals depicting Detroit industry painted in the 1930s by the Mexican artist Diego Rivera are indoors, at the Detroit Institute of Arts, outdoor murals are today part of the rejuvenation of the city. Such murals offer hope to residents of priority neighbourhoods where, to give an example, one project created murals on the walls of elementary schools (Rhea 2004). In Northern Ireland, due to the large number of murals there, it has been observed that Belfast and Derry/Londonderry could be the most famous murals destinations in Europe (Rolston 2010a). The political murals may be viewed as forming part of dark or political tourism (Simone-Charteris and Boyd 2010) and also reflective of the politics of community heritage (Crooke 2010). This is not always the case, however, as the meaning of murals can change over time, along with the community's identification with them. The development of the murals through Orgosolo shows a shift from political expression along the lines of resistance, war and internationalism (Rolston 2014) by left-wing artist and art teacher Francesco Del Casino in the late 1960s to contemporary satire, art competition and tourist commoditization in the past two decades. Anthropologist Tracey Heatherington (2002, 19) suggests that the murals have come to represent different identity narratives as though a form of structural nostalgia has taken place for the protests of old; the murals signify an idealized Orgosolo community that was at once exclusive and isolated, proud and independent; critics contend that this is the opportunistic imposition of an outsider's leftist agenda on the town (Rolston 2014, 83). This is how art becomes, according to Francesca Cozzolino who examined the production and heritagization of the murals between the 1960s and the 1990s. Such 'artification' leads to an 'anesthetization' of the politics surrounding their production (Cozzolino 2014, 175). The collective artwork nature of the unsigned original murals has been lost for newer individualized pieces mapped and labelled in tourist guide books. All

Figure 1.2 Mother teaching children about the Israel/Palestine conflict in Gaza through Orgosolo mural.
Source: J. Skinner, 2014.

are now protected by the municipality in defence of the burgeoning tourist trade. Gone is the grey tourism industry, diluted down from the kidnapping experiences or lunches with partisans, bandits and shepherds to posing for a selfie before one's choice *cause célèbre* (Figure 1.2).

Whether viewed as heritage asset, legacy leftover or contested art space, outdoor murals are complex and each is more than a simple tourist attraction or accidental aspect of material culture. Cultural tourists experiencing murals may be unintentional visitors, not planning to visit but nonetheless viewing murals, or intentional visitors, choosing to visit in order to view a mural or a series of murals, or to participate in a murals tourism experience. At many locations, murals have been linked together into tours, either as additional means for groups to get their political message across or just as tourism product and activity. The former has happened with well-known mural destinations such as Belfast and Derry (Londonderry) in Northern Ireland, and the latter with lesser-known locales. In Winnipeg, Manitoba (Canada), a tour of the murals commemorating the ethnic and cultural diversity of the west end of the city is offered daily during the summer tourist season providing an additional heritage tourism experience (Tourism Winnipeg 2016). The website promoting these murals tours states, "Murals are more than just a colourful piece of art painted on a wall. Murals are a great asset for the neighbourhood" (West End Business Improvement Zone 2016). Murals, therefore, not only take art out of the gallery setting, but they also bring them down to the community level where, as public art, they form part of the everyday life of residents. This sense of community embodied in an area's expression on walls is an important theme in the study of murals.

Murals located outdoors reflect a long tradition of mural painting, originating indoors, for example, in the churches and public buildings of the Renaissance period. Today's murals located outside are fragile works of popular art, as weather can be quite damaging to these expressions on walls. There is consequently often a need to restore them, or when the damage is beyond repair, or the message no longer deemed viable (by state entities) or indeed acceptable politically, many murals are just painted over with a new mural, as has often happened with the murals of Northern Ireland (Rolston 1970). The walls upon which some murals are painted also serve as barriers, between the inside and the outside of buildings and, in some cases, between geographic or secular areas of a town or city, as with the murals in Belfast, Northern Ireland along the parallel Falls and Shankhill Roads. Being outside and accessible, these works of art on walls have, as a result, become a heritage resource for the development of murals-related tourism.

Both the development of murals projects with touristic objectives and the bundling of existing murals not painted for the purposes of tourism have resulted in a niche form of cultural heritage tourism identified in this volume as 'murals tourism'. This form of niche tourism specifically consists of visiting locations and destinations with murals. A variety of organized murals tourism products have been developed for consumption, ranging from both guided and self-guided murals tours to murals festivals to murals souvenirs such as postcards, books and t-shirts. The small town of Chemainus, British Columbia (Canada), is our ideal example above of a place that has promoted the murals tourism movement with workshops, festivals and the establishment of the Global Mural Arts and Cultural Tourism Association.

The subject matter and content of murals may include heritage (images of the past), political messages, advertising messages and/or signage, and artistic and satirical images. It is therefore evident that the painting of murals has a variety of motivations to it, some of which may overlap, as in the case of individual murals (Table 1.1). For example, murals classified as political may become economic if through commodification they are used for the various forms of murals tourism. A primary example of this phenomenon is the use of the political murals in Belfast, Northern Ireland, for the development of a tourism product in the form of walking tours that include the murals (Skinner 2016; see also Brunn *et al.* 2010).

Around the world, visitors are therefore drawn to visit murals painted on walls that express something about the heritage and/or the politics that

Table 1.1 Typology of murals by motivation

Type	Motivation	Example
Economic	Development, beautification, urban revitalization	Murals in murals towns and on murals routes and trails
Political	Messaging, expression of political views and positions	Murals in conflict areas, murals as resistance, murals as part of election campaigns
Commemoration	Commemoration of events and people	Murals painted at a specific time to commemorate individual persons and events significant to the locale
Commercial	Promotion, advertising of goods and services	Murals on commercial buildings or in other locations carrying a commercial message
Artistic	Expression by artists	Graffiti

make up the identity of the locations being visited. The heritage theme of the volume is further explored below.

Heritage theme

From a heritage perspective, murals represent an accessible and popular form of the expression of local characteristics and identities. Unlike the painted murals in art galleries that often require an admission fee, the paintings on walls are accessible to whoever passes by them, and in many cases (as in Belfast, Northern Ireland) as a group they can be viewed as a kind of an outdoor art gallery. As a form of public art, the content of murals is less curated than that which is presented in museums and art galleries: outdoor murals can be more spontaneous, in some cases with only the artist and perhaps the owner of the wall determining the content. Where murals have been painted specifically for economic development purposes (Koster and Randall 2005), as with the Canadian examples given earlier such as Chemainus, British Columbia (Barnes and Hayter 1992), the subject matter is almost exclusively heritage focused. This occurs as communities use the murals as a means of expressing the past histories and interesting facets of their communities' heritage. Graham and Howard (2008) observed that heritage is one of the main means of establishing identity. In the case of Belfast, Graham and Whelan (2007) also examined the role of the murals in commemorating past events. Employing nostalgic heritage themes, the murals projects also therefore have the benefit of a particular locale developing a shared sense of community.

It is well known that heritage is used for place-making in tourism, and the murals movement is an interesting example of this phenomenon. A number of authors have acknowledged the power of narrative in shaping places as tourist destinations. Jamal and Hill (2004) discussed the role of place in developing authenticity in cultural and heritage tourism. It is this sense of place identity that is reflected by outdoor murals painted for various motivations. The nature of heritage at a particular place may be contested, as is often the case with former conflict sites such as those in Northern Ireland (see the final section in this volume).

Politics theme

The subject of murals can be seen as apolitical or political. Apolitical murals include heritage-themed murals painted for beautification or tourism purposes, as well as advertising murals. Political murals very often include slogans and/or symbolism in which the artist is using the mural as a means of communicating a particular viewpoint. In some cases, murals created for political purposes, to express a particular viewpoint, become a point of interest for visitors – again, the murals of Belfast, Northern Ireland, are an excellent case in point (Vannais 2012). Here, in some situations, the murals painted for political purposes are part of peace processes and related projects (Hill and White 2012). These political murals at sites of conflict are, in addition, transitioning to more secular messaging (often through government re-imaging programmes), and bundled and packaged as tourism products re-employed sometimes unintentionally, as instruments of economic development.

If the subject of murals is often political, the organized tours of them can also reflect politics. In Derry/Londonderry (Northern Ireland), tours are given by two groups: namely, The Bogside Artists and The Free Derry Museum. The Bogside Artists offer tours with one of the artists who created the twelve murals in the People's Gallery while The Free Derry Tours offers what they call 'authentic tours' that can be combined with a visit to the Free Derry Museum. Recent interviews with The Bogside Artists indicate that they feel politically discriminated against because of their claimed neutrality. Their desire is to not be co-opted into Republican politics. This has led to their work remaining unlit across the city, and to a lack of local acknowledgement as to their ability – despite their international acclaim and the iconic status of images such as the The Petrol Bomber depicting their cousin, Paddy Coyle, in the riots in the Bogside in August 1969 (painted in 1994 by Tom Kelly, Kevin Masson and William Kelly, see image) (Figure 1.3).

The Bogside Artists feel that their series of gable-end murals in Derry/Londonderry's Bogside quarter has been sidelined by the Arts Council of Northern Ireland, as well as civic and regional tourist boards that promote visits to the city's walls, Peace Bridge and other commissioned artworks. Their art transcends the parochialism of The Troubles, using their life experience growing up in this traumatic period of conflict to extraordinary effect. Their reaction is to create 'visual poetry' in their words (The Bogside Artists 2001, 47), a practice of political activism that reframes the conflict

Figure 1.3 Bogside residents viewing The Petrol Bomber: Battle of the Bogside.
Source: 1994, J. Skinner 2016.

with a vivid theatricality. Rather than mark territory in typical sectarian street fashion, their murals stand witness and commemorate insurgency, resistance, and socialism. There are twelve house-sized murals that constitute The People's Gallery, events that the artists personally lived through rather than heritage murals that they are recreating from history books. Here is the Troubles laid bare from the riots to the hunger strike. "How did he end up in this position to begin with?": in the Kellys' words, they are raising questions in the viewers' minds as to how the artists' subject, such as Paddy Coyle, got to be in that position. What prompted them? Does it happen to others and can it happen to them?

> There's different ways that people react and respond to conflict and violence and we could of went down a different road but we didn't. We decided to use art as a way of trying to make sense of the world in which we were growing up and actually be a voice for the community.
>
> (Tom Kelly interview with J. Skinner, February 25, 2016)

'Three ordinary blokes who've done an extraordinary thing' is how the artists characterize their mural work: art that has gripped their global audience; art that they have dedicated their lives to with conviction through conflict and post-conflict Northern Ireland. They have refused to compromise their work or to align themselves with the politics or politicians of the day. This lends weight to their claim that they are the authentic muralists of Northern Ireland, more so than the muralists of Belfast who are painting post-events, retrospectives on the Troubles or even glossing over it with new innocuous C.S. Lewis Narnia murals; this is despite academic Bill Rolston's (2010b, i) point that the murals tradition has been sustained since 1908 in the Loyalist community as part of their July commemoration of King William of Orange's victory in Battle of the Boyne in 1690 that secured a Protestant ascendancy. The Bogside Artists now operate out of their own studio where they display work and projects and sell posters and books about their work. This murals centre can be visited prior to or at the end of a tour of the murals themselves.

In Belfast, it is possible to take tours from groups with opposing views of the conflict (Skinner 2016). The tour guides use visits to the international wall of murals to weave a political narrative that reflects their own allegiance, although in some cases guides of the opposing tours and their groups meet briefly mid-point through the tours for a handshake and a handover. In terms of visiting murals, this political aspect of 'murals tourism' may be interpreted as either unique or more pronounced in the case of Belfast. The Bogside Artists would contest the suggestion that Belfast is the murals destination in Northern Ireland. While there are more murals around the streets, they are identifiers rather than works of art, reminders and warnings rather than imaginative alternatives. They are Unionist murals or Nationalist murals first. Public authority-commissioned work has no victims in it but also little identification with the art. When an innocuous jungle fantasy scene was commissioned across the walls of Springhill community, it was immediately disputed and defaced. Des Wilson (1983, 20) describes such external attempts to depoliticize murals as 'insipid, escapist and futile'. '[S]ymbolic war on the walls' is how Goalwin (2013, 213) characterizes this muralscape that people still want to see and live with – having lived through. He (2013, 199) makes the point that mural painting in Nationalist areas has been – and to some extent still continues to be – a critical opportunity to disseminate the Republican ideology, particularly when Republican activists have been censored in the past and banned from airing their views through the public media.

Identity theme

The medium of the mural painted on a wall provides an accessible means for the expression of local identity that can easily be communicated to both residents and visitors. There is a wide range in the relationship of murals to the identity of the places in which they are placed. In some instances, murals are painted as part of either beautification, celebration or economic development initiatives. Often with a nostalgic view to a better past, they link contemporary times to historic identities of communities; the murals in Canadian towns mentioned earlier (Chemanius, British Columbia, and Sussex, New Brunswick) present subjects harking back to the colonial pasts of both industry (sawmills, dairies) and local life (picnics). In other cases, murals are created with messages of resistance against the policies of local or even national authorities – this is particularly apparent in post-conflict environments such as the murals of Northern Ireland and South Africa (Crooke 2005).

The reflection of identity through the murals relates back to the earlier themes of both heritage and politics, as softer murals' subjects often take a nostalgic view of the communities past whereas harder murals' subjects with political viewpoints make more contemporary statements. As destinations seek to differentiate themselves from others' murals, even if not painted for touristic purposes, the murals of a place can be seen to be a public demonstration of the identity of the location and so be employed in tourism promotions. This latter phenomenon may be more common in terms of the softer nostalgic subjects portrayed than of the harder political messages, as destinations managers seek to promote the nostalgic and apolitical views (Yeh, Chen and Liu 2012).

Organization of the book

The focus of this volume is primarily on the 'visitation to murals', broadly defined as the viewing of expressions on walls. As outdoor murals are an accessible form of public art, they may either be viewed by the casual visitor who comes upon them during their exploration of urban environments or by intentional visitors viewing them as part of an organized murals tour – either using a self-guided map or guide book, or alternately accompanied by a tour guide who provides an interpretation of what is being viewed. Either way, if the visit is casual or intentional, visitors are participating in a form of 'murals tourism' that we referred to earlier, and in some cases responding to destination marketing that includes murals as forms of public art and cultural tourism activity. Within this context, the book traces the interconnecting themes of politics, heritage and identity and develops them all together in the extended section on the murals of Northern Ireland. It draws upon multidisciplinary perspectives from anthropology, geography, heritage studies, heritage management, history, leisure, museum studies, tourism, and other related disciplines, contributing new perspectives and theories related to the employment of murals for tourism. The book has six sections: Introduction, Heritage, Politics, Identity, Northern Ireland, and Conclusion.

In the Introduction, Chapter 1, by Jonathan Skinner and Lee Jolliffe, *'Wall-to-wall coverage': an introduction to murals tourism* introduces the justification behind this book project, which is to the knowledge of the editors the first one to focus on the theme of visitation to murals. As explored in this chapter, with varying motives for their creation, murals are a form of accessible public art, with broad appeal to communities, forming part of their everyday lives and identity. As a form of communication in public spaces, mural art on walls has often been used to communicate messages that are contested by the state who often respond with policies of either removal or re-imaging. However, murals convey a sense of place and, as such, have also transitioned as assets for the development of niche forms of heritage tourism including murals tourism, dark tourism and political tourism. The motives for mural creation range from political expression to commercial messaging to beautification and community improvement or economic development. Indeed, in the race for the differentiation of destinations, some murals have been created specifically with economic development in mind, making communities more attractive for tourism or known as 'murals capitals' of their own region. The contributions to this volume have been grouped in line with the themes of heritage, politics, and identity. We suggest that these themes are reflected in the creation of murals as well as their evolution over time as their functions evolve and the perceptions of them change in the eyes of both their creators, the communities where they are located, and the visitors who come to view them.

Heritage section

In the study of murals as sites to visit, heritage is a central theme. One finds that most murals reflect in some way the culture and heritage of those who construct them and the locales where they are situated. The subjects of murals may be celebratory, nostalgic, political or commercial and in certain situations some of their subject matter may be contested within communities and audiences, yet viewed by tourists as characteristic of the places visited. Visiting or viewing murals can, on a superficial level, reveal much about community heritage, while the study of their visitation – the subject of this volume – can delve into the complex layers of meanings that lie below the surfaces of these expressions on walls: in the memories of the artists who created them; of those who inherit them; of the community members who live with them on a daily basis; and of those who may visit them. Chapters 2 and 3 delve into and introduce the murals tradition by examining early murals painted and mosaics constructed on walls both inside and outside of buildings.

In the first contribution in this section (Chapter 2), *Mosaic and painted heritage murals as tourist attractions: artistic treasures, cultural identities and political statements*, authors Warwick Frost and Jennifer Laing provide a historical background to the development of painted and mosaic murals. They then proceed to consider a selection of historic European tile, mosaic and painted murals, including looking back at their political and cultural importance and considering the way in which they are interpreted to and consumed by contemporary visitors. Three comparative case studies include murals from different periods of European history: the mosaics of Ravenna, the painted churches of Moldavia and ceramic tiles in Portugal. The authors consider how these historic forms of murals reflect heritage and identity, as well as their role as public art within forms of religious tourism. It is argued that because the murals portrayed within this chapter are located in situ where they were created, they have continued meaning and authenticity for tourists as opposed to murals located in gallery settings that are viewed out of context. In terms of visitation to the murals, the authors note viewing the murals and the fascination with them as a connection to the past. They also appeal to those visiting geographic areas with concentrations of murals, collecting murals experiences, and perhaps leading to a more in-depth experience of and connection to the murals of the past.

In Chapter 3, the second contribution to this section, *From 'sacred images' to 'tourist images'? The fourteenth-century frescoes of Santa Croce, Florence*, author Russell Staiff further explores the transformation of one of the early forms of murals for mass consumption. In what will become a recurring theme within this volume, Staiff explores the contemporary touristic consumption of murals, in this case Giotto's frescoes in Santa Croce Church, created for one purpose and now being consumed for other purposes and contexts. Staiff observes that through heritage tourism the frescos have been repositioned as objects of the past that have survived and have been given new and contemporary meanings through the visitation of tourists. This reinforces the views of Frost and Laing (Chapter 2) that historic murals serve to connect visitors with the past.

The third part of this heritage section, Chapter 4, contributed by Martín M. Checa-Artasu, is entitled *The walls speak: Mexican popular graphics as heritage*. The author introduces the local Mexican traditions of painting graphics on walls, including popular or graphic art. Checa-Artasu considers murals to be part of the fabric of the urban city, reflecting the long tradition of popular graphic art in Mexico. The author finds that such graphics, while sometimes contained within districts with different socioeconomic profiles, have become part of the identity of the urban landscape of Mexican cities and towns. He contends that these graphic murals reflect the creativity and cultural wealth of the country, arguing that they now form part of the intangible cultural heritage. Today, popular graphics in Mexico are reflective of a long and evolving tradition of commercial messages painted on walls, now forming part of local heritage available for tourism.

In Chapter 5, the final part of this section on heritage, *Tourism, voyeurism and the media ecologies of Tehran's mural arts*, Pamela Karimi delves into the meaning of mural arts in Iran's capital Tehran. This contribution addresses a research gap in the literature about these murals and the relationship between the murals and how they are viewed. The murals of Tehran are profiled in terms of ideology and their connection to tourism (or lack of), leading to the portrayal of the murals through a global social media in what the author identifies as (dis)embodied tourism. In the absence of actual visitation in person to the murals by international tourists, at the time of this study, it is noted that the online portrayal of Iran's wall art plays a significant role in the country's post-revolutionary mural endeavours.

In summary, while this heritage section reflects the evolution of murals as both commercial and non-commercial messages, it serves to foreshadow the elements of politics and identity focused upon in the following sections. These contributions demonstrate that while murals have been painted for different audiences, including parishioners (Chapters 2 and 3), commercial entities (Chapter 4) and messages from the state (Chapter 5), all reflect situations where murals are increasingly being co-opted for the purposes of tourism visitation either in person or through social media.

Politics section

Murals in public spaces are inherently tied into politics, and there are many questions to consider here. What kinds of expressions and messages are suitable in public spaces? Who creates public murals? Are they mandated by the state? How do art and politics intersect in the case of murals (see Chapter 6)? How can a place improve its image through the use of murals for the benefit of both locals and visitors (see Chapter 7)? When the messages portrayed by the murals are not those put forward by the state, are the messages then erased, as is the case with the pixação in São Paulo (see Chapter 8)? Addressing these varied questions, the three contributions in this section – from Spain, Germany and Brazil – all deal with the transformation of urban public space through the use of murals as well as discussing the political implications of this trend.

In Chapter 6, *La Carbonería: an alternative transformation of public space*, contributor Placido Munoz Moran examines the relationship between art and politics in terms of the case of a mural on a particular building in Barcelona, Spain. Inherent conflicts between the visions of the urban planners and of the local populace are embodied in this mural case of La Carbonería. Constructed on a building occupied by squatters, for Barcelona residents this mural has become the subject of heated discussion and deliberation representative of contested individual and collective actions in connection with differing politics of representation in the city. Using ethnographic methods, the author is able to capture the rationale of the artists for constructing this painted wall, as well as to trace its influence on the public space around it.

Moving onto Chapter 7, Gareth Hamilton also delves into perceptions of public space in *Murals as sticking plasters: improving the image of an eastern German city for visitors and residents*. Again using an ethnographic approach, here we have a chapter that focuses on how murals have been used as a form of art in the public spaces of the city of Halle, Germany, in order to improve views of the place for both residents and visitors. In areas of the city that are in a state of disrepair, various forms of murals have been used to change perceptions of the built environment. With the city management being directly involved in many of these initiatives, the politicians of the place have therefore discovered a unique method for improving the image of Halle. However, as implied by Hamilton's title of 'sticking plasters', the improvement in appearance may be temporary at best. This leads nicely into the following Chapter 8 in terms of the preoccupation of politicians with the appearance of their cities, and the censoring or even eradication of messages on walls.

In the next contribution, Chapter 8, *Difference upon the Walls – hygienizing policies and the use of graffiti against pixação in São Paulo*, authors Paula

Larruscahim and Paul Schweizer introduce Brazil's distinctive city art movement of pixação or signatures on walls (see also Chapter 11). This exemplifies this book's key themes of heritage, politics and identity in terms of expressions painted on walls that are visible to the public. The authors both discuss and analyse the meanings of the recent 'hygienist policies' designed to repress and outlaw such expressions on walls in the context of perceived images of São Paulo within global city models.

In summary, this section on politics demonstrates that many murals are instruments of political messaging, expression and thought. Being for the most part in public areas, but often on private walls, murals and their messages are of interest and possibly concern to the state. However, in terms of their creation, local governments may on occasion be involved (see Chapter 7), but many murals are independently created with the government being on the receiving end of messages intended for them. Governments have adopted various approaches for dealing with messages that do not fit with the city-state viewpoint; one of them introduced in this section is the adoption of hygienist policies (see Chapter 8) that seek to oppress freedom of expression on walls.

Identity section

Murals are generally intrinsically linked to the identity of the places where they are created. This section of the volume thus encompasses contributions reflecting the theme from Africa and both North and South Americas where murals have been employed variously: to frame neighbourhood identity (Chapters 9 and 10); to heal divisions within communities (Chapter 10); to contribute to art appreciation (Chapter 11); and to reflect innovation (Chapter 12). In these contexts, murals often have an economic development context as they serve to attract visitors to their host communities and destinations.

More specifically and by order, the first contribution in this section, Chapter 9 by authors Lorenzo Cantoni and Marta Pucciarelli, is entitled *A journey through public art in Douala: framing the identity of New Bell neighbourhood*. This chapter explores a mural arts installation project in Douala, a port city in Cameroun in Africa. This project was established as a means of creating identity within shared public space in the new informally established neighbourhoods of the city. A particular case is examined: that of *Les Mots Écrits de New Bell*, a series of six murals produced for the SUD – Salon Urban de Douala 2010 – by a local artist and poet who lives and works in Douala's central district of New Bell. In this multi-methods study, the authors surveyed locals, interviewed artists, organizers and stakeholders and reviewed tourism guide reports in order to identify and discuss the differing views of the murals. The authors found that the presence of the murals not only defined the identity of the neighbourhood but also increased the mobility of inhabitants and visitors across the city, enhancing the cultural understanding of both groups. It is evident from this contribution that murals projects can have an impact on improving the quality of life of local inhabitants as well as break down the barriers that often exist between locals and visitors.

The second part of this section, Chapter 10, *Visiting murals and healing the past of racial injustice in divided Detroit*, is contributed by author Deborah Che. The author first examines the contested nature of publically visited murals. The chapter then moves on to consider the relationship of murals to community economic development, including both political empowerment and tourism benefits. The cases of two murals projects in racially divided Detroit, the Birwood Wall mural and the Detroit Chinatown mural, are then considered in terms of their efforts to heal the city overall and the neighbourhoods they are situated in. The author concludes that murals dealing directly with a community's contested heritage can bring the dual benefits of both healing and tourism to the host community.

In the next contribution, Chapter 11, authors Angela C. Flecha, Cristina Jönsson and D'Arcy Dornan contribute *Visiting murals and graffiti art in Brazil*. After a brief introduction to Brazil's tradition of mural arts that dates back to the 1940s, the authors move on to consider the development of street and urban art. They focus in particular on graffiti in São Paulo and Rio de Janeiro that reflects Brazilian identity (see also Chapter 8). The contribution of graffiti to creating art within the urban landscape has now been more accepted as a form of cultural expression. The authors also posit that the street and urban art movements are influencing art appreciation in Brazil.

Turning to another country in South America, in Chapter 12, authors María de Miguel Molina, Virginia Santamarina Campos, Blanca de Miguel Molina and Eva Martínez Carazo contribute *Balancing Uruguayan identity and sustainable economic development through street art*. This chapter examines the evolution of street art in public open spaces as an expression and consumption of popular art reflecting innovation and identity. This contribution also delves into the meanings surrounding street art in relation to both identity and economic development in Uruguay. Three cases of towns (Rosario del Colla, San Gregorio de Polanco and Pan de Azúcar) with mural developments are examined through interviews conducted regarding the murals. In summary, the authors found that mural arts here resulted in differing local developments that are nurturing identity, commemorating historical events, and beginning to contribute to developing the hospitality and tourism sectors.

This section on identity has amply demonstrated the varying roles of murals projects in relation to framing neighbourhood identity (Chapter 9), contributing to the healing of past injustices (Chapter 10), and the emergence of murals as street art affirming local identities (Chapters 11 and 12). It is evident from these contributions that murals as public art may provide a venue for the expression of local identities, potentially contributing to the authenticity of place that is sought both by local residents and by visitors. There is an inherent link with local economic development as murals are beginning to be both used by destinations to differentiate themselves from others and sought out by visitors at a number of locations as profiled in this section.

Northern Ireland section

It would not be possible to edit a book about murals and tourism without reference to the murals of Northern Ireland. Without a doubt, these are the most studied and written about of murals in works relating to the interwoven themes of this book - heritage, politics and identity. Elements of these themes are all found within the three contributions that make up this section on Northern Ireland while extending the study of murals tourism to the re-imaging of contested murals (Chapters 13 and 15), and how the murals are experienced by the communities where they are located (Chapters 14 and 15) and the tourists who visit them. These are also murals that, while first created during the years of the Troubles, have evolved with the times, incorporating as subject matter other areas of struggle to spawn an entire murals-related tourism industry in Northern Ireland complete with related tours, exhibits, souvenirs, books and theatrical productions.

Chapter 13, the first in this section on the murals of Northern Ireland, is *State intervention in reimaging Northern Ireland's political murals: implications for tourism and the communities*. In this contribution, author Maria T. Simone-Charteris introduces the background and the context of the murals of Northern Ireland with a particular focus on those related to the Troubles period of political conflict between Loyalists and Nationalists. Murals have been used as propaganda tools by both sides and today visitation is to some extent shaped along the political lines of the two groups. That the meanings of some of these murals have become embedded in the life of the communities where they are located will be further demonstrated in Chapters 14 and 15. However, Simone-Charteris deals with the intervention of the state in the re-imaging of the murals, aiming to sanitize those that are most contentious in terms of messaging, while discussing the implications of related projects on both communities and their political tourism prospects. However, despite efforts to eradicate the political messaging of the murals, the author argues that they are necessary as part of the ongoing dialogue between communities, and have become part of the distinctive resources for political tourism that is becoming increasingly popular with tourists, an appeal that would be lost if the murals are to become apolitical. This contribution provides a valuable context for the following chapters (14 and 15) that delve more deeply into the meanings of murals in particular neighbourhoods of Belfast.

In Chapter 14, *The Gaeltacht Quarter of Mural City: Irish in Falls Road murals*, author Siun Carden delves into the use of murals to create a cultural identity in the Gaelic (Irish) quarter of Belfast. As well as being a destination for the political tourism related to the Troubles documented by Simone-Charteris in Chapter 13, the area has, in recent years, been reimaged and marketed along Irish language themes as the 'Gaeltacht Quarter'. This practice has included not only bilingual signs and ads, but also the use of murals that emerged during the conflict period of The Troubles.

According to Carden, the re-imaging of the Quarter through the use of Irish in Gaeltacht local murals represents and celebrates both cultural difference and normalization. Efforts to portray the Quarter as a kind of Murals District are seen as emerging both for economic objectives of tourism and from a desire to be on a path to a normal life. The author also posits that the repositioning of the Irish language within the Quarter is important to tourism as the language is framed as a cultural resource for the whole city rather than an individual territory within. The next contribution, Chapter 14, further examines the issue of re-imaging of the murals in a Belfast neighbourhood, this time on a particular West Belfast estate.

In the third contribution in this section, Chapter 15, *Terror, tourism and re-imaging the mural in Belfast*, author Katy Radford examines the evolution over time of the murals at a case study location of a West Belfast housing estate. This follows up on the theme of re-imaging introduced in Chapter 13. This chapter further documents the complexities of the Belfast murals as their interpretation changes over time. The author employs ethnographic methods in examining perspectives of the tourists and guides (largely taxi drivers) as well as of the creators of the murals. A powerful personal active-researcher perspective is reflected here by the author having worked with conflict transformation programmes on the estate over the last 17 years. This practitioner-led view is significant in providing a nuanced counter-interpretation of the ongoing evolution of the Belfast murals.

In summary, this section on Northern Ireland has investigated the interplay of heritage, politics and identity in terms of the ongoing evolution of the murals of a particular place that is well known for murals-related tourism. Heritage is employed by the mural artists to get their message across, and those murals painted along political lines (Loyalist or Republican) have become representative of place identity, although state intervention has attempted to replace offending murals through re-imaging programmes. The murals here, which were once seen as expressions of the politics of a local conflict, have now evolved as a strong community-based resource for forms of heritage tourism (including murals tourism and political tourism). Some members of the related visitor industry are now using such tourism as a form of political messaging as the purpose of the murals of Northern Ireland as well as their use continues to change.

Conclusion

As murals as a means of communication continue to evolve, there is ample room for future research on murals creation and transformation, visitation and reception from a number of perspectives. This volume is only a beginning in terms of the study of murals by an interdisciplinary group of authors from the heritage, political and identity perspectives. There is no doubt that the concept of murals on walls that originated in ancient times

22   *Jonathan Skinner and Lee Jolliffe*

(see Chapters 2 and 3) will continue to develop in terms of the heritage they represent, the politics of their subject matter and the identity that they nurture, providing abundant subject matter for continued research.

Chapter 16, in the final section of this volume by Virginia Yeo, *Murals as a tool for action research,* represents one contemporary use of murals in work with the disability sector that could lead to other similar projects. It reflects the use of murals in action research so that the editors deemed it appropriate to conclude the volume with this particular chapter. The author situated the chapter within the broader field of visual imagery. In this contribution, instead of murals bearing a message intended for viewers, the iterative process of creating the murals is put forward as being researched for its potential as a research method and a process that can potentially act as a tool for social change. Yeo concludes that the appropriateness of using the creation of murals will depend on the goals of the research, but that there is potential, as demonstrated by the case in this chapter, for further delving into mural creation through action research.

A final word

In writing about visiting murals, we hope to have uncovered some of the meanings behind these expressions on walls, especially in terms of their contextual relationship to the heritage, politics and identity of their locales, as well as their connections to broader issues of freedom of expression. While there has previously been a plethora of literature examining the political murals of Northern Ireland and the community economic development murals of Canada, this volume addresses the gap in the literature regarding creation and visitation to murals in other parts of the world. Examining the phenomena of murals from different perspectives, both the editors and the contributing authors have explored the issues around the creation, evolution, documentation and consumption of murals and their role as ever-attractive forms of public art and communication.

References

Barnes, Trevor J. and Roger Hayter. 1992. "The Little Town That Did: Flexible Accumulation and Community Response in Chemainus, British Columbia." *Regional Studies* 26 (7): 647–63.

Brighenti, Andrea. 2009. "Walled Urbs to Urban Walls – and Return? On the Social Life of Walls." In *The Wall and the City/Il muro e la città / Le mur et la ville,* edited by Andrea Brighenti, 63–71. Trento: Professional Dreamers.

Brunn, Stanley, Sarah Byrne, Louise McNamara and Annette Egan. 2010. "Belfast Landscapes: From Religious Schism to Conflict Tourism." *Focus on Geography* 53 (3): 81–91.

Coffey, Mary. 2012. *How a Revolutionary Art Became Official Culture.* London: Duke University Press.

Community Tourism Foundations Programme. 2010. "Cowichan Region Tourism Plan, 2010–2015," accessed August 29, 2016, http://www.tourismcowichan. com/wp-content/uploads/2014/05/Cowichan_Region_Tourism_Plan_FINAL_ April2010.pdf.

Cozzolino, Francesca. 2014. "Observing the Artification Process: The Case of Murales in Sardinia." In *Popular and Visual Culture: Design, Circulation and Consumption*, edited by Clara Sarmento, Ricardo Campos, Rúben Pinho and Nuno Duarte, 167–90. Newcastle upon Tyne: Cambridge Scholars Publishing.

Crooke, Elizabeth. 2005. "Dealing with the Past: Museums and Heritage in Northern Ireland and Cape Town, South Africa." *International Journal of Heritage Studies* 11 (2): 131–42.

———. 2010. "The Politics of Community Heritage: Motivations, Authority and Control." *International Journal of Heritage Studies* 16 (1–2): 16–29.

Ellsworth-Jones, Will. 2012. *Banksy: The Man Behind the Wall*. London: Aurum.

Foster, Norman, Frederick Baker, Deborah Lipstadt and David Jenkins, eds. 2003. *The Reichstag Graffiti/Die Reichstag-Grafiti*. Berlin: Jovis Verlag GmbH/Foster and Partners.

Goalwin, Gregory. 2013. "The Art of War: Instability, Insecurity, and Ideological Imagery in Northern Ireland's Political Murals, 1979–1998." *International Journal of Politics, Culture and Society* 26: 189–215.

Graham, Brian and Peter Howard. 2008. "Heritage and Identity." In *The Ashgate Research Companion to Heritage and Identity*, edited by Brian Graham and Peter Howard, 1–15. Burlington: Ashgate.

Graham, Brian and Yvonne Whelan. 2007. "The Legacies of the Dead: Commemorating the Troubles in Northern Ireland." *Environment and Planning D: Society and Space* 25 (3): 476–95.

Heatherington, Tracy. 2002. "Murals and the Memory of Resistance in Sardinia." *Irish Journal of Anthropology* 6: 7–24.

Hill, Andrew and Andrew White. 2012. "Painting Peace? Murals and the Northern Ireland Peace Process." *Irish Political Studies* 27 (1): 71–88.

Historic Places.ca. 2007. "Sharp's Corner Drug Store," accessed August 29, 2016, http://www.historicplaces.ca/en/rep-reg/place-lieu.aspx?id=8716.

Jamal, Tazim and Steve Hill. 2004. "Developing a Framework for Indicators of Authenticity: The Place and Space of Cultural and Heritage Tourism." *Asia Pacific Journal of Tourism Research* 9 (4): 353–72.

Jones, Sam. 2005. "Spray Can Prankster Tackles Israel's Security Barrier," *The Guardian*, August 5, 2005, accessed August 6, 2016, https://www.theguardian. com/world/2005/aug/05/israel.artsnews.

Koster, Rhonda and James E. Randall. 2005. "Indicators of Community Economic Development through Mural-Based Tourism." *Canadian Geographer* 49 (1): 42–60.

Kunzle, David. 1995. *The Murals of Revolutionary Nicaragua 1979–1992*. Berkeley: University of California Press.

Lisle, Debbie. 2006. "Local Symbols, Global Networks: Rereading the Murals of Belfast." *Alternatives* 31: 27–52.

Marschall, Sarah. 2004. "Getting the Message Across: Art and Craft in the Service of HIV/AIDS Awareness in South Africa." *Visual Anthropology* 17: 163–82.

Mettler, Margaret. 2012. "Graffiti Museum: A First Amendment Argument for Protecting Uncommissioned Art on Private Property." *Michigan Law Review* 111 (2): 249–82.

Moreau, Terri and Derek Alderman. 2011. "Graffiti Hurts and the Eradication of Alternative Landscape Expression." *The Geographical Review* 101 (1): 106–24.

Murakami, Haruki. 2014. "Haruki Murakami: Racing to Checkpoint Charlie – My Memories of the Berlin Wall," *The Weekend Guardian*, Reviews, November 22, 2014, 18.

Parry, Nigel. 2005. "Well-Known UK Graffiti Artist Banksy Hacks the Wall," *The Electronic Intifada*, September 2, 2005, accessed August 6, 2016, https://electronic intifada.net/content/well-known-uk-graffiti-artist-banksy-hacks-wall/5733.

Rhea, Shawn. 2004. "Detroit Renaissance." *Yes Magazine*, May 10, 2004, 1–6.

Rolston, Bill. 1970. "Visions or Nightmares? Murals and Imagining the Future in Northern Ireland." In *Representing the Troubles: Texts and Images, 1970–2000*, edited by Brian Cliff and Eibhear Walshe, 117–28. Portland, OR: Four Courts Press.

———. 2010a. "'Trying to Reach the Future through the Past': Murals and Memory in Northern Ireland." *Crime, Media, Culture* 6 (3): 285–307.

———. 2010b. *Drawing Support: Murals in the North of Ireland*. Belfast: Beyond the Pale Publications.

———. 2014. "Resistance and Pride: The Murals of Orgosolo, Sardinia." *State Crime Journal* 3 (1): 73–101.

Silberman, Marc, Karen Till and Janet Ward. 2012. "Introduction: Walls, Borders, Boundaries." In *Walls, Borders, Boundaries: Spatial and Cultural Practices in Europe*, edited by Marc Silberman, Karen Till and Janet Ward, 1–24. Oxford: Berghahn Books.

Simone-Charteris, Maria T. and Stephen W. Boyd. 2010. "Developing Dark and Political Tourism in Northern Ireland: An Industry Perspective." In *Contemporary Issues in Irish and Global Tourism and Hospitality*, edited by Geraldine Gorman and Ziene Mottair, 106–23. Dublin: Dublin Institute of Technology.

Skinner, Jonathan. 2016. "Walking the Falls: Dark Tourism and the Significance of Movement on the Political Tour of West Belfast." *Tourist Studies* 16 (1): 23–39.

Sussex Murals. n.d. "The Mural Capital of Atlantic Canada," accessed August 29, 2016, http://sussexmurals.com/.

The Bogside Artists. 2001. *Murals*. Derry: Guildhall Press.

Tourism Winnipeg. 2016. "West End BIZ Mural Walking Tours," *West End BIZ Mural Walking Tours*, accessed May 12, 2016, www.tourismwinnipeg.com.

Vannais, Judy. 2012. "Postcards from the Edge: Reading Political Murals in the North of Ireland." *Irish Political Studies* 16 (1): 133–60.

West End Business Improvement Zone. 2016. "Murals," accessed August 29, 2016, http://www.westendbiz.ca/visiting-the-west-end/murals/.

Wilson, Des. 1983. "The Painted Message," *Circa Art Magazine* 8 (Jan–Feb), 19–20.

Yeh, Shih-Shuo, Chun Chen and Yao-Chung Liu. 2012. "Nostalgic Emotion, Experiential Value, Destination Image, and Place Attachment of Cultural Tourists." *Advances in Hospitality and Leisure* 8: 167–87.

Part II
Heritage

2 Heritage murals as tourist attractions in Ravenna, Moldavia and Istanbul

Artistic treasures, cultural identities and political statements

Warwick Frost and Jennifer Laing

Introduction

Murals are generally perceived as a picture created by the application of paint upon a surface, but also encompass *tile or mosaic* murals, where the design is created by small pieces of stone, glass or ceramic tiles. European murals have a long history, with mosaic techniques dating back to Roman times in the second century AD (Herrin 2007), while tiles were introduced into Spain and Portugal by the Moors from the thirteenth century AD. Murals were created for a range of different purposes including their aesthetic impact, the making of political statements through the depiction of rulers, battles and conquests, reinforcing the authority of rulers and as a means to create and entrench cultural identities. They remain under-researched in the context of their role in tourist experiences, as indeed does art in public spaces more generally, despite its potential appeal and high interest to those tourists 'who are tired of packaged and staged offerings and are looking for something more subtle, challenging and personally meaningful' (Frost, Laing and Williams 2015, 60). This chapter considers a selection of European tile, mosaic and painted murals as examples of heritage, taking a retrospective look at their importance from a political, artistic and cultural standpoint, and the ways in which they become markers of identity and are consumed by and interpreted to contemporary tourists.

Three comparative case studies are considered to illustrate the discussion. Each is based on qualitative data collected during fieldwork, outlined in the next section. The first case study involves the fifth- and sixth-century Byzantine mosaics in Ravenna, Italy. These mix religious and political imagery, particularly in how they portray and symbolize the imperial splendour and supreme authority of the Emperor Justinian and his wife Theodora, juxtaposed with Christian motifs. The second case study is that of the painted churches of Moldavia in Romania. Like the Ravenna mosaics, they are World Heritage listed. Built in the fifteenth and sixteenth centuries, these churches are fully adorned with colourful murals. Ostensibly religious and created to educate illiterate peasants, they also feature political messages and reinforce the power of local lords. The third case study concerns ceramic tile (*azulejo*) murals in Portugal, dating from the sixteenth century. These often represent important milestones or events in the nation's history and are found in public places such as the São Bento railway station in Porto, on the walls of churches and facades of houses and public thoroughfares in Lisbon. Each of these case studies focuses on murals that are featured as tourist attractions in most reputable guidebooks, such as the *Lonely Planet* series and the *Eyewitness* guides. Indeed, during our research at each of these sites, we witnessed many people consulting with guidebooks or their phones as they visited, perhaps because there is little interpretation available in situ unless the visitor is on a guided tour. We observed a number of tours at the Ravenna and Moldavian sites, but not at the São Bento railway station in Porto, perhaps because it was a working station and not suitable for large groups to congregate within its environs. The guidebooks may have encouraged tourists to seek out these sites, given that they stressed their importance as artistic and cultural heritage, and might also have mediated their meaning for these individuals (Bhattacharyya 1997; McWha *et al.* forthcoming; Mercille 2005).

Murals and public art

Murals can be considered to be examples of *public art*, which we define, following Miles (1997, 1), as 'making and siting art outside conventional art spaces'. As Frost, Laing and Williams (2015, 58) note: 'In its most literal sense, it refers to those art works and buildings that have been installed in the public sphere, such as squares, plazas and laneways', which includes art found in 'churches which were once free public spaces but may now only be accessible with the payment of an entrance fee'. Public art is therefore a useful lens for understanding the role and influence of murals as works of art intended for communal gaze or consumption; it is an integral part of urban tourist experiences.

Following Frost, Laing and Williams (2015), we note that destinations known for their public art can be conceptualized in at least five ways from a tourism perspective. Table 2.1 analyses the three case studies in terms of this conceptual framework. The case studies were selected to highlight *different ways* in which their public art (focusing on murals) is revealed to tourists, and each embodies *different dimensions* of the conceptual framework. The benefit of using comparative case studies, as opposed to a single case study, is that the former can illuminate issues that might be otherwise overlooked in the latter with its more limited scope (Verschuren 2003; Yin 2003).

The first dimension of this framework involves distinguishing those destinations that feature largely *commissioned* or planned examples of public art from those where the public art arises more *organically*. The murals discussed in this chapter have all been commissioned. The second and third dimensions consider the *purpose* of commissioning the public art and the *body or individual* who has provided the commission. The purpose of

Table 2.1 Comparison of case study destinations linked to murals

	Ravenna	*Moldavia*	*Portugal*
Commissioned or organic murals	Commissioned	Commissioned	Commissioned and organic
Purpose of commissioning murals	Political power Religiosity	Political power Religiosity	Political power Religiosity
Predominant commissioner of murals	Imperial rulers	Moldavian princes	Church Monarchy Government
Classification of art within the destination	Artistic heritage	Artistic heritage	Artistic heritage
Historical period	Late Roman Empire, Byzantine Empire	Late medieval	Post fifteenth century, particularly the Baroque period

commissioning murals can vary, as mentioned in the Introduction, and can also change over time. Thus, the political role of murals in modern times tends to be linked to urban regeneration strategies and a desire to promote place identity (Hall and Robertson 2001; McCarthy 2006) rather than a desire to symbolize political power and dominance over a population. Most modern murals are commissioned by governments, particularly local councils or municipalities, or private individuals rather than the religious bodies or rulers of the past.

The fourth dimension for classifying these destinations is to consider how they can be understood in terms of their art more generally. Those destinations that are known for their *artistic heritage* may have World Heritage listing as a consequence, which often reflects a city's status as a capital or former capital (Frost 2012). For example, as the capital of Portugal, Lisbon was at the centre of a trading and colonial empire that was instrumental in the Age of Discovery (roughly corresponding to the mid-fifteenth century). One could also consider the level of *monumentality*, the encouragement (or not) of *street art*, or whether the city itself can be regarded as a *work of art*, in the sense of 'deliberate artistic creations intended not merely to give pleasure but to contain ideas, inculcate values, and serve as tangible expressions of systems of thought and morality' (Olsen 1986, 4). The case studies in this chapter feature some monumental architecture connected to murals, including palaces, churches and railway stations. None of the murals discussed in this chapter could really be conceptualized as *street art* in that they are mostly publically sanctioned and commissioned, not clandestine or illegal. Of the three destinations we examine, two are regions or countries, and the only city (Ravenna) is not a *work of art*, nor is it an *historic gem* (Ashworth and Tunbridge 2000) given the lack of an intact heritage core to the city. The fifth dimension of the conceptual framework examines the *period in history* in which the public art was produced, in that 'certain eras were marked by a flourishing of public art, sometimes linked to a particular artistic movement' (Frost, Laing and Williams 2015, 62). The Ravenna mosaic murals were created during the Byzantine era, and the Moldavian painted churches in the fifteenth and sixteenth centuries, whereas Portuguese tile art reached its epoch during the Baroque period of the eighteenth century.

Methodology

Data in this study were collected using participant observation and field research (following Weaver 2011) by the authors during their site visits to the three case study locations – Ravenna, Moldavia and Portugal. At least one of the authors visited each individual site, and both authors simultaneously visited the Ravenna and Portugal sites. Each site visit lasted 1–2 days. The focus of this fieldwork was on the type of murals found in each destination, the level of interpretation available, and its potential contribution to the tourist experience and the observed behaviour of the visitors.

The mosaics of Ravenna

In the fifth and sixth centuries, Ravenna became one of the most important cities in the Mediterranean world. During that period, three regimes made it their capital. In contrast to Rome, it was considered to be impregnable and became seen as the key to controlling Italy. After the Battle of Pollentia between the Romans and the Visigoths in 402 AD, the Emperor Honorius shifted his capital to Ravenna. Whether a wise move or not, he was able to defend Ravenna, whereas Rome was sacked by the Visigoths in 410 AD. With the forced abdication of the Emperor Romulus Augustulus, a power struggle ensued amongst the Goths to rule Italy. Ultimately, Theodoric the Ostrogoth was successful, establishing his capital at Ravenna in 493 AD. Within half a century, the Byzantine Emperor Justinian mounted an expedition to reclaim Italy, capturing Ravenna in 540 AD. The city remained the centre of Byzantine power in Italy until it fell to the Lombards in 751 AD (Norwich 1990).

All three regimes engaged in public building works that would both cater for the needs of imperial courts and demonstrate their power and legitimacy as rulers. Most prominent were large churches, richly decorated with coloured mosaics. For both the Western and Eastern Roman Empires, mosaics were the peak of their artistic culture. Though characterized as a barbarian, Theodoric also shared this cultural capital. As a princely hostage, he had spent 10 years of his youth at court in Constantinople. Accordingly, he too knew the value of the artistic trappings of imperial rule.

Today, Ravenna is a medium-sized regional city. Much of its architecture is recent, but it still retains eight sites from the fifth and sixth centuries that are World Heritage listed. These were inscribed in 1996 by 'virtue of their supreme artistry of mosaic art' (UNESCO 2015a). Scattered throughout the modern city, they are the main tourist attraction of Ravenna (Frost, Laing and Williams 2015). We observed both tours and independent tourists during our field work in Ravenna. Visitors took many photographs and the lack of in situ interpretation meant that many were overheard discussing what they were viewing with other tourists in an attempt to understand what they were looking at. Others preferred to sit in quiet contemplation, particularly when they were not part of a tour group. The tourist was therefore largely forced to co-create or co-construct their own tourist experience (Chronis 2005).

The oldest of the sites we visited was the Mausoleum of Galla Placida, dating from 450 AD. Galla Placida was the sister of the Emperor Honorius and mother of Emperor Valentian III. Though small and unprepossessing from the outside, the building is richly decorated with interior mosaics. It is particularly noted for the many abstract designs and clever mosaic effects, such as the contrasting representations of daytime and night. On a much grander scale is the Basilica of Saint Apollinare Nuovo (Figure 2.1) built by Theodoric around 500 AD. It is richly decorated with massive mosaics running down both sides of the interior. These show Jesus being adored by the apostles and a range of saints. Appropriately for an important trading hub, there are contemporary references in the works. The port is shown juxtaposed with Jerusalem. The Three Wise Men are represented not as kings

Figure 2.1 Basilica of Sant' Apollinare Nuovo Ravenna.
Source: J. Laing.

but as wealthy merchants. Matching this Basilica is an even larger Church of Saint Apollinare in Classe. This imposing structure was opened in 549 AD to serve the port area of Classe. However, that port eventually silted up and the church remains isolated in the country some 5 km out of town. Its main mural is a massive mosaic of Jesus in its apse.

While many inhabitants of Ravenna were Orthodox Christians, the Ostrogoths tended towards Arianism. This creed held that Jesus was not equal to God, but rather essentially human. The Arian Baptistry, built around 500 AD, served the needs of the Arian Ostrogoths. Its main mural is on the ceiling and shows the Baptism of Jesus. Appropriately for the Arians, he is depicted fully naked with genitalia like any male human being. Adding to its distinctiveness, Jesus is attended by John the Baptist and a venerable bearded character. This unknown figure is thought to be a representation of the river god or spirit and reveals the maintenance of some animist beliefs amongst the worshippers. That the Arian Baptistry has survived throughout the centuries when its core beliefs were seen as heretical is testament to the tolerance of the diverse cultures that were drawn to this imperial capital and port.

The murals most associated with the Byzantines are in the Basilica of San Vitale. Completed in 547 AD, the colourful mosaics mainly depict Biblical scenes. The most well known are on either side of the altar. On one side is the Emperor Justinian, on the other the Empress Theodora. Unlike many medieval portraits, these are meant to be accurate representations of the rulers. The imperial couple are richly dressed and bejewelled, attended by clergy and ladies-in-waiting. It is most likely that similar mosaics were incorporated into the Hagia Sophia Church in Constantinople that Justinian built just a few years earlier (Norwich 1990 – and to go further than Norwich, it seems likely that the Ravenna mosaics were a copy of those done for Constantinople). It is, however, the Ravenna mosaics that survived the iconoclasts, again testament to a tradition of tolerance arising from this era of multiple rulers and cultures. It is these lifelike portraits that are perhaps the best-known examples of Byzantine mosaic art in the world. They send a clear message of the legitimacy of the Emperor that, following the collapse of Rome and the rule of the Ostrogoths, the rightful Emperor has returned from the east to continue imperial rule. Enigmatic and personal, the mosaic portraits are open to a variety of interpretations. Norwich, for example, reads a great deal into them:

> Of all the Emperors of Byzantium, he [Justinian] is the one whom we find the easiest to imagine – thanks to the great contemporary mosaic … his face … is plain and unidealized: a portrait clearly taken from life … It is not a fine face … nor indeed a particularly strong one. Certainly, it bears no comparison with that of Theodora on the opposite wall … No wonder, one feels, that her husband was easily led – if it was she who was doing the leading.

> (1990, 263)

To conclude with the Ravenna murals, it is instructive to consider two examples of how they have influenced later artists, which mirrors their fascination and enduring appeal for tourists. First, inspired by a visit to the Mausoleum of Galla Placida, Cole Porter wrote the song *Night and Day*. Second, following a similar visit to Ravenna, Gustav Klimt adapted the style of the Theodora mosaic for his portrait *Adele Bloch-Bauer I*; in 2006, it sold for $135 million USD, the highest reported price paid for a painting.

The painted churches of Moldavia

Eight churches were listed as World Heritage in 1993, which are often referred to collectively as the Painted Churches or Painted Monasteries of Moldavia, now modern Romania. They were all built in the fifteenth and sixteenth centuries, a period of expansion and conflict in Moldavian history. Under leaders like Stefan cel Mare (Stephen the Great), the principality of Moldavia was involved in constant warring with the Hungarians, Poles and Ottoman Turks. After success in battles, victorious rulers established churches as thanksgiving and penance – Stefan cel Mare is reputed to have established forty-four churches in this way. These new churches also had a role in anchoring settlers to the frontier, either through fortified monasteries or villages. They are distinguished by large coloured murals in their interior porches and on the external walls. The massive murals in the porches portray the Crack of Doom or Last Judgement. Such representations are found in churches across Europe, though in most cases only fragments of the paintings remain. An interesting example of a recent restoration is at the Holy Trinity Church in Coventry, UK. There, the mural of the Last Judgement dates from the mid-fifteenth century, making it contemporaneous with and quite similar to those of the Moldavian churches. Possibly covered up in the Reformation, the mural at Holy Trinity was long thought to be beyond repair, but test cleaning in the 1980s led to a full restoration in 2004 (McGrory and Gill 2014).

For most of the churches, these murals completely cover their exterior, providing a colourful and exotic image for the viewer. Whereas the porch murals all depict the Last Judgement, those on the outside cover a varied range of biblical stories. In some cases, the imagery relates to the patron saint of each individual church, though in most instances no pattern is apparent and the choices must have been subjectively made by individual priests or artists. Sadly, the names of the artists are largely unknown, unlike the great Italian Renaissance fresco artists of the same period, perhaps because they often worked in teams or were local masters without a strong individual reputation. We know, however, that Toma from Suceava painted the exterior of the Dormition of the Mother of God Church (Humor Monastery) and included his own portrait on the southern wall, while Dragoş Coman of Iasi, a well-known mural artist of the sixteenth century, painted the exterior of the Beheading of St John the Baptist Church at Arbore.

The bright and stunning paintings are reminiscent of both cartoons and the works of Hieronymous Bosch (who painted at the same time). The church murals are public art created in the late medieval period to be 'read' and understood by a predominantly illiterate audience. The imaginative and explicit Day of Judgement in the porches tells churchgoers what will ultimately happen to them: as the earth cracks open, the dead rise from their graves. Furthermore, those who have drowned at sea return from the mouths of large fishes. Similarly, those devoured by wild beasts, for example, bears, now magically issue forth. As the populace await judgement, hordes of impish devils attack them, prodding with pitchforks – again reminiscent of Bosch. While the lords and other elite members of society are ushered through to heaven, whole ethnic or religious groups are sent straight to hell. These include the Muslims, Jews and Armenians. For the ordinary folk, there is an anguished wait as their sins are weighed against their loyalty and devotion to their faith.

Whereas the porch mural is widespread throughout Europe, the external paintings of the Moldavian churches are claimed to be unique and this is an integral part of their World Heritage listing (UNESCO 2015b). Any such claims of uniqueness must be treated with care and consideration is required of what special conditions were in play in late medieval Moldavia to explain why they only occurred there. Certainly external illustrations occur elsewhere, as in the examples of Notre Dame in Paris and Reims Cathedral. These, however, were carved in stone rather than painted. More importantly, they do not cover the whole exterior, as in Moldavia. The external murals cover a wide range of topics from the Old and New Testaments. Representations of Jesus are prevalent, usually associated with a wide array of saints. Pictures of the latter are important within the Orthodox tradition, as each individual has a saint who they are named after; they wish to see and identify with *their* particular saint during their visits. As in the porch, these murals are intended to be viewed and 'read' by a predominantly illiterate local audience. Old Testament imagery includes Jacob's Ladder, the Tree of Jesse and the Siege of Jericho. These detailed and colourful images complemented oral storytelling by priests and village elders, providing an aid to understanding complex religious concepts. Thus, for example, the biblical narrative of Jacob dreaming of a ladder to heaven is represented quite vividly and literally.

The World Heritage listing of the Painted Churches is based on their religious significance, recognizing that 'far from being mere wall decorations, the paintings form a systematic covering on all facades and represent complex cycles of religious themes' (UNESCO 2015b). However, seeing these murals purely from a religious perspective misses a great deal of their significance and subtlety. These are the product of a frontier zone. Each was built to give thanks for a victory and to further safeguard the region. Villagers settled around the churches looked to the vivid paintings to reinforce their identity and provide social bonding and unity in the face of likely attacks by their enemies. References to the contemporary are visible throughout the murals. Princes and lords are shown gifting these churches to God – this recognition of patronage is common in Orthodox churches. On Judgement Day, the elite are shown as ascending to heaven, reinforcing the natural order of society. Most importantly, they are accompanied by the ordinary folk who have been pious and loyal. The message is clear. The ordinary folk must be both good Christians and good subjects. Reinforcing this is the depiction of those who will go to hell. Prominent here are the enemies – foreigners who threaten to attack. External murals representing conflict have a dual narrative. This may have been made explicit by the storytellers, particularly when people came together to shelter around the churches when the risk of attack was high. Biblical battles come complete with cannons and medieval-style clothing. Jericho falling to Joshua also serves as a parable to the Ottoman conquest of Constantinople in 1452, a warning of what might happen if the defenders are ill-prepared. As with Ravenna, the Painted Churches of Moldavia are visited by both tour groups and independent tourists, with attention drawn by guides to their World Heritage status, as well as the symbolism of the murals. These Churches lack visual interpretation in the form of signage. And so, it could be argued that this adds to the attraction of these sites, appealing to those tourists who prize discovery and challenge on their vacations; individuals we have labelled *explorer travellers* (Laing and Frost 2014, 2015).

Ceramic tiles in Portugal

While the Portuguese did not invent the ceramic tile or *azulejo*, it forms part of the country's artistic and cultural heritage (Calado 1989). These tiles often covered a whole building or interior rather than just being a decorative flourish. There was also the fashion for creating large-scale pictures or murals based on these tiles that adorned churches, palaces and monasteries. The history of these tiles can be traced back to the introduction of mosaics, through the influence of the Moors (Coentro *et al.* 2012; Vaz, Pires and Carvalho 2008). The earliest example of this can be seen on the floors of the Mosteiro de Alcobaça in Portugal, dating back to the thirteenth century (Vaz, Pires and Carvalho 2008). During the fifteenth century, ceramic tiles rather than mosaics became more widespread and were imported from Spain, Italy and Flanders. The *azulejo* are 'square ceramic plaques glazed on one side, and have larger dimensions than mosaics' (Vaz, Pires and Carvalho 2008, 270). They were made using the techniques developed by the Moors in Spain. The first tile manufacturing in Portugal was started by artists from Antwerp in the latter half of the sixteenth century (Vaz, Pires and Carvalho 2008). In the seventeenth century, the shift of the court to Spain led to an economic downturn. Thus, tiles, which were cheap to manufacture and durable, replaced the use of tapestries hung from the walls of churches (Coentro *et al.* 2012) and were applied to both the interior and the exterior of buildings such as churches, palaces and monasteries (Portela and Queiroz 2010). While some started out mimicking tapestries with simple patterns, they eventually became more ambitious and figurative in scope, representing 'hunting, battles, religious and mythological scenes' (Vaz, Pires and Carvalho 2008, 270). Some were copies of famous paintings or prints of these paintings (Da Silva *et al.* 2011). Examples of figurative designs include the life of St Clare depicted on the walls of the Monastery of Santa Marta de Jesus in Lisbon and the tile painting of the Adoration of the Shepherds that was formerly part of the Church of Santo André in Lisbon and is now displayed in the Portuguese National Tile Museum.

The shift towards creating tiles in blue and white occurred in the second half of the seventeenth century and was ascribed to the Dutch influence (Portela and Queiroz 2010; Vaz, Pires and Carvalho 2008). One example is the eighteenth-century tile painting that adorns the interior of the southern gate, *Porta da Vila*, into the town of Óbidos (Figure 2.2). It depicts the Passion of Christ. There is also a series of these blue and white *azulejo* in the refectory of the *Mosteiro dos Jerónimos* – Monastery of the Hieronymites – in Lisbon, dating from 1780–1785, which portray the miracle of the loaves and fishes from the New Testament and scenes from the life of Joseph in Egypt from the Old Testament. The most famous exhibit of Portugal's National Tile Museum is a 23-metre-long mural of Lisbon's skyline, made in 1738 before the Great Earthquake and composed of 1,300 blue and white painted tiles.

Large-scale production of tiles occurred after the Great Earthquake of 1755 in Lisbon when there was an urgent need to recover buildings that were

Figure 2.2 Tile painting on the Porta da Vila, Óbidos, Portugal.
Source: J. Laing.

destroyed or damaged. Tiles were 'easy to clean and maintain' (Portela and Queiroz 2010, 5). The eighteenth century saw a divide in the type of designs adorning tiles between the Church and the ruling classes. The former still mainly clung to religious themes, including the Christian recapture of Lisbon from the Moors in 1147, exemplified by one of the tiled panels on the wall of the Church of Santa Luzia in Lisbon. Royalty and the aristocracy preferred landscapes or scenes from mythology or warfare, as exemplified in the *Palácio Fronteira* in Lisbon with its Battles Hall depicting the War of Restoration when Spanish rule was overthrown. The eighteenth-century tile paintings from the *Palácio Nacional* or Royal Palace of Sintra, which was a favoured summer retreat for the Portuguese monarchy, depict bucolic pastoral and hunting scenes, flanked by beautiful maidens and cherubs. The University of Évora is graced by *azulejos* representing famous teachers of the ancient world such as Plato and Aristotle. There was now a greater variety of colours used for these tile paintings, although the traditional blue and white colour scheme was still favoured (Portela and Queiroz 2010).

From the nineteenth century, the bourgeoisie or nouveau riche returning from Brazil used tiles to cover the facades of their houses (Vaz, Pires and Carvalho 2008), 'trying to imitate, on a smaller scale, the most lavish renaissance and baroque palaces' (Portela and Queiroz 2010, 6). The upper classes, in contrast, abandoned this architectural style around this period, perhaps to distinguish themselves from those who would seek to emulate them (Portela and Queiroz 2010). Despite the functionality of the tiles in architectural construction, they were not divorced from general artistic trends of the twentieth century. Thus, the town of Aveiro contains numerous tiled buildings in Art Nouveau style, including motifs such as birds, flowers and insects (Gomes and Lourenço 2014) which create ambience for those walking through town or eating in their many restaurants. Throughout the twentieth century, tiles continued to be used to commemorate events such as the appearance of the Virgin Mary to three children in Fátima in 1917 and the visit of Pope John Paul in 1982.

Some of the finest use of these tiles in contemporary public spaces has occurred in Portuguese train stations. The station of São Bento in Porto, opened in 1916, has a number of tile murals created by Jorge Colaço that depict scenes from the history of Portugal, such as the Battle of Valdevez in 1140 and the meeting of the knight Egas Moniz and Alfonso VII of León in the twelfth century, as well as pastoral scenes. In the 1950s, those involved in designing the first underground station in Lisbon sought 'a low-maintenance, easy way to have the underground spaces feel less separate from the outside world' (Whitely 2014). The Oriente train station in Lisbon, constructed as part of the hosting of Expo by the city in 1998, is the backdrop for a series of stunning contemporary tile murals that were commissioned from five international artists. Featuring motifs such as pirates and various sea creatures, the murals are linked by the Expo theme 'The oceans, a heritage for the future' – a nod to the fact that 1998 was the 500th anniversary of Vasco da

Gama's arrival in India and the United Nations' 'Year of the Oceans'. The murals were therefore designed to salute the city's maritime heritage and its role in global maritime exploration. While we did not observe tour groups in the stations, we did see visitors gazing entranced at the station murals. Some of this would have been serendipitous, as tourists arrive at or depart from these stations. In other cases, individuals armed with guidebooks appeared to have made a specific visit to the stations and were taking photographs of what they were gazing upon.

The use of tiles in twenty-first-century Portugal is less to educate the masses than to delight them. It is often carried out with a playful or whimsical touch, as illustrated by the tile murals in Oriente Station discussed above. Whitely (2014) refers to the 'surreal' mural by Pomar at the entrance to the Museu da Cerveja in Lisbon, including a rabbit eating a watermelon, and reproduces the words of a sign nearby that makes the rationale for the mural clear: 'What has been painted on the wall is there to entertain – a juggling trick; a street performance. It's as simple as that'. There is no overt political agenda behind their existence, and thus no conflict or dissonance associated with them on the part of the visitor. Tourists passing by these murals when taking the train around the city were observed taking photographs of them but also smiling at this distinctive twist on the usual grey environs of railway stations in other parts of the world.

Sustainability of these tourist drawcards, however, is an issue for various cities. The *azulejo*, both old and new, form a decorative backdrop to many street scenes in Portugal and make them attractive places to visit and gaze upon by tourists. At the same time, there is disquiet over the number of thefts of *azulejo* from Portuguese streets, leading to the SOS Azulejo project in 2007 that aims in part at 'raising people's awareness of the value of Portuguese historic tiles', as well as preventing the stealing and neglect of these treasures (European Heritage Association 2014). Concerns over potential degradation of these tiles in situ were also part of the rationale behind the creation of the National Tile Museum in Lisbon in 1971 (Calado 1989). While a number of interior examples of *azulejo* are subject to World Heritage listing in Portugal, such as those in the town of Sintra and Porto and the Monastery of the Hieronymites, those in public streets are not similarly protected. Interestingly, the azulejo on facades of buildings developed as part of Portuguese colonial rule contributed to the Historic Centre of São Luís do Maranhão in Brazil receiving World Heritage listing in 1997.

Discussion

It is tempting to categorize these murals as another manifestation of cultural heritage. They were created in the past and continue to exist and be valued in the present. However, there are some difficulties with such an approach. As has been widely argued, heritage is usually underpinned by a personal connection with the visitor (Poria, Biran and Reichel 2009). Does that connection exist in these case studies? There are local communities that see these murals as part of their regional – perhaps even national – identity. This may attract tourists, even where there is no personal connection. Portugal is probably a good example of this. Nonetheless, tourism is usually better understood as a validation of *identity* rather than identity being a driver of tourism (Frost and Hall 2009; Pretes 2003). Certainly in Portugal, the murals may be seen as a component of a portfolio of experiences and features that make up the Portuguese culture. In contrast, the Moldavian murals are confined to a small and peripheral regional area, dwarfed by the more widely known cultural attractions of neighbouring Transylvania. The Ravenna mosaics, while placed in one of the most tourist-focused economies on earth, derive from the Ostrogoths and Byzantines – cultures which may be more difficult for modern tourists to identify with. An alternative is to consider these murals in terms of religious tourism. In his typology of religious tourism, Ron (2009) identifies visits to Christian sites of art and architecture. This certainly covers Moldavia and Ravenna and some of the murals in Portugal. Again, though, there are difficulties with applying this typology in this context. These visitors are not having religious experiences. They are drawn by the art, not by a pilgrimage to a sacred site.

To better understand the phenomenon of these murals as *tourist attractions*, we suggest consideration of three interrelated concepts. The first is that these are public art, which is 'consumed' differently than other forms of art. All of these murals were designed to be viewed and read in situ. Their placement – often in or on the outside of churches – was an important political statement. Local people saw them and were imbued with the messages they conveyed. Such messages related to identity: reinforcing groups and cultures within society, emphasizing who were the rulers and elites and proclaiming their legitimacy and wisdom. If taken away and placed in museums, such murals lose this power of place. That these murals are still where they were created gives them continuing meaning, resonance and authenticity for tourists.

Existing within the spaces of normal society – as opposed to within a gallery or museum – these murals are generally lacking formal visitor interpretation about them. This would affect how they are consumed and experienced. In many cases, the multiple murals spread across a geographical area provide a sort of treasure hunt. These are not neatly packaged or staged tourist experiences. With limited interpretation and often inadequate mapping and information, the tourist has to seek them out and then try to make sense of what they see. Our concept of the explorer traveller (Laing and Frost 2014, 2015) is particularly applicable here. Travelling independently, these tourists relish the challenge of finding their own way, acting as a *flaneur* or wanderer and overcoming difficulties. The existence of multiple sites raises the attraction of being a collector, ticking off the various murals to complete the set.

The final concept is the appeal of imagining the past as an antidote to modernity. Rather than being built on a personal connection, much history is fantasized about as a better – perhaps simpler – period and lifestyle than to-day. Many modern cultural heritage tourists are drawn by their fascination with past times. The medieval period, in particular, seems to hold a special place in their hearts and minds (Ashworth and Bruce 2009; Laing and Frost 2012). This may be seen as a function of popular culture, demonstrated by the popularity of books that were turned into recent films and blockbuster television series such as *Lord of the Rings* and *A Game of Thrones*. In the case of these murals, the appeal is that they are the tangible fabric of the past, vividly telling stories that the tourist finds interesting and relevant and worth travelling to.

Conclusion

The importance of heritage murals as tourist attractions has been largely overlooked in the literature. This chapter has helped to fill this gap by exploring their importance through three European case studies of Ravenna, Moldavia and Portugal. It has considered the different reasons for commissioning these murals throughout history. Many have been created for political purposes, often as a way of reinforcing the power of the ruling class, generally monarchical. They have also been used as markers of identity. Gazing upon the depictions of famous victories or events in history helps to embed national narratives into the public consciousness. In more recent times, it is their artistic merit that which is often emphasized, with murals used to make the urbanscape, notably train stations, less dreary and impersonal. Interestingly, the latter do not appear to be controversial or to feature contested narratives, unlike examples of contemporary murals in other parts of the world. For many visitors, the different backgrounds to the creation of these murals are often unclear, due to the lack of formal interpretation at the sites. On the other hand, this may boost their appeal to some tourists, who may enjoy the challenge of discovering the heritage for themselves and speculating as to the reasons for its existence.

Future research might examine the tourist experience involving these murals through the aegis of interviews with conservationists and tourists visiting these sites to augment the data gathered about observed behaviour in this study. For example, we know very little about the role that mobile phones play in potentially replacing the guidebook as a source of information about these sites, as well as whether the absence of formal interpretation enhances rather than detracts from these experiences (Frost, Laing and Williams 2015). It might also be useful to consider whether the lack of personal connection to these murals affects the profundity of these experiences or alternatively adds to their mystery and intrigue. The findings of this current study might be compared with other cases of heritage murals, particularly those which are potentially divisive and involve contestation. There is also scope for further research on public art more broadly, including its role in place identity and attachment, as well as the aesthetics and liveability of urban settings.

References

Ashworth, Gregory and David M. Bruce. 2009. "Town Walls, Walled Towns and Tourism: Paradoxes and Paradigms." *Journal of Heritage Tourism* 4 (4): 299–313. doi: 10.1080/17438730903118097.

Ashworth, Gregory J. and John E. Tunbridge. 2000. *The Tourist-Historic City: Retrospect and Prospect of Managing the Historic City*, 2nd ed. Oxford: Pergamon.

Bhattacharyya, Deborah P. 1997. "Mediating India: An Analysis of a Guidebook." *Annals of Tourism Research* 24 (2): 371–389. doi: 10.1016/S0160-7383(97)80007-2.

Calado, Rafael S. 1989. "The Azulejo Museum: A Unique Glazed Tile Collection in Lisbon." *Museum International* 41 (1): 10–12. doi: 10.1111/j.1468-0033.1989. tb00746.x.

Chronis, Athinodoros. 2005. "Coconstructing Heritage at the Gettysburg Story-scape." *Annals of Tourism Research* 32 (2): 386–406. doi: 10.1016/j.annals.2004. 07.009.

Coentro, Susana, João M. Mimoso, Augusta M. Lima, António S. Silva, Alexandre N. Pais and Vânia S. F. Muralha. 2012. "Multi-analytical Identification of Pigments and Pigment Mixtures Used in 17th Century Portuguese Azulejos." *Journal of the European Ceramic Society* 32: 37–48. doi: 10.1016/j.jeurceramsoc.2011.07.021.

Da Silva, Nuno Pinho, Manuel Marques, Gustavo Carneiro and João P. Costeira. 2011. "Explaining Scene Composition using Kinematic Chains of Humans: Application to Portuguese Tiles History." Proceedings of SPIE 7869, Computer Vision and Image Analysis of Art II, 786905. doi: 10.1117/12.872130.

European Heritage Association. 2014. "SOS Azulejo Project," accessed December 28, 2014, http://www.thebestinheritage.com/presentations/2014/sos-azulejo-project, 253.html.

Frost, Warwick. 2012. "Commemorative Events and Heritage in Former Capitals: A Case Study of Melbourne." *Current Issues in Tourism* 15 (1/2): 51–60. doi: 10.1080/13683500.2011.634894.

Frost, Warwick and Colin M. Hall. 2009. "National Parks, National Identity and Tourism." In *Tourism and National Parks: International Perspectives on Development, Histories and Change*, edited by Warwick Frost and Colin M. Hall, 63–77. London and New York: Routledge.

Frost, Warwick, Jennifer Laing and Kim Williams. 2015. "Exploring the Contribution of Public Art to the Tourist Experience in Istanbul, Ravenna and New York." *Journal of Heritage Tourism* 10 (1): 57–73. doi: 10.1080/1743873X.2014.945458.

Gomes, Ana and Andreia Lourenço. 2014. "Portugal: The Adoption of the Art Nouveau Movement by the Local Bourgeoisies." *Uncommon Culture* 4 (7/8): 182–187.

Hall, Tim and Iain Robertson. 2001. "Public Art and Urban Regeneration: Advocacy, Claims and Critical Debates." *Landscape Research* 26 (1): 5–26. doi: 10.1080/01426390120024457.

Herrin, Judith. 2007. *Byzantium: The Surprising Life of a Medieval Empire*, 2008 reprint. London: Penguin.

Laing, Jennifer and Warwick Frost. 2012. *Books and Travel: Inspiration, Quests and Transformation*. Bristol: Channel View.

Laing, Jennifer and Warwick Frost. 2014. *Explorer Travellers and Adventure Tourism*. Bristol: Channel View.

Laing, Jennifer and Warwick Frost. 2015. "The New Food Explorer: Beyond the Experience Economy." In *The Future of Food Tourism: Foodies, Experiences,*

Exclusivity, Visions and Political Capital, edited by Ian Yeoman, Una McMahon-Beattie, Kevin Fields, Julia Albrecht and Kevin Meethan, 177–193. Bristol: Channel View.

McCarthy, John. 2006. "Regeneration of Cultural Quarters: Public Art for Place Image or Place Identity?" *Journal of Urban Design* 11 (2): 243–262. doi: 10.1080/13574800600644118.

McGrory, David and Miriam Gill. 2014. *The Last Judgement: The Coventry Doom Painting and Holy Trinity Church*. Coventry: Holy Trinity Church.

McWha, Madelene Rose, Warwick Frost, Jennifer Laing and Gary Best. "Writing for the anti-tourist? Imagining the contemporary travel magazine reader as an authentic experience seeker." *Current Issues in Tourism* 19, no. 1 (2016): 85–99.

Mercille, Julien. 2005. "Media Effects on Image: The Case of Tibet." *Annals of Tourism Research* 32 (4): 1039–1055. doi: 10.1016/j.annals.2005.02.001.

Norwich, John J. 1990. *Byzantium: The Early Centuries*. London: Penguin.

Olsen, Donald J. 1986. *The City as a Work of Art: London, Paris, Vienna*. New Haven and London: Yale University Press.

Poria, Yaniv, Avital Biran and Arie Reichel. 2009. "Visitors' Preferences for Interpretation at Heritage Sites." *Journal of Travel Research* 48 (1): 92–105. doi: 10.1177/0047287508328657.

Portela, Ana M. and Francisco Queiroz. 2010. "Ceramics in Portuguese Architecture (16th-20th Centuries)." Paper presented at Qualicer 10, XIth World Congress on Ceramic Tile Quality, Castellón, Spain, February 15–16, accessed January 4, 2015, http://www.qualicer.org/recopilatorio/ponencias/pdf/2010097.pdf.

Pretes, Michael. 2003. "Tourism and Nationalism." *Annals of Tourism Research* 30 (1): 125–142. doi: 10.1016/S0160–7383(02)00035-X.

Reijnders, Stijn. 2011. *Places of the Imagination: Media, Tourism, Culture*. Farnham: Ashgate.

Ron, Amos S. 2009. "Towards a Typological Model of Contemporary Christian Travel." *Journal of Heritage Tourism* 4 (4): 287–297. doi: 10.1080/17438730903045548.

UNESCO (2015a). "Early Christian Monuments of Ravenna," accessed January 15, 2015, www.whc.unesco.org/en/list/788.

UNESCO (2015b). "Churches of Moldavia," accessed January 15, 2015, www.whc.unesco.org/en/list/598.

Vaz, M. Fatima, João Pires and Ana P. Carvalho. 2008. "Effect of the Impregnation Treatment with Paraloid B-72 on the Properties of old Portuguese Ceramic Tiles." *Journal of Cultural Heritage* 9: 269–276. doi: 10.1016/j.culher.2008.01.003.

Verschuren, Piet. 2003. "Case Study as a Research Strategy: Some Ambiguities and Opportunities." *International Journal of Social Research Methodology* 6 (2): 121–139. doi: 10.1080/13645570110106154.

Weaver, David B. 2011. "Contemporary Tourism Heritage as Heritage Tourism: Evidence from Las Vegas and Gold Coast." *Annals of Tourism Research* 38 (1): 249–267. doi: 10.1016/j.annals.2010.08.007.

Whitely, David. 2014. "The Story Behind Lisbon's Beauty." BBC Travel, May 24, 2014, accessed December 27, 2014, http://www.bbc.com/travel/feature/20140515-the-story-behind-lisbons-beauty.

Yin, Robert K. 2003. *Case Study Research: Design and Methods*, 3rd ed. Thousand Oaks, CA: Sage.

3 From 'sacred images' to 'tourist images'?

The fourteenth-century frescoes of Santa Croce, Florence

Russell Staiff

Introduction: a radical disjunction?

In 2006, Cambridge University Press published a collection of essays entitled *Renaissance Florence: A Social History*. Many of the leading Florentine scholars working in English are represented in this volume and together they build on the historical research that has been undertaken about the Tuscan city in recent decades and extend this work by assembling a composite picture of the social life of the city from the fourteenth to the sixteenth century CE. This time frame is, of course, the three centuries synonymous with Florence's reputation as the crucible of the Italian Renaissance. In his conclusion, Jonathan Nelson's contribution about sacred spaces and the memorial chapels in Florentine churches notes the radical disjunction between the family chapels of the distant past – with their decorations, sacred objects and rituals – and what they have become in the present.

> Today, most physical signs of individual and family ownership in Florentine churches are lost, faded, or forgotten, and the adaptation of these buildings to mass tourism further complicates our efforts to understand these spaces. Not surprisingly, we often conflate these ecclesiastical settings with modern temples of culture – the museums – where the paintings and sculptures once found in chapels are now conserved in environments radically different from those with which they were intended.
>
> (Nelson 2006, 374)

Presumably, Nelson is, in the main, referring to those artworks and objects that have been removed from the chapels and placed in museums, but he could also be referring to the frescos, altar pieces, painted crucifixes and sculptures that today remain in situ. Nelson's perspective is that of the historian with their attempt to reconstruct the past in order to understand it. He appreciates only too well how subsequent centuries of use and change so alter the 'original' that historical explanations can often stand in contradistinction to contemporary meaning-making, and perhaps this is especially so in a city like Florence with its multiple millions of visitors per annum (see below).

This chapter explores an entangled conundrum common to so many cultural heritage sites: the 'radical disjunction' between historiography and tourism in relation to the fourteenth-century chapels clustered around the high altar of Santa Croce, a Franciscan church in the southern part of the medieval core of Florence (Figure 3.1).

In particular, the focus is on the famous fourteenth-century CE murals that adorn the walls of the choir, chapels and sacristy. The first part of the chapter is concerned with the current interpretations of the frescoes as understood by historians and art historians. The second part examines the contemporary transformation of the murals into aesthetic objects of 'Art' under the aegis of both museology and tourism. The argument is essentially thus: what was once an integral part of family and city-wide identity at the time of execution, and what was significantly sacred in nature (and well into the sixteenth century) has given way to murals now regarded, via the agency of city and national identity formation, and magnified by tourism, as symbolically synonymous with the Italian Renaissance. This shift seems to indicate a substantial change in the interpretation and experience of the murals. By the twenty-first century, the frescoes of Santa Croce carried multiple meanings: historical, theological, bearing high heritage significance,

Figure 3.1 Santa Croce, Florence.
Source: Wikimedia Commons, image licensed under a Creative Commons Attribution-ShareAlike 4.0 International License.

masterpieces of European art and as an integral part of the identity of contemporary Florence.

By way of a conclusion, I muse upon the multiple meaning-making enterprises at work in Santa Croce through the prism of a recent revisionist interpretation of Renaissance images that offers a very different slant to the perceived disjunction between 'sacred image' and 'tourist image' (Nagel and Wood 2010). Thus, in the title of the chapter, the inclusion of a question mark. Nagel and Wood (2010) propose that images like those in Santa Croce can be considered as having 'plural temporality', and so the disjunction between 'sacred' and 'tourist', between the points of view of the fourteenth century and those of the twenty-first century, is not necessarily oppositional. They reject linear chronology as the foundational epistemology for the experience and cognition of Renaissance art. Instead, they propose that artworks are set free from their historical anchorage and are apprehended in circumstances far from the contexts of their creation (Nagel and Wood 2010).

In this analysis, I have conflated the terms 'mural' and 'fresco'. They are almost interchangeable, both referring to an image on a wall, but 'fresco', in terms of technique, relates to painting on a wall surface rather than other mural making techniques like printing (using stencils) or tiling a wall with mosaic or aerosol spraying. So, the images on the walls of Santa Croce are both murals and frescoes.

The church Santa Croce, the Holy Cross, as we see it today, replaced an earlier much smaller church that had been given to the Franciscan friars who established themselves in Florence in 1228 CE, just 2 years after the death of their founder St Francis of Assisi. The massive expansion via the building of the 'new' Santa Croce began in 1294–1295 CE (Brucker 1983). Originally outside the walls of the city, it eventually became part of the city with the building of the third set of city walls built between 1299 and 1333. The church, in the shape of a Tau-Cross a symbol of St Francis, is 115 metres in length and, notably, has 16 chapels. It is the largest Franciscan church in the world. The conglomerate of patrician families who owned the chapels was responsible for their fresco decorations that began in about 1310 CE and was completed by the 1330s. Famously, it was the workshop of the Florentine painter Giotto that painted the frescoes in the Bardi and Peruzzi family chapels, the nearest to the high altar on the southern side (Najemy 2008) (Figure 3.2).

The choir was decorated by the workshop of Agnola Gaddi in the 1380s with the depiction, appropriately, of the legend of the True Cross. But that was then. Today, Santa Croce has been transformed into a quasi-museum with special lighting, entrance fees, booking systems, audio guides, interpretation panels (conventional and digital), a circulation system, security, bookshop and so forth, and caters for over one million visitors annually. As Jeni Ryde has asked, in her recent research in the phenomenon of church transformation in Florence, is Santa Croce church or museum? (Ryde 2009, 2013).

Figure 3.2 Apse of Santa Croce, Florence. The Bardi Chapel is to the right of the high altar.
Source: the author.

The frescoes of Santa Croce

The extent, scale and diversity of the fourteenth-century CE frescoes of Santa Croce are such that, for the purposes of this chapter, it is impossible to consider them as anything other than a generalized category. For reasons that will become apparent, my focus will be on the Bardi Chapel and, to a much lesser extent, the Peruzzi Chapel, both decorated by the workshop of Giotto – most probably in the 1320s CE or the decade before (Stubblebine 1985). Both the Bardi and the Peruzzi families were wealthy and highly influential banking families that lived in extended family enclaves within the Santa Croce quarter of the city. The Bardi's were the Papal bankers and, probably, this was the reason why they were able to obtain the chapel closest to the high altar – the most prized location – over the more powerful Peruzzi family. By the 1320s, the two families owned Europe's leading banking companies, the source of their enormous prestige, power and status within and without Florence (Najemy 2008; Herlihy and Klapisch-Zuber 1985).

The Bardi family purchased the Santa Croce chapel in 1310 and had an especially close relationship with the Franciscans, particularly Louis of Toulouse, the Franciscan bishop who was canonized in 1317. Given the location of the chapel, next to the choir in a major Franciscan church, and the Bardi family's relationship with the Franciscan friars, the theme of the fresco cycle of their chapel is to be expected: six narrative scenes from the life of St Francis of Assisi (Bellosi 1981). On his death in 1299, the Peruzzi family scion, Donato di Arnoldo, left money for the purchase of a family chapel in Santa Croce. The Peruzzi chapel was decorated with scenes from the lives of St John the Baptist (the patron saint of Florence) and St John the Evangelist (Bellosi 1981). The Bardi and Peruzzi chapels were not just prestigious accoutrements but were also family tombs.

Giotto's involvement with both of these chapels is known only by tradition. In the Western art canon, Giotto is often heralded as the 'revolutionary' painter that instigated a type of realism and expressiveness into his dramatic narrative scenes that broke with the two-dimensional and coolly abstract painting style of the late Medieval period (Cole 1976). There is no surviving documentation that specifically links Giotto with the Santa Croce commissions (Norman 1995). The earliest extant references are from the fifteenth and sixteenth centuries by the sculptor Ghiberti and the painter and biographer Vasari who wrote a 'life' of Giotto (Cole 1976). According to Vasari, Giotto's workshop was responsible for the fresco decoration of four chapels in Santa Croce (Vasari 1965). Sadly, little remains except those pictorial programmes in the Bardi and Peruzzi chapels. The Bardi frescoes are 'true' fresco, that is, the murals were painted onto wet plaster and so the compositions have dried within the plaster layer. In the Peruzzi chapel, the technique was *al secco*, the paint pigment applied to dry plaster so the paint layer sits on top of the plaster and, as a result, has faded much more quickly over time than the murals in the Bardi Chapel. The painted narrative cycles in both chapels were painted over in the eighteenth century and hidden from view during a time when fourteenth-century CE images were considered somewhat unsophisticated and 'old-fashioned'. They were 'rediscovered' in the nineteenth century. In other assaults on the integrity of the painted murals, tombs were set into the walls, severely damaging images like the justly famous 'Death of St Francis' in the Bardi Chapel. Restoration occurred in the 1950s only to have this work literally inundated by floodwaters in the disastrous River Arno flood of 1966, bringing a torrent of mud and water into Santa Croce and submerging the lower scenes of the fresco cycles. The subsequent restoration took decades. Somewhat perversely, the Florence flood heightened media attention about the 'art treasures' of Florence and their heritage value by re-rehearsing the idea of Florence as the crucible of the Italian Renaissance and using the deluge to raise the spectre of loss, threat and destruction of invaluable patrimony. *Life* magazine called Florence the 'ravaged realm of art', 'treasures ... devastated' and 'much of the city's most precious heritage ... of the Renaissance lay submerged in water and mud' (Velon 1966, 121–126).

Today, the visitor to Santa Croce is directed by guidebooks, guides, the internet and the travel industry to three main attractions housed by the Santa Croce complex. The first relate to the funeral monuments of famous Florentine citizens including Alberti, Bruni, Ghiberti, Michelangelo, Machiavelli, Galileo, Rossini and Marconi. The second are the fourteenth-century murals. The floor-to-ceiling mural decorations are concentrated in the eastern part of the church in the choir, the family chapels (especially the Bardi, the Peruzzi, the Baroncelli, the Bardi di Vernio and the Guidalotti-Rinuccini chapels), the sacristy and the old refectory. Although frescoed over a number of decades, there is a common emphasis on narrative cycles depicting the lives of the saints: the Virgin Mary (twice), Mary Magdalene, John the Baptist, John the Evangelist, St Francis, St Sylvester, St Lawrence and St Stephen. The third attraction of Santa Croce is the Renaissance works of art of the fifteenth century, especially the sculpture of Donatello and the Brunelleschi-designed Pazzi Chapel.

Santa Croce and Florentine historiography

When nineteenth-century scholars began to privilege Florence as the centre of the Italian Renaissance and to support the boasts the Florentines had often made for themselves about their crucial role in the 'rebirth' of Classical culture in the fifteenth century, they were instrumental in the foundations of the 'myth of Florence'. This myth – expressing the exceptionalism of Florence, and the belief that, beginning in the fourteenth century under the power of humanist rhetoric hinged to the study of Greek and Roman literature – claimed that the city broke with earlier so-called 'medieval' traditions and ushered in a new golden age of civilization (Brucker 1969). The self-belief of the Florentines had an enormous power over European historians and art historians. Giotto, the early fourteenth-century Florentine painter, was singled out as a mural painter whose workshop introduced a 'new' style of painting that turned its back on the Byzantine influenced art of previous decades, taking it from ornate abstraction of divine figures to a more 'naturalistic' style based on observations of the 'real' world (Norman 1995). Giotto's fame and brilliance were established early in the writings of Dante and Vasari. By the mid-twentieth century, under the influence of the idea of a 'Renaissance', Giotto had been transformed into 'an Artist' and words like 'revolutionary style' were attached to the works he had supervised (see Cole 1976). This was despite the fact there was no word in fourteenth- and fifteenth-century Italian for 'artist' in the sense that we use it today. The closest was what, in English, translates as 'artisan', something quite different to contemporary usage (Larner 1971).

These shifts in art historical discourse – the fusion of scholarship with the myth of 'Renaissance Florence' – had a profound effect on the way that the Bardi and Peruzzi chapels in Santa Croce were regarded. They had become part of a galaxy of star attractions in the story of 'Modern' Europe, a watershed moment in time when image and vision heralded a new society and culture that challenged, and eventually eclipsed, medieval feudalism (for an overview see Graham-Dixon 1999). Art historians saw a lineage of realism/naturalism in Western painting that stretched from Giotto to Cezanne (Norman 1995). Historians saw a new humanist spirit fed by classical knowledge that stressed individualism over the collective; much of this was epitomized by the nineteenth-century writings of the influential Swiss historian Jacob Burckhardt (Burke 1974). However, by the end of the twentieth century, the exceptionalism of Florence was being challenged on a number of fronts. It is beyond the scope of this chapter to describe these in detail. Suffice it to point to a number of research directions that have substantially modified the nineteenth-century and early- to mid-twentieth-century conception of Renaissance Florence. I will touch on just two dimensions that pertain to the fresco decorations in Santa Croce: (1) image, theology and religious ritual (2) family patronage and devotions.

Image, theology and religious ritual

In his groundbreaking study of public life in Renaissance Florence, Richard Trexler (1972, 1980) offers a wealth of evidence illustrating that sacred images, like the frescoes in Santa Croce, were considered in the fourteenth century to be 'power-laden'. This was a time when devotional practices were fuelled by the belief in the omnipresence of the supernatural, and this presence had its locus in sacred objects like the Host (of the Eucharist), relics and pictures (Trexler 1972, 1980). In a chapel, like the family chapels of Santa Croce, all three were present in a potent matrix whereby God's power, for the supplicant, could be defined in quite precise physical terms. In the fourteenth century, Florentines would not speak about 'going to church' or 'going to Mass' but, rather, would say they were 'going to see the "Body of Christ"' or they were 'going to see God'. There are also many examples in contemporary chronicles of images speaking or supplicants speaking to images (Trexler 1980; Eckstein 2006). Indeed, the whole mission of St Francis of Assisi was initiated, according to his contemporary biographer the Franciscan St Bonaventure, by an image that spoke to him while he was praying before it (Jørgensen 1955). Sacred pictures were a gateway to the divine, a portal that connected the earthly with the heavenly. The frescoes of the Santa Croce family chapel were, to use the words of Nicholas Eckstein, 'living places' in 'active dialogue' (Eckstein 2014, 6) with the community of friars, with the families who came to worship in their chapels and bury their dead; with the wider congregation – the chapels were not completely sealed away but consciously visible in their magnificence to those who could access the choir; with the neighbourhood within which Santa Croce stood; with other Florentines; and with visitors to the pre-eminent city of banking, manufacturing and mercantile activities (Eckstein 2014). The frescoes, then, were commingled with the constant dynamism of the social and religious rituals of which they were a crucial part.

The very 'life-like' renderings by Giotto's workshop in the Bardi and Peruzzi Chapels – the qualities of 'realism' and 'naturalism' commented upon by the Florentine chroniclers – is a testament to the way in which the images interacted with and within the communal life they inhabited. Their 'realism' enhanced their efficacy and the intimacy supplicants brought to the encounter (Sinding-Larsen 1984). Like the population of the city, the frescoes were actors in the cosmic drama. Florence could be regarded, with no sense of irony, as the 'New Jerusalem' precisely because the border between the sacred and the profane was porous in the extreme (Trexler 1980). Thus, the images were much more than narrative scenes of the lives of the saints, much more than theological instruction for the viewer, more than the communication of Franciscan orthodoxy for the community of friars (Goffen 1988); these images collapsed time and space. In these chapels – as in all churches in Florence – the whole history of God's creation, the earthly incarnation of God/Christ, the presence of the Divine in the present and the future salvation of the sacred city at the end of time, came together in a mystical union epitomized by the frescoes.

Family patronage and devotions

One of the fundamental understandings of recent Florentine historiography is the notion that a triad defined the social environment of the inhabitants of the city throughout the fourteenth and fifteenth centuries: kinship, friendship and neighbourhood (Kent 1977; Kent and Simons 1987; Burke 2004; Eckstein 2006). The Florentine urban world was one where everything was personalised. Commerce, politics, culture, religious observance and so on were characterized by intimacy and a sense of personal obligation. Patronage was a central dynamic of the kin, friend and neighbour trio of social bonds: individuals were motivated to seek wherever possible dealings with family, friends and neighbours. The system also had a sacred dimension. What defined the moral climate of clientage was fraternal love, respect and loyalty between patron and client, a due and deferential sense of subordination of lower to higher, of son to father. Patronage employed the language and imagery of saintly intercession; the idea of heavenly intercession was replicated in the social world of the Florentines. Indeed, there was a general expectation that, come the Day of Judgement, those redeemed would rise with their familial and neighbourhood networks entirely intact. The family tomb being located within their chapel was thus highly significant.

Patricia Simons has suggested that artistic patronage should be considered more as a process rather than a system (Simons 1987). The patron, she argues, was a go-between mediating between kinsmen, the friars of the church and the artist's workshop. This helps explains that the pictorial programmes within the chapels fused the social orbits of the Florentine patricians and the liturgical life of the church. But the magnificence of the chapel decorations – certainly an important statement about the power, wealth and status of the family – was only part of the patrician family's concern. The overriding consideration was the family's salvation. Chapel endowments included liturgical rituals and the insistence that masses for the salvation of the family linage be regularly performed within the ancestral chapels. In the private chapel, the cult of the family clan was powerfully tinctured with ancestor reverence and the Catholic cult of the dead (see Kent and Simons 1987).

By way of illustration, I want to consider just one of the narrative scenes in the Bardi Chapel fresco programme: Francis's *Renunciation of Worldly Goods* (Figure 3.3). Putting aside the specifically hagiographic elements, the scene consists of well-dressed patricians gathered in a public place witnessing an argument between two family members, father and son. Francis is shown publically renouncing the material world of his father and, in so doing, bringing shame to his father as head of the family. Such a renunciation in the eyes of a patrician Florentine involved the abrogation of family tradition. The Church, represented by the Bishop of Assisi, has been dragged into the dispute. The anger of Francis's father is understandable when it is recognized that the 'good name' of the family was hugely important to these

Figure 3.3 Renunciation of Wordly Goods. Giotto fresco, Bardi Chapel.
Source: the author.

mercantile patricians. By openly disobeying his father, Francis has breached family solidarity, an action that struck at the very heart of patrician power. Florence, in the fourteenth century, was a society that distrusted and kinship was all that often stood between order and anarchy. Indeed, the setting that Giotto uses reinforces this very point. The building is certainly not an ecclesiastical structure; if anything, it is a patrician palace with a sort of loggia facing onto the street. The very public nature of the dispute is a vital aspect of Florentine justice – it is public so that family, friends and neighbours can witness the outcome and thus sanction whatever results arise. In this case, the Church, which was one of the important judicial instruments in northern Italian city-states, is present as an arbitrator. That the outcome (Francis getting his own way) was unacceptable is underlined by the two children depicted as either being severely reprimanded or having their gaze forcefully averted from the shocking breach of family honour.

Goffan (1988) suggests that while the saint's renunciation of his father's material possessions is an abnegation of worldly values; the scene, nevertheless, is in homage to the merchant class who are displayed in all their finery. The Franciscans had reconciled the merchant-banker with the Christian church and the strength of this belief is to be found in the nature of the patronage at Santa Croce and, in particular, in the identification in the composition of Ridolfo Bardi, the patron of the chapel (Goffan 1988).

Santa Croce, tourism and the Renaissance myth

Any cursory examination of guidebooks and coffee table books about Florence quickly reveal that the art of the fourteenth to sixteenth centuries has come to stand for the preeminent cultural achievements of the city, an embodiment of the 'golden age' of the Renaissance. This is the myth of the Renaissance: Florence, the crucible of the rebirth of the classical culture of ancient Greece and Rome, the recovery of the languages and learning of antiquity, the production of timeless masterpieces by creative (male) genii (Giotto, Masaccio, Donatello, Brunelleschi, Botticelli, Leonardo da Vinci, Michelangelo and so forth) and the advent of 'modern' society (as opposed to the medieval world of Europe). In an essay for *Tourism Analysis* in 2010, I attempted to analyse the mediation of the tourist Florence by the discourse of the Renaissance and attempted to untangle some of the strands of intertextuality at work in the (ongoing) cultural productions of tourist Florence (Staiff 2010). I do not want to re-rehearse the specifics of my argument here except to underline how pervasive the myth has become and how the recent developments at Santa Croce, now a major tourist attraction, are a response to the myth/tourism nexus rather than a response to recent Florentine historiography and art historical research.

Currently, according to an article by Emily Payne in the *Daily Mail* (April 16, 2015) (Payne 2015), some sixteen million tourists visit Florence every year. *Tourism-Review.com*, however, reported that 8.5 million tourists (domestic and international) stayed overnight in 2014 and another 4.5 million visited (but stayed elsewhere). Given the population of the Commune of Florence is approximately 381,000 (2014), no matter the source of tourism statistics, the numbers are extremely high. The Basilica of Santa Croce is the fifth most visited attraction in Italy (Ryde 2009) and any survey of tourist guides to Florence will include Santa Croce in a list of 'top things to do'. *Lonely Planet's* online guide is typical of the English language guides:

> Most visitors come to see the tombs of Michelangelo, Galileo and Ghiberti inside this church, but frescoes by Giotto in the chapel's right of the altar are the real highlights. (www.lonelyplanet.com/italy/florence, accessed April 3, 2015)

Given such exhortations, and given the numbers of tourists to Florence, the issue of visitor management at Santa Croce (and other Florentine churches) became increasingly pressing. Jeni Ryde's work (Ryde 2009, 2013) is crucial to understanding the responses of religious orders and civil authorities to tourism. She has analysed the transformation of churches in Florence into quasi-museums in response to, first, the appropriation of the myth of the Renaissance into tourism culture (experiences, representations, discourse, marketing and so forth) and, second, the number of tourists and their impact on highly sensitive heritage environments like the frescoed chapels in Santa Croce. The contemporary 'Santa Croce experience' is the result. In 2002, the *Opera di Santa Croce*, a lay organization that administers the funds of the Basilica for maintenance and conservation, initiated a series of visitor management measures: an entrance ticket (bought online before visiting and with timed entry); the division of the internal church space into secular and sacred (as theologically peculiar as that may be); roping off areas of significance and/or fragility; special lighting to illuminate artworks of importance; an outsourced security firm and an alarm system plus visitor facilities/services – including a shop, toilets, audio guide, interpretive panels (both conventional signage and digital installations), and the provision of local guides (Ryde 2009, 2013).

One of the fundamental spiritual and cultural shifts that has occurred, because of the deepening power of the myth of the Renaissance, has been the metamorphosis of the frescoes of Santa Croce into secular objects under the aegis of Art. This process is not recent and one can point to a number of historical factors for its occurrence. It had its origins in the fifteenth century when painters and sculptors began to assert their status as 'Artists' and not craftspeople. The profound and enduring effects of the Reformation and the Counter-Reformation with their disputes about the role and function of religious imagery gave the process further impetus. The Enlightenment and the doctrine of the separation of church and state increased the momentum. By the nineteenth century, at the very time the modern myth of the Florentine Renaissance established itself, Romanticism and then Modernism in the

visual arts, both movements promoting a very different form of spirituality/
transcendence, largely, but not completely, subsumed the religious power
of paintings. The creation of the public art museum in the late nineteenth
century and the removal of many works of art from churches to galleries –
in the case of Florence, the (re)creation of the Uffizi collections – was yet
another form of the secularization of religious art. Audiences to the Bardi
and Peruzzi chapels were no longer experiencing the images as portals to the
divine, as sacred objects, but as emotional experiences (sometimes overpow-
ering ones) governed by or alongside formal analysis (style, colour, composition, iconography) and the (historical) lives of the artists.

This far-reaching shift is perfectly captured in E.M. Forster's 1908 novel
A Room with a View: 'The traveller who has gone to Italy to study the tactile
values of Giotto ...'. Forster observed, '... may return remembering nothing
but the blue sky and the men and women who live under it' (Forster 1955,
19–20). Lucy Honeychurch on her visit to Santa Croce to see the Giotto frescoes, minus her Baedeker guidebook, and thus rather afraid to experience
art without reference to dates and authorship and authoritative explanation,
makes a discovery. '... [T]he pernicious charm of Italy worked on her, and
instead of acquiring information, she began to be happy' (Forster 1955, 25).
The modern travellers, in their multitude, are quite remote from the world
that produced the frescoes upon which they gaze; they are more closely
aligned with the world of Lucy Honeychurch. In the 1985 movie version of
the novel, a tour group is in the Bardi Chapel listening to a tour guide identifying the subject matter of the scenes and Lucy Honeychurch is listening
to the atheist ideas of Mr Emerson.

Whether Santa Croce is a church or museum is a moot point. Mass attendance is low (about 200 at the mid-morning service on Sundays and an
average of 4 at weekday masses), local parishioners preferring to go to small
churches that are outside the tourist trail and the number of Franciscan
Friars in the attendant community is less than ten (Ryde 2013). In this way,
it is arguable that the secularization of the Giotto frescoes of the Bardi
and Peruzzi Chapel is complete. Tourists marvel at artistic invention and
achievement: Giotto's genius, the story of St Francis (one of Italy's patron
saints), a famous film set, damage by the 1966 flood, the Bardi family, Papal
bankers, their disastrous loans to Edward III of England and the marriage
of a daughter into the Medici family in 1415. It is the 'time of the Renaissance' that now permeates the interactions between the frescoes and their
contemporary viewers. And so, whatever interpretation is given tourists, the
frescoes of the Bardi and Peruzzi Chapels are frozen in time, locked in the
past (cf. Staiff 2010).

Heritage tourism as a cultural production invariably attempts to expel
the contemporary (or at least bracket it out) in the act of beholding the objects and material culture of the Renaissance. The frescoes of Santa Croce
have been repositioned in four ways. First, they are regarded as objects of a

particular past (the golden age of the Florentine Renaissance) to be venerated in this way. Second, they are regarded as objects of survival: the frescoes are still here in the twenty-first century, and so we are aroused by the time scale involved in this survival, some 700 years. Third, and as a result of one and two, the frescoes are given new contemporary meanings: they are a masterpiece, a treasure, an invaluable remnant of 'our' past that have endured the ravishing effects of chronological time. Fourth, the chapels are projected into the future as something to be protected for generations to come, not as sacred spaces but as historical objects that have remained in situ seven centuries after Giotto and his workshop created the images that adorn their walls. The inscription of Florence onto the World Heritage list has underscored and reinforced this repositioning (cf. Nagel and Wood 2010).

Conclusion: anachronic time and the sacred/tourist image disjunction

I began this chapter by suggesting, along with others, a radical disjunction between the 'living images' of the Giotto frescoes at the time of their creation and the 'tourist images' of the present; between the family chapel of the fourteenth century and its current function as a viewing gallery for artworks; between contemporary historical research and tourism representations and interactions (Staiff 2010). However, as I intimated in the introduction to the chapter, I want to conclude by changing the register of the debate and the way we perceive this apparent dichotomy.

In 2010, two American art historians, Alexander Nagel and Christopher S. Wood, published *Anachronic Renaissance*. This extremely important work begins with a series of propositions. The first of these is a rejection of linear chronology as a foundational epistemology in the interpretation of art works. As part one of my exposition illustrates, the Santa Croce frescoes have been treated by scholars as images to be understood in their own time. The research has focused on the social world that produced the paintings and the iconography of the images as a fusion of the artist's commission, the theological and ritualistic role of the images at the time and their place within a family chapel and tomb. It is, however, a twentieth- and twenty-first-century research agenda of recovery: recovering original meanings, original artistic intentions and the recovery of social relationships in a world long gone. Linear time is crucial to this endeavour.

The second proposition of Nagel and Wood (2010) considers works of art as 'generating the effect of a doubling or bending of time' (9). It follows on from their rejection of linear time as an underpinning epistemological structure. Time, instead, is deemed as being flexible and so they embrace the term 'anachronic time' to describe the potential of art works to be dislodged from Western chronological time and for the art work to be interpreted/appreciated/affecting in circumstances radically different to those of its execution in the early fourteenth century. Scholars, they argue, tend to overlook the possibility of the life-force of images, like the Santa Croce frescoes, beyond the time of their creation. Consequently, later interpretations and symbolic renderings are considered as a 'disjunction'.

The third proposition flows from the idea of anachronic time: artworks can reference multiple historical moments *in* the present, and so the viewer can find in any one historical image a number of temporalities and a number of past events but not apprehended as a line stretching back through time but as a synchronous moment of perception and effect/affect.

In the Bardi Chapel, the events depicted in the narrative scenes of the life of St Francis were events presumed to have occurred some 100 years before Giotto's pictorial realization. And yet, in the confines of the family chapel, they are both of the past and, for the Bardi family gathered in their chapel, of the present (see the discussion of the *Renunciation of Worldly Goods* above). On another level, the paintings replicate the function of the chapel they adorn – the interred members of the Bardi family venerated by the living family members just as Francis, dead since 1226 CE, is venerated in the frescoes. Furthermore, given the celebration of the Mass in the chapel, the temporal shifts are manifested on a number of planes: the living Christ of the Eucharist in the present, reenacting the historical event, the Last Supper, thirteen centuries in the past. But Francis, the first saint in recorded history to miraculously receive the stigmata, the wounds of Christ's crucifixion and a phenomenon depicted in the frescoes, brings another temporal dimension to the image-ritual relationship. So, following the argument of Nagel and Wood (2010), multiple historical moments/events are operating simultaneously in the fourteenth century, even though these events are, in fact, dispersed and separated across linear time and dispersed and separated spatially.

Zooming forward to the twenty-first century, these anachronic dimensions continue on but with important variations. The celebration of the Eucharist in Santa Croce still harkens back to historical events, now twenty centuries ago, whereby the divine mysteries at the centre of the Catholic Mass connect the past with the present: the historical Christ *and* the living Christ of the Eucharist in the twenty-first century linked to the life, death and mission of the Franciscans. The Bardi Chapel images connect three temporalities: the historical Francis, the Franciscans, and their newly built church in the early fourteenth century when the frescoes were painted, and the present day community of friars, the ongoing custodians of the basilica (the Franciscan Order does not own Santa Croce). But this axis of meaning and significance is not the only one operating. Giotto's frescoes have been given a different but synchronous identity precisely because they are not anchored to the moment of their rendition. Tourism and the museumification of Santa Croce is built upon the survival of Giotto's frescoes and their absorption into contemporary life as 'artistic masterpieces', as symbols of the Florentine Renaissance, of Florence the city, of a particular art historical narrative, as part of a World Heritage designation and as oft-reproduced images in photography, postcards, books, all manner of digital formats, cinema, documentaries and, above all, as a tourist encounter. The frescoes of Santa Croce have a vibrant 'life' in the present and thus bear witness to Nagel and Wood's view that '"Art" is the name of the possibility of a conversation across time' (Nagel and Wood, 18). In this calculus, 'radical disjunction' may not be the only way to consider the perceived disconnect between recent historical research into Renaissance Florence and the frescoes of Santa Croce with their contemporary tourist publics.

References

Anonymous, *Lonely Planet*. Introducing Florence, accessed April 3, 2015, www.lonelyplanet.com/italy/florence.

Anonymous, *Tourism-Review.com*, accessed May 8, 2015, www.tourism-review.com/florence-a-record-year-for-the-tourism-industry-news.

Bellosi, Luciano. 1981. *Giotto*. Florence: Becocci Editore.

Brucker, Gene. 1969. *Renaissance Florence*. Berkeley: University of California Press.

Brucker, Gene. 1983. *Florence 1138–1737*. London: Sidgwick and Jackson.

Burke, Jill. 2004. *Changing Patrons: Social Identity and the Visual Arts in Renaissance Florence*. University Park: Pennsylvania State University Press.

Burke, Peter. 1974. *Tradition and Innovation in Renaissance Italy*. London: Fontana/Collins.

Cole, Bruce. 1976. *Giotto and Florentine Painting 1280–1375*. New York: Harper and Row Publishers.

Eckstein, Nicholas. 2006. "Neighborhood as Microcosm." In *Renaissance Florence: A Social History*, edited by Roger Crum and John Paoletti, 219–239. Cambridge: Cambridge University Press.

Eckstein, Nicholas. 2014. *Painted Glories: The Brancacci Chapel in Renaissance Florence*. New Haven and London: Yale University Press.

Forster, Edward M. 1955. *A Room with a View*. (First published 1908). Harmondsworth: Penguin Books.

Goffen, Rona. 1988. *Spirituality in Conflict: Saint Francis and Giotto's Bardi Chapel*. University Park and London: Pennsylvania State University Press.

Graham-Dixon, Andrew. 1999. *Renaissance*. London: BBC Worldwide.

Herlihy, David, and Christina Klapisch-Zuber. 1985. *Tuscans and Their Families*. New Haven and London: Yale University Press.

Jørgensen, Johannes. 1955. *St Francis of Assisi: A Biography*. New York: Image Books/Doubleday.

Kent, Francis W. 1977. *Household and Lineage in Renaissance Florence: The Family Life of the Capponi, Ginori and Rucellai*. Princeton, NJ: Princeton University Press.

Kent, Francis W. and Patricia Simons, eds. 1987. *Patronage, Art and Society in Renaissance Italy*. Oxford: Clarendon Press.

Larner, John. 1971. *Culture and Society in Italy 1290–1420*. London: BT Batsford Books.

Nagel, Alexander and Christopher Wood. 2010. *Anachronic Renaissance*. New York: Zone Books.

Najemy, John. 2008. *A History of Florence 1200–1575*. Oxford: Blackwell.

Nelson, Jonathan K. 2006. "Memorial Chapels in Churches: Sacred Spaces." In *Renaissance Florence: A Social History*, edited by Roger Crum and John Paoletti, 353–375. Cambridge: Cambridge University Press.

Norman, Diana, ed. 1995. *Siena, Florence and Padua: Art, Society and Religion 1280–1400. Vol. 2, Case Studies*. New Haven and London: Yale University Press and The Open University.

Payne, Emily. 2015. "Save Florence From Mass Tourism." *Daily Mail*, April 16, accessed May 8, 2015, www.dailymail.co.uk/travel/travel_news/article-3041513/.

Ryde, Jeni. 2009. "Church or Museum? The Case of Santa Croce, Florence, Italy." *The International Journal of the Inclusive Museum* 2 (2): 39–50.

Ryde, Jeni. 2013. *Church or Museum? Tourists, Tickets and Transformations*. Unpublished PhD dissertation, Sydney: Western Sydney University.

Simons, Patricia. 1987. "Patronage in the Tornaquinci Chapel, Santa Maria Novella, Florence." In *Patronage, Art and Society in Renaissance Italy*, edited by Francis W. Kent and Patricia Simons, 221–250. Oxford: Clarendon Press.

Sinding-Larsen, Staale. 1984. *Iconography and Ritual: A Study of Analytical Perspectives*. Oslo: Universitetsforlaget As.

Staiff, Russell. 2010. "History and Tourism: Intertextual Representations of Florence." *Tourism Analysis* 15 (4): 601–611.

Stubblebine, John. 1985. *Assisi and the Rise of Vernacular Art*. New York: Harper and Row Publishers.

Trexler, Richard. 1972. "Florentine Religious Experience: The Sacred Image." *Studies in the Renaissance* XIX: 7–41.

Trexler, Richard. 1980. *Public Life in Renaissance Florence*. Ithaca, NY and London: Cornell University Press.

Vasari, Georgio. 1965. *Lives of the Artists*, trans. George Bull. Harmondsworth: Penguin Books.

Velon, Victor. 1966. "Ravaged Realm of Art." *Life Magazine* 61 (21): 121–126.

4 The walls speak

Mexican popular graphics as heritage

Martín M. Checa-Artasu

The observation of movement in cities reveals the existence of a whole series of complex and dynamic scenarios. Urban centres tend to be loci for noisy cacophonies often mixed with varieties of odours and, almost always, a veritable flood of visual stimuli that catch one's attention. For purposes of this analysis, this will be called the landscape, and it is eminently anthropic. Thus, the landscape as the visual reflection of an urban space contains numerous elements that we can detect and decode, actions which assume that these visual images are signs that must be understood if one is to fully appreciate that the landscape determines how to move within it and comprehend the diverse characteristics of cities (Arias 2003, 131–132).

Visual elements can and have been categorized by social scientists that study urban landscapes. Bailly (1979, 161), for example, offered a diaphanous, bipolar classification that highlights both unique and constant elements. The former include different kinds of monuments, buildings and unique spaces. The latter consist of other natural or constructed elements that form part of the city's fabric: this includes the publicity and the materials that support it, which manifest typical features such as communications intended to persuade people to buy products and so stimulate production or to inform and contribute to the socialization and integration of urbanites (Molero 1995, 56). That said, we must remember that diverse forms of publicity became established in European cities through a long historical process. This began in the eighteenth century amidst the turmoil of the Enlightenment and the French Revolution and were handed down to us through distinct moments or periods. In the mid-nineteenth century, for example, signs painted on walls were antecedents of popular graphics that evolved into poster art. Both expressions later became forms of publicity par excellence that endured into the mid-twentieth century. At that point, new mediums of expression like billboards, canvases, monopoles, UIPI (urban installations that present information) and IPO (illuminated publicity objects), among others, progressively appeared in urban spaces. Parallel to their emergence, design – gradually consolidated as a discipline – began to elaborate new theoretical conceptualizations including *visual design* and techniques that continued to expand with the advent of new technologies and digitalization.

This was a global evolution, but one marked by disparity when we consider the different geographical areas of the planet that have emerged as a result of capitalist development, market economy, colonization, trade expansion and industrialization, the transmission of ideas, construction of the urban phenomenon and the effects of globalization (Pacheco 2007, 121–123). This disparity explains the persistence of diverse support for publicity that exists in the same temporal framework throughout history, a kind of stratigraphic sequence that reveals multiple supports that have led to a high degree of graphic contamination and an excess of messages whose meanings must be discerned. It is precisely amidst this maelstrom that signs painted on walls, a form known as commercial art, can be found. They are also called, in some Latin American countries, 'popular art' or 'popular graphic art' or, as in Brazil, 'popular or vernacular typography' (Guimarães 2005).

This chapter analyses popular graphic art in Mexico, a place where this form of advertising has a long tradition and its presence is widespread across cities and towns. The professionals who produce graphic art are called *rotulistas*, a term that broadly encompasses what in English are painters, letterists and graphic artists. Likewise, their varied production, in Spanish *rótulos*, will be referred to as popular graphics, signs and paintings on walls. In Mexico, popular graphic art is a communicative artefact that conveys a concrete and synthetic message. It is a painting technique that combines lettering and drawing and is presented on a lintel or on a wall close to a commercial establishment. The messages conveyed are purely commercial, and popular graphic art must not be considered an artistic mural, such as those realized by the great Mexican muralists (Rivera, Orozco, Siqueiros). It probably does not follow the same Mesoamerican tradition. However, it is painting on a wall using letters, typographies, colours and drawing with the intention of transmitting a message. Furthermore, although the commercial requirements leave little room for artistic expression, these advertisements can convey a secondary, parallel message where the *rotulistas* express irony, humour, sensuality, social constraints and other such themes. This following chapter analyses popular graphics arts in Mexico while taking into consideration the graphic artists and their work and techniques, and the conceptual meaning of this form of publicity.

Popular graphics in Mexico

The last 15 years in Mexico have seen several attempts to recover popular graphics that go beyond simple compilations. Particularly notable is the study coordinated by two graphic designers, José Carlos Mena and Oscar Reyes (2001) entitled: *Sensacional de diseño Mexicans*. This is an exhaustive compendium of popular graphics from central Mexico. They published and presented this as an exhibition that toured several cities in the USA and some in Europe, but is rarely seen in Mexico (Mena and Reyes 2001).

Though it includes diverse elements that appear in Mexico's urban spaces under the heading 'graphics', it is highly suggestive and rich in nuances and a meritorious pioneering work.

Four similar studies – photographic collections of murals artwork – have appeared in the last 15 years. The first was by the photographer Germán Montalvo (2002) where the image of the Popocatépetl volcano, one of Mexico's most representative symbols, is transformed into a recurring icon on walls and other surfaces of schools, houses and businesses, as well as on buses and advertisements for bottled water. The second, also by a photographer, Rafael López Castro (2006) is entitled *Vestida del Sol*. It presents an extensive series of images of the Virgin of Guadalupe from walls throughout Mexico that reflect devotion and the significance of religion among Mexicans. The third contains an exhaustive collection of images from the city of Puebla and its neighbouring municipalities by Enrique Soto Eguibar (2003, 2009), an amateur photographer, biochemist and university professor. After 20 years and thousands of images photographed, he published a compilation of them. His work shows the ephemeral nature of these graphic representations but simultaneously allows these images of faith to reveal the richness of this resource. The most recent work is compiled by the North American writer and editor Phyllis La Farge and presents images taken by the Swedish photographer Magdalena Caris. Entitled *Painted Walls of Mexico* (2008), it contains a collection of samples of graphics from Mexico City and the states of Yucatán and Veracruz. It is a collection narrated in colloquial language reminiscent of the style of travel books, and its great merit lies in presenting works by several graphic artists. This book rescues these artists from anonymity while elucidating the meanings of their graphic art through a primarily semiotic approach that allows the authors to penetrate into the sociological elements underlying the scenes depicted.

Several studies also emerged recently from the academic world with reflections on the characteristics of popular graphics in Mexico. Particularly important is the research of the graphic designer and professor at the *Universidad Autónoma de Aguascalientes*, Mónica De la Barrera Medina (2005), based on paintings from markets in San Luís Potosí. We should also include the exceptional 2006 BA Thesis, *Tipografía y gráfica popular Mexicana como influencia para el Diseño Gráfico*, by the designer and plastic artist from Coahuila, Patricia Hernández, a graduate of the *Universidad Iberoamericana (La Laguna)*. Additional work, such as the collection of images by two graphic designers from the *Universidad de las Américas* (Puebla), Alejandra Escamilla Yarahuan (2004) and Liza Bueno Linero (2005), focuses on popular graphics in Veracruz. Finally, it is worth mentioning a study by the graphic designer Pilar Castro, and the author of this article (Checa-Artasu 2008; Checa-Artasu and Castro 2009, 2010). This study takes a cultural geography approach to the analysis of popular graphics and its presence in the urban landscape. All of these scholars seek to identify the characteristics of graphic expressions and to find a way to incorporate them within the parameters of academic design from a historicist perspective. The undercurrent is one that seeks to vindicate this form of popular design.

Often, these graphics are not only collected but also become sources of inspiration or even a resource that stimulates new typographies, especially in today's digital environment. In this regard, the work of Mena and Reyes (2001) is an excellent attempt to reutilize sources that emerged from popular graphics. Perhaps the most successful such attempt is found in the journal *Tiypo* which, in its eleven issues, presents diverse typographies created by young Mexican designers, including some that emanate directly from popular graphics. These 'figures' include the so-called *Santa Clara* typography devised by Ángeles Moreno in her study of hand-painted graphics in downtown Puebla (Peón 1999, 31), and the *Luchita Payol*, a font derived from prints that advertise wrestling matches that uses movable type made of cut linoleum to rescue the textures and imperfections of printing on low-quality paper.[1]

The characterization of popular graphics

Popular graphics are a set of communicative artefacts that transmit messages that are synthetic and easily understood. These two features are key to identifying the essence of this form. Popular graphics are typical of cities where they were born and flourished in response to commercial flows derived from capitalist expansion. Cities also concentrate the most diverse expressions of human activity. Their technique and material supports – of being paintings on walls or glass, concrete or sheeting – and their permanence in urban landscapes is determined by their resistance to inclement weather and the more or less frequent renewal of paintings by whoever sponsors them.

Perhaps the most inherent, typical feature of popular graphics, and what differentiates them from other communicative artefacts, is that they cannot be automatically copied, unlike prints, lithographs, linotypes, serigraphy or offset. They are described as 'popular' because of the characteristics of the agents who create them – designers (graphic artists) – and the party that commissions them. The former are artisans, 'masters' of a trade learned through tradition and experience that, through the techniques employed, seems to approach the academic postulates of the field of graphic design – though their work is not included in it. The clients who commission such works expect the artefact to solve their need to communicate, especially in an effort to sell products or services, but also to transmit information on ludic activities, announce public policies or publicize institutional campaigns.

Formally speaking, works of popular graphics consist of four interconnected elements: lettering, drawing, colour and support. Of these, the first is the essential component for without it, popular graphics would not exist due to the fact that its messages would be diluted and easily misinterpreted. The companion of the lettering is the drawing which may be figurative or caricaturist. This is the second primordial element and is inextricably linked with the lettering in a union that explains the communicative function of popular graphics. This makes it relevant to the typographic characteristics of the words and the concrete characteristics of the image which appear together in vignettes on the walls where they are painted. The wording on its own – depending on the target population sector – cannot assure communicative and functional success, so the drawing is a complement that corroborates the function of the sign and assures that it is fulfilled effectively (Kerlow 2001, 9; Checa-Artasu and Castro 2010, 28).

Two additional elements complete the artefact: colour and the support where it appears; i.e. a wall, facade, fence, metallic curtain or other flat surface. Formally speaking, these four elements – wording, drawing, colour and support – characterize popular graphics. However, often these graphic expressions transcend the purely functional purpose of transmitting certain information to introduce elements. This is especially the case with images that convey humour, irony, desire, vanity, irreverence, covert sexuality or social criticism. This gives the resource added value and expands its dimension as a sociocultural artefact. The transcendence that derives from the creativity of graphic artists proclaims their artefacts as an inexhaustible source of typographical solutions with a broad panoply of drawings, logotypes and caricatures. These are all created by individual initiative or copied from foreign models adapted from globalized or local cultures (García Canclini 1990, 68; Monsivais 1978, 104). In light of these considerations, we can say that this is a manifestation of an unofficial form of communication if by this we understand that it is not framed within any specific discipline such as graphic design. It would appear that popular graphics is exempt from the academic conventions that govern plastic composition (typography, the use of colour, etc.), though skill is clearly reflected in the use of these elements (Mena and Reyes 2001, 12). A detailed study of the work of popular graphic artists reveals that in many cases they do take into account the tools typical of academic conventions, but that they readapt and re-comprehend them as a function of the greater efficiency and resolution of their work (Troconi 2009, 44; Populardelujo 2009, 12–56; Cárdenas 2009; Checa-Artasu and Castro 2009, 2010).

Both the creators of popular graphics and those who demand their services come from the popular classes, and it is there that this form has developed. It is assumed to be *their* form of communication. This explains why popular graphics may be created, assumed or used by other social sectors that need to communicate with those classes: for example, the political or governing class that wishes to send messages, business people of all economic levels who publicize products or services or even university centres that paint on walls their lists of undergraduate courses. All of them use popular graphics to reach a broader public and transmit messages to large segments of the population. Likewise, popular graphics is a perfect example of hybrid culture and a referent of multidimensional heterogeneity, to use

García Canclini's expression (1990, 71). By drawing on resources, messages and artefacts from the mass media and global cultural industries, it is possible to claim that popular graphics symbols have originated in cultured art. They then assimilate, alter and adapt them to transmit messages that incite people to consume.

The creators: graphic artists

Rotulistas hide behind three names: graphic artist, letterist and painter. These are synonyms that recall the figure of a 'master' who teaches a trade learned through tradition and experience. Indeed, the fact that it *is* a trade leads to the belief that those professionals are anonymous and invisible, an opinion held by those who analyse and vindicate popular graphics as an element of visual urban culture. Actually, upon deeper understanding of this profession, anonymity was found to be relative. These graphic artists are professionals who are sought out – like plumbers, carpenters, bricklayers or locksmiths – by an astounding variety of clients who require the kind of communicative artefacts they create. Over time, they may become well-known in local circles through word of mouth as their reputation for excellence spreads. However, this does not mean that none aspire to be artists someday and that some have actually already achieved that 'status' (Populardelujo 2009). To the trained eye, it is possible to recognize their style and identify them. Some graphic artists are better at lettering. Others are more gifted at drawing. While others are extraordinary caricaturists. Certain constant elements are integrated into the artists' work: for example, the use of diverse typographies taken from manuals or created freehand; realistic drawings copied from a broad range of everyday objects; characters from comic books or animated drawings; attempts to caricature public figures; animation of inanimate objects; and the use of colour contrasts that do not obey the canons of correct combinations. Moreover, *rotulistas* work outdoors and, despite the anonymous nature of their trade, they may become public figures.

Significantly, this trade emerged in various cities in Europe and colonial America in the eighteenth century when it was known as 'sign-painting', but it underwent a transformation as it expanded in cities due to the processes of industrialization in the second half of the nineteenth century (Combier and Merou 2007, 44; Vitta 2003, 245). Professional sign-painters were trained through the typical guild sequence of apprentice-official-master. They became more dexterous through practise, direct instruction and systematic repetition. Their methods conferred a singular ability to draw images or trace different typographies. While, today, these popular graphic artists tend to work individually because the popularity of their trade is declining, they were once organized in workshops where they accumulated professional experience and handed it down from one generation to the next. Serigraphy (silk-screen printing) later challenged their trade, but graphic artists were able to adapt and carry on, though the same cannot be said of the more recent challenge of digital graphic design with its novel techniques and resources that threaten the future of popular graphics. At present, unfortunately, the emphasis is on producing large volumes, rather than on the quality of the finished product. In large cities in Mexico, the decline of this trade is reflected clearly, for example on *República of Perú* street in Mexico City: once lined with numerous graphic workshops, now there are only three left (Cárdenas 2009, 43).

Graphic artists and their procedures

Though at first sight the technique seems simple, when asked to describe their trade, graphic artists discerned five stages. At this point, I must say that several *rotulistas* were interviewed in situ in cities such as Chetumal, Puebla and Mexico City over 2007 (Checa-Artasu 2008; Checa-Artasu and Castro 2009):

1   The commission, or order, is the first phase in the process. It begins when a potential client contacts the graphic artist. Usually, it involves identifying the place where the image will be painted, perhaps the facade of the business, part of a building or an unoccupied wall or concrete surface in the urban geography. It is important to mention that these surfaces are now often rented for this purpose, but occasionally there are free spaces that do not require payment, mostly along communication routes between different municipalities. During this phase, the characteristics of the painting are discussed so that the artist can calculate how much of the work will be original, how much copied, and the ratio of lettering-to-drawing, while devising the drawing system she/he will propose.

2   The sketch is the key element presented before work begins. Usually, it is a simple sketch on paper where the artist outlines a proposal for the mural that takes into account the client's requirements. Often, the client will participate actively in elaborating the sketch, or may even develop it her/himself to show the graphic artist.

3   The base step consists of applying gypsum or plaster to fill holes and imperfections in the wall chosen for the work, and then covering the surface with a base coat of white paint. This often covers up an existing drawing that is in some stage of deterioration.

4   Tracing the design and lettering with pencil and ruler. This stage involves two procedures performed simultaneously once the white base paint is dry. The objective is to orient the drawing(s) and lettering in the space destined for the mural. The graphic artist must calculate the distribution of the pieces of the mural and then pencil them in. Of course, this follows the sketch given by the client or drawn by the artist in tune with the client's needs and requirements. The outlines of the different objects or figures are first traced in pencil, and a technique called *reglado* is used to position the letters that will appear in the mural. To

this end, the artist uses a ruler or straight strip of wood and draws two parallel lines similar to what graphic designers call the 'body', though some artists prefer to draw only one baseline.

5   Painting or colouring depends on the level of complexity involved. The graphic artist proceeds to paint the definitive form of the pieces of the mural, including drawing(s) and lettering. In many cases, she/he paints the entire surface area with one, or various, colours over the white base. This use of colour is one of the primordial characteristics of popular graphics, and the technique requires either a roller or some kind of pressure-applied painting (Figure 4.1).

With respect to the drawings, brushes of distinct thicknesses are used for different types of images, including very fine ones for extremely detailed

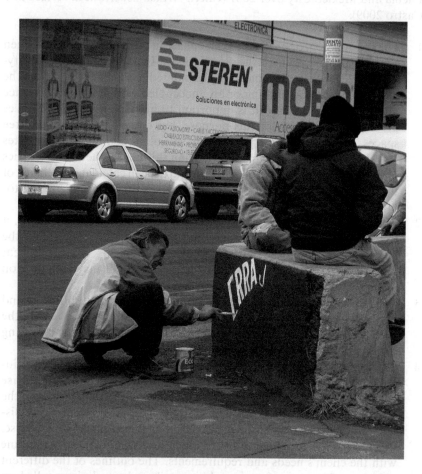

Figure 4.1 Rotulista in action. Puebla, México.
Source: Martín Checa-Artasu, March 2012.

paintings. For the lettering, a medium brush is used because it allows the artist to trace firm, homogeneous lines. In some cases, especially large-format works, the thin side of a flat brush is employed in an up-and-down motion. The colours, finally, are applied in a series of layers carefully calculated by the graphic artist, who first paints one and then allows it to dry before applying the following colour. The result is a combination of nuances that often give a gradient effect or transition from one colour to another. This technique is often used for especially large signs or panels because it allows several graphic artists to work simultaneously.

The lettering as key to popular graphics

In the popular graphics documented in cities in Mexico, lettering is virtually omnipresent because it is almost impossible to assure that the message communicated is exactly what the client wishes to transmit without the help of a written message. A more thorough analysis shows that lettering represents not only language, but also expresses the creativity that the artist adds to the desire to transmit a specific message. In popular graphics, the lettering governs the graphic space occupied by the words of the message, but it is often stylized into images that give the walls and streets of cities a certain 'flavour' (Millán 2008). Through this metamorphosis, letters cease to pertain to language and become part of the city itself. The visual impact accounts for this art form being currently recognized, revalued and reutilized by professionals in graphic design eager to find new ideas and sources of inspiration (Huerta 2008, 67–78). This conversion of series of letters into images is not separate from the technique employed by graphic artists. In fact, they first elaborate the sketch and then carefully determine the size of the phrase, the spacing and the interlineations. It is precisely this preparatory phase that explains how this conversion is achieved (Figure 4.2).

Upon analysing the forms of the construction of lettering, it becomes clear that the typographies reveal great freedom. In general, graphic artists seem not to be hindered nor constrained by the norms that regulate the use of typographies and their constituent structural or stylistic elements in other contexts. However, many popular artists also purchase books with font-types and symbols (published by *Mecanorma*) and use them as models for their freehand reproductions. One specific form whose use has spread extraordinarily, and that fits perfectly into current popular Mexican culture, is called *Blackletter* or Gothic minuscule. The origins of this style of lettering can be traced back to the twelfth century, but it began to appear in Mexico with the arrival of the first movable-type printing presses in the second half of the sixteenth century. The abundant use of this font, whether it be in religious books, public announcements, pamphlets or early newspapers led to its assimilation into Mexican popular culture so that today it can be seen in tattoos, murals painted on pick-up trucks, popular graphics and painted posters. Its application reflects certain values linked to the concept

Figure 4.2 Typography and lettering play announce this copy shop in San Andres Cholula, Puebla.

Source: Martín Checa-Artasu, January 2008.

of tradition and its now widespread use is a living example of the freedom characteristic of the work of graphic artists (Paoli 2006).

Strictly speaking, in the vast majority of cases, the lettering is of a basic type, though one perceives an extraordinary degree of diversity. In not a few examples, shanks and stems are painted in bright tones with fading, while in others, the letters contain a series of effects so that they appear to be in low or high relief, but they tend not to technically reflect the formal construction of typography. In other samples, the width of the letters may be compacted, stretched, normal or widened in order to adapt them to the space available on the surface. One might say that most are variations of a basic type that are applied according to the features that each graphic artist wishes to include in their work while respecting the constraints imposed by the space available, the message, and the client's specifications. This variability in lettering provides a richness made possible by the dexterous use of techniques of calligraphy that graphic artists (sign-painters) learn through practise. However, they must never lose sight of the fact that the final product has to fulfil the functional goals of maximizing legibility, clarity and simplicity.

The indispensable drawing

The drawing is the indispensable complement to the message transmitted in letters in works of popular graphics. It transmits such features as humour, irony, double-meaning, desire, vanity, mockery of something or someone, sexual innuendo or 'jabs' thrown at the desire for wealth or power. In popular graphics, drawings are elaborated on the basis of a series of graphic resources that run from virtually identical copies of logotypes and trademarks, to reproductions of characters from comic books or cartoons, to the creation, sui generis, of figures invented by the graphic artists themselves. These drawings can be grouped into five categories. The first includes images taken from, or inspired by, the world of animated drawings and comics. The use of these elements reflects a degree of familiarity, or perhaps humour, which is easily appreciated by real or potential clients. This form is especially characteristic of the walls of kindergartens or primary schools, for example, though we also see it in other kinds of establishments. Wherever it appears, it lends a jocular, humorous or playful tone to paintings (Figure 4.3).

The second type includes human figures drawn in caricaturized styles. The use of these drawings fosters identification with the public to whom the advertisements are addressed, so these images are often used in portraits like those seen in beauty salons and barbershops where the objective is to demonstrate how a particular hairstyle or haircut may look. They tend to feature highlighted faces with highly stylized wavy hair that brings to mind the promotional photographs displayed by cosmetics companies. A third group consists of caricaturized drawings of edible animals and everyday objects. Almost all the images in this category combine and transmit a sense of humour and irony. Unlike the first two groups, they appear in more diverse contexts, postures and actions: butcher shops, poultry shops, locksmiths' shops, seafood restaurants, or diners and cafeterias, among other establishments.

The fourth group includes graphic representations of foods, drinks and prepared dishes. Clearly, they are characteristic of businesses in the food sector such as vegetable booths, taco stands and grocery stores. Typically, they include various lines of text that describe the range of products offered, reinforced by graphic elements that inform clients of the products that are available, and/or emphasize the optimal quality and characteristics of the merchandise they offer.

The last group consists of drawings of machinery, tools, construction materials or automobile parts, typically seen at businesses related to the purchase and or sale of replacement parts, automobile repair, tire stores, locksmiths' shops or companies that rent industrial machinery, or sell construction materials or wood, among other items. The artistic merit of these paintings is quite remarkable since they reproduce on a large scale – but with impressive precision – real-life objects that are quite small (e.g. nuts

Figure 4.3 Lettering, drawing, cartoon characters, colour and branding are combined in this groceries shop at Calzada de los Milagros in México DF.
Source: Martín Checa-Artasu, November 2007.

and bolts), or medium-sized such as shock absorbers, table saws or car batteries. An attempt at a semiotic reading of these forms might reveal that, above all, they seek to assure that potential clients or consumers will be able to easily identify and discern stores where they will find professionals perfectly familiar with the merchandise or service offered, whether it be machinery, tools, or some kind of utensil. Here, the painting is a synonym for a specialized service.

Popular graphics as cultural heritage in Mexico

Popular graphics on walls contain two clearly determined denominators: drawing and lettering. Together, they close a communicative circuit that transmits the desired message. To accomplish this, popular graphics relies on creativity that transforms sign-making into an exercise of synthesis that strives to solve a challenge; namely, how to transmit messages effectively (Boden 1994). However, despite the supposed anonymity in which its creators work, producing popular graphics is an exercise that entails risks associated with several techniques that may be considered elements of the discipline of graphic design. Risk is present in the act of learning this amalgam of elements that, through the interplay of combinations, experiments with the role of lettering. Another risk is the characteristic variation in the use of colour, form and type. Nor is the act of using this form exempt from subversion, provided by its capacity to appropriate and reinterpret through drawings that can represent numerous elements of the *mass media*, global culture, local cultures and conventional publicity. Additionally, graphic artists must seek to comply with the functional requirements of communicating a message with clarity. It is important to note that both concepts – subversion and risk – are implicit in the elaboration of creative processes, as in the case of popular graphics. If the clients are not pleased with the advertisement, they have it painted again.

Simonton (1999, 201–206) writes that creativity is multidimensional and based on experience and different influences. Analyses of the panels of popular graphics indicate that streets in Mexican cities often agglutinate examples of multidimensional creativity visualized through popular graphics created by a series of anonymous artists who, after long processes of apprenticeship of this craft, become capable of expressing it on walls, concrete fences, shop lintels and other public surfaces. But, of course, we must not let ourselves be fooled during analysis. Creativity is present, no doubt, but cannot always be freely expressed since the graphic artist is subject to the strictures of demand. The possibility for multifaceted and subversive creative play depends on them, such that it might be possible to establish gradients of degrees of creative development dependent on economic availability and the criteria and rules established by clients.

In Mexico, popular graphics on walls must be seen as a social phenomenon because it extracts a series of resources from society to be used in its construction. It is well known that creativity flourishes in environments marked by type of activity, the capacity for intellectual reception, ethnic diversity and political aperture – the latter understood as stability (Florida 2010, 77). But how much of all this can be seen in popular graphics found in Mexican cities? Without probing too deeply, it could be argued that this activity is, in essence, creative, be it through the knowledge acquired by the graphic artist her/himself while practising this art, or through the paintings commissioned. Ethnic diversity and social plurality are inherent to Mexican society where miscegenation of all types has left diverse marks and scars, especially where different ethnicities coexist in urban centres. In light of these components, one might say that popular graphics in Mexico is becoming a form of cultural heritage, one both tangible and intangible. This is particularly so when it is concluded that the graphic artist offers services that are required by a broad layer of society – the so-called popular classes – which understands that the communicative technique it offers is both economically more affordable and intellectually more understandable. This consideration of popular graphics as heritage is confirmed by both its geographical distribution and its progressive extinction. This art form is systematically excluded in towns throughout Mexico, preponderantly in neighbourhoods or zones called 'popular' and less so in historical downtown areas, bustling financial centres or new commercial spaces. Furthermore, it seems clear that the distribution of popular graphics in the city is a function of socioeconomic aspects that segregate urban populations. If publicity is associated with the segmentation of publics for the transmission of messages, then, in this case, the opposite is true: the publicity element, popular graphics, is a reflection of the segmentation of urban residents into social classes.

Linked to this, the wall or façade where these advertisements are painted has become an economic resource, as are the surfaces that support other types of publicity. Today, clients who need a wall to advertise their products or services through popular graphics must rent that surface. In this way, walls around empty lots awaiting urbanization, or abandoned fields along roads and highways, acquire value for their owners who can rent them out to be painted with murals. Thus, the use of popular graphics in the urban landscape is neither random nor isolated from the economic features associated with other forms of publicity. And this economic factor, its capacity to segment the population and the characteristics of popular graphics used in the murals itself mean that this is a form of publicity that is habitually found in urban landscapes in cities and towns in Mexico that we may justifiably consider part of Mexico's cultural heritage.

Conclusion: overlooking the obvious

This chapter has defined and explained each and all of the components of popular graphic arts as murals in México. Due to its formal features and its generating process, popular graphics is very well represented in the urban landscape of Mexican cities and towns. However, this presence does not quite depict the configuration of the urban environment as far as social classes are concerned. *Rotulistas* paint their work in those neighbourhoods and districts considered popular. We must not forget that they are part of a profession that arose in popular neighbourhoods to a need of the residents of these neighbourhoods. Thus, this is one of the main conclusions that stem from the analysis of popular graphics in Mexico since it is an indication of socioeconomic aspects that segregate the urban population. If publicity is associated to the segmentation of the target public, in the case at hand, the commercial element is a reflection of the economic segmentation of the city.

Additionally, the location of the commercial element reflected in graphic murals in certain areas that are part of the urban landscape is not random. The façade and the fence where these graphic signs can be found are the support turned into an economic resource that blends with the process of generation and reproduction of the commercial element analysed in this chapter. These wall surfaces on fences are rented to clients who want to advertise their business or merchandise by means of popular graphic art murals. Thus, the fences that surround unused land waiting to be urbanized, and the walls around those lots along frequently used routes, see their value enhanced as their owners use them for publicity purposes. Consequently, the distribution of graphic art in the urban landscape is closely associated to the economic characteristics of other commercial elements. This economic factor in terms of its capacity of segmentation and above all the intrinsic characteristics of popular graphic arts make the subject of this chapter a commercial element closely related to the urban landscape of Mexican cities and towns. It is indeed similar to the experience of urban areas in other latitudes, but it contains part of the idiosyncrasy, creativity and cultural wealth of Mexico, reflecting identity through the graphic arts murals. All these justify a deeper study, like the one presented here, and point to considering popular graphic arts as another one of the features of the rich, intangible cultural heritage of Mexico.

Note

1 This font was presented at the congress *Mexico, Forging the Character,* organized at *TypeCon 2007* in Seattle, Washington, by the Mexican designers Marina Garone, Isaías Loaiza, Gabriel Martínez Meave and Leonardo Vazquez. New typographies can be consulted at: http://www.flickr.com/photos/mexicoforgingthecharacter/.

References

Arias Sierra, Pablo. 2003. *Periferias y nueva ciudad: el problema del paisaje en los procesos de dispersión urbana*. Sevilla: Publicaciones de la Universidad de Sevilla.

Bailly, Antoine. 1979. *La percepción del paisaje urbano,* Madrid: Instituto de Estudios de la Administración local.

Boden, Margaret. 1994. *La mente creativa: mitos y mecanismos*. Barcelona: Gedisa.

Bueno Linezo, Liza. 2005. "Gráfica Jarocha." BSc diss., Department of Graphic Design, Universidad de Las Américas Puebla.

Cárdenas, María Luisa. 2009. "Oficio: rotulista. Entrevista a Manuel Velasco." *Artes de México, El otro muralismo* 95: 42–45.

Checa-Artasu, Martín Manuel. 2008. "Tras la gráfica popular de Chetumal." *Revista Río Hondo* 65: 32–35.

Checa-Artasu, Martín Manuel and Pilar Castro Rodríguez. 2009. "Deje que la barda hable." *Artes de México, El otro muralismo* 95: 48–57.

Checa-Artasu, Martín Manuel and Pilar Castro Rodríguez. 2010. "El olvido de lo obvio: La gráfica popular, un elemento de publicidad en el paisaje urbano de México." *Diseño y sociedad* 29: 24–33.

Combier, Marc and Henri Mérou. 2007. *Typos en liberté*. Barcelonnette: Atelier Perrousseau editeur.

De la Barrera Medina, Mónica S. 2005. "Mensajes gráficos en los mercados de San Luis Potosí." Paper presented at 1º Congreso Estatal: "La Investigación en el Posgrado." Aguascalientes, Universidad Autónoma de Aguascalientes, 28–30 November 2005.

Escamilla Yarahuan, Alejandra. 2004. "Quinto Patio. Apuntes de la gráfica popular." BSc diss., Department of graphic design, Universidad de Las Américas, Puebla.

Florida, Richard. 2010. *La clase creativa*. Madrid: Editorial Paidós.

García Canclini, Néstor. 1990. *Culturas híbridas. Estrategias para entrar y salir de la modernidad*. México DF: Grijalbo.

Guimarães Martins, Bruno. 2005. *Tipografía popular. Potências do ilegível na experiência do cotidiano*. PhD diss., Universidade Federal de Minas Gerais.

Huerta, Ricard. 2008. *Museo tipográfico urbano. Paseando entre las letras de la ciudad*. Valencia: Universitat de Valencia.

Kerlow, Issac V. 2001. "Gráfica funcional popular mexicana." In *Sensacional de Diseño Mexicano*, edited by Juan Carlos Mena and Oscar Reyes, 7–11. México DF: Trilce Ediciones.

López Castro, Rafael. "Vestida del Sol." *México, Ediciones Era*, 2006.

Mena, Juan Carlos, and Oscar Reyes. 2001. *Sensacional de diseño mexicano*. México DF: Trilce Ediciones.

Millán, José Antonio. 2008. "La letra y su imagen. La rotulación figurativa popular." *Páginas de Guarda* 5: 114–120.

Molero Ayala, Victor M. 1995. *Publicidad, marketing y comunicación. Herramientas para la pequeña empresa*. Madrid: Editorial ESIC.

Monsivais, Carlos. 1978. "Notas sobre cultura popular en México." *Latin American Perspectives* 5 (1): 98–118.

Montalvo, German. 2002. *Popo-pop. Imágenes de la urbe volcánica*. México DF: Secretaría de Cultura del Gobierno del Estado de Puebla.

Pacheco Rueda, Marta. 2007. "La ciudad como escenario de la comunicación publicitaria." In *Publicidad y ciudad. La comunicación publicitaria y lo urbano: perspectivas y aportaciones*, edited by Antonio J. Balandrón, Ester M. Pastor and Marta P. Rueda, 132–145. Sevilla: Comunicación Social Ediciones y Publicaciones.

Paoli, Cristina. 2006. *Mexican Blackletter*. New York: Mark Batty Publisher.

Peón, Ignacio. 1999. "Mexican Letras." *Revista Dx. Estudio y Experimentación en Diseño* 1: 29–33.

Populardelujo Cooperativa. 2009. *Jorge Montesdoca, Roberto Ayala, Arnulfo Herrada*. San Juan de Puerto Rico: Trienal Poli/Gráfica de San Juan and Instituto de cultura puertorriqueña.

Simonton, Dean Keith. 1999. *Origins of Genius: Darwinian Perspectives on Creativity*. New York: Oxford University Press.

Soto Eguibar, Enrique. 2003. *Gráfica Popular Mexicana*. Puebla: Volkswagen de México.

Soto Eguibar, Enrique. 2009. "Un guiño en la pared." *Artes de México, El otro muralismo* 95: 14–23.

Troconi, Giovanni. 2009. "Rótulos para toda ocasión. Entrevista a Adán Navarrete." *Artes de México, El otro muralismo* 95: 44–47.

Vitta, Maurizio. 2003. *El sistema de las imágenes. Estética de las representaciones cotidianas*. Barcelona: Editorial Paidós.

5 Tourism, voyeurism and the media ecologies of Tehran's mural arts

Pamela Karimi

The history of modern institutionalized tourism in Iran dates back to the early twentieth century. After the Pahlavi dynasty defeated the Qajars in 1925, the traditional ritual of *ziyarat* (Shiite pilgrimage to sacred sites) was gradually replaced by the modern secular task of *siyahat* (touristic explorations). Until 1937, Western travellers were not welcomed in religious mausoleums such as Imam Reza's shrine in Mashhad, arguably the most important Shiite pilgrimage site after Iraq's Karbala (Grigor 2009, 33). However, in the later years of Reza Shah's reign and the succeeding rule of Mohammad Reza Shah, many religious sites were, for the first time, defined as historical and tourist destinations and they subsequently attracted thousands of visitors from around the world.

Iran reached its height as a site of tourist attraction in the 1970s when the country became more prosperous thanks to its spectacular oil boom. During the same decade, the master plan for the development of tourism in Iran was completed by a Geneva-based Iranian architectural firm, Zanganeh Consulting Engineers (Sazman-e Barnameh va Boodjeh 1972). The plan, which was submitted to the Iranian National Tourist Organization, outlined the government strategy to expand Iran's tourism to the end of the 1990s. This was an all-encompassing initiative addressing all strata of tourism in Iran, including public entertainment. However, it was halted after the Islamic Revolution of 1979, and tourism increasingly declined. Moreover, following the Iran hostage crisis, involving the holding of 52 American diplomats and citizens for 444 days (November 1979 to January 1981), Iran became an antagonistic place for Westerners. Indeed, overnight, Iran went from a pleasant 'hippie trail' to a hostile zone, and in the following decades it appealed only to a few brave and adventurous travellers whose trip was carefully coordinated in prearranged groups. After the start of the Iran-Iraq war in September 1980, local tourism waned as well. Tourist destinations became grim and art became predominantly political. Equally, Tehran's public places were not intended for pleasure or tourism; rather, the public space of the city became primarily a vehicle for communicating revolutionary and war propaganda messages via larger-than-life murals.

There is a relatively ample body of literature on the raison d'être of murals in Tehran (Chelkowski and Dabashi 2002; Gruber 2008; Karimi 2008;

Marzolph 2013; Grigor, 2014, 25–91). However, little is known about the relationship between these murals and how visitors experience them. In what follows, I first introduce some aspects of murals in relation to the Islamic Republic ideology, and then move to Tehran's aestheticization movement (involving murals) and its connection to local and regional tourism or the lack thereof. Subsequently, I turn my attention to the social media networks to discuss a lesser-known aspect of the experience of viewing murals in the context of global tourist voyeurism and what I call (dis)embodied tourism.

Tehran murals and local tourism

Soon after the Islamic revolution of 1978–1979, the Ministry of Islamic Guidance and the Ministry of Culture and Higher Education, in conjunction with other parastatal organizations (*buniyads*) and the municipal governments (*shahrdari mantagheie* and *basij-e mahalli*), began to sponsor all the political propaganda and slogans that appeared on the walls of Tehran (Gruber 2008, 16; Zangi, Ayatollahi and Fahimifard 2011, 85–101). The government changed the façades of existing buildings by covering them with murals depicting anti-East and anti-West as well as anti-Saddam and anti-Zionist propaganda. There was also a corpus of Shiite-inspired imagery showcasing martyrs of the Iran-Iraq war in larger-than-life proportions side by side with the leaders of the fundamentalist movement such as Ayatollah Khomeini (Chelkowski and Dabashi 2002, 39–40).

After the Iran-Iraq war (1980–1988), the themes of the murals began to shift, slowly but surely. In the early 2000s, the Beautification Bureau, or *Sazman-i Ziba Sazi Shahr-i Tehran*, began to sponsor what they called 'artistic murals'. This was concurrent with the completion of the first draft of Iran's Tourism Master Plan (circa 2000) after the Islamic Revolution and President Khatami's call for the 'dialogue of civilizations' that hoped for better cultural connections between Iran and the outside world (Vafadari and Cooper 2010, 172–173). In keeping with the shared desire to turn Iran into a more open and attractive place for global audiences, one of the first achievements of the mural section of the Beautification Bureau was to licence no further propaganda murals, nor would it protect the already existing ones.

For more than a decade, local media have consistently communicated how the Bureau-sponsored murals have made Tehran more attractive. In addition to local newspapers and online news outlets, several books have been dedicated to these works. *Naghghashihay-e divari Tehran: Panj sal baray-e tasvir gari yek shahr* [*Tehran's Wall Paintings: Five Years of Effort towards Illustrating a City* (2013)] and *Majmooeh maghalat hamayesh elmi avvalin dosalaneh divar negari shahri va gerafik-e mohiti* [*Proceedings of the Biannual of Public and Mural Arts* (2014)] are two handsome volumes enlivened by colourful images on glossy paper. While only marginally addressing the propaganda murals that were sponsored by the Islamic Republic regime, the two volumes are primarily focused on the aesthetic dimensions in murals such as issues of colour and lighting, or how a mural must correspond with its surrounding environment. To make the text more informative for Iranian readers, the latter volume also highlights examples of well-known unconventional murals and public art projects from the USA and Europe, including, for example, Jaume Plensa's 2004 video mural/sculpture, *Crown Fountain*, in Chicago's Millennium Park (Davarian 2014). Correspondingly, the Chief Director of the Beautification Bureau has expressed the organization's interest in expanding the scope of mural arts to turn them into wall sculptures (*divarnegareh*) involving ornamental materials from traditional Iranian architecture such as the ceramic/brick/mirror-work (*seramikkari, ajaorkari, ayneh kari*) (*Goftegoo* editorial 2012). Due to their exotic value for non-Middle Easterners, traditional decorative patterns have long been of more interest to foreign visitors. As such, there is an implicit desire for the expansion of foreign tourism in the capital. However, what is often openly articulated is not tourism, but rather 'the right of the citizens to beauty' (*zibayi va hagghe shahrvandi*) (*Goftegoo* editorial 2012). Indeed, almost four decades after the revolution, the word tourism – *san'at-i tourism* or the industry of tourism, especially as it refers to foreign visitors – is still somewhat of a taboo.

Ironically, however, more than ever before, the emerging mural artists in Iran want to use their art to liven up the city for visitors. Exemplary is the work of Mehdi Ghadyanloo, who takes his cue from renowned Western artists such as David Hockney (Ghadyanloo 2007). Among Ghadyanloo's Beautification Bureau-sponsored murals are those that have added to the tourist attractions of old Tehran. For example, one of his trompe-l'œil murals enlivens the entrance to the Marvi Passageway near Tehran's old bazaar. Appropriated subject matter from nineteenth-century Iranian photography animates empty spaces between rows of traditional brick and ceramic arches, resembling actual arches in and around the passageway (Figure 5.1). In conjunction with the city's efforts to clean up this area, where drug users used to congregate, Ghadyanloo's mural has since served to brighten the surrounding environment and draw tourists.

The desire to attract tourists has also surfaced in religious sites. Prime examples include colourful murals painted in a Cubist style depicting mosques and other sacred buildings on the side of the walls in the holy city of Mashhad, home to Imam Reza's Shrine (for images, see Rustin Zarkar 2014). These added attractions licence a kind of 'non-serious behavior and ... unconstrained social togetherness', thus assuring a more enjoyable public life for citizens, tourists and pilgrims alike (Urry 2002; Deeb and Harb 2013; Zamani Farahani 2010, 211–13). This is particularly important considering that much of local and regional tourism in Iran is religious tourism. According to a recent census, more than five million domestic tourists visit major Shiite sites in Mashhad, Qom, Shiraz and Tehran. In 2008, pilgrimage to Shiite sites was the most prominent purpose of travel after family and recreational visits (Zamani Farahani 2010, 206). These sites also attract the Shiites of the neighbouring countries in the region, especially Bahrain,

Figure 5.1 Mural by Mehdi *Ghadyanloo*, Guzar-e Khatereh, Kucheh Marvi [*Path of Memory, Marvi Alley*], Marvi Quarter, Tehran, District 12, 2006.
Source: Photograph courtesy of Mehdi Ghadyanloo.

Iraq and Lebanon. However, the majority of local and foreign pilgrims are low-income tourists and this limits their spending. Religious tourism is therefore not a huge source of income for the government. Its ideological value is probably more significant than its financial worth.

(Dis)embodied tourism and the lure of Iran's walls

As mentioned earlier, in the 1930s mosques and shrines became official places of tourism where foreign tourists could enjoy the dazzling architectural achievements of the medieval period. These places generated pleasurable visual experiences for foreign tourists of all strata, from anthropologists and ethnographers to casual visitors and photographers. Among them were some photojournalists working for Western mainstream media who followed in the footsteps of Orientalist travel photographers, as well as Orientalist painters who had heightened the mysterious and sensual character of the Middle East (Trivundza 2004). To varying degrees, these photojournalists presented the old codes of dominance and subjugation, difference and otherness. A case in point is the work of the renowned fashion and celebrity photographer Henry Clarke who was commissioned by *Vogue* in 1969 to shoot a spread for the magazine at historic locations around Iran. Conjuring a nostalgic sense of the colonial era for his viewers, Clarke captured his Western female models against the walls of old buildings, including mosques. Akin to Orientalist paintings, notably Jean-Leon Gerome's 1860 *Snake Charmer*, Clarke's photographs reveal the detailed decorative patterns of the walls against partial nudity, thus eroticizing Iran. Similar to art historian Linda Nochlin's assertions in her widely cited article, 'The Imaginary Orient', one may posit that by virtue of the posing model, the ceramic and brick or the wall of mirror-work in Clarke's photographs were 'a project of imagination, a fantasy space or screen onto which strong [erotic] desires ... could be projected with impunity' (Nochlin 1989, 41).

As we look at Clarke's pictures, we think about two visible elements – an old oriental wall and a modern Western female model. Alternatively, and following again in the footsteps of Nochlin's readings of nineteenth-century Orientalist paintings, Clarke's pictures also permit us to think about things that are hidden from the gaze: local people, contemporary life in Iran and so on. Thus, the process by which tourist voyeurism in Iran is ratified in these Pahlavi images can be thought of as part of the colonial practices of subjugation. This approach lingered even when Iran's tourism became increasingly limited to a remote visual experience rather than direct involvement with people and sites. As mentioned before, after the Islamic Revolution of 1979, few foreign visitors could delight in actual tours of Iran.

As an alternative, Iran's locales were mainly observed by foreigners through a repertoire of images in the media. These images often spotlighted the barren, exotic and abnormal characteristics of Iran, dismissing other aspects of everyday life in Iran. Of particular interest to Western media were Tehran's political murals that featured propaganda messages and revolutionary slogans as well as themes from the Iran-Iraq war (1980–1988). Art historian Margaret Olin writes how this form of gaze (i.e. one with absent eyes) is more significant than one with present eyes. She refers to a passage in Sartre's *Being and Nothingness* where the shame of being watched is deemed to be more powerful than the actual experience of seeing someone see us. If you see the eyes, Sartre writes, you cannot see the gaze (Olin 1996, 218). Therefore, 'the felt gaze is more powerful than the seen one', Olin concludes. Sightseeing in Iran has been largely centred on the 'absent eye'. While the citizens of Tehran – a city whose mural real estate was, for decades, exclusively dedicated to the Islamic Republic's ideology – often ignored and still overlook this heavily political scenery, foreign viewers found, and still find, them oddly interesting. Even travel websites encourage visitors to Iran not to miss them. A caption to an anti-American mural painted on the former US embassy's wall featured on a German travel blog reads: 'The former American Embassy is probably one of the most famous sights in the Middle East [...] The walls of the former embassy are painted with anti-American slogans. It's a nice place to visit and you can take some great photos there' (Cahill 2014). And, it is this foreign attention that is often 'felt' by the locals.

In other words, they become more conscious of themselves as they increasingly 'feel the shame of being seen'.

'Shame' might be too strong as a term to connote the impact of this form of visiting, but it is nonetheless applicable; many Iranians – including security guards, police officials and even ordinary passers-by – warn against taking photographs of ideological murals, reasoning that these pictures will circulate on the web, enhancing Iran's poor reputation in the West. In 2006, I was urged to stop photographing an anti-Zionist propaganda mural. The guard justified himself by saying: 'You take pictures of these murals and put them on the web. Then, the US officials will be persuaded to come and bomb us'. Indeed, in both conservative and liberal Western media, Tehran's murals have been continually used to encapsulate Iran's ideological stance. Attracting the attention of US officials aside, the global spectacle of the mural industry has made the Iranian capital a voyeuristic Mecca. And to borrow from John Urry, a sociologist known for his scholarship on tourism (in *The Tourist Gaze*), and John Berger (in *Ways of Seeing*), this form of voyeurism or tourist gaze is not 'a matter of individual psychology but of socially patterned and learned "ways of seeing"' (Urry 2011, 2).

But the reaction to being subject of the gaze does not always involve shame, embarrassment, fear or intimidation. There are other ways through which Iranians react to the so-called 'felt gaze'. Taking note of the global gaze, Iran seeks to discern its own future. In 2013, Tehran's anti-American murals attracted the mainstream media's attention more than ever before, owing to a large banner of Barack Obama that appeared in one of the busiest spots in Tehran, making Iran again a spotlight in the news. To contextualize the Obama banner, the mainstream media showcased many other anti-American murals in Tehran. Notable among them were a skull-faced Statue of Liberty (probably an imitation of a WWII Italian poster, see *Gettyimages* 2015) and a gun animated by the stripes and colours of the American flag set against a backdrop of a seemingly traditional Iranian geometric tile pattern, both adorning the outer walls of the former US embassy.

Unlike these bold murals, the new anti-American banner seemed more complex in terms of its iconography. The banner showed Barack Obama standing next to Shemr (a character from the story of Hussein's martyrdom at the Battle of Karbala in 680). Shemr's killing of Hussein was an ordeal that split Muslims into Sunni and Shia sects. The caption that appeared below the Valiasr Square banner, ascribing to each man, in his own time, the years 'late 2012' and '680 CE', read 'Be with us, be safe'. This mural became the focus of numerous mainstream Western media, each alluding to how Iranians began to lose hope in Obama after the economic sanctions against Iran took a firm foothold. Roland Elliott Brown of *The Guardian* explained the context and meaning of the mural as follows:

> In the mural, Shemr extends a similar letter to the viewer, as he and Obama [who attracted the attention of the Iranian regime, because of

his middle name – Hussein – which he shares with the central martyr in Shia theology, the prophet Muhammad's grandson] utter the words *Ba ma bash* – 'be with us' – playing on the president's name [o ba ma], and insinuating that anyone who still likes Obama in the wake of tightening sanctions – or who advocates meeting American, EU, or International Atomic Energy Agency demands over Iran's nuclear programme to avoid conflict – is a traitor to the faith. Obama, the state insists, is a 'Hussein' unworthy of loyalty.

(Brown 2013)

The main message that Iran insists on in its nuclear development, despite the sanctions, was intended for local audiences. Similar meanings were envisioned for Western onlookers. But when Western media pinpointed this image, they contextualized it within the larger anti-American atmosphere in Iran, drawing attention to Iran's resentment towards the USA. Meanwhile, instead of expressing their own opinions about this image, reporters inside Iran were mostly focused on the ways in which the Western press interpreted it. *Diplomacy-e Iran [Iran's Diplomacy]* and *Bashgah-e Khabarnegaran [Reporters' Club]* paid close attention to the aforementioned *Guardian* article, obsessing over how the West sees Iran's nuclear programme after having stumbled upon this gigantic mural (Eftekhari 2013). This method of interpretation – seeing themselves as others see them and rediscovering the meaning of a propaganda after having encountered the explanation of it by the 'other' – attests to how Iran seeks out its potential on a global scale. In his seminal 1978 book, *Orientalism*, Edward Said writes that European knowledge was established as 'truthful' by the authority of a system of representations, which bolstered Western hegemony. But this authoritative knowledge also informed the discourse of nationhood and became an authoritative base for the self-definition of many postcolonial countries (Ludden 1993). Iran was never officially colonized, however; inadvertently perhaps, its attitude toward Western knowledge perpetuates, to follow historian David Ludden, the epistemological authority of Orientalism.

John Urry uses the term 'tourism reflexivity' to describe the urge for places to turn themselves into tourist destinations (Urry 2002). He writes that this reflexivity derives from 'the set of disciplines, procedures and criteria that enable each … place to monitor, evaluate and develop its "tourism potential" within the emerging patterns of global tourism' (Urry 2002, 2). In a similar vein, both philosopher Jean Baudrillard and sociologist Chris Rojek have argued that through visual culture, tourism is 'frequently promoted as a seduction process' (Baudrillard 1981; Rojek 1995). Endorsing these views in the introduction to their edited volume *Visual Culture and Tourism*, cultural geographer David Crouch and art historian Nina Lubbren have concluded that the act of remote viewing forestalls the actual experience of walking in the city and viewing things up close (Crouch and Lubbren 2003, 8). The propaganda murals in Tehran do not necessarily anticipate what Urry calls 'embodied tourism'. Rather, they construct a form of sightseeing mediated by image and language (Crouch 2000; Urry 2002). Their circulation on the 'street' context of the web turns Tehran into a site for voyeurism, a destination for disembodied sightseeing made possible through virtual and allegorical reality (Buhalis 1998). To expect foreign tourists to come visit Iran's murals after having seen the images of them on the web is an overstated presumption. However, we might posit that the circulation of their images on the internet grants the murals some sort of display value or spectacle agency.

Reworked as tools of resistance against both the dominant sociopolitical atmosphere and cultural mores, Tehran murals have become even more influential in the past few years. Indeed, these countercultural works have formed another category of mural arts that is both fabricated for and consumed by disembodied sightseeing. Unlike the old propaganda murals that showcased Tehran as a site of autocracy, this latter group of murals present the capital as a site of resistance, turning it into an all the more attractive and exotic place. Featuring murals of countercultural 'underground' artists substantiates the failure of the Islamic Republic's ideological programme. Consequently, since Iran's 2009 Green Movement, the countercultural murals have gone viral in social media spheres where local and diasporic Iranians, as well as those interested in change in Iran, (re)produce and consume such imagery.

The global media flow of Tehran's countercultural murals

Until the late 1990s and before thriving domestic computer and internet usage, most of the Iranian media were controlled by the state and used to advance government interests while often ignoring and negatively covering public opinions. By contrast, in today's age of online social and global media networking, anyone can participate in the production and dissemination of news and information or use media to promote social movements and popular social transformation. Facebook, Twitter, Instagram, YouTube, cell phones and other social media allow Iranians to document graffiti art with sensitive and anti-establishment themes. There are institutions in Iran, virtual or otherwise, that regulate standards for such injunctions. *Akhareen akhbar va etelaat- e hozey- e amaliyat- e ravani va jang- e narm [Soft War: The Latest News and Information in the Field of Psychological Operations and Soft War]* is a an official Islamic Republic website that warns against the West's 'soft war' and raises awareness about the soft war as its 'critical cultural mission' (Akhavan 2013, 102). It defines 'soft war' as a wide range of 'cultural, literary, artistic, propaganda, linguistic, and communication' practices that aim to transform a society's 'way of thought' (Akhavan 2013, 102).

Despite efforts to discourage people from using social networks, Iranians are able to access them by installing a software programme known as *ghoflshekan* [lock breaker]. Furnished by *ghoflshekan*, street artists in Tehran often document and feature their art through social media networks because the actual life of their ostensibly unofficial work is too short – they are frequently defaced by the authorities shortly after they appear on the walls. Douglas Kellner, a leading voice in theories of media culture, asserts that 'social networks help construct a new media ecology in which individuals can consume and help produce multiple media in a wide range of platforms and sites, thus becoming ever more immersed in media environments' (Kellner 2012, xi). While earlier Iranian media (TV and the printed press) involved top-down communications, 'the new media ecology' is participatory, dispersed and 'ever shifting and mutating', even despite the above-mentioned sanctions (Kellner, Ibid). Thus, to reiterate, in Iran, art activists use social networking for validating popular resistance and democratic discussions. Since the 2009 Green Movement, they have become fully mindful of the ability of art to function as an arena and medium for political protest and social activism. This is not to say that this phenomenon is exclusive to the post-Green Movement or its successors. Before mural art was institutionalized by the Islamic Republic government, many independent artists expressed their views on the walls of the capital. The message of their work was not always pro-Islamic Republic. For example, the revolutionary female muralist, Nilufar Qadarinejad, was inspired and informed by historic leftist figures such as Diego Rivera (Grigor 2014, 36–37). Because of her gender, Qadarinejad's career as a public artist ceased after the Islamic Republic regime took a firm foothold over the country. As with Qadarinejad, contemporary mural activists are inspired by foreign movements in street art. Even more so, they want to change the propaganda mural system or the general political and social conditions by means of creating alternative modes of street art. Instead of focusing on foreign politics, today's mural artists try to draw attention to the restrictive local sociopolitical atmosphere. They embody the desire for the collapse of the ideological stances of the Islamic Republic regime, even reversing the messages of state murals. They also speak, in a larger sense, to the generation of their parents or grandparents who facilitated the creation and sustenance of this system. Hence, they address those with power as well as to those who permitted the existence of those with power – whether by deliberate approval or submissive acceptance – evoking Václav Havel's 'The Power of the Powerless' in which he highlights the role of those who inadvertently submit to power by simply ignoring it (Keane 2012, 270). On the other hand, they also communicate with a global audience that anticipates seeing unusual things on Iran's walls.

Black Hand is a Tehran-based artist who, like the renowned British graffiti artist Banksy, has expressed his sentiments through his graffiti and mural arts. He paints his graffiti on the walls of Tehran during the quiet hours of the night. Usually, by the next morning, his graffiti has been eliminated by the authorities. Despite erasure, there are photographic records of the actual and the defaced graffiti and these photographs are often widely circulated via Facebook and other social media forums. Because of the sensitive aspects of his work, Black Hand and other Tehran-based graffiti artists – Nafir, Icy and Sot, GhalamDAR, and Alone, to name a few – use pseudonyms and refuse to reveal their identity even during email interviews. Although street art continues to be a crime, the public consensus of opinion is that it does not fit the traditional framework of crime (Zarkar 2014). Even if the political message of the graffiti is subtle, it has to be removed as it is considered vandalism. Because of the subversive and anarchic nature of his work, Black Hand's murals are doubly unlawful.

A characteristic that makes Black Hand's work timely is his urge to remain anonymous. The notion that the artist has the right to remain anonymous aligns an intellectual trend that has surfaced in art circles since the 2011 Occupy movements (Loock 2012). In these artistic circles, the choice between 'opacity' and 'transparency' has become the subject of increasing critical engagement in contemporary art and politics (prime examples are works by Zach Blas, Hito Steyerl and Adam Harvey, which employ various techniques of masking and concealing the face). Should artists reveal their identities? Should their artworks necessarily reveal cultural, racial and ethnic origins? It seems that Iranian graffiti artists have entered a new phase wherein their artwork is simultaneously autonomous and tied to global art. Even more so, these street artworks are as much a part of the world as they are its replica. The artists are not exclusively tied to the traditions of Iranian art, neither in their stylistic approach nor in their ideas (Black Hand 2015). They can best be placed in the category of global counterculture art (for example, the work of the Situationist International, a group that defied the rudiments of mid-twentieth-century advanced capitalism) or cultural-appropriation artists (such as Cooper Greene, the anonymous creator of the 2004 controversial New York posters that appropriated the well-known iPad campaign placards, protesting the then-recent revelations of the mayhem committed by US soldiers in Abu Gharib). Defying established laws and authority, the graffiti work of Black Hand is above all in line with the motifs of global street art popularized by Banksy. Sanaz Farazi's timely translation of *Banksy: Wall and Piece* has added to this interest, making Banksy's ideas even more accessible to Farsi readers (Farazi 2010). Despite being 'opaque', Iranian countercultural graffiti artists have become part of the global art scene; their work is increasingly circulated in mainstream media and social media networks. Recognized as the 'Banksy of Iran', Black Hand has attracted the attention of many local/unofficial websites (*Asr-e Anarchism* editorial 2014; *Fararoo* editorial 2014), none of which end with .ir, a domain designation for government-sponsored sites.

In April 2014, Black Hand showcased a body of graffiti in a dilapidated historic house in central Tehran. The property was under the protection of the Historical Preservation Society for its unique early-twentieth-century architecture. But to make room for a new development, the authorities decided to tear it down. In recent years, artists, architects and activists have protested governmental decisions to demolish historic buildings in Tehran to create taller modern buildings, thus increasing real estate profits. So, the act of showing street art in an abandoned yet historically valuable and architecturally significant house is in and of itself a way of protest – if not on ideological grounds, at least on the basis of civil rights. Whether intended or not, Black Hand helped increase the value of some of the old houses of Tehran, pushing them into the centre of attention for both national and international tourists and tourist specialists alike, even if only seen second-hand via online venues such as a Facebook group dedicated preserving Tehran's old homes with more than 10,000 followers (Tehran Historic House Committee 2014). In 2015, the group protested the plan for the destruction of an early-twentieth-century home, seemingly a replica of the White House, which had served as the venue for the First World War II conference held between the "Big Three" Allied leaders.

Most of Black Hand's other works emerge in visible public places, encouraging intelligent involvement and even active participation by the general public. Even before the artist posts the images on his own Facebook, Twitter or Instagram pages, passers-by record them on their iPhones and post their photographs on the web. Thus, the work becomes an object of media spectacle preceding its defacement. Thus, in addition to providing an aesthetic backdrop to the concrete edifices of urban Iran, Black Hand challenges the authorities, albeit subtly. Whereas the real Banksy shows authority figures (politicians, police, military men) in satirized positions, Black Hand portrays random everyday people in subtle poses, leaving it open to interpretation (Zarkar 2012). Despite his elusiveness, Black Hand is seen as a vandalistic artist. In response to the barring of Iranian women from sports stadiums in the summer of 2014, a mural by Black Hand went up on one of the busiest spots in central Tehran. It depicted a woman wearing the national jersey triumphantly holding up a bottle of dishwashing liquid as if it were the World Cup itself. It was signed by Black Hand and dated 2014. The graffiti showed a timely and important response to women's human rights in Iran. Although it went viral on social media networks, notably *Ajam Media Collection, Reorient, Iranwire, BBC* and *PBS*, it only took a few days before the authorities covered the whole mural with red paint (see, for example, Zarkar 2014; Morris 2014) (Figure 5.2).

Iranian women have long been banned from watching football matches in stadiums. In 2012, this ban was extended to volleyball games and, with the World League currently under way, many Iranians were not happy. 'It's very cruel, it's unbelievably cruel. Why would you not let them in?' These are the words of Sarah Ahari who played basketball for Iran's national team, as reported by the *BBC* (Rakusen 2014). Shortly following the ban, to make matters worse, the Iranian authority arrested a 22-year-old British/Iranian girl, Ghoncheh Ghavami, whose aim was to watch a game despite the newly sanctioned ban on attending matches. Amid the international urge to release Ghavami and to allow women to have access to sport stadiums, the authorities – some of them women – dismissed the idea. For example, a female Member of Parliament, Fatemeh Alia, asserted, 'Women's duty is

Figure 5.2 Black Hand's mural showing a woman holding up a 'World Cup' in the shape of a washing-up liquid bottle.
Source: Image courtesy of Black Hand.

to raise children and take care of their husbands, not to watch volleyball games ... the woman whose main concern is to go to [the] stadium ... would not be able to fulfill her duties' (Fardad 2014). Regardless of such commentaries, the enthusiasm for encouraging the Iranian government to change its regulations was reinforced worldwide. The texts in support of this cause were often accompanied by Black Hand's iconic image which was and still is truly 'worth a thousand words'. The graffiti lives on in social media as it is still being 'shared' and viewed. It continues to resonate on the 'street' of the web, gaining an even greater global audience.

Despite ongoing attempts by the state to limit the bounds of acceptable public art, by producing unregulated art, artists like Black Hand carry on. The social media have been useful, not only in terms of featuring the photographs of actual short-lived graffiti, but also with regard to providing alternative (virtual) walls for creating them. Hamed Safaee's work is particularly stimulating in this regard. Instead of painting the murals on the actual walls of Tehran, he creates imaginary murals on photographs of Tehran walls, manipulating them in Photoshop. The images – now occupying the space of the social media networks – are realistic, making the viewer second-guess their authenticity. Women in sensual poses and erotic attire appear incongruously side by side with street name plaques that read, for example, The

Islamic Revolution Street (Figure 5.3). Because of their sensual appeal, it would be impossible to imagine the actual execution of Safaee's murals on the streets of Tehran. Nonetheless, these virtual murals promote the quest for freedom of expression, the quest for reviving all the things that have been strictly banned since the Islamic Revolution.

Of course, the figure of an erotic woman exudes an air of self-Orientalization (Behdad 2001), bringing to mind the *Vogue* photographs by Clarke. But the Gramscian notion of hegemony, emphasizing that power is negotiated among all strata of society helps us understand how this is not necessarily the main point of the image (Gramsci 1971). Safaee does not speak just to the dominant ideology, but with a whole host of audiences (Hall 1993, 90–103). Most significantly, he speaks to his young artist friends on Facebook. He gives ironic meanings to the walls of Tehran that have always been a place of ideology for him and his peers, a generation of Iranians born after 1979 (Black Hand 2015). There is indeed a limit to the explanatory agency of the members of this group: rather than confusing Safaee's work with self-Orientalizing and sexual or sexist imagery, they read it primarily as reversing the meaning of the wall. With regard to the supremacy of their spectacle in a virtual context, Safaee's murals perfectly capture the mood of our time: that is the notion that we are becoming increasingly hooked onto machines

Figure 5.3 Hamed Safaee's 2014 imaginary mural applied to the corner of a street with a street plaque that reads *enghelab-e eslami* [The Islamic Revolution].
Source: Image courtesy of Hamed Safaee.

for our sensory input. Safaee's imaginary murals are thus all the more germane; they embody Guy Debord's widely quoted point in *the Society of Spectacle*: 'When the real world changes into simple images, simple images become real beings and effective motivations of a hypnotic behavior. The spectacle ... naturally finds vision to be the privileged human sense which the sense of touch was for other epochs' (Debord 1994, 18).

However, Debord has also stated that aestheticization and spectacularization divert attention away from the practical goals of political protest (Groys 2014). Thus, the use of art for political action necessarily defeats its goal. Over the years, many have taken this assertion very seriously. The seventh Berlin Biennale curated in 2012 by Artur Żmijewski provoked criticism for its approach to activism. Lack of engagement and participation by the audiences led some critics to call the show a zoo for art activists (Maak 2012). By this account, one can posit that, at least for the global audience, the immediate spectacle of Tehran's countercultural street art is much more pertinent than its latent political implications. In other words, by default, these murals are there to charm and entertain rather than engage the audience in a serious political discussion. Thus, whether negatively or positively influencing Iran's reputation in the outside world, Tehran's murals have played a part in the country's disembodied tourism. Mindful of the powerful 'display value' of murals in general, the officials in Tehran are turning towards purely artistic murals. In May 2015, in an unprecedented move, the Mayor of Tehran decided to replace the common billboard ads with artworks by renowned local and foreign artists. For ten days, images by the likes of many local artists as well as Pablo Picasso, René Magritte and Henri Matisse turned the capital into a giant urban art gallery and thousands of social media networks and major news agencies, ranging from *New York Times* to *The Guardian*, turned the city into a virtual tourist destination (see, for example, Erdbrink 2015).

Conclusion

Tehran murals – real, temporary, virtual, political or apolitical – invite outside viewers to a kind of attractive destination that will presumably give them a glance into one of the few places far from the homogenizing forces of capitalism where commercial murals take over everything else. Time and again, images of Iran's murals are juxtaposed with photographs of its historical sites, not only on tourist websites, but also in travel and food documentaries made by such iconic figures as Anthony Bourdain, whose episode 6 of CNN-sponsored *Parts Unknown*, recorded in summer 2014, opened with a brief tour of streets of Tehran including its political murals. Besides its undoubtedly valuable historical attractions, Iran's contemporary exotic art scenes made it to the list of the top 2014 destinations picked by travel industry leaders. Thirty-five years after it disappeared from the tourist map,

Iran returned to the top of the 'must-visit' list in 2014, according to multiple recent news posts (Porter 2014). Most tourist agencies list a variety of venues as prime sightseeing destinations, from historic mosques and ancient archaeological sites to ski resorts (Cornet 2015) and art scenes, including propaganda and artistic murals (Brown 2013). Wild Frontiers, the London and Philadelphia-based adventure travel specialist, has already seen a 30 per cent rise in bookings for Iran (*Wild Frontiers* editorial 2015). '… [W]e expect there to be a surge in demand similar to when Aung San Suu Kyi changed the stance on travel to Myanmar', says John Bealby, the founder of Wild Frontiers (*Financial Times* editorial 2014).

Between 2005 and 2006, Iran saw an unprecedented number of tourists with over two million inbound tourists (Vafadari and Cooper 2010, 161). This was following the 2004 merge of the Iran Cultural Heritage Organization with the Iran Tourism Organization that allowed an emphasis on the role of Iran's heritage in the promotion of tourism and the tourist economy (Naghi 2001). However, from July 2013 to January 2016 – when the USA toughened sanctions on Iran – a financial exchange with Iran has become almost impossible, thus discouraging visitation to the country (*Euromonitor* editorial 2015; Fayazmanesh 2003). Even so, online venues portraying wall art continue to play a significant role in promoting Iran's rich post-revolutionary mural enterprise and may, in due course, help bolster the country's tourist industry.

References

Akhavan, Niki. 2013. *Electronic Iran: The Cultural Politics of an Online Evolution.* New Brunswick, NJ: Rutgers University Press.

Asr-e Anarchism editorial. 2014. "Bansky Irani dar Shabakeh-haye Ejtemaie [The Iranian Banksy in the Media]," *Asr-e Anarchism*, August 17, 2014, accessed 10 January 2015. http://fararu.com/fa/news/194341/.

Baudrillard, Jean. 1981. *For a Critique of the Economy of the Sign.* St. Louis, MO: Telos Press.

Behdad, Ali. 2001. "The Power-Ful Art of Qajar Photography: Orientalism and (Self)-Orientalizing in Nineteenth-Century Iran." *Iranian Studies* 34 (1/4): 141–151.

Black Hand. 2015. *email* message to the author, January 29, 2015.

Brown, Roland E. 2013. "Iran's Obama Billboard: What It Really Means," *The Guardian*, January 20, 2013, accessed January 21, 2013, http://www.theguardian.com/world/shortcuts/2013/jan/20/iran-obama-billboard-tehran-propaganda.

Buhalis, Dimitrios. 1998. "Strategic Use of Information Technologies in the Tourism Industry." *Tourism Management* 19 (5): 409–421.

Cahill, Josh. 2014. "Guide: Travel to Tehran – the Real Middle East," March 11, 2014, accessed March 30, 2014, http://www.gotravelyourway.com/2014/05/14/travel-to-tehran-the-real-middle-east/#.VLfzWZwk8zo.

Cornet, Laurence. 2015. "Could Tehran (Yes, Tehran) Be the Next Aspen?" *Vogue Magazine*, January 28, 2015, accessed January 30, 2015, http://www.vogue.com/9003569/skiing-in-tehran-iran/.

Crouch, David and Nina Lubbren, eds. 2000. *Leisure/Tourism Geographies*. London: Routledge.

———. 2003. *Visual Culture and Tourism*. Oxford, UK and New York: Berg.

Chelkowski, Peter and Hamid Dabashi. 2002. *Staging a Revolution: The Art of Persuasion in the Islamic Republic of Iran*. London: Booth-Clibborn Editions.

Davarian, Shadi. 2014. "Estefadeh fanavari digital dar naghashi divari [Use of Digital Technology in Mural Arts]." In *Majmooeh maghalat hamayesh elmi avvalin dosalaneh divar negari shahri va gerafik-e mohiti [Proceedings of the Biennial of Public and Mural Arts]*, edited by Sayyed Mohammad Fadavi, 181–188. Tehran: Beatification Bureau Press.

Debord, Guy. 1994. *The Society of Spectacle*. New York: Zone Books.

Deeb Lara and Mona Harb, eds. 2013. *Leisurely Islam: Negotiating Geography and Morality in Shiite South Beirut*. Princeton, NJ: Princeton University Press.

Eftekhari, Azadeh. 2013. "Payam-e billboard Obama va Shemr dar khiyabanhay-e Tehran chist? [What is the Message behind the Obama and Shemr Poster on the Streets of Tehran?]," *Diplomacy-e Iran*, January 30, 2013, accessed March 2, 2015, http://www.irdiplomacy.ir/fa/page/1911824.

Erdbrink, Thomas. 2015. "Suddenly, Tehran's Mayor Becomes a Patron of the Arts," *The New York Times*, May 7, 2015, accessed May 20, 2015, http://www.nytimes.com/2015/05/08/world/middleeast/suddenly-tehrans-mayor-becomes-a-patron-of-the-arts.html?_r=0.

Euromonitor editorial. 2015. "Country Report: Travel and Tourism in Iran." *Euromonitor*, May 10, 2015, accessed May 30, 2015, http://www.euromonitor.com/Travel_And_Tourism_in_Iran.

Fararoo editorial. 2014. "Banksy Iran: Divarha-ye shahr-e man boomi baray-e naghashihayamand [Banksy of Iran: The Walls of my City are my Canvases]," *Fararoo*, July 20, 2014, accessed August 10, 2015, http://asranarshism.com.

Farazi, Sanaz. 2010. *Banksy: divar va asar-e honari*. Tehran: Ketab Aban Publications.

Fardad, Mani. 2014. "Iranian Women Still Banned from Stadiums," *Almonir: Iran Pulse*, July 3, 2014, accessed May 2, 2015, http://www.al-monitor.com/pulse/originals/2014/06/iran-womens-volleyball-barred-entry.html#.

Fayazmanesh, Sasan. 2003. "The Politics of US Economic Sanctions against Iran." *Review of Radical Political Economics* 35 (3): 221–240.

Financial Times editorial. 2014. "Top 2014 Destinations, Picked by Travel Industry Leaders," *Financial Times*, January 3, 2014, accessed January 30, 2015, http://www.ft.com/cms/s/2/e4f47a04-6972-11e3-89ce-00144feabdc0.html.

Gettyimages. 2015. "Italian World War II Poster: 'Here Are the Liberators'." Last Modified June 6, 2015, accessed June 20, 2015, http://www.gettyimages.co.uk/detail/news-photo/italian-world-war-ii-poster-here-are-the-liberators-shows-news-photo/113633792.

Ghadyanloo, Mehdi. 2007. Personal interview with the author, March 29, 2007.

Goftegoo editorial. 2012. "Doctor shooshtari dar goftegoo ba pajoohesh honar: honarmandan beh ma etemad konand [A Conversation with Dr. Shooshtari: 'Artists Must Trust Us'," *Goftegoo: Majalleh Pajuhesh Hunar [Goftegoo: A Research Bulletin]* 1 (1): 19–22.

Grigor, Talinn. 2009. *Building Iran: Modernism, Architecture, and National Heritage under the Pahlavi Monarchs*. New York: Periscope Publishing.

————. 2014. *Contemporary Iranian Art: From the Street to the Studio.* London: Reaktion Press.

Groys, Boris. 2014. "On Art Activism," *e-flux* 56, accessed May 10, 2015, http://www.e-flux.com/journal/on-art-activism/.

Gramsci, Antonio. 1971. *Selections from the Prison Notebooks*, trans. Quintin Hoare and Geoffery Nowell-Smith. New York: International Publishers.

Gruber, Christiane. 2008. "The Writing is on the Wall," *Persica: Uitgave van het Genootschap Nederland-Iran* 22: 15–46.

Hall, Stuart. 1993. "Encoding, Decoding." In *Cultural Studies Reader*, edited by Simon During, 90–103, New York: Routledge.

Karimi, Pamela. 2008. "Imagining Warfare, Imaging Welfare." *Persica: Uitgave van het Genootschap Nederland-Iran* 22: 47–63.

Keane, John. 2012. *Vaclav Havel: A Political Tragedy in Six Acts.* New York: Basic Books.

Kellner, Douglas. 2012. *Media Spectacle and Insurrection, 2011: From the Arab Uprisings to Occupy Everywhere.* London: Bloomsbury Academic.

Loock, Ulrich. 2012. "Opacity," *Frieze* 7, accessed June 5, 2015, http://frieze-magazin.de/archiv/features/opazitaet/.

Ludden, David. 1993. "Orientalist Empiricism: Transformation of Colonial Knowledge." In *Orientalism and the Postcolonial Predicament: Perspectives on South Asia*, edited by Carol A. Breckenridge and Peter van der Veer, 250–274. Philadelphia: University of Pennsylvania Press.

Maak, Niklas. 2012. "Kritik der zynischen Vernunft," *Frankfurter Allgemeine Zeitung*, May 9, 2012, accessed May 10, 2015, www.faz.net/berlin-biennale-kritik-der-zynischen-vernunft-11731589.html.

Marzolph, Ulrich. 2013. "The Martyr's Fading Body: Propaganda vs. Beautification in the Tehran Cityscape." In *Visual Culture in the Modern Muslim Middle East: The Rhetoric of the Image*, edited by Christiane Gruber and Sune Haugbolle, 164–186. Bloomington: Indiana University Press.

Morris, Natasha. 2014. "Iran: Unedited History," *Reorient Magazine*, September 16, 2014, accessed October 10, 2015, http://www.reorientmag.com/2014/09/iran-unedited-history/.

Naghi, Simin. 2001. "*Tourism Development and Management Plan for the Islamic Republic of Iran, Activity* 1.1.3." Tehran: Unpublished report for the Iran Tourism & Touring Organization.

Nochlin, Linda. 1989. "The Imaginary Orient." In *The Politics of Vision: Essays on Nineteenth-Century Art and Society*, edited by Linda Nochlin, 33–59. New York: Harper Row.

Olin, Margaret. 1996. "Gaze." In *Critical Terms for Art History*, edited by Robert Nelson and Richard Shiff, 208–219. Chicago: The University of Chicago Press.

Porter, Lizzie. 2014. "Iran is 2014's Surprise Tourism Hit," *The Telegraph*, April 1 2014, accessed August 10, 2014, http://www.telegraph.co.uk/travel/travelnews/10736532/Iran-is-2014s-surprise-tourism-hit.html.

Rakusen, India. 2014. "Iran's Washing-Up Liquid Protest," *BBC Trending*, July 14, 2014, accessed July 20, 2014, http://www.bbc.co.uk/news/blogs-trending-28293818.

Rojck, Chris. 1995. *Decentering Leisure: Rethinking Leisure Theory.* London: Sage.

Sazman-e Barnameh va Boodjeh. 1972. *Tarh-e jami' tose'he jahangardi dar iran* [Master Plan for the Development of Tourism in Iran], 1972 (Final Report,

Phase II). Unpublished Document Available at *Sazman-e barnameh va boodjeh* [The Organization for Planning and Finance].

Tehran: Beatification Bureau. 2013. *Naghghashihay-e divari Tehran: Panj sal baray-e tasvir gari yek shahr* [*Tehran's Wall Paintings: Five Years of Effort towards Illustrating a City*]. Tehran: Beatification Bureau Press.

Tehran Historic House Committee, *Facebook*, accessed March 20, 2014, https://www.facebook.com/injatehran.

Trivundza, Ilija T. 2004. "Pictorial Representations of the US Attack on Iraq in Delo." *Journalism: Theory, Practice and Criticism* 5 (4): 480–499.

Urry, John. 2002. *The Tourist Gaze*. London: Sage.

Vafadari Kazem and Malcolm Cooper. 2010. "Japanese Tourism in Iran." In *Bridging Tourism Theory and Practice: Tourism in the Islamic World*, edited by Noel Scott and Jafar Jafari, 160–179. Bingley, UK: Emerald.

WildFrontiers editorial. 2015. "Iran: Persian Explorer," *WildFrontiers*, May 2, 2015, accessed May 25, 2015, http://www.wildfrontierstravel.com/en_GB/destination/iran/group-tours/2000787/iran-persian-explorer-5.

Zamani Farahani, Hamira. 2010. "Tourism, Heritage and Religion." In *Bridging Tourism Theory and Practice: Tourism in the Islamic World*, edited by Noel Scott and Jafar Jafari, 205–218. Bingley, UK: Emerald.

Zangi, Behnam, Habibollah Ayatollahi and Asghar Fahimifard, 2011. "*Barresi moghiyyat-e naghashi divari pas az enghelab dar Iran be rooykard-e jame'eh shenakhti Pierre Bourdieu* [An Analysis of Mural Paintings after the Revolution (Based on Pierre Bourdieu's Anthropological Theories)]." *Negareh* 24: 85–101.

Zarkar, Rustin. 2012. "Taking Back the Streets: Iranian Graffiti Artists Negotiating Public Space," *Ajam Media Collective*, November 5, 2012, accessed January 10, 2015, http://ajammc.com/2012/11/05/taking-back-the-streets-iranian-graffiti-artists-negotiating-public-space/.

———. 2014. "A Mural Erased: Urban Art, Local Politics, and the Contestation of Public Space in Mashhad," *Ajam Media Collective*, March 30, 2014, accessed March 30, 2014, http://ajammc.com/2014/03/30/a-mural-erased-urban-art-mashhad/.

Part III
Politics

6 *La Carbonería*

An alternative transformation of public space

Plácido Muñoz Morán

The contemporary space of Barcelona is mainly designed and ordered according to the principles of the 'Barcelona Model'. The aesthetic of this model can be linked to what Tim Edensor (2005) refers to as 'normative and modernist aesthetic' (2005, 73), a regulation replete, in the case of Barcelona, with architectural and urban design codes to embody and evoke specific imaginaries of the city. These ordered worlds coexist with the urban life and its constant processes of adaptation and transformation in the city. Mass tourism illustrates the tension between the aims of the 'Barcelona Model' and the everyday life of the local inhabitants in the city. In this chapter, I see the case of the mural on the façade of the squatted building of *La Carbonería* as a visual subject that is both an object of discussion and debate, and the contested arena of individual and collective actions in connection with different political representations of the city, contributing to the discussion in this edited volume on the politics of the mural.

The building: between art and politics

Space, and how it is linked to modernity and ways of making politics in democratic societies through the conception of public space, is central in my argument. At the end of the nineteenth century, the military walls that surrounded and limited the expansion of Barcelona were broken and the city began to expand towards its present-day spatial dimensions. The engineer Ildefonso Cerdá designed the *Eixample* (extension) urban plan of Barcelona, approved in 1860. One of the aims of this plan was to create more public space to facilitate the mobility and circulation of bodies in the new modern city of Barcelona. In this chapter, I describe the creation of a graffiti mural so as to explore further the meanings of making public space in relation to the politics of graffiti murals in this city.

According to the local statues and most of the graffiti artists that I interviewed, the practice of graffiti in the public spaces of Barcelona is illegal if it is done without a permit from the council. Nevertheless, throughout my fieldwork, I observed particular places and situations where graffiti artworks had not been erased and the authorities did not stop their creation.

To analyse how this was the case – in spite of contravening local civic ordinance – I am going to use the example of a collective mural painted by local graffiti artists in the squatted building of *La Carbonería*. I collaborated in this mural and experienced how its images were not only painted but also discussed and debated in assemblies and commented on by the inhabitants of the neighbourhood and the council's representatives.

My participation in this mural arose from my collaboration with 'Grafforum', a section of a TV hip-hop programme focused on graffiti that was part of an alternative local TV channel broadcast on the local TDT, called 'La Tele'. It allowed me to get into contact with members of the local graffiti and street-art scene and record and edit videos about their work. One of those encounters was with the squatter collective of *La Carbonería* which had its headquarters in a squatted building in the centre of the city. They got in contact with 'Grafforum' for the 'covering' (filming and dissemination) of the painting process of a new mural on the façade of their building. I ended up filming the painting of the mural for more than 3 weeks as a collaborator and researcher.

Moving around the wide and transited public space that surrounded the building of five floors occupied by squatters for more than 5 years, I realized how the actions of a collective of squatters and graffiti artists had transformed the sensory order of public space that surrounded the building. Drawing on Ranciére's (2004) work and his idea of the 'distribution of the sensible', I argue that public space is shaped by a dominant sensory order that conditions its transformation and the way in which people can participate in it. This distribution determines what can be said, done and made in public space, establishing a particular 'aesthetics'. The disruption of this 'aesthetics' is, according to Ranciére (2004), at the core of politics and a form of experience. In referring to the aesthetics, I am using Ranciére's (2004) conception of this term as follows: 'aesthetic encloses not only perceptive qualities but also practices and performances, production of places and fostering of social and political relations' (2004, 10).

This allows me to address a question about why the people from *La Carbonería* were able to create their mural without any authorization? They were painting the mural for almost 3 weeks during the daytime, closing off half of the sidewalk and hanging from ropes at great heights and the police never intervened to stop them or issue them with an appropriate penalty. The significance of these actions is open to multiple interpretations.

The building was located between the 'Carrer Comtes d'Urgel' and 'Floridablanca' in the central district of 'Ciutat Vella' and was one of the first architectural works developed within the *Eixample* urban plan at the end of the nineteenth century. Its geographical location, in the centre of the city, and its big façade made the building a good communication tool for social and political movements, and the mural was an example of it. In the building, the squatter collective organized vegan dinners, informative talks concerning issues such as ecological and social, and meetings and

Figure 6.1 Mural painted in 2009.
Source: Plácido Muñoz Morán.

gatherings with other collectives. In summary, many projects discussed in this centre were made viable thanks to its location, and this made it a reference point for the anti-capitalist movement in the city.

There were an average of fifteen to twenty, mainly young, people living permanently in *La Carbonería*. One of the floors was a communal area where they had a kitchen, a dinner room with long tables, a living room and a gym. On the ground floor, they had three independent spaces with a free shop and a library where people could donate or get free clothes. In addition, they also hosted a public vegan dinner every Thursday, as well as occasional music concerts and poetry readings. All of these workshops and activities were open to the 'San Antoni' neighbourhood and its inhabitants.

As a collective action, the painting of the mural in 2009 and its renewal in 2013 was a way to interact with, and bring their project ideals closer to, the people of the city. But what did the squatters want to transmit through the murals, and how did different people understand the content and painting of the murals on the building? To try to answer these questions, I should like to treat murals as textures which stimulate different forms of making graffiti, seeing the city and living within it. Can we use murals to reflect and critique on the dynamism of life in the city across spaces and times?

The assembly: ways of seeing and socialising

It was in one of their weekly assemblies at the end of February 2013 that they began to discuss the creation of a new mural. There were two main reasons behind this initiative. The most important was linked to the eviction notice that they had received from the lawyers of Barclays Bank, the official owners of the building. The second reason was based on a sentiment that some of the members of the collective had about the old mural – they thought that it had become another of Barcelona's tourist attractions at which people stopped to take photographs. In this sense, I argue that the mural was understood in the context of the visuality of the city, as part of its architecture, when architecture is appreciated and embodied in terms of surfaces and textures, but also symbolically as signs of the city.

For three weeks, the painting of the new mural in public space without an official permit became the symbol of their campaign, *No Encadenado Nuestro Vuelo* ('Let us fly without chains'), to protest against their eviction and to find social support. Within this context, the participants in the assembly began to discuss the content of the new mural. They were aware of the potential of the new mural to make their claims visible and to give voice to their cause.

The *CSO* (*Centro Social Ocupado*), 'Squatted social centre' assembly, was constituted when they moved into the building in the November of 2008. Before it was squatted, the building had been bought by a real estate construction company that had evicted the old tenants. The construction company's plan was to demolish the old building and build new apartments. But the financial crisis meant that this never happened as it eventually caused the bankruptcy of the company.

The CSO assembly was formed by a diverse group of people of different ages, genders, nationalities and with various occupations. Among them, there were artists with experience in fields such as fine arts, mural painting and graffiti. When they squatted in the house in 2008, it was these artists who immediately saw the possibilities that the building's surface had for testing and putting into practice their artistic skills. Deru (http://www.ekosystem.org/tag_big/deru), one of these artists, explained this to me in the following way:

> Only a few times you have the chance to paint a wall of such dimension in the centre of a big city. And we wanted to try and see how it would be, the experience and the result. Finally, it was very well accepted and the police did not stop us; we skipped like eighty thousand civic and security ordinances of the council, but we did not have any problem and we achieved our goal.

The debate in the assembly was focused on what message they wanted to communicate through the renewal of that first mural. For the members of the CSO assembly, that first mural of big black and white roots growing out of a tree house symbolized their birth as a collective which was materialized when they arrived and squatted in this neighbourhood building. The semiotic content of graffiti is part of a complex, dynamic and nonlinear process where the meanings of the environment are actively coproduced by the people who create and experience it (Iddings, McCafferty and Teixeira da Silva 2011, 5).

The first time I saw the old mural, it was a great surprise to me. It was in 2010, and I was walking around the area when suddenly, there it was, an alien figure in front of me on one of the buildings in the city space. The massive scale of the mural and the contrast that it made with the rest of the buildings was what really hit me. This first shock of the encounter and my corporeal interaction with the mural did not fit at all with the meaning of the symbolic content that the mural had for the members of *La Carbonería* collective. As W. J. T. Mitchell (2002) argues about images, the image of the mural in the public space mediated between ways of seeing and ways of socialising in the city. It takes us to look at the mural in terms of the every-day, seeing in the city or what Mitchell defines as "vernacular visuality" (2002, 178). In this sense, the mural acted as an interface between individuals who shared the same space and the different visual conceptions about the construction of it. I suggest that collective murals in Barcelona foster the creation of a symbolic landscape with political signifiers.

For some of the collective's members, the new mural needed to express their disappointment towards the urban speculation in the city and the local council regulations of public space. There was a collection of the assembly that had a more radical and aggressive posture and proposed to paint a big rose in flames, making reference to the *Rosa de Fuego* (Rose of Fire). This was the symbolic name that the city had received at the start of the twentieth century due to the fame of its social uprisings and resistance mobilizations against the dominant economic and state powers. Another group formed by the graffiti artists made the case for a more conciliatory attitude based on collective and creative action with other artists.

In *La Carbonería*, although the council accepted the mural – and by this I mean simply that the police did not intervene to stop it – there was a tension and crucial differences between the understanding and making of graffiti in public space. As this chapter shows, one of the tensions is related to how the space, the times of making and the content of the mural were established by the collective and followed by the council, not the other way around. The success of the action, therefore, was conditioned by a balance and productive tension between their capacity to communicate with the public and their collective organization and intervention in public space. This made me think, as Gell (1998) states about artworks, that the mural acted as anonymous mediators of social relations with other individuals. Using Gell's terms, the mural can be seen as a form of 'distributed person-hood' which enclosed explicit dynamic agencies connected with image making and collaborations.

From the outset, the idea of the graffiti artists was focused not only on *La Carbonería* and its claims, but also on the people of the neighbourhood and themselves as actors of a collaborative art project. The previous mural had ended up becoming a symbol for the collective members themselves and for most of the inhabitants of the neighbourhood who accepted and recognized it as part of their urban landscape.

Neil Jarman (1998) argues in his study about the political murals in the city of Belfast that their significance is generated through a semiotic dynamic in which the images take meanings from the location and, at the same time, the location takes meanings from the images (1998, 5). Making reference to the mural in *La Carbonería* and placing it within the particular context of Barcelona, where the creation of graffiti in the public space is not allowed and sanctioned with high penalties by the city council, I think that there is a level missing in Jarman's argument linked in this case to the actual act of making those images in the public space of Barcelona without a permit from the council. The painting of this mural not only transgressed the council's civic ordinances, but also created an arena within which to debate and discuss them. Although in the assembly there was more than one proposal, eventually they agreed that the new mural should represent the conflictive relationship between different conceptions of the city. These different conceptions included ideas about collectivism linked to the collective members themselves and the self-managed and collaborative projects developed in the squatted building. Then, there was the local council and the economic powers in the city that tried to establish a kind of absolute control over the public spaces and their inhabitants.

The texture of corporeal vision: painting of the mural

The generalized and abstract idea of representing the antagonistic relationship between the dominant political and economic powers of the city and the squatter collective began to take form with a small drawing made by Fran (http://basuravisual.blogspot.it/), one of the graffiti artists. Then, the members of the collective started to interact with the surface of the house and the new mural started to take form. Some of the participants began to paint the wall from the windows of the building. When the ropes were ready, they began to descend and hang from them with harnesses and other climbing gear so as to reach the entire wall. Overall, it was a complex process that sometimes flowed and sometimes was blocked by logistical and participation problems. As a researcher and participant, I found this period of transformation between the old and the new murals very intriguing and I gained a particular insight through my role as cameraman filming the whole process.

During the first stage of the mural, it was possible to see how the communicative aspect of it was differentiated. There was a focus on the content of the mural addressed in the assembly debates. But the mural was also conceived and used as a symbolic object that was part of a wider context than the one limited to the physical boundaries of its image. This first stage could be defined as the rough draft in which they mainly erased the old mural, covering it with the background colours. For this task, they used different kinds of devices, from normal brushes to brushes attached to big sticks and various types of spray guns filled up with paint. Some of the people wore overalls, and soon after they started everyone who was painting or helping began to get covered by paint.

The new images did not begin to take form until a few days after they started to paint. During this time, there were all kinds of speculations among the people passing by. It could be said that the semiotic dynamic of the mural images began in people's heads as they imagined into being what they could not see. They imagined themselves into the actions of the artists and the surface of the wall. This imagination formed part of a broader game of the visible and the invisible in a public space that both approved and disapproved of the mural's 'distribution of the sensible'. Although most of the people with whom I spoke supported the creation of the mural, there were also people who disapproved of the creation of images without an official permit on the surface of a public wall. Thus the creation of the mural staged the overlapping of different forms of politics of representation in public space.

As we have seen, the mural at *La Carbonería* fostered not only collaborative and collective relationships, but also antagonistic and contradictory ones. The 'distribution of the sensible' around the mural represents something more than a shared sensible world. It encloses different distribution of modes of being and occupations. There were two separate parts to the new mural. On the lower side of the building, there was a city skyline made up of grey buildings in the form of padlocks. These buildings were attached with a chain that metaphorically represented the economic and state power and its control over society. On the other part, above the city skyline, the chain was broken by air balloons that had escaped from the city. But, as we have seen in the description of the process of its recreation, the mural was not only about what the images represented and where they were made, but it was also about how they were made. This brings us to forms of corporeal vision and the textural qualities of the surfaces of these walls which are ways of understanding sensory relations in the city space.

Deru explained to me the strategy that they used to paint the mural as follows:

> We did it in a clever way, thinking and planning everything very well to reduce the possibilities of police intervention to stop the painting of the mural. Thus in our two murals interventions on the building, we began using harnesses and ropes and hanging on the wall. It allowed us to get into the house through any of the windows if the police tried to stop or identify us.

This interaction between the artists and the surface of the wall allows us to think in terms of sensory relations within and around the painting of the mural. Here, we can recognize how the texture of the mural was formed, not only by the material images, but also by the particular way of making them

Figure 6.2 Painting of the new mural.
Source: Plácido Muñoz Morán.

and being at the wall. For the artists, being attached to the wall involved close contact with it, to the degree that they were literally part of the mural and they were able to even enter into it in order to escape. Using David MacDougall's (2006) concept of 'corporeal vision', it can be said that the mural was formed by 'corporeal images' which carry the imprint not only of the bodies who make them but also of the ways in which these images are seen by other bodies who interact with them. Therefore, the texture of the mural is an abstract form which contains not only images but also social relations that are shaped by ways of seeing and ways of making images.

These actions with the ropes also turned the street into a situation akin to a circus performance where the graffiti artists were in the air hanging from ropes, and a guessing game went on at street level where people guessed what it was that they were painting. At one level, this situation was about the artists reclaiming public space through transgressing the boundary practices of bodies and surfaces, and the horizontal, walking forms of mobility. At another level of interpretation, these actions can be understood as extending the spectacular nature of the modern city and its visually determined image (Debord 1994; Lefebvre 1991). Drawing on Vanessa Chang's (2013) argument regarding the work of the Italian street artist Blu, where she says that 'Blu's work reminds us that urban inscription is at once an act and an aesthetic, and that it is necessary to engage our urban environments in all the ways available to us' (2013, 232), it could be argued that the participants in *La Carbonería*'s mural used the vertical hanging spectacle as an aesthetic tool to inscribe and reimagine the city. Thus, their radical position in the public space, suspended in the air and attached to the ropes, posited an ethereal departure point for the mural. It highlighted the mutable nature of the city and showed different possibilities for multidimensional experiences of moving and interacting with its surfaces. The properties of the building's surface and therefore its texture emerges in the same way that the anthropologist Tim Ingold (2007) discusses the properties of artistic Neolithic stones: 'through the stone's involvement in its total surroundings'. He concludes his analysis, 'the properties of materials, in short, are not attributes but histories' (2007, 14). Thus, the painting of the mural was a process that also drew the attention of the general public just as the surfaces of the urban landscape were actively changing in front of them.

This active attention from the public took different forms. There were verbal exchanges that involved the artists breaking off from the actions of making and reconfiguring their working space with the surface of the wall to talk with the passers-by. These verbal interactions took place on the sidewalk next to the building and between the artists who were painting the lowest side of the mural and some of the pedestrians who passed by during most of the day. Another form of interpretation was photography, which was a form of *capture*, one that transferred the surface material textures of the wall into digital textures (pixels) and into virtual (digital) space of the photograph. Photography has been used as a medium not only to document and study graffiti from an art history perspective (Stewart 2009), but also to explore it as part of the social and political contexts of the city, closer to the visual studies frame of interpretation (Cooper and Chalfant 1988). The way in which photography was used to capture the mural by passers-by can be approached from different perspectives. From one perspective, the old mural, as some of the squatters stated, had become part of what John Urry (1990) defines as 'the tourist gaze'. This means that the mural was one of the signs that the tourists collected through photography as part of the touristic image of the city and not a political statement against the council's promotion and regulation of public space. Graffiti artists have expressed this tension with the tourist in the city through specific artworks in public space. For instance, the graffiti 'Tourist go Home' keeps appearing periodically on the walls of streets transited by tourists. Inspired by the same issue, there are other examples of more elaborate and permanent graffiti murals like the one next to the squatted building and social centre of 'La Montaña'. Here, the mural represented the relationship between tourist and local residents claiming: 'Good for the tourists, Bad for the Neighbours' and 'Tourist you are the terrorists'.

The urban space around the mural is therefore constantly being subjected to different forms of visual construction and shaped sensorially by a great variety of people and their ways of seeing and interacting with the mural. Saying this, I want to highlight "…the potential inherent in bodies to shape space" (Chang 2013, 223). As I described above, the aerial displays of the members of *La Carbonería* collective challenged the official order of the public space through the ways in which they became part of the 'spectacle' of the city (Debord 1994) in a manner that was not part of a pedestrian view from the ground but was created through suspension in the air.

This suspension was created by experienced climbers who attached ropes with special knots to an iron cable on the terrace and set up a whole system of ropes with climbing gear. Their knowledge and experience of climbing made it possible to produce an alternative distribution of the public space of graffiti. The graffiti artists began to paint the mural while being in touch with the space of the wall aerially rather than being grounded from the pavement. This position fostered new interactions with the space, with other participants and with their ways of painting, all of which added to the textural dimension of the mural. On each rope, there was a permanent communication and involvement between three people: one on the terrace to move the rope to the right or to the left, another painting and a third at one of the windows filling up the buckets with paint and passing them to the painters. In one of the two ground floor premises of the squatted building, which had a large gate onto the street, they mixed and created the colours for the mural. The graffiti artists were in charge of this task. They used plastic white paint and mixed it with other colours and colour powder. There they created the general palette of colours for the mural based on grey for the city skyline, light yellow and light red for the sky and blue for the big balloon. These were the main background colours. Once they had painted the background, they started to use spray can colours as well.

Trying to represent the transformation process, I created time-lapses, made photographs, records video sequences and edited two videos throughout the whole process. These videos reflected on the forms of collaboration that were going on between 'La Tele', an alternative local channel from Barcelona, and myself as a volunteer and researcher. The use of visual methods is by nature collaborative and involves ethical, social and practical relations between the researchers and the different participants. My previous collaboration in 'La Tele' shaped my access to, and interaction and collaboration with the collective members of *La Carbonería*. Then, the edited videos allowed me to represent my view of the creation of this mural and to share my involvement with the participants and get some feedback from them. My aim was to approach the public space with a sense of plurality in which the bodies and their movements shape the space in which they live and interact (Chang 2013, 215). My images of the mural represented my way of looking at the images made by others on the surface of the city and in connection with its everyday life. The graffiti mural formed part of an 'ocean of materials' in which human beings, like other organisms, were immersed, generating and transforming the city (Ingold 2007, 7).

The anthropologist Michael Taussig (1991) draws on the distinction made by Walter Benjamin in his complex essay "The Work of Art in the age of Mechanical Reproduction" (1931) between 'contemplation' and 'distraction'.

He proposes the study of everyday life in the modern city through analysing the 'distracted' almost unconscious perceptions of individuals instead of the 'contemplative' attitude. Taussig states that this distracted, peripheral-vision perception is 'unleashed with great vigour by modern life at the crossroads of the city, the capitalist market and modern technology' (1991, 7). Thus, the analysis of everyday life has to take into consideration the tactility of vision and other senses to overcome the obvious and reach the 'flash of a profane illumination' (ibid. 152). The tactility of perception implies looking at the moment in which the meanings of the mural images emerge from experience as 'corporeal images'. In this sense, MacDougall (2006) notes, 'as we look at things, our perception is guided by cultural and personal interests, but perception is also the mechanism by which these interests are altered and added to' (2006, 2). Analysing the process of the mural painting at *La Carbonería* allows us to uncover the symbolic and cultural sensory order that is behind everyday contemplative life, and at the same time we can question its meanings.

As mentioned, *La Carbonería* is at a busy intersection of four streets where cars, people, cyclists, motorbikes and also the police continually passed by every day. On Sundays, the stalls of the 'San Antoni' market were erected in one of the streets next to *La Carbonería*. This is a historic city market. Every Sunday since 1886, this market has been a meeting point for sellers, buyers and collectors, and lately even some curious tourists. Here, it is possible to buy all kind of books, magazines and comics from among the numerous stalls of the market or exchange your cards and stamps with other collectors in the market side stalls. On market days, the space around the mural changed and there were more people moving around than during the rest of the week. The council sets up portable toilets in the street next to the market and in front of the mural. There are also police who controlled the road traffic which was not allowed to pass through the main street of the market.

Furthermore, the police also mediated in possible conflicts, and their presence was intended to counter the pickpockets in the area. And yet, the people in the squatted building continued painting the mural as if it were an extension of the market: people also stopped to look at it, wonder and take some photographs.

Around the camera: the mural and its somatic plurality

All of these observations were collected while I filmed and took photographs in *La Carbonería* over the time that the mural was being painted. The camera not only acted as an extension of my presence, but it also allowed me to produce a representation and foster interpretations of the mural among different viewers. Overall, this practice and experience provided me with a multidimensional view of the mural and the space that surrounded it.

One of my aims was to capture the temporal transformation of the public space through the creation of the mural and for this I made a series of time-lapse films. In the same way that the camera could not focus on all of the social events and material objects that occurred around it, the outcomes of the time-lapses shaped new ways of seeing the mural that had escaped my perception during the making process. It was a mural in fast motion in which cars, people, sunlight, shade, the clouds in the sky and the painting of the mural seemed to flow and interact with each other. But these time-lapse videos were something more than a new way of seeing the creation of this mural in Barcelona. The time-lapses formed part of a greater compound of multiple images of people, objects and relations that I selected throughout my fieldwork in the city.

The images coexisted in the same space but in different temporalities or what Bergson calls 'durées'. This idea posits looking at these images according to 'intuitive' insights as part of multiple presents with different, multiple pasts (Bergson in Mullarkey and de Mille 2013, 1). They were part of my fieldwork and memories, but they enclose information that reflects on public space and the use of the camera and my role as an anthropologist throughout this process. The graffiti murals are not only isolated images, but they also form part of the fluidity of the city. The images of graffiti coexist not only with the presence of the buildings and the people, but also, as Bergson argues, with their multiple pasts. This fluidity can be broken with the interactions between different bodies such as the ones between photographer and subject. It fosters perceptions that are, as Baraklianou (2013) states, reading Bergson, 'a possibility amongst other possibilities, that the body, through its action, has chosen in relation to other bodies, to other matter' (2013, 142). Therefore, the phenomenological approach applied in this research implies multiple embodiments within different contexts.

If we analyse the mural in *La Carbonería* from the perspective of the council institution of *Paisatge Urba* ('Urban Landscape'), we can find a quite particular way of understanding this mural as part of the public space. This institution is in charge of the regulation and use of the public space in Barcelona. In this sense, the painting of this mural was a reflection of the competence of the council. Following the official regulations, 'Paisatge Urba' had a duty to disallow the painting of the mural and to fine the people who were painting it. Thus, when I interviewed Xavier Olivella, the Director of 'Paisatge Urba', I asked him, 'why was the mural in 'La Carboneria' allowed?' His answer was quite a surprise to me. He said that '"Paisatge Urba" respects the elements of public space that belonged to the historical and collective memory of the city'. From his point of view, the mural had achieved a level of historical memory in the city within the 4 years of its creation. This response is intriguing when one considers that the new mural implied the erasing of the old one which in theory was also part of the historical memory of the city. His answer suggests the old mural was not extinguished but lives on as a layer of the new one as part of the collective memory.

In this perspective, the mural could be seen as part of the city palimpsest that encrypted a plurality of relations and stories over time. Perhaps this is what the representative of 'Paisatge Urba' meant when he said that the murals were part of the historical memory of the city. But for whom was – and which perception of – the city is linked to this memory? I argue that the institutional position in this case can be understood in terms of Benjamin's phantasmagoric sensorium of modernity in which human experiences are impoverished by the daily shocks of the modern world (Benjamin in Buck-Morss 1992, 24). Following Freud, Benjamin argues that the surface of the human body mediates between the external world and the internal ego of the individuals. In Freud's (1960 [1923]) words, the human ego 'may be thus regarded as a mental projection of the surface of the body' (1960 [1923], 15–6).

Can we approach the surface of the city in similar terms, and is this surface of the city a projection of something? The fact that the council's representative understood the mural, which is part of the surface of the city, as an element of the city's historical memory makes me look at the inner realm of the city. It could be argued that the historical memory of a city contains its traditions, customs or buildings and how they are linked to its everyday life. But the city's urban life also exists, according to the anthropologist Manuel Delgado (2002), upon 'unstable structures spread out of differentiated spaces and heterogeneous societies' (2002, 8). For the Director of 'Paisatge Urba', the painting of the new mural on the squatted building represented the repetition of the old one on the same building and on the same surface.

In contrast, the members of La Carbonería collective saw the mural as a way to directly participate in and transgress the order of public space and to explore new possibilities within it. They wanted to transform everyday life and, through their actions, obtain social support for their cause and effectively leave traces of these actions on the surface of the city. These transformative actions had to be limited to the space-time framework of the mural painting and ultimately derived from the bodily sensations of the participants in this process. During that time, the surface of the city changed its 'phantasmagoric' and permanent reality. This temporal situation fostered the imagination of the people who were involved in the mural, and incorporated the outside world as a form of empowerment and reflection in contrast to the mimetic adaptation of the life in the city (Buck-Morss 1992, 17). In this case, Benjamin's claims about 'phantasmagoria' as a quality of modernity were overturned through the practical experimentation and transformation of the city space by some of its inhabitants.

The overflow of stimuli in the city and its supposedly anaesthetic effects on the experiences of the city's inhabitants are not always produced with the same aims for all their attempts to create alternative experiences. The texture of cities such as Barcelona, as Wegenstein (2010) states with regard to the human skin within the relationship between body and media, is 'porous and fluid, the site of encounter and exposure' between the different inhabitants of the city 'rather than a site of exclusion and closure' (2010, 33).

In conclusion, I argue that the mural encloses multiple traces shaped not only by ways of making graffiti images but also by politics, financial and economic relations in the city. The world economic and financial crisis that hit Spain, deflating its housing bubble, left this building empty. Then, the collective of squatters and graffiti artists used it as medium for their political claims through the painting of the mural. The representative of the council, 'Paisatge Urba', probably did not think about these kinds of circumstances as part of the historical memory, although it is embedded in the texture of the mural.

The surface of the city, in this case represented by the mural of *La Carbonería*, mediates between the external and internal worlds of the city through institutional statements to filter and communicate only certain narratives. To explore the different narratives of the mural, I have used the ethnographic work on landscape and the Western Apache by the linguist and anthropologist Keith Basso (1984), who made use of Bakhtin's idea of 'the chronotope' to discuss Western Apache stories linked with places. Basso states that the geographic features in the Western Apache landscape are 'chronotopes' where their stories and memories make that 'time take on flesh' and allow listeners to place themselves in relation to particular features of the landscape, which are charged and responsive to the movements of time (Bakhtin 1981, 84, as cited by Basso 1984, 44–5). I see the mural in public space as a 'chronotope' where different narratives make the everyday life in the city 'take on material grounds' through multiple actions and participants.

Thinking in terms of the porous and fluid nature of the city textures allows us to consider other possibilities and to think of the mural as the writing of a new layer on the city palimpsest. It can be said then that the mural on the building mediates between multiple perceptions and understandings shaped by the fluidity of everyday life. For instance, the building was seen as a social centre and as a platform of political communication for the squatter collectives in the city as it was simultaneously seen as a source of economic income for the bank or as part of the collective and historical memory for the council. These examples show the separation between the historical and institutional meanings linked to the space and the perception of it according to a plurality of identities, political and economic relations within the city's everyday life.

If we focus our interpretation of the mural on its collective aesthetics, it is possible to arrive at the following conclusions. The fact that a collective of the city painted the mural seems to be a key factor in understanding its existence in the public space. In this sense, most of the squatted buildings that I visited and knew in Barcelona such as 'Los Bloques' in Vallcarca and 'Can Vies' in Sants had their façades painted with graffiti murals. Making reference to Ranciére (2004), it can be argued that the squatted buildings of Barcelona enclose their own 'distribution of the sensible' that transgresses the official order over the public space around them. Thus, using the process of the mural painting in the squatted building of *La Carbonería*, what I am proposing here is an understanding of the politics of graffiti in the public space of Barcelona in terms of its practices, sensorialities and contexts. Therefore, the 'aesthetic' regime and the murals of the squatters' movement in Barcelona are contained in political claims towards the use and transformation of the public space and end up being visible and experienced through the creation of big graffiti murals on the surfaces of squatted buildings.

References

Baraklianou, Stella. 2013. "Pasearse: Duration and the Act of photographing." In *Bergson and the Art of Immanence*, edited by John Ó Maoilearca and Charlotte de Mille, 131–47. Edinburgh: Edinburgh University Press.

Basso, Keith. 1984. "'Stalking with Stories': Names, Places, and Moral Narratives among the Western Apache." In *Text, Play and Story: The Construction Society and Reconstruction of Self and Society*, edited by Edward M. Bruner, 19–55. Washington, DC: Proceedings of the American Ethnological Society.

Buck-Morss, Susan. 1992. "Aesthetics and Anesthetics: Walter Benjamin's Artwork Essay Reconsidered." *October* 62: 3–41.

Chang, Vanessa. 2013. "Animating the City: Street Art, Blu and the Poetics of Visual Encounter." *Animation: An Interdisciplinary Journal* 8: 215–33.

Cooper, Martha and Henry Chalfant. 1988. *Subway Art*. New York: Thames & Hudson.

Debord, Guy. 1994 [1931]. *The Society of the Spectacle*. New York: Zone Books.

Delgado, Manuel. 2002. *Etnografía del espacio public*. Barcelona: Universitat de Barcelona.

Edensor, Tim. 2005. *Industrial Ruins: Space, Aesthetics and Materiality*. London: Berg.

Freud, Sigmund. 1960 [1923]. *The Ego and the Id*, trans. Joan Riviere. London: W.W. Norton.

Gell, Alfred. 1998. *Art and Agency: Towards an Anthropological Theory*. Oxford: Clarendon Press.

Iddings, Ana C.D., Steven G. McCafferty and Maria L. Teixeira da Silva. 2011. "Conscientizacao Through Graffiti Literacies in the Streets of Sap Paulo Neighbourhood: An Ecosocial Semiotic Perspective." *International Reading Association* 46–1: 5–21.

Ingold, Tim. 2007. "Materials against Materiality." *Archeological Dialogues* 14: 1–16.

Jarman, Neil and Anthony D. Buckley. 1998. "Painting Landscapes: The Place of Murals in the Symbolic Construction of Urban Space." In *Symbols in Northern Ireland*, edited by Anthony D. Buckley, 81–98. Belfast: Institute of Irish Studies.

Lefebvre, Henri. 1991. *The Production of Space*, trans. Donald Nicholson-Smith. Oxford: Blackwell.

MacDougall, David. 2006. *Film, Ethnography and the Senses: The Corporeal Image*. Oxford: Princeton University Press.

Mitchell, William J.T. 2002. "Showing Seeing: A Critique of Visual Culture." *Journal of Visual Culture* 1–2: 165–81.

Mullarkey, John and Charlotte de Mille. 2013. *Bergson and the Art of Immanence: Painting, Photography Film*. Edinburgh: Edinburgh University Press.

Ranciére, Jacques. 2004. *The Politics of Aesthetics: The Distribution of the Sensible,* trans. Gabriel Rockhill. London: Bloomsbury Revelations.
Stewart, Jack. 2009. *Graffiti Kings: New York City Mass Transit Art of the 1970s.* New York: Abrams.
Taussig, Michael. 1991. "Tactility and Distraction." *Cultural Anthropology* 6–2: 147–53.
Urry, John. 1990. *The Tourist Gaze.* London: Sage.
Wegenstein, Bernadette. 2010. "Body." In *Critical Terms for Media Studies,* edited by William J.T. Mitchell and Mark B.N. Hansen, 19–34. Chicago: University Chicago Press.

7 Murals as sticking plasters

Improving the image of an eastern German city for visitors and residents

Gareth E. Hamilton

Introduction

Halle an der Saale, the city which is the focus of the chapter, is a settlement of approximately 230,000 located in the former GDR (German Democratic Republic) but is now the largest city of the federal German *Bundesland* of Saxony-Anhalt. In this chapter, I show how murals have been used in the city, which has a somewhat complex reputation for visitors (and residents), to persuade these to take on a set of certain positive views of it throughout time. Considering GDR-era murals and their function, I move on to show how this form of public art has been used in contemporary Halle in symbolic and key areas of the city, yet which are simultaneously in a state of disrepair. Via the optic of a rhetoric culture approach, I show how murals become 'sticking plasters' on parts of the built environment that would otherwise be regarded as negative. While I do focus principally on the period of fieldwork there from 2008 to 2009, I take into account that the past is not far from view, especially in the minds and expressions of visitors. Images of persons in the past and the present feature not only in murals but also negative views of the city that these mural-based efforts positively attempt to counteract. The content of this chapter is not only based on my experiences in Halle visiting the places involved and talking to those involved; rather, I adopt an approach which also draws on mediated images of the city as these contain impressions that are both widespread and persistent but also reveal some of the issues that those attempting to improve the image of Halle both inside to residents and outside to visitors, whether via murals or not, must deal with.

Halle: a city underestimated?

The revelatory starting point – and one that provides readers of this chapter with the type of complex impression of Halle that people may have – is a travel article for potential visitors which appeared in 2015 in the prestigious national *Die Zeit* newspaper (Kraft 2015). The article, by journalist Nadine Kraft in a series called 'Underestimated cities', asks why people visit Halle's

Figure 7.1 Händel mural on leaving the 'Potemkin village' (*pace* Kraft 201) railway
     station.
Source: the author.

larger and more prosperous neighbour, Leipzig, instead of it. She notes positively that, despite its reputation, 'the city belongs more to architecture,
music, the arts, knowledge, technology, ecclesiastical history and nature
than it ever did to the [city's erstwhile principal] chemical industry' (ibid.).
Despite the auspicious beginning, Kraft then describes the visitor's arrival
by train (which she recommends, despite what follows!). The station itself is
described as a '*Gründerzeit* mid-to-late nineteenth century building in which
life pulses'. However, in a somewhat 'warts-and-all' description of exiting it,
when the automatic doors open, Kraft suggests that the visitor might think
they have been in some variety of 'Potemkin village': 'outside, the horrific
urban reality presents itself', as 'over the entry to the city there are two wide
flyovers and decrepit leftovers of the socialist planned economy'. She continues, 'junk shops and *Jugendstil* [*art nouveau*] facades secured by large nets
set the scene'. While Kraft displays the view of a visitor, here is a very similar narrative for comparison from an interview I conducted in Halle during
fieldwork on the self-employed and rhetoric of personhood:

> Tourists, guests, commuters arrive at station and have to go past ne-
> glected/run-down high-rises and empty shops, and that it their first
> view of Halle, and that is a problem. And the problem is because the
> station is so far away.

This interview was with a representative of the municipal *Stadtmarketing* (city marketing) department, making it clear that Halle people are also aware of the shortcomings of the area involved. As this chapter progresses, I show how *Stadtmarketing* and others, via the medium of murals, and principally those featuring persons from Halle of various levels of fame and from different time periods, are used to present a more positive view of the city. This occurs despite the negative-sounding built environment as presented above. For a preview of what follows, consider Figure 7.1. This is what Kraft (and other visitors) would have seen on leaving the station on the wall behind tramlines which lie to its front. It is a long and vivid mural of composer Georg F Händel. He is regarded as perhaps the city's most famous former inhabitant. Indeed, on Halle's main square, there is a famous statue of him that is its equivalent of a 'national thing' (Zerilli 2000, 177). Furthermore, people come to Halle due to Händel, and there are annual concerts (*Händel-Festspiele*) in his memory. This mural appeared after I left Halle in 2009, so the murals I refer to below were erected before it. However, I was not surprised to see it on returning, especially given the similar murals I had witnessed earlier.

Further setting the scene

While Kraft suggests that she has 'set the scene', before moving on to more murals, it is important to consider more of the historical and socioeconomic context into which visitors to Halle arrive and residents live within. Halle has been a place of relative prosperity throughout its history, for example, having a thriving salt industry in the Middle Ages. Its prosperity increased in the early twentieth century based on heavy industry and chemical production. Once called 'the middle German Essen' (Tullner 2007, 98), it suffered from wartime damage and also post-war industrial degradation through reparations to the Soviet Union. Despite this, it rebuilt its chemical industry under a controlled economy, supplying the GDR with petrochemicals and polymers it needed for its industrial recovery and for export. Halle's heavy industry gave it a reputation for pollution and urban degradation, even during the GDR period (1949–1990) – an informant who grew up there told me he thought snow was brown as a child due to the grime – coupled with one as a 'concrete jungle'. This was due to the so-called concrete panel buildings areas built during the GDR period to service this industry's workers. A large part of this was in a separate new town and municipality (Halle-Neustadt), while the original centre's buildings declined. German reunification from 1990 onwards brought further issues. Its population decreased as the industry it was famous for was reduced to a fraction of its former self due to a population decrease of 25.4 per cent by 2008 (Stadt Halle/Saale 2009, 37). These concrete areas are now also partly decaying, giving it a reputation for physical urban decline, as are parts of the centre which have not (yet) been renovated. Some of these feature in Kraft's description. Other indicators

114 *Gareth E. Hamilton*

are also stark: in 2009, Saxony-Anhalt had the second highest per capita rate of basic subsistence unemployment welfare claimants of all Germany's *Bundesländer* at 17 per cent (Die Welt 2009). These are typical indicators and fit into the eastern German popular (and academic) trope of a 'shrinking city' (e.g. Dietzsch 2010) alongside the empty, decaying or demolished buildings.

These figures are telling in themselves but, in terms of both the lived experience and of attracting people either to live there, or even visit as tourists, they should be taken alongside other softer factors. Readers of the German-language *Men's Health* magazine placed Halle forty-fifth in terms of male quality of life among German/Austrian cities. Shortly after I arrived there, a newspaper interview by the head of DHL in nearby Leipzig, who moved to Halle, complained that, even though there were benefits of living there, the attitude of the local people was negative and always put itself down (Freitag 2008b). However, *Stadtmarketing* does advertise the city towards outside visitors. There is even an amateur website, *Halle is beautiful* (*Halle ist schön* [Stein n.d.]), which shows pictures of Halle places that the editor suggests are picturesque, as might be expected from the name. Yet, the image is not as clear-cut as it seems. The website owner, Sebastian Stein, states that

> You may notice that I do not show pictures of problem areas and I also do not discuss such thing in the picture descriptions. Of course Halle also has some problem areas and things not that good. However, *I think we already talk too much about bad things, so I like to provide a counter balance by not broaching the issue at all.* [sic, emphasis added]
>
> (Stein n.d.)

From such impressions from various sources, it is clear that Halle has problems not only in socioeconomic terms, but that these terms become linked to the state of its built environment. Klein, *Stadtmarketing* and I have not left these out of all our accounts. However, Stein introduces a more complex question: that of representation. It is easily argued that he ignores the negative, but it is more an issue of editing. A website is easily edited. In comparison, in Halle, it seems that the built environment is not so easily brought into the state some might like. Consider below a further example from Halle-Neustadt, likewise connected to murals, in the formerly independent new town but which was made part of the Halle municipality after reunification.

Figure 7.2 shows two rather large murals almost equal to the height of the building by José Renau (Halle-im-bild.de 2015) and Lothar Scholz (Pasternack 2012a) from 1974 on the wall of the building where non-EU citizens go to register their residency status. The right-hand mural, entitled *Die Einheit der Arbeiterklasse und Gründung der DDR* ('The unity of the working class and foundation of the GDR'), features Karl Marx, 'who appears to watch over Neustadt' on this 'seemingly futuristic majolica painting' on tiles (Halle-im-bild.de 2015). Whereas the Händel mural features a character

Figure 7.2 The foreign citizen registration building, with mural featuring Marx.
Source: the author.

with seemingly long-lasting and wide international appeal, this example is somewhat more contentious. While no longer the regime's ideological archetype, the murals have not yet been, almost 20 years hence, 'edited out' of existence. The *Halle is beautiful* website does not feature them but, in the built environment itself, these murals still exist and, furthermore, on a building housing local civil servants. The mural could have been painted over, obliterated in some way, or the building even knocked down at the extreme end of possible options. Even today, GDR-era murals and their removal can provoke stark public debate (Piontkowski and Reißmann 2011), but knocking down buildings takes considerably more effort and a great deal more time – and importantly, money in a relatively poor area – than editing a website. Despite this, 'visitors' still come to see Marx, even if unexpectedly, when they register as immigrants. Yet, these murals have much more to reveal.

Persuasive murals

Although arguing it was not ultimately effective, Bytwerk (1999) highlights the GDR's extensive propaganda system. Feldtkeller notes that murals 'belonged to the important artistic media' of the GDR but 'had to promote the socialist state, had to grace the socialist residential areas' (2008, 282). According to sociologist Pasternack, the murals in Figure 7.2 were among

184 public artworks in Neustadt, and he places these among 25 in the category of '*agitatorisch*' (Pasternack 2012a), the Communist concept of intentionally persuasive 'agitation'. He further notes that public art in Halle-Neustadt was used to foster identity (2012b, 39). It is clear that there is a function within these GDR examples that aims to persuade domestic and foreign viewers of a certain point of view, in some sense, to create a sense of what society is like. Marx is metonymic for a Communist-based society and the benefits to residents of such states (and their cities) this form of government was to bring. Due to the intended persuasive nature of these murals, and given the preponderance of examples from the GDR era (and after) featuring people, I approach them and those viewed below through the theoretical optic of a rhetoric culture approach (represented by, among others, Fernandez 1986, 2009; Strecker and Tyler 2009; Carrithers 2005b) and especially that espoused by Carrithers on the rhetoric of personhood (2005a, 2008). Rhetoric culture theory assumes that persuasion is a widespread and fundamental phenomenon, the base of human interaction itself. Carrithers suggests that persuasion is fundamental to human social life, which is composed of overlapping rhetorical situations (2005b). Our understandings of situations are initially inchoate but, through persuasive explanations of situations, become clear(er) as does the necessary action to be taken to take the situation out of a state of inchoateness and opaqueness (2008). There is rhetorical 'movement' towards a 'performance' being made. This performance is not necessarily linguistic; it can be artistic or gesture-based too.

The tools of the rhetor aiming towards performance might include the use of narrative of various lengths, including the very short (2009), telling a story to explain a situation and persuade others of how to interpret a situation. Another tool that is relevant here is the use of persons being used strategically within such narratives where persons 'move the at-first-unknown persons into an understandable narrative' (Carrithers 2008, 163), placing characters in a story. Even though we may have to deal with what Schütz (1962, 1967) would call *Nebenmenschen*/contemporaries rather with *Mitmenschen*/consociates in complex society, humans are able to use knowledge of the latter to deal with the (personally) unknown former because they can make inferences to deal with various 'types' they may meet. A further important aspect to rhetoric culture is called to mind by Bailey who reminds readers that 'all rhetoric is palaestral' (2009, 107) in its attempt to persuade as part of a 'battle' between competing opinions, to win over others, persuade and supply a certain message. There are also a number of persons involved. There are those depicted on the murals, equally those who have created them. However, there are also the viewers who Carrithers would, after Lienhardt (1961), call 'agents-cum-patients' of the rhetoric. The 'agents' who create rhetoric in general – in this case, the mural creators or commissioners – might be acting on the 'patients' (here, the mural viewers), but these 'patients' may make their own interpretations of situations they are in. The Halle-visiting 'patients' may already possess views on Halle before arriving as the following examples show, or reject the murals' messages. Even when in Halle, opinions visitors have about 'types' of people can confirm and reinforce their views on seeing the built environment. Rather than passive, these 'agents-cum-patients' can act while other actors act on them.

The visiting mathematician, the set-theorist, the Scots and the Russians

When I returned to the UK from fieldwork in Halle, I discovered that a BBC television programme featuring Halle existed (Berry 2008). Presented by celebrity academic mathematician Marcus du Sautoy, this programme on set theory, entitled *To infinity and beyond*, provides another example of a visitor's impressions of Halle. Despite its mathematical theme, this visitor came to view murals, or rather a mural-like bas-relief of Georg Cantor in Neustadt. Cantor developed set theory at the local university, and four of its historically famous thinkers feature in bas-reliefs on the GDR-era *Wissenschaftler-Würfel* ('cube of scientists') designed by sculptor and graphic designer Gerhard Geyer. Beginning at the statue of Georg Händel found on the main square, du Sautoy travels by tram to Neustadt. He seems annoyed that he 'had to take a tram way out of town', telling viewers wryly that 'Communists' loved to celebrate their famous scientists and placed the image of Cantor on a large 'cube', 'but being Communists, they did not put the cube in the middle of the town but out amongst the people'. In fact, the cube was quite central in the GDR-era in independent Neustadt. There follows a succession of standard 'former Communist country' cliché sounds and images: sad music, windows with broken glass, high-rise concrete buildings like those seen in Figure 7.2 but unoccupied and burnt out. Du Sautoy wonders if he is in the wrong place, thinking this is 'the most unlikely place for a statue of a mathematician'. When he finds the statue, he is somewhat impressed by its stature, but there is still a certain gratuitous presentation of Halle given via these clichés.

While Neustadt has problematic buildings, Pasternack suggests that initial post-reunification feelings of malaise about Neustadt came from persons viewing it from outside, and as evidence quotes prestigious news magazine *Spiegel* that only dynamite would help it (2012b, 55). Yet, the documentary also indulges in negativity as a mini-travel report in its own right, while also being a product of editing like the *Zeit* article or the *Halle is beautiful* website. It expresses much more clearly and gratuitously the 'Cold-War binaries' (Berdahl 2000, 1) when these had little to do with mathematics in general, let alone set theory. However, it also throws in a 'type' of person into a historical narrative, relatively personally unknown to most viewers in the UK: the 'Communists' who become linked to Halle's apparently grey, decrepit urban landscape where public art is located in bizarre locations. I realised when watching this that I had heard something similar while in Halle where other visitors also used group nouns in a negative way.

This observation was of a group of otherwise all-inclusive bus-touring Scottish pensioners who needed to purchase lunch in Halle one Sunday. I was in a café and thought it would be interesting to hear their views as visitors – these were not positive. Alongside Halle's apparent tourist unfriendliness, architecture received their ire. They were disappointed by the buildings near the café, blaming another unknown third-person-plural entity – this time, the 'Russians'. These 'Russians' had apparently quite typically left no money for anything when they departed; no wonder Halle looked the way it did. Ironically, in terms of this chapter, one of the other sides of the bas-reliefs features philologist Viktor Klemperer, famous for his analysis of Nazi discourse and exposition of their manipulation of language for negative political purposes (1947). Though from a different era, the repetition by these elderly Scots of the language of Cold War enmity shows how deep-lasting the effects of political language can be. Further in this train of irony, the café where the Scottish pensioners were was not only rather central in the negative narrative portion of the article written by Kraft, but also in an area that had faced relatively recent renovation compared to its GDR-era appearance. Additionally, the area was connected to a particularly interesting mural-based action by *Stadtmarketing* to counteract negative impressions of Halle by those arriving as Kraft did.

The *palaestra* of persons

To take up the combative metaphor of rhetoric suggested by Bailey, the area around the train station is a palaestral place in that strong rhetorical effort has been made to create a positive impression and to fight the negative – and this via mural decoration. The area from the station to the flyovers and over to the net-covered *Jugendstil* buildings is occupied principally by Riebeckplatz square, and Leipziger Straße ('Leipzig street') which connects it to the main square with the Händel statue. Leipziger Straße is nicknamed the 'Boulevard' and is split into two pedestrianized parts where it is cut by Halle's inner ring road. One kilometre long, the end towards the main square is called the 'Lower Boulevard'; the other, towards Riebeckplatz, and where the café I met the Scottish pensioners is located is the 'Upper Boulevard'. Riebeckplatz had been renovated in the mid-2000s, including the removal in 2002 of a statue of paleastral fists punching towards the sky to celebrate the victory of socialism. Along with the renovation of the underpass, local government buildings had gained new facades. The access from the station to the square had been simplified, the tram connections improved, and new, small shopping units had been built below the underpasses and inside the square.

Riebeckplatz itself is named after a famous Halle industrialist but had been 'usurped' from 1945 to 1991 by Ernst Thälmann, former German Communist party leader, presidential candidate and Nazi concentration camp martyr. Leipziger Straße had also been renamed after the Communist Czechoslovak leader Klement Gottwald. In these names, there is an attempt to bring inferences from people and their fame or attributes to this important gateway to the city. Bodenhorn and Von Bruck suggest that it is their 'detachability that renders names a powerful political tool for establishing or erasing formal identity, and gives them commodity-like value' (2006, 4). It is not only in these locations in Halle that this occurs: Cantor has a prestigious school named after him. Likewise, the university where Cantor developed set theory is named after Martin Luther. Names seem to be freely detached from their original owners and then reattached to other entities at will to bring the attributes of one to the other where these neither explicitly nor even necessarily exist. However, on Riebeckplatz and on the Boulevard, much more noticeable was that this occurred upon their walls in a visual way. Within the area under the flyovers – whose shop units were often unoccupied – were images of 'famous' people who had hailed from Halle including Klemperer, Cantor and Riebeck who had been placed on the walls at the entrance to the square. Text with their names, dates of birth and death, and a small explanation of who the people were had been placed beside their photographs. Interspersed with these were the city coat of arms and the names of various industries in Halle's past and present. Larger text had also been used in order to engage in some playful use of plural nouns, for Halle has three denonyms. These are *Hallenser*, *Halloren* and *Hallunken* that refer to local people on a scale from native born to having moved there, respectively. Linking these personalities and its industry directly with the city itself and its other people, and the use of these playful demonyms, is simultaneously both ludic – intentionally attention-grabbing – and entertaining in itself. There is a deliberate rhetorical use of persons to create an impression of a dynamic Halle throughout the ages for visitors and city-dwellers in spite of what else surrounds the square.

At the time of my fieldwork, however, there was still building work to be done on Riebeckplatz. Awaiting removal were the '*Riebecktürme*', two twenty-three-floor towers, empty and decaying. At the bottom of these towers was a former club, more recently a steak restaurant. Attached to these was a supermarket at the start of the Boulevard, still in operation and intended to remain in place. The Boulevard might be called Halle's version of a '*Prachtstrasse*' (literally 'street of splendour') with connotations of finery and grandeur. Such streets are often the main shopping 'drag' of a settlement. This, historically, has been Leipziger Straße's role. Yet, when the *Zeit* journalist mentions junk shops, they are principally on its upper part. It was not only visitors who saw this and once, in an article in the local edition of the national *Bild* tabloid newspaper, other names were used for it: 'Bankrupts' boulevard' and '*Ramschmeile*' ('junk mile') (Freitag 2009a). This was in the context that the Boulevard, or here, 'Boulevard of the bankrupt' (ibid.) was in need of 'saving' (Freitag 2009b). However, at that time, the world economic crisis was in its early stages, businesses were closing in places more prestigious than Halle's boulevard. In one sense, the business owners were investing and coming together to attempt to improve the area. The joint owner of the café where I met the Scottish pensioners had bucked the trend, opening this, his second location, not far from where Riebeckplatz meets Leipziger Straße. I interviewed him and he revealed that he saw this as a long-term investment and part of longer-term improvements. Nevertheless, the area needed something more acute, and this café owner 'played a part' in this issue.

The boulevard of stars

The placing of 'playing a part' at the end of the previous paragraph in inverted commas is for two reasons. The first is that this café owner, Dirk, was involved in an action to help improve the area, and in a way that employed murals. The second is that these murals took the form of a film metaphor in which people like Dirk played a 'starring role' in cleverly edited photographs. This can be seen in showing *Halleywood Boulevard*, punning the name of the famous Los Angeles street. The ground has also been painted with a red strip, alluding to a red carpet and the presence of 'stars'. A large set of tarpaulins has been stuck over the tower façade carrying the murals. Above the supermarket, various 'stars' appear along with an inscription that reads: 'Halleywood Boulevard/A silent film on the moving history of the Upper Boulevard'. There are traders, businesspeople and those involved in commercial-related activity in the city, but especially the section of the Boulevard beginning at Riebeckplatz. Municipal housing company staff are pictured with a large key. The editor of a free sheet is located in a mock-up edition. DJs from a local radio station sit upon a large representation of its logo. Dirk sits on a large coffee bean with one of his waitresses, Jenny, portrayed inside a coffee cup he is holding. In visual wordplay, the Rotes Ross ('red steed') hotel manager sits on such an equine. The 'credits' for the murals are given along with the inscription mentioned above: *Stadtmarketing*. I interviewed the representative from the department shortly after it had rebranded Halle a *'Händelstadt'* (Händel Town) – persons used again to represent Halle – but conversation moved onto this particular set of murals.

In terms of the approach to the murals and to Halle's general advertising, he said that 'it would be nonsense to write "Halle is super!". We need to show that Halle is super, but more subtly and less directly'. Given the other murals featuring people, I asked him why the murals featured these particular people. He replied,

> that is what wakens Halle up. The chemist up there is a friend of mine and it is like that for many [Halle people], that they know someone. In Halle everyone knows everyone else. That is a very nice feeling, a fine feeling, the village character in a large city. [...] There are personalities whom everyone knows.

Even I, as a relative newcomer, had met people like Dirk. People arriving in Halle could also meet him or the other 'stars' if they spent time in a café or shop on their way to the main square. The tourism representative went on to talk about the murals with an explicit reference to consociates – here, demonstrated by pronouns – suggesting that:

> It is the nice thing that it shows the you [*du*] to you [*du*], it shows a social note. It shows the persons behind the pronouns. It is social; there are no machines, no buildings.

I have suggested elsewhere (Hamilton 2014) that east German people value the accentuation of personal relations and social closeness in what I called a (partly rhetorical) 'consociational personhood' ideal. In this example, in this vein, it is important to note that German is a 'T-V' language (Brown and Gilman 1960), meaning that it marks the distinction between formal and informal second-person pronouns. *Du* is the informal form suggesting such familiarity. For the resident, there is social proximity, people they may know, creating a sense of solidarity within the town amid the negative – or, rather, negated – urban environment. However, while this analysis based on what *Stadmarketing* claims may make sense for residents, what about for the visitors?

In our conversation, there were various themes, including the value of the 'personality' in the sense of someone who is widely known being employable as an icon to represent places. Given the presence of Marx, Cantor, Klemperer *et al.* on murals throughout the city, this is something not lost to Halle people of various time periods from the GDR to the present day. Indeed, *Stadmarketing* staff are dressed in Händel's contemporary fashions on the *Halleywood* murals suggesting the strong linkage between the town's image and the composer. Dirk placed Händel on murals inside both of his premises. In the Boulevard branch, Dirk claimed a mural of the Händel statue forms part of a spatial metaphor for the street itself. Reflecting the actual direction a pedestrian would walk, the physical locations of an ancient tower located at the point where the inner ring road intersects the Boulevard, and the train station are represented by murals upon the respective walls of the café. Dirk said he 'wanted simply to show this Boulevard has existed for an eternity and has had a certain course through history', expressed via these murals. Händel, the celebrity representing Halle, though, stands symbolically in the middle.

Murals as sticking plasters

In terms of the physical environment, what Dirk has done with his indoor café murals is to 'edit out' the unfortunate aspects of Leipziger Straße, much like the *Halle is beautiful* website does for the whole city. Indeed, the murals themselves represent the landmarks in their pre-war state, the pre-'Communist' and 'Russian' era, which can be seen as ignoring the negative aspects of the built environment of Riebeckplatz and the Boulevard in their current state and the historical processes that brought these about. He was able to do this inside his premises. Outside, this was a task that seemed to require municipal action taken by *Stadtmarketing*. It is clear that the distance is not alterable so the space itself must be dealt with. It was a matter of waiting until the towers had gone, and these were hardly the type of thing one could go and takes one's own dynamite to. Rather, part of the rhetorical effort in the square was the murals themselves as a form of *materiél* in their arsenal, in the form of tarpaulins. The representative first called the tarpaulins a 'disguise for the many ugly buildings' which is true in terms of physically covering what is not desired to be known or seen. He went on, more interestingly, to describe them in a metaphorical form: *Trostpflaster*. This word, etymologically consisting of words for 'consolation' and 'sticking plaster', means something offering consolation for small troubles or difficulties. There is a, perhaps, ironic aspect to this metaphor, but the image of a sticking plaster describes these murals rather well. They have been stuck over things that, like the idea of the disguise also suggests, people do not want to be seen. However, the idea of something that needs to be healed and cured is also visible. From the negative impressions of Halle, perhaps consolation is needed? It is an editing out of the bad, and covering over with the good. This is consoling. But what is this 'good'? On the Riebeckplatz *tarpaulin* murals, the viewer (visitor or resident) sees people used to create an impression of Halle. This is true also in the other mural examples: whether on Riebeckplatz with miscellaneous famous people, or outside the station with Händel, with the scientists in Neustadt in the GDR period and likewise Marx. These people are internationally famous. This is not to say that everyone in Halle knows the history of Cantor, for example, or even cares, but their achievements or fame can be transferred to Halle. The examples on the tarpaulins are not people visitors to Halle would know personally, rather they fit into schemes of plural nouns just like the du Sautoy 'Communists' or Scots' 'Russians'.

These murals fight back against negative stereotypes expressed by plural nouns, the 'Cold War binaries' which can be quite readily it seems be evoked by the decaying urban-built environment. Riebeckplatz's murals are an attempt to enforce a counter-narrative of the city into people's minds before they have the chance to walk down the full length of the Boulevard where negative images might be reinforced in a space which concentrates in a narrow quasi-tube what has been viewed before (un-plastered) and confirms negative preconceptions. In Carrithers' terms, the murals act as 'story seeds' (2009) – micro-sized items which unfold longer narratives in the mind. This is coupled with the images of people used strategically, important in rhetoric. Thus, more than 'plastering' occurs. The persons themselves (those on the murals) are key in this (rhetorical) situation. For an eastern German audience, these are capitalists who are friendly, open and not too self-important, as I have elsewhere suggested (see Hamilton 2014), and an important image for them to project in public. For visitors, they are an addition to the railway station-Boulevard-main square narrative as seen in the *Zeit* article, but also recognised by *Stadtmarketing*. Instead of 'Communists', such murals show many active 'capitalists' working together (with others, like the municipality) to create a vibrant business (and social) community despite the surroundings. They might even be the successors of the other famous persons met on the murals closer to the station. In these, the Marx mural, or the scientist cube, images of people are used to show what type of positive, active place one has arrived in – and that is not to be 'overlooked'.

The prince and the Potemkin tarpaulins

Ironically, many murals in Halle are not things people deliberately come to the city to see. They get presented with them as part of a strategy to create a better image of the city. While du Sautoy sought out Cantor's symbolic bas-relief for the purposes of televisual mise-en-scène, it was Cantor himself that drew the mathematician there. Even visitors for the *Händel-Festspiele* get to visit murals, whether or not they arrive by train or intended to view them or not; this set of 'sticking plasters' tarpaulin murals on Riebeckplatz were not the only examples. The 200th anniversary of Händel's death was 2009. That year's *Händel-Festspiele* was to be a gala event. The local press reported that the British monarch Elizabeth II was to attend, given Händel's adopted British citizenship and role in royal music. This was later played down to entail a visit from her son instead (Wätzold 2008). In the end, neither attended, but the notion of decrepit buildings causing a bad impression – this time between the main square Händel statue and the house of his birth (now a museum) close by – was brought up. Halle's oldest, yet endangered, example of wooden beam architecture on the route was seen as particularly shameful. Reminiscent in a similar vein to Riebeckplatz and its towers, money had apparently become available for renovation, but time was needed. To hide ongoing works, tarpaulins bearing local advertising were to cover the façades of the buildings en route. Even at this point, the newspaper was unimpressed, comparing these actions to the GDR-era practice of painting over ruins in Leipzig before the annual fairs, commenting:

> Basically it means this: The ramshackle buildings should, if-you-please, disappear behind construction tarpaulins. Rather than a "masterplan" it sounds more like Potemkin villages.
>
> (Freitag 2008a)

even this did not happen. The tarpaulins were to be used to cover up the non-renovated ruins and, bizarrely, the oldest building would feature a ghost image-based light installation.

One thing brought out in the newspaper article noted above is that, evidenced by Leipzig, perhaps there is a somewhat negative history of covering up the built environment in eastern Germany. Potemkin villages as an image is something also invoked by the Kraft in *Die Zeit* to describe the train station, and it might also be a valid critique of the way 'Halle' employs such techniques as 'plastering over' the remnants of the GDR era with the neglected 'leftovers' not renovated since those times. These are temporary solutions, as one might place a tarpaulin over a leaking roof. However, at least something was being done in a difficult situation. Even in less symbolic parts of Halle, or its neighbouring towns, it was possible to come across temporary murals used to similar effect (see Hamilton 2010). In Halle, there was a shop on a principal street which nonetheless had many dilapidated and net-covered buildings that bore a verbal artistic mural installation mimicking shop signage. Designed to be provocative, the name 'Bin Laden' was interposed into the German for 'I am an empty shop and am searching for someone who will make something out of me' [*Bin* is the first person singular of the verb *sein* (to be) and *Laden* means 'shop']. The second, from Naumburg an der Saale, approximately 40 kilometres south of Halle, was also an example where the building had been made to appear to address someone. There, red, eye-catching tarpaulins were attached to buildings to encourage persons to actually renovate them. They also represented an interesting use of persons as the buildings themselves seemed to speak via these murals. Or rather, someone decided to cause the buildings to do so, and dialogically. While one building might say, via the medium of tarpaulin, 'this house wants to LIVE!', another adjacent building would declare 'Me too!'. It is the creation of a conversation between objects not given to conversing, evocative in itself. These examples were not necessarily for visitors but recall that these locations are also places in which people have to live and work. Further, as in Riebeckplatz in Halle, they are a sign of something being done to solve a situation that both visitors and residents view as problematic and disheartening. Visitors are welcome to see this effort being made.

Concluding remarks: magic plasters

Throughout this chapter, I have shown how public art, and principally murals in the form of bas-reliefs, tiles, paintings and tarpaulins have been used to reimage a town and persuade people about what to think of it over time. However, to return to an important point, many people visiting Halle are unlikely to be coming to visit murals as a genre of artistic endeavour. Rather, these are murals that have been set in place by those who attempt to alter the impression of Halle that would otherwise be much more negative without the presence of those murals. While, on a basic level, the murals do attempt to mimic the metaphorical medical bandages, these are more than 'sticking plasters' given the playful, clever and artistic or conceptual motifs upon them. To take an example from the domain of sticking plasters, on the Halle Boulevard, like elsewhere, it is possible to purchase Hansaplast plasters featuring Walt Disney princesses. They have no extra medical properties compared to other plasters, but I have met children who seemed to think the presence of these characters provided some almost fetishistic or magic power to them. In the same vein, the Naumburg buildings have been rendered animistic by their murals, telling people of their desire to live. In comparison, the Halle examples feature people in the form of people themselves. Nevertheless, the presence of Halle people on murals seem designed to provide some persuasive feature for visitors and residents viewing them, as the princess plasters do towards the children with some minor cut gained through the 'vicissitudes of life', as Carrithers (2009) might call them. The people on the murals provide consolation to the residents to a city which has faced many vicissitudes, showing them that, despite the difficulties of the past and the present, Halle has and has had people who have overcome adversity and have been successful and certainly not been 'overlooked' in the world. Likewise, Halle should not be ignored today either. This is the message to the visitor too. When I returned to Halle at the same time as I first saw the Händel mural at the railway station, the Riebeckplatz 'Halleywood-Boulevard' murals were still there, although the film strip motif was somewhat truncated: the towers had gone. For me, as a newly re-arrived visitor, it seemed that the 'stars' of this action were to keeping shining – and persuading.

References

Bailey, F.G. 2009. "The Palaestral Aspect of Rhetoric." In *Culture, Rhetoric, and the Vicissitudes of Life*, edited by Michael Carrithers, 107–120. Oxford and New York: Berghahn.

Berdahl, Daphne. 2000. "Introduction: An anthropology of postsocialism." In *Altering States: Ethnographies of Transformation in Eastern Europe and the Former Soviet Union*, edited by Daphne Berdahl, Matti Bunzl and Martha Lampland, 1–13. Ann Arbor: University of Michigan Press.

Berry, David. 2008. "To Infinity and Beyond." In *The Story of Maths*: BBC Four.

Bodenhorn, Barbara and Vom Bruck. 2006. "'Entangled in Histories': An Introduction to the Anthropology of Names and Naming." In *An Anthropology of Names and Naming*, edited by Barbara Bodenhorn and Gabriele vom Bruck, 1–30. Cambridge: Cambridge University Press.

Brown, Robert and Albert Gilman. 1960. "The Pronouns of Power and Solidarity." In *Style in Language*, edited by Thomas A. Sebeok, 253–276. Cambridge: Technology Press of Massachusetts Institute of Technology.

Bytwerk, Randall L. 1999. "The Failure of the Propaganda of the German Democratic Republic." *Quarterly Journal of Speech* 85 (4): 400–416.

Carrithers, Michael. 2005a. "Anthropology as a Moral Science of Possibilities." *Current Anthropology* 46 (3): 433–456.

———. 2005b. "Why Anthropologists Should Study Rhetoric." *Journal of the Royal Anthropological Institute* 11 (3): 577–583. doi: http://dx.doi.org/10.1086/428801.

———. 2008. "From Inchoate Pronouns to Proper Nouns: A Theory Fragment with 9/11, Gertrude Stein, and an East German Ethnography." *History and Anthropology* 19 (2): 161–186.

————. 2009. "Story Seeds and the Inchoate." In *Culture, Rhetoric, and the Vicissitudes of Life*, edited by Michael Carrithers, 34–52. Oxford and New York: Berghahn.

Die Welt. 2009. "Hartz-IV-Empfänger sollen mehr fürs Alter sparen," *Die Welt*, October 8, 2009, http://www.welt.de/wirtschaft/article4782802/Hartz-IV-Empfaenger-sollen-mehr-fuers-Alter-sparen.html.

Dietzsch, Ina. 2010. "Perceptions of Decline: Crisis, Shrinking and Disappearance as Narrative Schemas to Describe Social and Cultural Change." *Durham Anthropology Journal* 17 (1): 11–34.

Feldtkeller, Julia. 2008. *Wandmalereirestaurierung: eine Geschichte ihrer Motive und Methoden*. Vienna: LIT Verlag.

Fernandez, James W. 1986. *Persuasions and Performances: The Play of Tropes in Culture*. Bloomington: University of Indiana Press.

Fernandez, James W. 2009. "Tropological Foundations and Foundational Tropes of Culture." In *Culture and Rhetoric*, edited by Ivo Strecker and Stephen Tyler, 166–181. New York and Oxford: Berghahn.

Freitag, Uwe. 2008a. "Alle Ruinen weg bis zu Händelfest!" *Bild-Zeitung (Halle)*, November 17, 2008, 3.

Freitag, Uwe. 2008b. "Was ich an Halle liebe und hasse." *Bild-Zeitung (Halle)*, March 25, 2008, 3.

Freitag, Uwe. 2009a. "Boulevard der Pleiten." *Bild-Zeitung (Halle)*, July 14, 2009, 3.

Freitag, Uwe. 2009b. "Rettet der Schoko-König den Oberen Boulevard?" *Bild-Zeitung (Halle)*, August 13, 2009, 3.

Halle-im-bild.de. 2015. "Einheit der Arbeiterklasse und Gründung der DDR." Last modified 2015, accessed July 5, 2015, http://www.halle-im-bild.de/fotos/wandgestaltungen/einheit-der-arbeiterklasse-und-gruendung-der-ddr.

Hamilton, Gareth E. 2010. "Rediscovering Our Shared Qualities in Ever-Changing Situations: Why Postsocialist Anthropologists Should (and Do) Study Rhetoric." *Durham Anthropology Journal* 17 (1): 35–64.

Hamilton, Gareth E. 2014. "Selling, Yet Still Social: Consociational Personhood among the Self-Employed in Eastern Germany." In *Neoliberalism, Personhood, and Postsocialism: Enterprising Selves in Changing Economies*, edited by Nicolette Makovicky, 17–35. Farnham: Ashgate.

Klemperer, Viktor. 1947. *Lingua Tertii Imperii: Notizbuch eines Philologen*. Berlin: Aufbau.

Kraft, Nadine. 2015. "Halle: Es muss nicht immer Leipzig sein." *Die Zeit*, March 11, 2015, http://www.zeit.de/reisen/2015-03/halle-saale-unterschaetzte-stadt.

Lienhardt, Godfrey. 1961. *Divinity and Experience: The Religion of the Dinka*. Oxford: Clarendon.

Pasternack, Peer. 2012a. "Künstlerische Stadtraumaufwertung als pädagogische Politik: Die künstlerische Bewirtschaftung des Ideenhaushalts Halle-Neustadts." *Bundeszentrale für politische Bildung*, accessed July 4, 2015, http://www.bpb.de/geschichte/zeitgeschichte/deutschlandarchiv/147746/kunst-im-stadtraum-als-paedagogische-politik?p=all.

Pasternack, Peer. 2012b. *Zwischen Halle-Novgorod und Halle-New Town: Der Ideenhaushalt Halle-Neustadts, Der Hallesche Graureiher*. Halle (Saale): Martin-Luther-Universität Halle-Wittenberg Institut für Soziologie.

Piontkowski, Torsten and Martin Reißmann. 2011. "Debatte um Wandbild aus DDR-Zeiten: Schulleiterin Brigitte Schmutzler versteht die Welt nicht mehr."

Vogtland-Anzeiger, March 25, 2011, http://vogtland-anzeiger.de/Vogtland_
Anzeiger/cms-nachrichten/entgegengesetzt/debatte-um-wandbild-aus-ddr-
zeiten.html.
Schütz, Alfred. 1962. *Collected Papers 1: The Problem of Social Reality*. The Hague:
Martinus Nijhoff.
Schütz, Alfred. 1967. *The Phenomenology of the Social World*, trans. George Walsh
and Frederick Lehnert. Evanston, IL: Northwestern University Press.
Stadt Halle/Saale. 2009. *Statistisches Jahrbuch der Stadt Halle (Saale) 2008*. Halle
(Saale): Die Oberbürgermeisterin, Stadt Halle (Saale).
Stein, Sebastian. n.d. "Halle ist schön," accessed July 3, 2015, http://www.halle-ist-
schoen.de/index_84_de.html.
Strecker, Ivo and Stephen Tyler. 2009. "The Rhetoric Culture Project." In *Culture
and Rhetoric*, edited by Ivo Strecker and Stephen Tyler, 21–30. New York and
Oxford: Berghahn.
Tullner, Matthias. 2007. *Halle 1806 bis 2006: Industriezentrum, Regierungssitz,
Bezirkstadt: Eine Einführung in die Stadtgeschichte*. Halle (Saale): Mitteldeutscher
Verlag.
Wätzold, Jan. 2008. "Prinz Charles kommt nach Halle!" *Bild-Zeitung (Halle)*,
September 15, 2008, 3.
Zerilli, Linda. 2000. "Democracy and National Fantasy: Reflections on the Statue
of Liberty." In *Cultural Studies & Political Theory*, edited by Jodi Dean, 167–188.
Ithaca and London: Cornell University Press.

8 Difference upon the walls

Hygienizing policies and the use of graffiti against pixação in São Paulo

Paula Larruscahim and Paul Schweizer

Introduction

Brazil is widely discussed as an emerging economy or 'threshold country'. In this context, São Paulo is prominently presented as the pioneering city. Contrasting the threshold narrative, Caldeira (2000) focuses on its condition as a 'city of walls', divisions and closures. Mainstream media and politicians present São Paulo as the very symbol of Brazil's 'developedness', having achieved 'Western standards' of '(world) city-ness' and 'urban economic dynamism' (Robinson 2002). This 'modernist' achievement is often connected to and mediated through a literal cleansing of the city. Dirt, deviance and even the bodies of the poor are being dragged and pushed to the outer limits of the city, into invisibility. In this chapter, we highlight one practice of opposition to these policies of cleaning and cleansing, by visually intervening on walls in São Paulo's public space. Pixação is a typical style of graffiti writing in Brazilian cities originally practised by marginalized youth in São Paulo since the mid-1980s. The simple line, muddled typography, commonly painted with black latex ink, evades hegemonic aesthetics. Pixação writers aim to spread their signatures, generally not containing explicit political content, across the whole city, but particularly in representative places such as the centre's skyscrapers' façades. Though pixação is clearly distinct from muralism, it ties in with the theme of this edited book as it evokes its own issues of politics and identity through painted interventions on walls in public space.

Based on ethnographic fieldwork conducted with pixadores between 2013 and 2015, interviews with policy makers (March–April 2015) and media analysis, we show how pixação is discursively framed as 'sujeira' – dirt, filth – or 'visual pollution'. As such, it calls into question São Paulo's status as a modern world/global city. City's authorities, as well as private real estate owners, make enormous efforts to combat pixação through harsh policing, legally prosecuting writers and large-scale grey painting. After giving a brief historical review of 'hygienizing' policies of São Paulo's public space, we show how recent policies now especially focus on pixação as one of the most important threats to 'modern' São Paulo. In contrast to this framing of pixação, we propose to understand it as the struggle for recognition, across and through difference, in a context where urban theory and policies largely tend to deny the right to, or even existence of difference, in 'modern' metropolises. To conclude, we argue that it is first of all necessary to overcome role models based on Western modernist aesthetics in urban studies, planning and policy making to be able to acknowledge heterogeneity and difference within 'the 21st century metropolis' (Roy 2009).

São Paulo: pioneering modernity?

Stefan Zweig's 1941 (2015) designation of Brazil as 'a Land of the Future' has been commonly cited in recent economic literature on Brazil. Recent enthusiasm has seen it being called a 'booming economy' (Rohter 2012), a 'Global Power' 'on the rise' (Reid 2014). Many of these commentators underline that economic progress in Brazil is accompanied by 'Good Governance', 'higher-quality democracy' and 'innovative social policy' (Montero 2014), as if to prove that capitalism is a philanthropic mode of production, even in the dictatorship-plagued problem child of Latin America.

In this developmental narrative, São Paulo steadily appears as the pioneering city. Having been crucial to the Brazilian economy during the last two centuries – from agricultural to industrial exports, to finance markets (see Ana Fani A. Carlos 2004) – in the current discourse, São Paulo is not only considered 'Brazil's economic powerhouse' (Yang and Anaya 2014, 12) but also its very 'business, financial and cultural capital' (Reid 2014, 14).

Cities such as Salvador and Rio (both the former capitals) are often presented as being 'marvellous', 'exotic' and 'tropical', characterized by Afro-Brazilian culture, beaches, favelas and carnival. Salvador has become popular amongst western tourists especially for its '"Black Culture" and "Black Bodies"' (Calvo-Gonzalez and Duccini 2010) and its Afro-Brazilian popular culture like ubanda and capoeira. Several travel agents and hostels promise to provide the tourist with an authentic experience in one of Rio's famous favelas (see Frisch 2012; Steinbrink 2014). The contrast could not be harsher, while Lonely Planet praises Rio de Janeiro – the marvellous city – in its own guidebook, the website chapter on São Paulo begins: 'São Paulo is a Monster' (Lonely Planet 2015b). São Paulo has a long tradition of being presented as a Brazilian island of Euro-American modernity: a developed, economically prosperous, prosaic city where it is 'all about business' instead of party and beaches (Reid 2014, 14). These discourses are often related to and mediated through racial categories of 'whiteness' or culturalisms, reinforcing the middle-class condition which Paulistans nowadays supposedly live in. Weinstein (2015) has shown how regional identity in São Paulo emphasizes European origins as aptitude for modernity and progress. This racialized regional identity serves not only to naturalize the enormous disparities between Brazilian regions but also to identify poorer, darker-skinned populations within São Paulo as foreign, culturally different, 'backward', 'non-modern' and a potential threat to Paulistan modernity (Weinstein 2015).

In the last two decades, theorists and political actors have been progressively led by a new paradigm to pigeon-hole São Paulo's 'modernness' and pivotal position in the Brazilian economy. Urban scholars, along with urbanists and politicians, had long searched for the right term to characterise this city region and started to discuss São Paulo as a 'world city' or 'global city'. Besides the use of these concepts as analytical frameworks, they are applied as 'strategic paradigms' guiding urban policies, aiming to consolidate São Paulo's position in global economy (Sousa 2008, 197). The World Bank-financed study 'Rio-São Paulo, world cities' is just one example for research explicitly encouraging such policies (Rezende and Lima 1999). Consolidating São Paulo's world/global city status is here understood as the necessary step to place Brazil in a leading position in the globalized economy. Carvalho (2011) appoints 'urban tourism' one of the most important factors for the economic development of global cities. In fact, the municipality's 2015–2018 Tourism Plan adopted the idea of tourism policies as a major tool to improve the city's profile as 'Latin America's business capital' (São Paulo Turismo S/A 2015b, 70).

'Other' São Paulos

'We live in "fortress cities" brutally divided between "fortified cells" of affluent society and places of terror where the police battle the criminalized poor'.

(Davis 1992, 224)

While the 'threshold' narrative paints a picture of an open door to the middle class for all Brazilians, or at least for all Paulistanos, reality for the vast majority of the city's population looks fairly different; it is walls equipped with electric fences rather than open thresholds that divide the upper and middle classes from the vast rest of the population. Mike Davis' description of Los Angeles might well be used to describe socio-spatial segregation in São Paulo – the 'City of Walls' as Caldeira (2000) has called it. The richer parts of Paulistan population – those that might actually feel like living in a world/global city – live in gated communities in the suburbs or closed apartment complexes in the central neighbourhoods, both equipped with leisure facilities, shopping malls and in some cases even office spaces inside the complexes (Freeman 2003, 183). The other part of the population stays cut off from the 'modern' São Paulo by walls, electric fences and security guards, but also through the 'mere distance' combined with inflationary prices for public transport.

Caldeira describes how recent urban planning and policies incited by crime discourses lead to the rejection of public space as the place where heterogeneity and difference may appear, encounter and become explicit. Instead, the most feasible way to keep the 'world city São Paulo' thesis reliable seems to be through a total denial of difference. São Paulo's topology and history offer quite different conditions regarding the visibility of difference and poverty – thus the incoherence of the thesis – than, for example, the nearby metropolis of Rio de Janeiro (Carreras 2004, 313). But, besides that, concrete measures have been undertaken to keep these incoherencies as hidden as possible.

São Paulo's visible and invisible (non-)modern

If São Paulo is understood as a metropolis of a 'fragmented first world' as Carreras (2004) has suggested, these wide-ranging 'others' are all living within it. Thus, they keep disturbing the image unless as they are made completely invisible. O'Dougherty (2002) declares her astonishment when realizing that 'tourist maps show only the central zone and adjacent middle- and upper-class areas of the south and west zones as "São Paulo"' (O'Dougherty 2002, loc 452). The contradictory coexistence of various urban realities and their corresponding conflicting imaginaries might be dealt with by policies of obscurement. It is in that sense that Tiburi, in her reflection on pixação and the 'Visual Right to the City', claims that 'the façade of the white wall' has actually become an ideology in cities like São Paulo. She describes a 'closed block of neat, clean persons' being protected by 'the hate of the other, the different, the excluded' (Tiburi 2011, 43). In her study of São Paulo, Silveira (2004, 67) points out how the world/global-city model necessarily comes along with new norms in urban policies and planning.

Hygienist policies then and now

A famous historic example of policies and urban development projects aimed to actively reinforce São Paulo's status as a 'modern' metropolis are the hygienist measures applied during the first decades of the Republic in the late nineteenth and early twentieth centuries. A range of urbanistic and social policies, in the name of prevention of 'plagues and diseases', was supposed to gain control over 'dangerous classes' (Carpenter 2013). Inspired by its European predecessors, namely Haussmann's urban development projects in Paris (see Harvey 2003) and driven by the same ideal of metropolitan modernity, these policies, in the Paulistan context, affect especially poor urban populations living in tenements (cortiços) and favelas (Sobrinho 2013).

At the start of the twenty-first century, we can observe certain policies aiming to aestheticize the city's public spaces, especially in the most representative 'Big Centre'. That includes not only the historic centre but also the two business districts aggregating big companies' offices in modern glass-and-steel skyscrapers around Paulista and Berrini avenues (Carreras 2004, 314). The latter two are kept 'clean' more or less successfully, free from all-too-visible evidence of usages not compatible with the 'all about business' São Paulo. Contrary to this, the historic centre has long been the place where one can encounter multiple different São Paulos. On the one hand, it still contains an important share of business and administrative offices and the main architectonic and urbanistic symbols of São Paulo's economic rise and 'modernization': Luz Train Station (1901), Municipal Theatre (1911), the Municipal Market (1933), Italy Circle (1965), Brazil's second highest skyscraper and Oscar Niemeyer's Copan Building (1966). The centre of São Paulo was also the location for the telenovela 'Tempos Modernos' ('Modern Times'). In order to make the scene compatible with the telenovela's title, the film crew used litres of disinfectant, ten cleaning trucks and had to 'gently request' homeless people to evacuate the area. 'And it was like this, last Saturday, that the sun had hardly risen and a big part of the centre's problems had been resolved' (Folha de São Paulo, 2009). As general Director Villamarin states, 'The centre has been revitalized, like Soho, like Barcelona. It is human and aesthetically marvellous' (Folha de São Paulo 2009). On the other hand, it concentrates elements of what are often considered a 'backward São Paulo', most prominently represented by the presence of over 3,000 people sleeping in the centre's streets every night (Fórum Centro Vivo 2006, 123) and the infamous Crackolândia, an area close to Luz Station that is largely occupied by crack users, commonly 'considered one of the centre's biggest problems' (Raupp and Adorno 2011, 2615).

During the last decade, a range of policies promoted a rhetorics of 're-vitalization' and 'cleanliness'. Extremely repressive measures were applied to control and expel popular groups from the centre of the city, executing a 'true hygienization and social cleansing' (Fórum Centro Vivo 2006, 12). Especially affected was the Luz Station area which was planned to be 're-generated' through the urban development project 'New Luz'. Under the name of 'Operação Limpa' ('Operation Clean'), Gilberto Kassab, then vice-mayor, increased police pressure on the homeless population, informal street vendors and waste collectors and used the occasion to 'criminalize poverty, social movements and human rights activists' (Fórum Centro Vivo 2006, 185ff.). Other hygienist policies in the following years – like the 'Integrated Operation Nice Centre' (Operação Integrada Centro Legal) in 2009 and the 'Operation Suffocate' (Operação Sufoco) in 2012 – employed similarly repressive measures (Carta Maior 2014).

As Raupp and Adorno stress, these hygienist policies claim to 'cleanse the Centre from degradation' by expanding the concept of cleansing 'to persons and activities exercised in these spaces' (Raupp and Adorno 2011, 2620). Conversely, it is quite surprising that Caldeira, when comparing Paulistan hygienist policies from the early twentieth century with contemporary cleansing policies, states that in 'contemporary São Paulo the project of cleansing the city is quite different from the ones put forward a century ago'. Its principal target is not the 'control of epidemics, not even the control of the dangerous classes. Rather, it is controlling the mass of signs that both the administration and the citizens believe are visually polluting the city' (Caldeira 2013). What Caldeira refers to is the discourse in which the passage of the 2006 'Clean City' bill was embedded.

'Clean City'

The Clean City Programme was launched in 2006 during the administration of Mayor Gilberto Kassab. According to the dispositions of the Municipal Legal Act 14.223–2006, the programme seeks to 'order the elements that make up the urban landscape'. While the overall effect of the law would be to prohibit publicity in public space, the discourse in which it was embedded focused significantly on issues of 'dirtiness'.

Regina Monteiro (2013), Director of the Department of Environment and Urban Landscape in the Municipal Company of Urbanization, and principal creator of the Clean City Programme, declares São Paulo's urban landscape to be one of the city's most dignified assets: 'We will wage an urban war to guarantee our civility'. Elaborating on the need for such cleaning policies, she poses the rhetorical question why Brazilians commonly undertake the long, wearying travel to Europe while not even knowing the cities of their own country. She answers herself: 'It might be our desire to get to know structured, organized cities, rife with characteristics that make us dream'. (Regina Monteiro 2013).

The Clean City Programme has attracted the attention of urban planners throughout the world and won several awards in the United States, Germany, Shanghai and London. Nevertheless, summarizing the programme's achievements regarding graffiti and pixação, Caldeira notes that,

'[...] while the city has been remarkably successful in dealing with ads and commercial signs, it has failed as remarkably in controlling more transgressive practices such as graffiti and pixação. As advertisements are removed and buildings painted anew, they are graffitied and tagged.'
(Caldeira 2012)

This leads us to a phenomenon specific to São Paulo's urban landscape – pixação. Often being referred to as 'dirt' or 'filth', sometimes as 'epidemics', calling to mind the rhetorics of early twentieth century hygienist discourse, city authorities officially approach pixação as 'visual pollution'. Indeed, Regina Monteiro affirms that: 'More than ever before, pichação is responsible for a major part of the visual pollution in the City' (Prefeitura da Cidade de São Paulo 2007).

Pixação

Pixação, or 'pixo' (what it is often abbreviated to by practitioners), is one of a variety of visual interventions in Brazilian urban space. While most of these are influenced by and clearly comparable to visual interventions like graffiti, street art or muralism in other urban contexts around the world, pixação differs from those in multiple ways: its stylistic pattern; the way it is criminalized; and the techniques developed to adapt to the financial condition of the practitioners and the specificities of the Paulistan urban landscape. Given these particular qualities, pixação has long been unique to the Brazilian metropolises. In fact, increasing interest in pixação from international social scientists, artists and the art market within the last few years indicates that this time it might be the São Paulo experience that will influence similar practices elsewhere (Figure 8.1).

The term 'pichação' derives from 'piche', which means pitch or tar, but is nowadays commonly used to designate 'scribblings' or 'scrawlings'. The

Figure 8.1 Praça Ramos Square in the very centre of São Paulo.
Source: Larruscahim and Schweizer.

orthographic subversion – from 'pichação' to 'pixação' (the pronunciation does not differ) – indicates a subcultural practice that follows certain internal codes and exhibits a distinct stylistic pattern: a simple line, muddled typography, commonly painted with black latex ink, evading hegemonic aesthetics. Pixação (with an 'x') originates from São Paulo in the middle of the 1980s and went viral in the early 1990s. Ever since, pixação writers (pixadores) aimed to spread their signatures, not necessarily containing explicit political content, across the whole city.

Many of the first pixadores worked in São Paulo's central business districts. Pixadores from the most distant suburbs and peripheries of São Paulo started to meet up in the centre of the city. They 'institutionalized' these weekly meetings as 'points', places to organize themselves in groups or crews, so called 'turmas' and 'familias', to promote their logos (grifes) and signatures throughout the city. The pixação gained special attention due to the adventurous acts of scaling skyscrapers' façades that pixadores perform in order to place their signature on the most visible and prestigious spots in the city's central neighbourhoods. This feature – a way to relate with the physical spatial conditions that São Paulo's urban landscapes offers – distinguishes Paulistan pixação from similar practices in other Brazilian metropolises such as the pixação in Salvador or xarpi in Rio de Janeiro (Pereira 2013).

Social scientists debating the political dimension of pixação attribute ambitious titles like 'The Politics of the Poor' (Franco *et al.* 2012), 'urban protest' (Larruscahim 2014) or even 'An Alphabet of Class Struggle' (Warsza 2012) to it. Snider (2012) claims attention to pixação as a powerful tool to denunciate social inequality:

> [not] the painting itself is the explicit political message; rather, it's the painting's location, on buildings and spaces that are economically and politically out of reach for virtually all of Brazil's urban poor, that makes the statement political.
>
> (Snider 2012)

While it is actually hard to find any point of view within the city region from which the viewer will not see any pixação, in regard to the location's importance to grasp pixação's potential political relevance, we might mention some interventions that, due to their location, claimed special attention in public discourse. Pixação legends from the early 1990s like Tchentcho and Krellos had already placed their signatures on the most prestigious spots of the city, including the very symbols of 'modern' São Paulo: the Italy Circle, the Bank of Brazil's and the Itaú bank's headquarters and Oscar Niemeyer's Copan Building ('Lendas Da Pixação – Tchentcho E Krellos', 2015). More recently, media-savvy pixadores effectively scribbled on spots like the Municipal Theatre (Folha de São Paulo 2013) and the São Paulo Biennials of 2008 and 2010. When pixadores 'attacked' the Bandeiras Monument with phrases like 'Bandeirantes Assassins', they referred explicitly to the bandeirantes' role in the violent colonization of the São Paulo region since the seventeenth century. They drew attention to these Portuguese settlers, gold seekers and Indian-hunters who had been honoured by an enormous monument in front of the famous Ibirapuera Park's entrance (Estadão 2013).

Talks on pixação

'A spectre is haunting Brazil: the spectre of pixação'. (Tiburi 2011, 40). In this quote, Marcia Tiburi uses Marx and Engels' famous metaphor to indicate how pixação seems to hit the sore point of Brazilian bourgeois society, causing debate and demand for repressive interventions just like the spectre of communism in nineteenth-century Europe. The analogy might be exaggerated but, indeed, pixação causes controversies with commentators showing themselves to be variously enthusiastic, distressed, hectored or furious.

Since its very first appearance in the mainstream media in the late 1980s, the dominant media discourse has tended to frame pixação (then called pichação) as 'dirt', 'vandalism' or in many cases even as 'terrorism'. In hardly any report in São Paulo's main newspapers is the term 'sujeira' ('dirtiness', 'filth') not mentioned when writing about pixação. Titles like 'Monuments of SP [São Paulo] deal with problems like pichação, excrements, urine and filth' (Folha de São Paulo 2012) indicate to the reader how to perceive pixação. Some reports even paint a picture that reminds us of late-nineteenth-century hygienist discourses when affirming that: 'Pichação and the pichadores have turned into a social epidemic and they should be treated as such' (Correio Popular 2003). Moreover, pixação is often discoursively connected to issues of fear, insecurity and insufficient interventions by the authorities and impunity. Consequently, policymakers have long been stipulated to act against the 'nocturnal vandals' and 'enemies of the City' (GSA 1989). Carlos Zaratini, Secretary of the District Councils, denounces three great problems of contemporary São Paulo: 'pichação, the scattered waste, and theft of cables and wires' (Folha de São Paulo 2004). During the last three decades, we can identify several strategies to cope with the first of these 'great problems'.

Criminalization and repression

In 1988, Mayor Jânio Quadros had announced a war on pixadores. In the Official Gazette of the Municipality of São Paulo, he claimed that they would be 'processed with the utmost rigor' and would soon 'scribble on the chain [in prison]' (Suplemento do Diário Oficial do Município de São Paulo 1988). From the late 1970s until the late 1990s, although pixação has never been criminalized with a specific legal act, it was always repressed, fined and framed as a crime of damage against property. In 1998, after nearly seven years of debate in the National Congress, the Environmental Crimes Bill (Law 9605/1998) was enacted. This defined both graffiti and pichação as acts of 'conspurcação' – 'defilement' and 'soiling' – and as acts 'against the urban order and cultural heritage'. In 2011, the original text of the legal act 9605/98 was modified to establish two different legal categories of visual interventions in public space: graffiti and pixação. According to this act, the practice of graffiti, when allowed by the property's owner 'performed with the objective to artistically valorize' the painted object, is not considered to be a crime. Pixação, on the other hand, is still considered a crime as to defile, to soil, to pollute are associated with being continually criminalized.

Caldeira's observation on the growing concern in 'controlling the mass of signs' is surely valid. Nevertheless, the conclusion that authorities have lost interest in controlling the bodies of the dangerous classes seems premature to us. As shown above, policies such as 'Operation Clean' still target the poor as dangerous classes. The same can be affirmed for repression against pixadores. During the early twentieth century, the supposedly diseased bodies of the poor, framed as dirt, illness and contamination, represented a threat. Nowadays, the poor's presence in the metropolis might be most successfully visualized through inscriptions in urban space. Understood as such, pixação can be conceived as the very portrayal of this threat. Furthermore, it is important to note that even though pixação's subversive potential might be situated in the domain of signs, this by no means assures the integrity of pixadores' bodies. Serious cases of police violence against pixadores recurrently prove the opposite.

Acts of police violence range from psychological abuse to the harshest physical violence. The most typical one is the famous 'ink shower' which consists of pixadores having their bodies painted with their own paint or even being forced to drink it. One of the most serious cases of violence against pixadores was the murder of Alex Dalla Vecchia Costa (whose pixo was ALD, from the JETS familia) and Ailton do Santos (NANI, from ANORMAL) in July 2014. They were supposedly murdered by five military police officers when caught red-handed scribbling on the rooftop of a building in São Paulo's East Zone.

Cleaning policies

Besides criminalization and repressive policing of the very bodies of pixadores, the second extensive strategy against pixação is to push pixadores back into invisibility – that is, through immediate cleaning or grey-painting the surfaces. Since the campaign against visual pollution manifested through the Clean City Programme, the municipal government has engineered enhanced measures to clean the city's walls. The Department of Historic Heritage states that 'every one of the 31 districts has an anti-pichação truck on its disposal to clean up the filth ... Monuments, frequent targets of pichadores, receive special treatment', being cleaned up to once a week (Jornal da Tarde n.d.). In 2007, the municipal government instituted the Antipichação Programme in the Municipality of São Paulo

(Lei n° 14.451, de 22/6/2007) to assure 'the recuperation of façades of public and private real estate which has been scribbled on' (Prefeitura da Cidade de São Paulo 2007). Despite all endeavors made by local authorities, at the end of Mayor Kassab's term, pixação was as omnipresent in São Paulo's urban landscape as it was 10 years earlier. This might be one reason for current Mayor Haddad (Workers Party – PT) to focus on another strategy of fighting pixação; repressive and cleaning measures keep being applied to the city, its civic landscape and citizens. As some protestors already knew more than a decade ago: 'Until now grafite is the only resort' (Correio Popular 2003).

Prettify the city with 'graffiti' in public space

For an understanding of the relationship between pixação and muralism, it is important to distinguish different aspects or movements within muralism. Originally, contemporary muralism is understood as an artistic and political movement that uses pictorial language to denunciate or to give voice to social and cultural matters.

As mentioned elsewhere (Larruscahim 2014), in Brazil graffiti – or 'grafite' – is tolerated and almost completely decriminalized; what people and authorities cannot stand is 'pixação'. Thus, the authorities and urban social policymakers have been using graffiti to avoid pixação. Combining the special style of Brazilian graffiti (see Chapter 11 of this volume), which is remarkably figurative, with social policies and legal measures that are implemented to fight pixação, one of the results is the emergence of a new type of 'grafite murals' in Brazil, and especially in São Paulo City. Since 2002, a series of graffiti murals commissioned by the Council Hall and the Secretaries of Tourism, Culture and Youth started to appear in São Paulo's urban setting: 'The Murals of 23 de Maio Avenue' (Prefeitura de São Paulo 2014), 'The Murals of Arcos do Jânio', 'The 4km Graffiti Project', 'MAAU – Open Museum of Urban Art' ('MAAU' 2015) and more recently (October 2015) the 'O.bra Festival' ('O.bra Festival – São Paulo' 2015) commissioned by private companies. Alexandre Youssef, at that time representative of the Municipal Coordination for the Youth, stresses that besides 'immediate painting over' there is a second way to combat pixação. He suggests that the city 'invest in urban art and grafite' (Folha de São Paulo 2004). Even though the repressive discourse has always been the most dominant one, already in the early 1990s, there emerged other ideas as to how to cope with pixação. Based on the same assumption that pixação was 'dirtiness', some commentators and policymakers saw the possibility to use the 'beautiful' to fight the 'ugly' – employing 'art' in public space. This is transcribed into policies at two levels: firstly, using projects of art in public space to occupy walls, assuming that pixadores will not dare to write over them; and secondly, by using graffiti as an educative means to bring 'errant youth' back on the right path.

Brazilian and especially Paulistan 'grafiteiros' and 'street artists', like Os Gêmeos, became world-famous and their work sold at high prices worldwide during the last decade. As current mayor Fernando Haddad proudly emphasises (Jovem Pan 2015), 'Our grafite is recognised in the whole world'. He followed this stating that 'besides Europe and the United States, São Paulo's [artistic] heritage is one of the biggest in the world. [...] Not even Tokyo has an archive like that of São Paulo.' Recently, the municipality's agency of tourism, São Paulo Turismo S/A, has started to promote urban art in sights such as Vila Madalena as one of São Paulo's 'must-sees' (São Paulo Turismo S/A 2015a, 36f.), and even published a guide for a thematic tour on urban art (São Paulo Turismo S/A 2014b). As 'urban art', or graffiti, has now been recognised as potentially promoting São Paulo's 'world/global city-ness', São Paulo's Council Hall, under Mayor Haddad, has also begun to promote a range of projects on graffiti or art in public spaces. In order to fit São Paulo to the image of a clean and pleasant – but also colourful – cosmopolitan, cool and arty city (Reid 2014, 14), urban policymakers have been reinforcing the opposition between graffiti and pixação, framing graffiti as 'art' and rigorously differentiating it from pixação – still understood as 'dirt' (and crime). While no guidebook on São Paulo will lack indications and pictures of urban art or graffiti in neighbourhoods like Vila Madalena, Santana or Santa Cecília (St. Louis 2014; Wikitravel 2015; Lonely Planet 2015a), surprisingly, there is no pixação apparent in the information offered by São Paulo Turismo S/A (see São Paulo Turismo S/A 2014a, 2015a). Even in the thematic tour guide 'Viewpoints', the large images of São Paulo's concrete jungle have been photoshopped – no pixo, just uniform, 'clean' grey (São Paulo Turismo S/A 2014c). To dismiss criticism concerning the murals along 23 de Maio Avenue commissioned by the municipality, Mayor Haddad notes that the respective walls were formerly 'full of dirt and pichação' and had to be cleaned by the city's anti-pixação trucks every month. Thus, graffiti turns into an instrument for 'modernization', attracting 'tourists who come to São Paulo to see its grafites' and preventing pixação at the same time (Jovem Pan 2015). Over time, the team in charge of cleaning and grey-painting São Paulo's urban landscape accidentally erased several authorised murals, some even financed by the Council Hall. 'The employees decide what is grafite and what not. He might look at it and say: "That is ugly, I'll erase it"', explained a municipal officer (Folha de São Paulo 2014). After some public quarrels between graffiti artists and the Council Hall, representatives pledged to improve the distinction and develop 'precision' within the cleaning policies. Municipal Secretary of Culture, Juca Ferreria affirms: 'The order is: pixação is erased and grafite is kept' (Folha de São Paulo 2014).

Assuming that Paulistan 'modern' public space is a place full of 'citizenship', 'participation' (though not for homeless people, crack users and pixadores) and 'art', what would it be without the 'modern' subjects to live in it? As early as 1988, Juneca, one of the most infamous old-school pixadores, was cited in a local newspaper as follows: 'It's a year that I don't do pixação, now I make only art' (Folha de São Paulo 1988). Even years later, newspapers talk of Juneca as the 'regenerated pichador' who, 'now that he turned into artist, scribbles on those who soil the city' (Jornal da Tarde 2002). This model has been applied in educational policy programmes for civic education focused on behaviour in public space. These point out the importance of 'understanding differences between pichação (closed code with little variation, used by specific groups to demarcate an area) and graffiti (language developed by artists to transmit an ideology)' (Araújo 2007). An educational booklet published by the Foundation Educating Dpaschoal tells the story of the city's children guided by protagonist 'Felício Happy', deciding 'to tell all their friends that the inks used to scribble on walls and monuments should be used to prettify the city' or be delivered to teachers so that they could 'use them to teach grafite, an art form that is expressed on the streets ...' (Secco 1999, 12f).

Conclusion

In this chapter, we discussed urban policies in São Paulo from a postcolonial perspective. We showed how current cleansing policies frame certain populations and activities in semantics of 'dirtiness', implying not only these elements' 'backwardness', but also a potential threat to 'modernness' that might emanate from them. Recent hygienist policies regulate among other things visual interventions on walls in public space. While graffiti is decriminalized or even actively promoted by urban policies, different expressions are harshly repressed.

Pixação – spread wide across São Paulo's urban space – evades unidimensional interpretations, but is here conceptualized as an expression of difference in the twenty-first century metropolis (Roy 2009). Focusing on public policy responses to pixação, we showed how measures of repression and immediate cleaning, as well as 'beautifying' through 'art' and mural projects and, finally, educational policies, are applied to create compliant images of a 'clean', 'modern', 'rife with art' world/global city, and the corresponding 'clean' civic subjects.

As Tiburi suggests, we understand 'the white façade' as suppressing 'other' truths and different realities. In that sense, we propose understanding pixação as a 'struggle for social visibility' (Franco 2010) of difference. As such, its subversive potential lies exactly in its capability to evade simplistic explanatory approaches, to 'undermine modernist dichotomies' (Varley 2013) and to express the 'heterogeneity and multiplicity of metropolitan modernities' (Roy 2009, 821). In this sense, it is invigorating to see how irritated commentators react when having to admit that pixação reached the middle classes, that the 'urban tribe' was 'no more only of youth from the periphery' (Folha de São Paulo 2003), as simplistic interpretations commonly suggested. In the context of this edited book on 'Visiting Murals' pixação might thus be read as an invoking to consider the 'other' murals, 'other' aesthetics, 'other' claims, to be visited on the walls of our cities.

References

Araújo, Paulo. 2007. "Grafite: Traços Da Cidadania." *Nova Escola*, April. http://revistaescola.abril.com.br/arte/pratica-pedagogica/tracos-cidadania-429583.shtml.

Caldeira, Teresa. 2000. *City of Walls: Crime, Segregation, and Citizenship in São Paulo*. Berkeley: University of California Press.

———. 2012. "Imprinting and Moving Around: New Visibilities and Configurations of Public Space in Sao Paulo." *Public Culture* 24 (2): 385–419. doi: 10.1215/08992363-1535543.

———. 2013. "Rewriting the City – São Paulo's Ubiquitous Graffiti and Pixação Are Subverting Notions of Power and Authorship in the Production of Urban Public Texts." *Cityscapes – Re-Thinking Urban Things* 3, http://www.cityscapesdigital.net/2013/05/12/rewriting-the-city/.

Calvo-Gonzalez, Elena and Luciana Duccini. 2010. "On 'Black Culture' and 'Black Bodies': State Discourses, Tourism and Public Policies in Salvador Da Bahia, Brazil." In *Tourism, Power and Culture: Anthropological Insights, Tourism and Cultural Change*, edited by Donald V.L. Macleod and James G. Carrier. Bristol, UK and Buffalo, NY: Channel View Publications.

Carlos, Ana F.A. 2004. "São Paulo: Do Capital Industrial Ao Capital Financeiro." In *Geografias de São Paulo   A Metrópole Do Século XXI*, edited by Ana Fani Alessandri Carlos and Ariovaldo Umbelino de Oliveira, Vol. 2, 51–84. São Paulo: Editora Contexto.

Carpenter, Mary. 2013. *Reformatory Schools: For the Children of the Perishing and Dangerous Classes, and for Juvenile Offenders*. 1st Reprint edition. Cambridge: Cambridge University Press.

Carreras, Cares. 2004. "Fragmentos de São Paulo, Metrópole de Um Primeiro Mundo Fragmentado." In *Geografias de São Paulo – A Metrópole Do Século XXI*, edited by Ana F.A. Carlos and Ariovaldo Umbelino de Oliveira, Vol. 2, 307–20. São Paulo: Editora Contexto.

Carta Maior. 2014. "Braços Abertos E Sufoco: Sobre a Situação Na 'Cracolândia'." *Carta Maior*, accessed February 11, 2014, http://cartamaior.com.br/?/Editoria/Direitos-Humanos/Bracos-Abertos-e-Sufoco-sobre-a-situacao-na-Cracolandia-/5/30235.

Carvalho, Mariana Aldrigui. 2011 "Cidade global, destino mundial: turismo urbano em São Paulo." PhD dissertation, Universidade de São Paulo.

Correio Popular. 2003. "Pichação Já Se Tornou Uma Epidemia Social: Cada Vez Mais Ousados – Pichadores Contribuem Para Aumentar a Poluição Visual Da Região Central E Dos Bairros de Campinas." *Correio Popular*, March 16, 2003.

Davis, Mike. 1992. *City of Quartz: Excavating the Future in Los Angeles*. Reprint. New York: Vintage.

Estadão. 2013. "Bandeirantes Assassinos," accessed October 4, 2013, http://cultura.estadao.com.br/blogs/marcelo-rubens-paiva/bandeirantes-assassinos/.

Folha de São Paulo. 1988. "Jânio Ordena Processo Contra Dois Pichadores." *Folha de São Paulo*, October 5, 1988.

——— 2003. "Cidade Suja – Pichadores Ousam E Chegam à Classe Média   Tribo Urbana Começa a Usar Até Escada E Andaime Para Pichar; Prática Não é Só Mais de Jovens Da Periferia." *Folha de São Paulo*, June 30, 2003.

————. 2004. "'É Vandalismo Mesmo', Diz Grafiteiro – Prédios E Espaços Públicos São Marcados Com Símbolos de Indivíduos E Gangues Que Disputam Espaço E Visibilidade." *Folha de São Paulo*, accessed October 3, 2004, http://www1.folha. uol.com.br/fsp/cotidian/ff0310200415.htm.

————. 2009. "Globo Desinfeta Praça Do Centro de SP Para Gravar Nova Novela." *Folha de São Paulo*, accessed November 10, 2009, http://www.google.de/url?sa= t&rct=j&q=&esrc=s&source=web&cd=1&ved=0CCIQFjAA&url=http%3A% 2F%2Fwww1.folha.uol.com.br%2Ffsp%2Filustrad%2Ffq1011200918.htm&ei= HhSVVdGkNqXPygO68bDIDw&usg=AFQjCNFuDJzHuEz-zYS3CDvw0OM_ QJ0IpA&bvm=bv.96952980,d.bGQ.

————. 2012. "Monumentos de SP Têm Problemas Como Pichações, Fezes, Urina E Sujeira." *Folha de São Paulo*, accessed May 28, 2012, http://www1.folha.uol.com. br/fsp/cotidiano/45495-monumentos-de-sp-tem-problemas-como-pichacoes-fezes-urina-e-sujeira.shtml.

————. 2013. "Theatro Municipal de SP é Pichado; Limpeza Será Concluída Quinta." *Folha de São Paulo*, accessed October 16, 2013, http://www1.folha.uol. com.br/cotidiano/2013/10/1357796-theatro-municipal-de-sp-e-pichado-limpeza-sera-concluida-amanha.shtml.

————. 2014. "SP Vai Orientar Funcionários Sobre a Limpeza de Grafites E Pichações." *Folha de São Paulo*, accessed August 2, 2014, http://www1.folha. uol.com.br/cotidiano/2014/08/1494860-sp-vai-orientar-funcionarios-sobre-a-limpeza-de-grafites-e-pichacoes.shtml.

Fórum Centro Vivo. 2006. "Violações Dos Direitos Humanos No Centro de São Paulo: Propostas E Reivindicações Para Políticas Públicas – Dossiê de Denúncia." Dossiê de Denúncia. São Paulo: Fórum Centro Vivo. http://www.polis.org.br/ uploads/977/977.pdf.

Franco, Sérgio. 2010. "Pixação E as Aves de Rapina – Le Monde Diplomatique Brasil." *Le Monde Diplomatique Brasil*, accessed November 1, 2010, http:// webserver.diplomatique.org.br/artigo.php?id=821.

Franco, Sérgio, Djan Ivson Silva, Rafael Pixobomb and Joanna Warsza. 2012. "The Politics of the Poor – in Conversation, March 29, 2011, São Paulo." In *Forget Fear – 7th Berlin Biennale of Contemporary Art*, edited by Artur Żmijewski and Joanna Warsza. Köln: König.

Freeman, James P. 2003. "Review: City of Walls – Crime, Segregation, and Citizenship in São Paulo. Teresa P. R. Caldeira." *Urban Geography* 24 (2): 183–84. doi: 10.2747/0272-3638.24.2.183.

Frisch, Thomas. 2012. "Glimpses of Another World: The Favela as a Tourist Attraction." *Tourism Geographies* 14 (2): 320–38. doi: 10.1080/14616688.2011. 609999.

GSA. 1989. "Grafismos E Pichações – Arte E Sujeira. Pichadores – A Mediocridade Em Ação." *GSA*, February 11, 1989.

Harvey, David. 2003. *Paris, Capital of Modernity*. New York: Routledge.

Jornal da Tarde. n.d. "1° Passo Contra Pichações – Parceria Com Iniciativa Privada Para Limpar Cidade. Portal Da Prefeitura Da Cidade de São Paulo." *Jornal Da Tarde*. http://www.prefeitura.sp.gov.br/cidade/secretarias/cultura/bibliotecas/ bibliotecas_bairro/bibliotecas_m_z/marioschenberg/?p=717.

————. 2002. "O Pichador Regenerado – Agora Que Virou Grafiteiro, Juneca Fica Pichando Quem Suja a Cidade." *Jornal Da Tarde*, December 14, 2002.

Jovem Pan. 2015. "Entrevista Entrevista Com Prefeito Haddad." *Jovem Pan – Jornal Da Manhã*. São Paulo, http://jovempan.uol.com.br/programas/jornal-da-manha/confira-versao-completa-da-entrevista-com-prefeito-haddad-no-jornal-da-manha.html.

Larruscahim, Paula. 2014. "From Graffiti to Pixação – Urban Protest in Brazil." *Tijdschrift over Cultuur & Criminaliteit* 4 (2): 69–84.

Lendas Da Pixação – Tchentcho E Krellos. 2015. *Beside Colors*, accessed June 30, 2015, http://besidecolors.com/lendas-da-pixacao-tchentcho-e-krellos/.

Lonely Planet. 2015a. "Private Street Art Tour of São Paulo." *Lonely Planet.* http://www.lonelyplanet.com/americas/activities/private-luxury/private-street-art-tour-sao-paulo.

———. 2015b. "São Paulo, Brazil." *Lonely Planet.* http://www.lonelyplanet.com/brazil/sao-paulo.

MAAU. 2015. *Museu Aberto de Arte Urbana*, accessed December 1, 2015, https://museuabertodearteurbana.wordpress.com/category/arte-urbana/

Montero, Alfred P. 2014. *Brazil: Reversal of Fortune.* 1. Auflage. Cambridge and Malden: Polity Press.

O.bra Festival – São Paulo. 2015. Accessed December 1, 2015, http://obrafestival.com/.

O'Dougherty, Maureen. 2002. *Consumption Intensified: The Politics of Middle-Class Daily Life in Brazil.* Durham, NC: Duke University Press.

Pereira, Alexandre Barbosa. 2013. "Cidade de Riscos: Notas Etnográficas Sobre Pixação, Adrenalina, Morte E Memória Em São Paulo." *Revista de Antropologia Da USP* 56 (1): 81–110.

Prefeitura da Cidade de São Paulo. 2007. "Prefeitura Cria Programa Antipichação Para Recuperar Muros E Fachadas." *Portal Da Prefeitura Da Cidade de São Paulo*, accessed June 15, 2007, http://www.prefeitura.sp.gov.br/cidade/secretarias/comunicacao/noticias/?p=131144.

Prefeitura de São Paulo. 2014. "Muros Da Avenida 23 de Maio Começam a Ser Grafitados Com Apoio Da Prefeitura," accessed December 6, 2014, http://capital.sp.gov.br/noticia/muros-da-avenida-23-de-maio-comecam-a-ser.

Raupp, Luciane, and Rubens de Camargo Ferreira Adorno. 2011. "Circuitos de Uso de Crack Na Região Central Da Cidade de São Paulo (SP, Brasil)." *Ciência & Saúde Coletiva* 16 (5): 2613–22.

Regina Monteiro. 2013. "Criadora Da Cidade Limpa Quer Guerra Urbana Em Defesa Da Lei." *Época SP*, accessed October 8, 2013, http://epoca.globo.com/regional/sp/blogs-epoca-sp/adote-sp/noticia/2013/10/criadora-da-cidade-limpa-quer-bguerra-urbanab-em-defesa-da-lei.html.

Reid, Michael. 2014. *Brazil: The Troubled Rise of a Global Power.* New Haven, CT: Yale University Press.

Rezende, Fernando and Ricardo Lima, eds. 1999. *Rio-São Paulo, Cidades Mundiais.* Rio de Janeiro: IPEA – Instituto de Pesquisa Econômica Aplicada, http://www.ipea.gov.br/portal/index.php?option=com_content&view=article&id=5368.

Robinson, Jenny. 2002. "Global and World Cities: A View from off the Map." *International Journal of Urban and Regional Research* 26 (3): 531–54.

Rohter, Larry. 2012. *Brazil on the Rise.* Reprint. New York: Palgrave Macmillan.

Roy, Ananya. 2009. "The 21st-Century Metropolis: New Geographies of Theory." *Regional Studies* 43 (6): 819–30. doi: 10.1080/00343400701809665.

São Paulo Turismo S/A. 2014a. "Guia / Guide – São Paulo 2014 – Global City, the Land of Soccer – Cidade Global, Território Da Bola." Prefeitura de São Paulo – Turismo. http://imprensa.spturis.com.br/downloads/GuiaSP_Ingles_BonecoTotal_BX_V01.pdf.

———. 2014b. "Arte Urbana – Street Art – Roteiro Temático." Prefeitura de São Paulo – Turismo, http://imprensa.spturis.com.br/wp-content/uploads/downloads/2014/08/Arte-Spread.pdf.

———. 2014c. "Mirantes – Vistas – Roteiro Temático'. Prefeitura de São Paulo – Turismo,"http://imprensa.spturis.com.br/wp-content/uploads/downloads/2014/08/Arte-Spread.pdf.

———. 2015a. "Cidade de São Paulo – Guia Da Cidade – City Guide." Prefeitura de São Paulo – Turismo, http://imprensa.spturis.com.br/wp-content/uploads/downloads/2015/04/Guia-da-Cidade_ING_bx.pdf.

———. 2015b. "Platnum 2015–2018 – Plano de Turismo Municipal – Cidade de São Paulo." Prefeitura de São Paulo – Turismo. http://imprensa.spturis.com.br/wp-content/uploads/downloads/2015/06/platum-2015-2018.pdf.

Secco, Patrícia Engel, ed. 1999. *Felício Feliz da Silva Feliz presenta: Muita água e sabão… mas pichação não! Cidadania preservação do patrimônio e respeito ao próximo*. Série Felício Feliz, o ratinho cidadão / Patrícia Engel Secco[…]. Campinas: Ed. Fundação Educar.

Silveira, Maria Laura. 2004. "São Paulo: os dinamismos da pobreza." In *Geografias de São Paulo. Representação e Crise da Metrópole*, edited by Ana Fani Alessandri Carlos, and Ariovaldo Umbelino de Oliveira, vol. 2, 59–72. São Paulo: Editora Contexto.

Snider, Colin M. 2012. "Street Painting and Social Inequality in São Paulo." *Americas South and North*, accessed May 24, 2012, https://americasouthandnorth.wordpress.com/2012/05/24/street-painting-and-social-inequality-in-sao-paulo/.

Sobrinho, Aafonso Soares de Oliveiro. 2013. "São Paulo E a Ideologia Higienista Entre Os Séculos XIX E XX: A Utopia Da Civilidade." *Sociologias* 15 (32): 210–235. http://www.scielo.br/pdf/soc/v15n32/09.pdf.

Sousa, Rosangela Silva. 2008. "Uma Investigação Sobre as Teorias Da Cidade Mundial, Cidade Global, Cidade Pós-Moderna E Sua Relação Com a Cidade de São Paulo." Dissertação de Mestrado, São Paulo: Universidade de São Paulo (USP).

Steinbrink, Malte. 2014. "Festifavelisation: Mega-Events, Slums and Strategic City-Staging – the Example of Rio de Janeiro." *DIE ERDE* 144 (2): 129–45.

St. Louis, Regis, ed. 2014. *Brasilien*. 3. dt. Aufl. *Lonely Planet*. Ostfildern: MairDumont.

Suplemento do Diário Oficial do Município de São Paulo. 1988. "Juneca E Bilão Vão 'pichar a Cadeia'". *Suplemento Do Diário Oficial Do Município de São Paulo*, October 4, 1988, 1 ed., sec. 105.

Tiburi, Marcia. 2011. "Direito Visual à Cidade – A Estética Da PiXação E O Caso de São Paulo." In *Filosofia Pop*, 39–53. Editora Bragantini, http://www.redobra.ufba.br/wp-content/uploads/2013/12/revista_redobra12_virtual.pdf#page=40.

Varley, Ann. 2013. "Postcolonialising Informality?" *Environment and Planning D: Society and Space* 31 (1): 4–22. doi: 10.1068/d14410.

Warsza, Joanna. 2012. "An Alphabet of Class Struggle." In *Forget Fear – 7th Berlin Biennale of Contemporary Art*, edited by Artur Żmijewski and Joanna Warsza. Köln: König.

Weinstein, Barbara. 2015. *The Color of Modernity: São Paulo and the Making of Race and Nation in Brazil*. Durham, NC: Duke University Press Books.

Wikitravel. 2015. "Vila Madalena and Pinheiros Travel Guide," accessed September 23, 2015, http://wikitravel.org/en/S%C3%A3o_Paulo/Vila_Madalena_and_Pinheiros.

Yang, Philip and Emilia Patiño Anaya. 2014. "Dawn of the Smart City? – Perspectives from New York, Ahmedabad, Sao Paulo and Bejing." Washington, DC: Woodrow Wilson International Center for Scholars. http://www.newsecuritybeat.org/2014/06/dawn-smart-city-perspectives-york-ahmedabad-sao-paulo-beijing/.

Zweig, Stefan. 2015. *Brazil: A Land of the Future*, trans. Lowell Bangerter. Riverside: Ariadne Press.

Part IV
Identity

9 A journey through public art in Douala

Framing the identity of New Bell neighbourhood

Marta Pucciarelli and Lorenzo Cantoni

Me voici donc à Douala. Douala, océan de bonheur immense. Douala, ville improbable, du magnifique tiers-monde. Douala, avec ses hauts et ses bas. [So here I am in Douala. Douala, ocean of an immense happiness. Douala, improbable city, of magnificent third-world. Douala, with its with its ups and downs]

—Oho Bambe 2014

Introduction

We have to admit that we barely visit an African city for cultural or artistic purposes, unless we are (or feel like) critics, researchers, curators, anthropologists or experts in art with a specific interest in the African art production. Compared to what happens to other developing countries, the African cities' artistic sphere is often ignored and moved to the background. Going to Berlin without visiting the Wall or to Venice without considering the dates of its biennial festival limits our knowledge about the city immediately, not only from the artistic and cultural point of view but also from that political and social ecosystem which these kinds of events represent. Even if we are not art experts, we do need to experience such an important area or event, but this feeling of being included or excluded from the city is not considered when we think about developing countries.

Cities like Douala, Dakar, Johannesburg or Luanda, for example, have a huge contemporary art production, both in public art and in the organization of international events, starting from the 1990s (the Biennial of Dakar is in its twelfth edition, while the Triennial of Luanda and the SUD – Salon Urbain de Douala have around 10 years' experience). In spite of this, communication at an international level is lacking, except for few experts, and these festivals have no impact on people's perception of the African reality.

This does not happen just because it is hard to find information concerning these countries on the Internet (Douala shows more than 300 pictures on Wikipedia), but because such information has very low impact on the collective unconscious. Thinking about an African city from the point of view of contemporary art produces a change in the perception that people have of reality in cultural, geographical, economic and social terms, and this means leaving the stereotypes which make us think about a poor, rural and static Africa. In artistic terms, the African unconscious is still deeply linked to masks, wooden sculptures, rituals or traditional ceremonies.

In spite of this, the artistic and cultural landscape has shown a striking growth in the last 20 years, especially around the expanding metropolis. Douala, for example, has experienced an impressive growth in the production of site-specific public art installations (including around 40 works such as monumental, architectural, murals and small scale installations) and in the organization of international event (the Triennal SUD – Salon Urban de Douala).

This chapter examines one of these installation: *Les Mots Écrits de New Bell*, a series of six murals produced for the SUD 2010 by the artist and poet Hervé Yamguen, who lives and works in the district of New Bell, the largest popular settlement of the centre of Douala. *Les Mots Écrits de New Bell* are fragments of texts extracted from songs by two local rappers, Picsou and Moctomoflar, that highlight social and safety issues affecting the districts. This study is based on several sources: a field trip done by its first author and a survey of locals aimed at exploring their understanding of Douala's public art installation; interviews with the commissioner (the president of doual'art), artist and rappers who produced the murals; and reports from tourist guides. The chapter is organized as follows. First of all, it provides an overview on Douala, its neighbourhoods and dynamic environment; then, it focuses on New Bell, to present and discuss the murals, and their role and interpretations according to different stakeholders – this chapter's authors, visitors and inhabitants.

Framing Douala and its neighbourhoods

Douala is considered the economic capital of Cameroun and the most populated city of the country. It is usually defined by inhabitants as a cosmopolitan city, constantly growing and attracting every year thousands of national and international young people looking to emerge, economically and socially, within the metropolis. The 'dreamt Douala' (Simone 2005) offers a wide spectrum of job opportunities, a dynamic lifestyle, and freedom from rooted traditions. Its harbour is indeed the largest of central Africa, strategically placed between the mouth of the Wouri River and the Atlantic Ocean. However, it doesn't produce enough employment for its 3 million inhabitants (while the last census dates back to 2005, this is the most likely estimate for 2015), and often immigrants' expectations remain unsatisfied (Sween and Clignet 1969; Séraphin 2000b).

Tourism, especially business tourism, is playing a key role in the city. Douala offers hospitality solutions for the two classes of tourists it attracts: top-level hotels addressed to international business tourists and low-medium hostels for missionaries and adventure tourists stopping-off in

Douala before moving to the inner Cameroonian's regions. In both cases, hotels, hostels and restaurants are concentrated within the four costal and most prestigious neighborhoods: Bonapriso, Bali, Bonanjo and Akwa. These areas constitute respectively the residential (Bonapriso and Bali), administrative and commercial centres of the modern/western-style Douala inhabited by the richest class of the city.

The flourishing economy around the harbour has attracted many new inhabitants who can't afford to live near to the rich dockland but instead live in the popular neighbourhoods spontaneously grown around it. After the economic boom of the 1960s, Douala is continuously extending horizontally, with 118 neighbourhoods divided into six districts (Evina Akam and Honoré Mimche 2009). Despite many social, economic and political problems, people in Douala do not like revolutions, after having experienced the dramatic consequences of failing revolutions (such as the *ghost cities* in 1991,[1] the *Commandement Opérationnel*[2] in 2000, and the *Emeutes de la faim* in 2008[3]) (Malaquais 2009). The community prefers to count on the 'genuinely endogenous strategy for change' (Bayat 2013). In particular, 'reunions', regular meetings held by associations, have been legalized since 1991 (Séraphine 2000a). They can have different goals (religious, developmental, educational). Often, the street is the place where these associations gather to discuss and to take popular decisions to face specific problems: this phenomenon has been labelled 'street politics' (Bayat 2003; Jones III 2000; Martin 2004).

The cultural boom

Since 1991, several cultural institutions and a collective of artists have operated in the urban space of Douala. First of all, doual'art has to be mentioned: it is the oldest art centre of Douala, addressing its work to the urban environment in order 'to provide the city with human identity'.[4] Doual'art, besides hosting an exhibition space, is a hub of experimentation for public art, inviting artists from all over the nation and the world to reflect on the city and to produce permanent or ephemeral public art installations. Since 2007, doual'art has been organizing the SUD – Salon Urban de Douala – a triennial contemporary urban festival in which permanent and ephemeral art installations are presented and offered to the city. Other important cultural institutions in the city are the MAM gallery, an exhibition space founded by Marem Malong Meslin Samb in 1996; Art-Bakery, an art centre located in Bonendale, a village outside Douala usually known as the artists' village; and the Cercle Kapsiki, a group of five Cameroonian artists in Douala who gathered as a formal group in 1998 to set up the K-FACTORY, a contemporary art space in the district of New Bell. After numerous cultural and artistic initiatives – started by doual'art in 1992 by promoting Art Venture, the first mural installation of the city (Babina and Bell 2008) – SUD 2010 promoted several public artworks, among them *Les Mots Écrits de New Bell* by Hervé Yamguen: a series of six murals and lighting installations located around the district of New Bell Ngangué. These installations showcase written messages coming from the lyrics of songs by two local rappers.

The cultural experience of visiting murals

Today, Douala's murals represent the main touristic offer of the city: we can define it as alternative cultural experience, and they are recommended to the few visitors who arrive in the city for business reasons, for a school trip or thanks to a doual'art invitation. It is no coincidence that the president of doual'art has a socio-economic education. In fact, she caught the 'human nature' of a city where beauty is hardly considered and not supported by the public authority, and she was able to transform not only the artwork but also the whole production project in an artistic and cultural proposal. These sociopolitical artworks are set in public spaces and clearly refer to the urban metamorphosis, which includes problems and hopes linked to Douala's nowadays life.

The power and the impression of the murals and of the artworks in public spaces do not depend only on the holiday package offered to visitors, which allows them to explore areas where they would never go alone, but also on the production process of the artwork: an artistic and cultural experience which, first of all, involves the locals, who experience it everyday as first addressees and beneficiaries. Even if the artworks have a different goal, a sequence of urban transformations have followed this effective production. That is the exceptional case of Douala: the urban and social impact of art becomes an essential part of the visit and makes tourists understand the artworks.

Consistent with Rasheed Araeen's postcolonial studies claiming to re-write history (Araeen 2010), the production of artworks, which are textual in this case, in public spaces allows for the writing of a real-time story of a city. Involving the community in the process means offering the locals an instrument to tell their own social wars and to express their fears and hopes through contemporary art. It is not the description of a past conflict; this is the present, everyday life's story told through rap music, murals, light installations, big and small sculptures, sometimes using agonizing words, sometimes showing lines full of hope.

Moreover, Douala's public administration intervention struggles to fight against this cultural system and, as we already know, it has silenced the insurrections generated by the locals' dissatisfaction. According to the inhabitants, the cultural institutions and the visitors, the real meaning of these artworks goes beyond the aesthetic of the city, showing clear political and social messages. On the other side, the public administration considers them as a mere urban decoration, which could be more or less likeable, that the authorities have made available to the city without taking on responsibility of them. Even if the artworks can be considered as permanent, their deterioration is fast, and it is not only due to the use but also due to the extremely damp weather during the arid season (90 per cent of humidity in the air) and to the exposure to the bad weather during the rainy season.

In few words, doual'art represents the only institution which provides maintenance to limit the artworks' deterioration, while the locals themselves handle the urban maintenance, in particular in New Bell, by taking care of the spaces where the artworks are set, by demanding the public administration intervention (concerning, for example, the garbage collection around the murals or the realization of new streets) and even by paying the electricity in order to allow the installations to work.

The exceptional case of New Bell

The district of New Bell in Douala represents one of the most exceptional cases where art participates directly in the citizens' life, assuming their political and social conditions and, at the same time, modifying the community's life through new forms of urban management. Set close to Bonapriso, the most fashionable residential area of the city, New Bell is the typical *kwatt* of Douala: an open-air slum where 'you're going to walk and fall down in the mud, you're going to cross dirty rivulets to go to the sub district, you're going to enter people's homes to go to yours'.[5] During the era of German colonization (1884–1916), the indigenous citizens were segregated in New Bell and isolated from Western settlements by a green area about one kilometre long in order to prevent any form of infection. After the French took over in 1916, the district became the main focal point for immigration of non-native people coming both from other regions of Cameroon and from abroad, especially from Nigeria, Ghana and Ivory Coast (Njoh 2007; Schler 2008). Today, the area's extension (including a total of 32 neighbourhoods) together with its population density have turned New Bell into one of the six administrative districts of the city.

Being historically the foreigners' district, New Bell has been completely excluded from any form of control and regulation, producing a seriously unhealthy and unsafe environment. In New Bell, sewers and gutters are open, used as garbage dumps, causing floods during seasonal rains. In addition, public fountains have been closed down and the community supplies water from shallow wells that are full of insects which cause infection and disease. At the same time, the widespread poverty and unemployment; the presence of the central jail and of the market of Douala, which are respectively the worst and the biggest of Cameroon (Amnesty International 2008; Loe, Meutchehé Ngomsi, and Nken Hibock 2007); the huge concentration of night clubs; and the absence of a public lighting system, of a police station and of any form of social control, are all factors which contribute to increase the risk of aggressions and the diffusion of criminality through the area.

In the district of New Bell, there is no centre. There is not a square or a public place devoted to entertainment, relaxation or civil discourse and the democratic exchange of ideas; it does not exist and it is even hard to imagine. In New Bell, as well as throughout the city of Douala, the concept of public space includes the idea of *shared space:* an area which is not private, which does not belong to anyone and, for this reason, anyone can take possession of in a completely free and anarchical way. The centre of New Bell is historically created by its streets where both commercial and non-commercial activities developed following the Douala's immigrant communities' lifestyle and/or their spirit of survival (Simone 2006, 2008a, b). New Bell's life is not concentric, but it's a flux (Malaquais 2005); it does not develop around a centre, but it expands inside a widespread and permeable network of physical and social intersections that follow the branches of paved streets as well as the entrances corresponding with the blocks of the neighbourhoods and with the so-called *mapans. Mapans* are a network of narrow streets connecting roads with the simple houses right inside and dividing buildings in blocks where people can pass only one after the other.

As an immigrant area, the district has a negative reputation. And yet, its lively art and cultural scene stimulates new interests, approaches and aesthetic visions of slum dwellers. From the 2000s, New Bell has become a theatre of art and cultural activities promoted by local and international institutions. Between 2001 and 2002, Cercle Kapsiki, in collaboration with Scu2,[6] proposed *Scenographie Urbaine* ('Urban scenography'), an itinerant festival devoted to urban art. This event was an exceptional success, so much so that it has been replayed in Alexandrie, Kinshasa, Johannesburg, Paris and Dakar. The triumph of *Scenographie Urbaine* is due to a special characteristic of the play; artists from all over the world were hosted by dwellers in their houses and got inspired by the sharing of living spaces for their art projects, so that several urban art installations – both permanent and ephemeral – were produced during the three weeks. The festival concluded with a fashion show that was also a resounding success, reaching a wide audience – both locals and people coming from the wealthiest areas of the city.[7] Following this exceptional event, the *Cinema du Kwatt* (2005–2006) was the second event achieving a relevant success involving the inhabitants of the districts and of the city. The goal of the shows was to invite people to reflect on the value of their popular culture, contemporary and decolonized, through the viewing of documentaries by Jean Rouch, certainly the most popular theorist of the visual anthropology. This was accompanied by works produced by African artists and intellectuals including Goddy Leye. At the start, the shows took place in Rue Napoleon, in New Bell Ngangué, but soon they had been moved out to the football field at the crossroads of New Bell Aviation and later to the CBC Babylon school courtyard. In addition to open-air shows, theater shows (like *Allah n'est pas obbligé* by Amadou Kouroum) and movies strongly related with the Cameroonian background (such as *Les Saignantes* by Jean-Pierre Bekolo) were all staged. Not long after they had started, the emotional charge and the intellectual value of these events – which took place in a district that was barely accessible at that time – started to attract not only a middle-class audience but also international promoters and financiers. The Institut Français (http://www. ifcameroun.com/programmation-culturelle.html) and the Goethe Institut jointly have funded the initiative to allow them to include international guests and troupes, thereby maintaining free access to the events.

This kind of activity allowed New Bell's inhabitants to overcome their troubled daily routines and to face afresh the external world, to reflect on their past and the forthcoming future, to develop new interests, and so – accordingly to an organizer's words – 'renewing the people's way of living'.[8] Moreover, this initiative allowed the inhabitants of the district to have an active role in the promotion of the city's cultural life, and to welcome people coming from different neighbourhoods and social classes, giving them the possibility to discover the liveliness of a district historically considered to be dangerous. Together with Cercle Kapsiki's work, doual'art selected New Bell as a privileged neighbourhood to host permanent art installations. Since the first edition of the SUD – Salon Urbain de Douala in 2007, New Bell developed a local pride in the presence of public artworks realized by internationally renowned artists. Among them, there are two monuments and several other installations: the *Njé Mo Yé* by Koko Komengé, considered to be the *father* of contemporary Cameroonian artists, and the *Colonne Pascal* by Marthine Tayou, one of the most famous African artists of the world. This is in addition to *New Walk Ways,* a 500-metre-long installation by Kamiel Vershuren, a Rotterdam-based artist; and two mural projects including *Oasis* by Tracey Rose (South Africa) enclosed in the walls of the CBC Babylon School, and *Les Mots Écrits* by Hervé Yamguen, artist, poet and member of the Cercle Kapsiki living in New Bell.

Les Mots Écrits de New Bell

The SUD2010 edition, dedicated to the theme of water, allowed the artist Hervé Yamguen to work on a pressing issue concerning his district. *Les Mots Écrits de New Bell* is a work composed by six wall installations which show segments of text extracted from the songs of two New Bell rappers employed by the artist. It represents the words on specific building's facades, using materials which are deeply linked to the context and to the audience. By doing so, *Les Mots Écrits de New Bell* describes the unhealthy situation in which the district is forced to live. The lack of an access to drinking water does not mean that there is no water in New Bell. Rivulets of polluted water overwhelmed by garbage cross New Bell and often define the borders between blocks. The songs that inspired *Les Mots Écrits* tell how pure and clean water reflects the population's wish to feel well, to live happily – a happiness which today is in decline because water pollution causes diseases and suffering and raises infant mortality rates. New Bell's rappers compare water with a thief; it is an element which escapes from the inhabitants in spite of its proximity and abundance. Artworks, which became part of the

Figure 9.1 Les Mots Écrits de New Bell – Entrée Source, Hervé Yamguen (2010).
Source: https://upload.wikimedia.org/wikipedia/commons/a/ad/OpeningenIMG_0728.jpg
(SUD Salon Urbain de Douala 2010. Triennial festival promoted by doual'art. Photo by
Sandrine Dole).

inhabitants' everyday life, converse with this public 'reflection' on their condition, their thoughts and deepest sensations, troubles and fears. On the
corner of Entrée Source of New Bell Ngangue, murals show lines such as
'*Se sentir bien*' (Figure 9.1) and '*La vie saine, la joie de se sentir bien, l'envie
de vivre de bonheur*'. The texts literally mean 'feeling good' in the first case
and 'The healthy life', 'The joy of feeling good', 'The desire to live happily'
in the second.

The choice of the place and of the material is never random. They are
placed at the entrance of the sub-district where, in the past, there was a public fountain that was then closed by the local administration. A big amount
of waste dominated the landscape of the Entrée Source and poured out in
the drainage canal, which follows the perimeter of the street a half metre
away from the wall where the artworks were installed. In this scenery, small
phrases patterned on an iron tube lie on a mesh made by a light blue wall and
four squared mirrors. The colour selected for the work completely changes
the look of the street, bringing a breath of fresh air to the place. It catches
the pedestrians' attention, inviting them to engage fully with the meaning
of 'feeling good' and the joy of conducting a happy and healthy life. The
use of mirrors is obviously linked to introspection and to the observation

of the surrounding environment: it invites the observer to change their own views, to wonder about the quality of life in a proactive way, producing a subtle and intimate impact at a personal level. *Les Mots Écrits* also shows the troubles that characterize the familial environment, such as the fears parents have about their sons who live in an uncertain society which does not assure a rosy and encouraging future. On the one hand, New Bell's sons and young people rebel, but, on the other hand, they try to be positive and to trust in a society which is going to change, mobilizing on the tiny streets of the neighbourhood, as reported in an artwork,[9] attempting to build their future and to establish themselves. At the same time, they are worried about how to reassure their parents about their ability to be independent and to survive in a society that is hostile to their future. Referring to this, the artwork set outside the CBC Babylon School says: *Apres le temps mort vient le temps vif. Comme un coup de foudre. Ne pleure pas maman. Tous les yeux de la ville pleuvent sur moi. Tranquille papa on ne panique pas* [*After the dead times, there are living times. Like a thunderbolt. Do not cry mom. All eyes of the city are raining down on me. Be calm, dad, do not panic*]. Ceramic – which in Douala is a synonym of hygiene – was used as the first material of choice for the mosaic as a channel of communication; flying swallows drawn by the text, together with the selection of pink and light blue as main colours, are all elements which refer to the essential need for self-awareness in the school's pupils who want to grow up and build their future in a healthy, transparent and encouraging environment.

This need is also narrated by the other artworks which show a rebellious, lively and dynamic youth who ask for a city finally cleansed and free from its rubbish, another synonym for its corruption, instability and illnesses. In this regard, a mural shows the pidgin text 'wash ma live, lave mon âme, wash mes ways, lave mon kwatt' [wash my live, wash my soul, wash my ways, wash my neighbourhood]. The pursuit of happiness is the *leitmotif* of *Mots Écrits*, an incitement to reflect, to fulfil personal growth and to react in spite of the dirty water of the district (*les eaux sales du quartier*) and the '*mousitques*' that cause malaria, from which people have to protect themselves in order to spend a safe and pleasant night ('*nuit de bonheur*').

Listening to the authors

Energie à Douala ... energie pour nous même ... la vie est belle à Douala!
[Energy in Douala ... energy for ourselves ... life is beautiful in Douala!]

These are the words chosen by Sadrake, the most famous Cameroonian rapper who lives in Germany, to spur the young people of his city while introducing his concert during the SUD 2013: *'tout le monde se plaindre de qui va nous sauver, il faut pas se negliger, on a tout à Douala!'* [everybody complains about what will save us, we should not neglect, everything is present in Douala] (Sadrake 2013). Sadrake gave his time and energies

to actively contribute to the production of the album *Wash mes ways* by
Picsou and Moctomoflar, the two rappers from New Bell. The album was
commissioned by the artist Hervé Yamguen, who extracted the lyrics for
his artwork *Les Mots Écrits de New Bell*. It featured two rappers and five
songs whose rhymes adopt a common ground language, often using the local pidgin dialect that combines words with a specific posture, to an intention or to an interpretation. The artist and poet Hervé Yamguen gathered
correctly the sociocultural value of this work, shaping it in a new language,
the language of visual art. That is why he involved the two rappers in his
project, allowing them to tell their own reality. Rap is characterized by a vo-
cal expressiveness which is rooted in the ghetto and, by its nature, criticizes
and contests society 'in an open and frank manner' (Harold Wentworth and
Stuart Berg Flexner 1975). According to Yamguen, a good artist is a good
citizen.[10] The idea of citizenship is really important in his work and his art
is inspired by the district's lifestyle. For this reason, the artist must have an
active role in the place where he lives and has to be a good citizen to be an
effective example for the inhabitants. This is an important role assumed by
the artist, in particular in a neighbourhood like New Bell, where the fact
that corruption is a consequence of the struggle for existence prevails on
the social sensitivity. The art value is, first of all, a human value. The artist
is never external from his work, and artworks have to be the representation
of the ethical space where the artist lives. Yamguen, who is living in New
Bell as well, believes that 'art has to feed the aptitude towards life, towards
community life'.[11]

   The participation of two local rappers was essential to the development
of the project that was two years in the making. They organized together
several performances and concerts in the district to allow the inhabitants to
familiarize themselves with the project, its actors and with an ever-growing
and ever more varied audience. Slowly, locals started to feel involved in
the event so that they made the facades of their houses available for hosting public art installations. Eventually, it reached the stage that the artist
felt embarrassed when he had to choose between so many offers. Dwellers
started to feel proud to give a concrete contribution to the artistic project,
increasing their self-esteem and their feeling of value at the same time. The
places chosen by the artist to install his artworks are mainly well-known
passageways, popular with the inhabitants; the specific intention was to introduce the district's reality to an international audience and to make the
inhabitants think about how to have a better everyday life. *Les Mots Écrits
de New Bell* was officially presented to an audience composed of inhabitants, government stakeholders and national and international visitors in
December 2010 during the SUD – Salon Urbain de Douala. At that occasion, a concert of the two local rappers was organized in the CBC Babylon
School's courtyard, a gathering with an estimated thousand of local and
international visitors.

Tourism in New Bell

In a city like Douala, where a city map is hard to find, tourism intended as a leisure experience is quite limited. Travel agencies mainly deal with flight tickets for business or migration, car hiring, accommodation services, airport assistance and travel insurance. Only in a few cases do they take care of tourist trips both to Cameroon and in Douala. Their mission is to draw the tourists' attention to the risks they can face within the city, providing information as to how to avoid them: for example, do not go around during the night, do not show your wallet in public places, do not leave the wealthy districts (such as Bonanjo, Bonapriso, Akwa), be always accompanied, catch only *à depot taxis* – better if reserved by the hotel – and do not even talk with the locals: sometimes communication could be difficult and, in some cases, aggressive. Even if this last advice could seem overstated, the others are good suggestions that an inexperienced tourist should consider to have a safe stay in Douala. When visitors decide to have a guided tour of the city, travel agencies turn to doual'art. In fact, travel agencies do not have tour guides and doual'art is the only tourism or cultural reference point for the city which can guide visitors to discover Douala. Together with their public artworks production and with the organization of SUD, doual'art invested a lot in tourism through the creation of a city map (the only one available), providing specific training for bilingual and expert tour guides, and proposing tours that go beyond the most wealthy areas, the only popular ones with Western visitors.

With reference to a survey realized in New Bell which sampled a group of 100 inhabitants, it is not only the tourists' flow that has grown considerably as a consequence of the installation of public artworks, but it is also constant (they suggest between three and five tourists per month) and, in addition to the peak of the flow reached during the SUD festival, 75 per cent of the interviewees believed that tourists are safe in the district.

Beyond this data, which refers to the individual perceptions of inhabitants, it is important to show that doual'art registered 77 guided tours for a total of 487 paying visitors in one year and a half (from May 2011 to December 2013). This is three times the level suggested by locals. Half of the visitors (49 per cent) came from Europe (mainly from France, Belgium and Germany), while the other half (45 per cent) consists of Cameroonian visitors, both from Douala and from the rest of the country. Within the latter statistic, half of the Cameroonian tourists are composed of groups of students on school and university trips coming from the only high school of art in Cameroon (300 kilometres from Douala) and from the University of Yaoundé. The remaining 6 per cent comes from the rest of the world, which includes 10 African countries, the USA, and China. The extraordinary nature of the tourism in a district like New Bell is not limited to artworks, whose contemplation by a foreigner results as fascinating and introspective; the arrangement of an artwork in New Bell becomes a chance to look around and to visit a district that a person would barely enter alone. Moreover, artworks interact not only with the environment but also with the inhabitants and with the owners of the buildings that host them. In this way, the tourist's experience in New Bell gives the possibility to observe the artwork giving an interpretation based on the personal cultural background, but it also allows one to deepen his knowledge through a direct dialogue with the actors involved in its production – sometimes visiting the atelier of the artist or discussing with the owners of buildings where artworks are arranged, together with local neighbours. Public art spurs the visitor to play an active role, to enrich their experience by discovering New Bell's *mapans* far and wide and to understand how, inexplicably, art succeeds gently in having such a strong impact on locals and on the urban transformation of the district.

Impact on locals

In New Bell, Yamguen's artworks have become part not only of the environment, improving it, but also part of people's mentality. They represent a real cause for cultural and educational reflection linked to the idea of beauty. Moreover, they allow the inhabitants to have a local and aesthetic reference point that they can imitate and transform as they like. Artworks are not elements which just beautify and decorate the district; rather, they become reflective of local aesthetic values that slowly and deeply transform the neighbourhood. In this case, they are still transforming the image of New Bell: one example is that homeowners have begun to paint their house walls blue after being inspired by the installations. As one teacher of the CBC Babylon School said, what really matters is that this kind of action *'Ça réveille. Ça réveille des grandes personnes, comme ça réveille des petits enfants'* [*It wakes. It wakes grownups as it wakes small children*].[12] The qualitative, personal and intimate impact that these artworks generated on people is clear, also considering the meaning that dwellers give to them. According to inhabitants, artworks express not only beauty but also innovation, education, reality and uniqueness. Some people[13] think that Yamguen's installations contributed to the requalification of the district: 'It makes the neighbourhood shine' ('Celà fait briller le quartier!'); 'It's the aesthetic to the service of society' ('C'est l'esthétique au service de la société'). Others think that artworks have made New Bell more modern – 'For our neighbourhood, this means opening to modernity, it is a rebirth!' ('C'est l'ouverture de notre quartier à la modernité, c'est une renaissance!') – modifying its external perception. 'It is the originality of a district considered as wild!' ('C'est l'originalité d'un quartier jugé sauvage!'), or even 'For me it represents the difference, as I do not see it everwhere!' ('Pour moi cela représente la différence, comme je ne vois pas celà par tout!'). Other inhabitants believe that installations have allowed them to disclose frankly the conditions of the district: 'It's another vision of our realities in terms of a shout of alarm' ('Une autre vision de nos réalités en terme de cris d'alarme'). But, at the same time, they represent a turning point: 'It is the young people's desire for awareness' ('C'est le désir de conscientisation des jeunes').

In New Bell, artworks did not revolutionize the environment and people's life; they rather influenced the citizens' capability to adapt themselves daily to the environment in innovative ways. Space metamorphosis represents the model on which people shape their lives. The director of the CBC Babylon School, where mural interventions were installed inside and outside, was inspired to plant flowers in order to improve the environment surrounding the school. She also put up signage in order to avoid people throwing garbage on the ground. The owner of the bar hosting the lighting installation *La nuit le bonheur c'est dans les moustiquaires* modifies the facade of his bar every year with new murals and is committed to pay electricity costs personally in order to maintain the installation on all night long, in a context where the electricity costs affect significantly the monthly cash outflow. Those kind of private activities (the school and the bar) have experienced a huge impact in terms of economic revenues. Since the installation of *Les Mots Écrits* outside the school, the number of students enrolled has doubled (passing from 200 students to 400 in 2012). The school has further invested the new income from the educational offer by introducing the Anglophone session, employing new teachers and funding a new wooden building. On the other hand, thanks to the earnings due to the increasing clientele, the bar owner could enlarge the surface of his bar, tile the floor and exchange old wood tables with plastic ones, more practical to move and to clean. Such examples show how people's sensibility towards urban space and artistic experience has changed: dwellers are no more extraneous with regard to the installations placed in the district but, on the contrary, they strongly demand them and ask for a renovation of art works and their surrounding space.

Conclusion

The presence of public art installations in the form of murals in the neighbourhood of New Bell contributes not only to define and reflect on the identity of the district, but also to increase the urban mobility of inhabitants and foreigners in and across the city of Douala. This mobility allows and makes sense to a process of city discovery, enhancing the cultural understanding of local and foreigners. From the locals' point of view, the role and the presence of artists into the district reveal to be really important to open young people to new experiences and new interests, and to prompt them to react. Experimenting the aesthetic of the 'ephemeral', they get in touch with the environment and they are inspired by it to react to its challenges, artistically or not, by questioning their own behaviour. Furthermore, the presence of public art enhances the inhabitants' possibility to expand their social and

162 *Marta Pucciarelli and Lorenzo Cantoni*

international networks; in Douala, expanding networks are a means to increase trust in other people, to improve self-esteem and to contribute to building individual identity.

From a foreigner's or tourist's point of view, the visit to public art installations in New Bell becomes something more than a guided tour of the city—it is rather an intense cultural experience reflecting the reality of a part of a city. New Bell, considered as one of the most dangerous district of Douala, has slightly changed its negative attitude to a positive one, thanks to the presence of public art in the form of murals. Tourists demand to visit the neighbourhood and to discover not only its public art, but also its *mapans* and its bars. They wish to visit to artists' ateliers as well. The character of being an immigrant district with murals has become an opportunity for New Bell, a factor that allows foreign visitors to feel welcomed by inhabitants, rather than rejected, even if what the neighbourhood can offer is still limited.

Notes

1 The Villes mortes ('Ghost cities') is the denomination of the historical period prior to the first multiparty election in Cameroon in 1991, characterized by a slaughter of the population, including arrests, violence, and tortures to the exponents of the opposition party.
2 The *Commandement Opérationnel* ('Operation command'), is a special paramilitary body instituted by the government of Cameroon the January 20, 2000 to fight insecurity and city banditry in Douala. The result was a second butchery, a legalized violence against the population including a thousand people fallen victim of extra-judicial killing, and an unknown number of people disappeared (Malaquais 2009).
3 The so-called Emeutes de la faim ('Hunger riots') are violent social movements organized by citizens of Douala in 2008 asking for a balance in the price of bread as a consequence of the strong inflation of the CFA franc and the diffuse unemployment rate. During these periods several thefts, rackets, armed violence, and burning shop were an everyday issue. Government repressed the manifestations with the army.
4 Personal conversation with Marylin Douala Manga Bell, President of doual'art, January 8, 2013.
5 Personal conversation with Junior Ndalle, journalist living and working in Douala, December 19, 2012.
6 scU2 is a collective of two scenographers, Jean-Christophe Lanquetin et François Duconseille.
7 Personal conversation with Hervé Yamguen and Hervé Youmbi artists and organizers of Scenographies Urbaines, January 9, 2013.
8 Ibid.
9 The mural text says 'Dans les eaux salles du quartier, dans ma ruelle ma jeunesse rebelle'. [In dirty waters of the neighborhood in my tiny streets my rebellious youth].
10 Hervé Yamguen, Personal conversation, November 19, 2013.
11 Ibid.
12 Personal conversation with teacher David from the CBC Babylon School, December 11, 2012.
13 Quotations from the survey.

References

Akam, Evina and Honoré Mimche. 2009. "Les Mouvements Migratoires Au Cameroun." In *L'état Du Cameroun: 2008*, Éditions Terroirs, 479–92. Yaoundé: Fabien Eboussi Boulaga.

Amnesty International. 2008. "Document – Cameroun: Prison Breack: Amnesty International Condems Use of Excessive Lethal Force and Calls for Independent Inquiry." *Amnesty.org*. July 3, 2008.

Araeen, Rasheed. 2010. *Art Beyond Art, Ecoaesthetics: A Manifesto for the 21st Century*. London: Third Text Publications.

Babina, Lucia and Marilyn Douala Bell. 2008. *Douala in Translation: A View of the City and Its Creative Transformative Potentials*. Rotterdam: Episode Publishers.

Bayat, Asef. 2003. "The 'Street' and the Politics of Dissent in the Arab World." *Middle East Report* 33 (1; ISSU 226): 10–7.

———. 2013. *Life as Politics: How Ordinary People Change the Middle East*. Stanford, CA: Stanford University Press.

Jones III, John Paul. 2000. "The Street Politics of Jackie Smith." In *A Companion to the City*, edited by Gary Bridge and Sophie Watson, 448. Malden: Blackwell Publishing.

Loe, Mamert Florent, Albert Claude Meutchehé Ngomsi and Marie Louise Nken Hibock. 2007. "Plan d'Action Strategique de Lutte contre la Delinquance Urbaine à Douala." UN-HABITAT, PNUD, CUD.

Malaquais, Dominique. 2005. "Villes Flux: Imaginaires de L'urbain En Afrique Aujourd'hui." *Politique Africaine* 100 (4): 15–37.

———. 2009. "Blood Money: A Douala Chronicle." *Chimurenga Magazine*.

Martin, Bradford D. 2004. *The Theater Is in the Street: Politics and Performance in Sixties America*. Amherst: University of Massachusetts Press.

Njoh, Ambe J. 2007. "Planning in the Cameroons and Togoland." In *Planning Power: Town Planning and Social Control in Colonial Africa*, 127–44. Boca Ratan, Florida: CRC Press.

Oho Bambe, Marc Alexandre. 2014. *Les chant des possibles*. La Cheminante.

Schler, Lynn. 2008. *The Strangers of New Bell: Immigration, Public Space and Community in Colonial Douala, Cameroon, 1914–1960*. UNISA Press.

Séraphin, Gilles. 2000a. "La Société Cvile Derrière La Communauté? Associations et Tontines à Douala." In *Le Désarroi Camerounais: L'épreuve de L'économie-Monde*, 193–215. Collection Economie et Développement. Paris: Karthala.

———. 2000b. *Vivre à Douala. L'imaginaire et l'action dans une Ville Africaine en Crise*.

Simon, AbdouMaliq. 2005. "'Reaching Larger World' Negotiating the Complexities of Social Connectedness in Douala." *Politique Africaine* 2005/4 (100): 38–53. doi: 10.3917/polaf.100.0038.

———. 2006. "Pirate Towns: Reworking Social and Symbolic Infrastructures in Johannesburg and Douala." *Urban Studies* 43 (2): 357.

———. 2008a. "Broken Links, Changing Speeds, Spatial Multiples: Rewiring Douala." *In Consuming the Entrepreneurial City: Image, Memory, Spectacle*, edited by Anne M. Cronin and Kevin Hetherington, 161–80. London: Routledge. http://eprints.gold.ac.uk/2825/.

———. 2008b. "Practices of Convertibility in Inner City Johannesburg and Douala." *In Gendering Urban Space in the Middle East, South Asia, and Africa*,

edited by Martina Rieker and Kamran Asdar Ali. Palgrave Macmillan. http://eprints.gold.ac.uk/2815/.
Sween, Joyce and Remi Clignet. 1969. "Urban Unemployment as a Determinant of Political Unrest: The Case Study of Douala Cameroon." *Canadian Journal of African Studies/Revue Canadienne Des Études Africaines* 3 (2): 463–87.
Wentworth, Harold and Stuart Berg Flexner. 1975. "Rap." *Dictionary of American Slang.*

10 Visiting murals and healing the past of racial injustice in divided Detroit

Deborah Che

> My thing is to saturate Detroit with as many murals as possible and try to reach young teenagers, teaching them that art is everything. My main goal is to have Detroit become the mural capital of the world.
>
> —Artist Chazz Miller (Lin 2005)

Murals, as a form of public art, serve multiple purposes including neighbourhood beautification, community and youth engagement, and tourism and economic development. However, murals, like other forms of public art, can redefine space and thus are subject to questions regarding what is art, who is it for, is it acceptable in the eyes of multiple audiences and/or stakeholders (i.e. artists, audiences, patrons) and what or who is represented? Public art has long spurred controversies in the USA, from a statue of George Washington commissioned in 1833 that depicted him as a bare-chested Greek god (Kammen 2006) to, more recently, Richard Serra's *Tilted Arc*, a 120-feet-long, 12-feet-high steel sculpture coated with brown rust commissioned for a new federal government building for which the process did not include any significant consultation with nor any public art education program for the government workers who had to use the space (Blake 1993; Levine 2002). Thus, given the public nature of murals, this chapter will first look at the contested content of visited murals. Then, it will examine how murals have fostered community economic development, including tangible economic benefits from tourism as well as intangible benefits such as political empowerment. It will then move to racially divided Detroit and two murals there, the Birwood Wall mural and the Detroit Chinatown mural that, in part, aim to heal the neighbourhoods they are situated in as well as the city overall.

Murals – who are they for?

As public art, murals painted on walls often reflect a community's taste, self-identity and communal heritage. For instance, Marling (1982) found the local content and style of US Post Office murals, funded by the US government as part of a Great Depression-era (1934–1943) Works Progress

Administration (WPA) program, expressed community attitudes and mythology, not reportorial accuracy. Technological optimism and images of an Edenic pioneer past, such as white clapboard farmhouses, shiny red tractors and people working harmoniously together which resulted in abundant agricultural production, were popular as they gave a reassuring sense of stability in light of the difficult present. In contrast, portraying natural disasters, work in a negative light, such as fatal mining accidents or struggling sharecroppers, and racial imagery outside small town norms, such as the inclusion of Native Americans in the recently Anglo-settled Southwest or a mulatto figure of justice in the segregated US South, were opposed and/or removed (Marling 1982).

While the taxpaying public was the implicit patron for the government-funded Post Office murals that were featured in WPA tour guides, public opinion has been important even with privately commissioned murals like artist Diego Rivera's controversial Rockefeller Center and Detroit Institute of Arts (DIA) projects that were also produced during the Great Depression. In the latter, Rivera similarly glorified workers and work in the Detroit Industry murals he painted in 1932–1934 in a city where only half the number of automotive workers were employed at half the wages they had been earning in 1929 (Downs 1999). The murals depict and exalt the evolution of technology, starting with agricultural production illustrated with nude female figures symbolizing the fertile earth and the crops of Michigan and Mesoamerica. They then depict the most modern, complex, sophisticated automotive technology and assembly line that Rivera marveled at the Ford Rouge Factory. In the murals, Rivera brought people together – workers of all races and management – in sharing Henry Ford's vision of the automobile industry as 'having power, breadth, and scope that went beyond the human scale of management, labor, and machines to take on a universal life of its own' (Downs 1999, 67). Even though in reality an ethnic and racial job hierarchy existed, Rivera portrayed the multiracial automotive workforce as Detroit's indigenous people of its industrial culture. When unveiled, the murals were attacked in the press for their portrayal of racial equality and for what were considered pornographic female nudes and sacrilegious caricatures of the Holy Family. They were also attacked because their creator was a foreign communist who prominently featured the working class and factories in the central court of the venerable DIA. The uproar over the murals, however, spurred attendance, with 10,000 people coming to view them on the Sunday (March 26, 1933) after their public unveiling. Amidst calls for the murals to be whitewashed, DIA Director William Valentiner stated that:

> Edsel Ford, the donor, was completely satisfied … I am thoroughly convinced the day will come when Detroit will be proud to have this work in its midst. In the years to come they will be ranked among the truly great art treasures of America.
>
> (Downs 1999, 177)

Indeed, the Detroit Industry murals, along with European masterpieces by Rembrandt, van Gogh, Bellini, Picasso and others, draw tourists to the DIA, one of the top ten art museums in the USA. Furthermore, they are treasured today by city and Metro Detroit area residents who see Detroit, the factory, the working class, machines, managers, industry and themselves in the murals.

Murals and community economic development

More recently, murals have been explicitly planned and developed with goals including tourism and economic development. Facing economic disaster with the closure of its sawmill, the town of Chemainus, British Columbia, commissioned murals featuring historical images of sailing ships, logging and mining, steam locomotives, pioneer families and First Nations tribes as part of a 1982 downtown revitalization program. Ten years after the first murals were unveiled, more than 70 businesses including restaurants, galleries, antique and gift shops had opened. These businesses served the nearly 300,000 visitors arriving in this artists' enclave located on the tourism corridor between the Vancouver Island ferry terminals at Nanaimo and Victoria (Patty 1992). Inspired by Chemainus' success, several Saskatchewan communities developed a murals approach to tourism. In their study and analysis of these communities, Koster and Randall (2005, 56) developed a framework to evaluate community economic development and the success of the mural projects based on the project objectives (i.e. tourism or community beautification), and intangible (i.e. community pride, knowledge, compliments) and tangible (i.e. number of visitors, number of jobs created, dollar value of tourist-related sales) measures of success. They found smaller rural towns considered the mural projects to be successful based on intangible attributes including community pride, levels of participation and fostering social linkages. Likewise, larger centres located on a major transportation route which had a variety of attractions including the murals were satisfied with the tangible economic benefits. However, smaller, more isolated communities with a more limited set of offerings had a more mixed view of the outcomes of the mural projects (Koster and Randall 2005).

Murals may also lead to intangible political or transformational benefits for communities. In Belfast, Northern Ireland, political murals were actively used by both Protestant Loyalists and Catholic Republicans to portray cultural myths that enabled more radical organizations to gather support from the broader nationalist and unionist communities for their political goals. These murals' symbols, themes and images fed myth and group-making on both sides of the conflict. For the Republican movement operating outside and against the government and status quo, the murals were particularly important in legitimizing its goals and methods (Goalwin 2013). In Belfast's working-class Nationalist districts, murals provide opportunities to present an alternative paramilitary narrative of the conflict and peace process, and also an alternative tourism product to that offered by the mainstream tourist industry which emphasizes natural and cultural heritage. This product includes the Protestant-owned Anglo-Irish mansions (Nagle 2012). In minority communities in the USA, murals produced in the last several decades increasingly incorporate community content and participation in the construction of the art to combat placelessness and provide transformative learning experiences for youth. While early Chicano murals in the 1960s drew on Mexican themes such as the mestizo, Mexican patriots, La Raza and the Virgin of Guadelupe to express political, social, ethnic and historical identity, by the 1980s murals incorporated local landmarks such as parish churches, skylines and tourist icons (i.e. cable cars in San Francisco). The latter Chicano murals embody Diego Rivera's sentiment that the muralist's intention 'must not lie outside the function of the place in which his painting has its being' (Arreola 1984, 418). They reinforce identification with place by involving local school youths under the supervision of an artist (Leesan and Agyeman 1986). In addition to having a transformative effect on youth, mural projects can revitalize communities. Boston's Dudley Street Neighborhood Initiative (DSNI) involved local youth in urban art and design projects including murals which identified and devised solutions to critical problems as part of revitalizing the thoroughfare (Breitbart 1995).

This chapter will now move back to Detroit and to the examination of two community-based public murals which serve multiple purposes, including:

- to reflect the attitudes and heritage of their Detroit neighbourhoods;
- to heal the past (and present) of racial injustice in the city;
- to spur community economic development through tourism, entrepreneurship and neighbourhood beautification.

The Birwood Wall mural is on a wall built in 1941 to separate a black community from an adjacent proposed housing development for whites so that the latter would be eligible for federal housing loans. The Detroit Chinatown mural features incidents important in Detroit's history, such as the bulldozing of the original Chinatown and two prominent African-American neighbourhoods for post-World War II freeway construction. This mural, which also references the racially-motivated murder of Chinese-American Vincent Chin, can be found in the remnants of Chinatown. Although designed by artists, these murals involved youth and organizations that aimed to address the problems facing their neighbourhoods and the city as a whole by using art as a way to stimulate community economic development. However, before discussing these murals in more detail, the history of residential segregation in Detroit must be examined as it is central to understanding the Eight Mile-Wyoming and Detroit Chinatown neighbourhoods where the murals are located.

Divided Detroit

Although Diego Rivera's Detroit Industry murals depicted a harmonious, multiracial industrial workforce, in reality, co-workers of different races live in very separate neighbourhoods. Given the city's racial neighbourhood boundaries, most African-Americans who came to Detroit during the Great Migration between 1916 and 1929, who were attracted by the unheard-of $5 per day wages at Ford and to escape the harsh Jim Crow segregation in the US South, were restricted to Detroit's overcrowded Black Bottom and Paradise Valley neighbourhoods (Figure 10.1). During World War II, another wave of black migrants who came for defence employment was also restricted to these same neighbourhoods. While Paradise Valley was home to nearly one-third of Detroit's black population, and was its commercial and cultural center with established and famous churches, social and business organizations and jazz and blues clubs, it, along with Black Bottom, contained some of the city's oldest, substandard housing stock (Sugrue 2005).

Federal government policy played a large role in limiting the quantity and quality of housing for blacks. The Federal Home Loan Bank Board created the Residential Security Maps and Surveys that were used to determine eligibility for federal mortgages and home loans. Designations were ranked from A (green) through D (red) based on the age and condition of buildings; the neighbourhood amenities and infrastructure; the neighbourhood's level

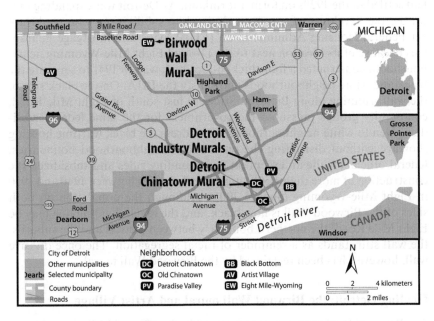

Figure 10.1 Map of Detroit, with featured neighbourhoods and murals.
Source: Cartographer Anne Gibson.

of racial, ethnic and economic homogeneity; and its absence or presence of 'a lower grade population' (Sugrue 2005, 44). The appraisal maps of Detroit assigned every African-American neighbourhood, or any neighbourhood with a black population from the Black Bottom ghetto to middle-class enclaves, as 'D' or hazardous. This made residents unlikely to qualify for mortgages and home loans that could enable them to upgrade or purchase housing. The designation also discouraged developers from building in those neighbourhoods. Conversely, white neighbourhoods whose properties were covered by restrictive covenants, such as the more than 80 per cent of property outside of inner city Detroit with Caucasian-only deeds, were given higher ratings (Sugrue 2005). Postwar highway and urban redevelopment projects further exacerbated Detroit's housing crisis, particularly for minorities. Paradise Valley, Black Bottom and Old Chinatown were levelled for the construction of the Lodge Freeway (M-10), the Edsel Ford Expressway (I-94), and the Chrysler Freeway (I-75) (Figure 10.1). While city officials claimed that the eradication of blight would increase tax revenue, revitalize the inner city and ultimately improve living conditions of their former residents (Sugrue 2005), the freeways actually facilitated 'white flight' to the new suburbs and left the displaced with limited places to go.

Opportunities to move out of the ghetto were restricted, although black enclaves outside of the inner city existed – including the Eight Mile-Wyoming neighbourhood (Figure 10.1) 10 miles north of Paradise Valley where blacks had settled in the 1920s on former farmland. As Detroit was expanding outwards, the developer of a proposed all-white subdivision, who could not get Federal Housing Administration (FHA) loans and mortgage guarantees because of its location next to the D-rated Eight Mile-Wyoming neighbourhood, constructed a foot-thick, 6-foot-high wall in 1941 to separate the black and white neighbourhoods and satisfy the FHA. On the black side of the wall, running along Birwood Street to just south of Eight Mile Road, community groups pressured the government for the same federal subsidies given to white neighbourhoods. To address the black wartime housing shortage without disrupting the city's racial neighbourhood boundaries, federal officials made an exception to its funding rules and subsidized the construction of more than 1,500 single family homes between 1940 and 1950 in Eight Mile-Wyoming (Sugrue 2005). Although the population on both sides of the Birwood Wall is now black, and the racial dividing line may be Eight Mile Road, the northern boundary between Detroit and the suburbs, the wall still stands as a reminder of racial segregation. The once divisive wall, however, has been reclaimed by the Birwood Wall mural.

Healing Detroit: the Birwood Wall mural and Artist Village

The Birwood Wall mural is part of artist Charles 'Chazz' Miller's goal to rejuvenate Detroit by changing its visual landscape and mindset through public community-minded art. As part of the civic healing, the Birwood Wall mural incorporates Detroit-specific issues of housing and segregation. This includes abolitionist Sojourner Truth leading the way to freedom out of the Underground Railroad, a reference to the nearby Sojourner Truth Public Housing Project located in the then-white Seven Mile-Fenelon neighbourhood where World War II black defense workers were harassed and attacked when moving in (Sugrue 2005). Additionally, the mural on the once divisive Birwood Wall draws on African-American history with Civil Rights icon and longtime Detroit resident Rosa Parks, a man with a Fair Housing sign, and the Spirit of Detroit statue leading a Great Migration family from the US South to Detroit. Images of houses and bubbles are included, as the latter, according to Miller, symbolize a form of creation that 'capture images and provide a new perspective' (Karoub 2013). Miller, the non-profit Motor City Blight Busters (MCBB) and neighbors and community volunteers, brought the 310-foot Birwood Wall mural to life in order to provide a new forum for discussing race. They also used the wall to help build a sense of place, shared purpose, community connections, and creativity in the youth and adults involved. MCBB founder John George said of the Birwood Wall mural, 'It's important to take something built to divide people and just flip the script and see if we can bring people together' (NBCNews 2006). The mural continues to receive publicity nationwide, most recently in a 2013 *USA Today* article (Karoub 2013), in part due to the need-to-be-seen-to-be believed nature of a wall built to divide blacks and whites in the USA.

In addition to the Birwood Wall mural, Miller, supported by community volunteers, business sponsorships and foundation grants, created a dozen murals in Artist Village (Figure 10.2) located in the Old Redford neighbourhood of northwest Detroit that are similarly rooted in the community's history and culture. They feature heroes like Martin Luther King, Jr, and themes such as mentoring and community gardening (Figure 10.2) (Lange 2006). Inspired by Diego Rivera's public art movement, Miller aims to create outdoor galleries with the goal of turning Northwest Detroit 'into a world class public art showcase using murals as the catalyst for change' (Terek 2010).

By building a sense of community and shared purpose, by beautifying the neighbourhood and by spurring small business creation, the transformative murals tie into local and regional community economic development aims and goals. Through his Public Art Workz! (P.A.W.Z.) project at Artist Village, Miller holds summer community art programs that impart art-related job skills such as computer animation, crafts and painting (Lange 2006). To this training, we can add life skills, because art is also about discipline (Miller, personal communication). According to Miller, such exposure to art and mural-making can foster in young people a sense of accomplishment, volunteerism and non-violence (Terek 2010); mural-making can develop their 'inner creativity (that) can empower, provide purpose and build confidence that cannot be broken' (Keane 2011). Artist Village operates on the principles that art can make the neighbourhood look better. Furthermore,

Figure 10.2 Artist Village.
Source: Deborah Che.

it functions better with art and can result in a growth in small businesses. Artist Village has studios with resident artists who mentor young people ('our most precious works of art' (Keane 2011), turning them into arts-based entrepreneurs. Artist Village has a gallery, computer lab for students, open-mic venue, a movie theater, a record company, an auto design shop, coffee house and Sweet Potato Sensations (an award-winning sweet potato soul food bakery). It is an arts-based neighbourhood that can bring visitors from metro Detroit and beyond.

Healing Detroit: the Detroit Chinatown mural

Like the Birwood Wall and Artist Village murals, the Detroit Chinatown mural was also envisioned as part of revitalizing the struggling neighbour-hood. Unlike other immigrant and migrant neighbourhoods in Detroit, Chinatown did not result from Chinese arriving for work in the manufac-turing or auto industries. Rather, they established businesses with lim-ited competition with the general population such as laundries or grocery stores that required little capital. They then went on to open restaurants after accumulating some wealth (Ohnuki 1964). The original, or Old Detroit Chinatown (Figure 10.1), peaked with approximately 2500–3000 residents. It was a popular exotic dining destination for the greater Detroit population

(The South End 2005). However, (Old) Chinatown and the surrounding Skid Row area were condemned in 1961 as part of a slum clearance project for the construction of Cobo Hall (Conference/Exhibition Center) and extension of the Lodge Freeway (M-10). Detroit Chinatown moved north to its present location centered at Cass and Peterboro (Figure 10.1) in 1963 after the On Leong Chinese Welfare Association purchased land for restaurants, storefronts, and a new Chinese school of Detroit. They also purchased buildings for senior housing and a community center (Gill 1962). Despite widening the sidewalks of Peterboro in the early 1980s to create a community space and walkway, the new Detroit Chinatown faltered. The new Detroit Chinatown was undermined by the forced move from downtown, Detroit's deindustrialization, the blighted condition of the Cass Corridor, the lack of a Chinese residential community, and increased suburbanization of whites, the Chinese, and increasingly blacks. After 50 years in business, first in Old Chinatown and then in the Cass Corridor location, Chung's, the last restaurant in Detroit Chinatown, closed in 1992. At the time of the unveiling of the mural, the only remnants of the Detroit Chinatown on the Cass-Peterboro block were a 'Welcome to Chinatown' kiosk and the Association of Chinese Americans' (ACA) Drop-In Center (providing hot lunches, English classes, computer literacy training for Chinese seniors, summer youth programming, gardening and Chinese language courses (Detroit Chinatown Revitalization Group 2006).

The Detroit Chinatown mural thus arose from community economic development concerns and from the desire for healing the legacy of racism. Following a 2002 event marking the twentieth anniversary of the murder of Vincent Chin, a group of community organizers and college students discussed possible projects in the Detroit area, including revitalizing the historic Chinatown district by highlighting its tourist potential and its historic nature as the only Chinatown in a US Midwest city existing since the early 1900s. The Detroit Chinatown Revitalization Workgroup (DCRW) – and Detroit Summer, an 'Intergenerational Multicultural Youth Program/Movement to rebuild, redefine, respirit Detroit from the Ground Up' – worked together to physically revitalize and repaint the remaining On Leong Welfare Association Chinatown buildings. With the help of visiting Los Angeles artists Tony Osumi and Jenni Kuida, Detroit Summer volunteers designed a 2,000 square foot mural reflecting the diverse history of Detroit and the Chinatown neighbourhood (Figure 10.3). The mural's main theme, the search for justice, connected the shared histories of Black Bottom, Paradise Valley and the original Chinatown, which were demolished for freeway construction. Justice, equality and diversity were represented through the following figures:

1   Martin Luther King, Jr, who led the march on Woodward Avenue and gave his first 'I Have a Dream' speech in Detroit on June 23, 1963;
2   Lily Chin, who sought justice for her son Vincent after two white autoworkers, who blamed the Japanese for their automotive industry job

losses, beat Vincent to death served no jail time (they received 2 years' probation and a $3,700 fine);

3   Helen Zia, one of the spokespersons representing the American Citizens for Justice that pushed for a federal trial charging the autoworkers with violating Vincent's civil rights, thus allowing for hate crimes to be pursued at the federal government level.

The mural speaks to the future with a street scene of Detroit Chinatown that includes a proposed Vincent Chin Museum. In the summer of 2003, volunteers from Detroit Summer, DCRW and the University of Michigan painted the mural on wood panels affixed to the former Chung's restaurant building owned by the On Leong Association (Lin and Suzuki n.d., Suzuki and Lin 2003).

Unlike projects in other Chinatowns, the Detroit Chinatown revitalization project that the mural was part of aimed to bring Chinatown and the scattered people back to the city (Lin, personal communication). The project would (re)establish a 'unique type of Chinatown' in Detroit 'with its post-industrial experience, along with its rich history of race relations', while 'attracting and catering to the Chinese community and population at large' (Detroit Chinatown Revitalization Group 2006). The visioning project included:

Figure 10.3 Detroit Chinatown mural.
Source: Deborah Che.

1   new grocery stores offering much-needed fresh produce in the food desert that characterized much of Detroit;
2   eateries and restaurants including the first sit-down, banquet-style Chinese restaurant in Detroit;
3   small business incubators to promote tourist shops, retail shops, Chinese/Asian bookstores, and other specialty stores;
4   senior and mixed-income housing;
5   a Vincent Chin Memorial Museum in Chinatown, serving as the hub for the community to mourn his racially motivated killing that had ignited the Asian-American civil rights movement and led to efforts to organize for a fair trial;
6   a community venue for celebrations and/or the streetscape for annual holiday events, public events or other traditional/folk celebrations; and
7   a historical designation for the neighbourhood.

The visioning project aimed to kick-start the rebuilding of the neighbourhood, which could attract the greater Detroit population and tourists as Old Chinatown had (Detroit Chinatown Revitalization Group 2006). While the physical infrastructure was part of the long-range vision (Lin, personal communication), the short-term focus was to work with Asian-American youth in exploring Asian-American history and to develop a curriculum giving them a sense of place in a predominantly black city (Detroit Asian Youth Project 2005). Echoing P.A.W.Z., art, history, community gardening and leadership development programs helped nurture this youth in Detroit.

Looking forward: murals, public art and the papillon effect

Murals dealing with the contested heritage of a host community can bring both healing and tourists to the community. Although seen by some as a pro-communist attack on capitalism, Diego Rivera's Detroit Industry murals are one of the primary reasons to visit the DIA. The Detroit Industry murals have been recognized nationally as a national historic landmark by the US National Park Service (NPS) that called them 'an exemplary representation of the introduction and emergence of mural art in the USA between the Depression and World War II' (Williams 2014). These murals and the three newly designated landmarks have been described by US Secretary of Interior Sally Jewell:

> … as diverse as our American heritage, telling stories of triumph and tragedy, of dedicated public service and artistic beauty. As part of a nationwide network of unique, historic sites, they help ensure the journey we have taken as a nation is remembered and interpreted both now and for future generations.
>
> (Williams 2014)

In Detroit, specifically, the Detroit Industry murals reflect the city's 'industrial presence in the central court of the city's art museum' and reaffirm its citizens 'work ethic and a certain toughness of spirit' (Downs 1999, 25). This toughness is especially needed given the city's historic municipal bankruptcy to restructure its debts that potentially posed a threat to the city-owned DIA. The DIA's unique setup as a city-owned art museum resulted when the booming city that was trying to be known as more than a factory town took possession of the DIA in 1920. The city funded it as 'a continuing asset' whose 'intrinsic worth' would continue to grow (Berman 2013). But the DIA was targeted by creditors that the city owes billions to. While the entire collection is valued at $4.6 billion today, the art bought with city funds and now valued at $900 million was the most vulnerable. Like the Detroit Industry murals, much of the DIA's collection had been acquired with private funds. To bolster city pensions and shield the art from sale by transferring ownership of the museum to an independent nonprofit, $815 million was pledged by foundations, the state government and the DIA (Stryker 2014). This has been considered to have been the only way in which the DIA can be preserved for residents and tourists alike.

While post-bankruptcy Detroit faces many challenges, changes are on the horizon. Downtown and Midtown have recently experienced an influx of investment, new businesses and new, mostly white professional residents. The gritty Cass Corridor where Detroit Chinatown is located is undergoing a land rush given its location both near trendy Midtown and on the northern edge of a 45-block, $650 million entertainment district. The Illitch family who own the Little Caesars pizza chain, the Detroit Red Wings ice hockey team, the Detroit Tigers baseball team and Olympic Entertainment (Motor City Casino, Fox Theater) has announced plans for a $450 million arena for the Red Wings (58 per cent publicly/42 per cent privately financed) and for another $200 million in private investment in an entertainment district that is expected to create "five 'new neighbourhoods' with hundreds of new apartments and a mix of national and independent retailers" (Reindl 2014). The land rush in Detroit Chinatown has resulted in the sale of some of the few remaining buildings still owned by Chinese Americans, including the former Chung's restaurant building on which the Detroit Chinatown mural can be found (Aguilar 2014). While the large number of parcels of land with unclear title, or that were tax-defaulted into the city's ownership, hampered the DCRW's efforts to revitalize the neighbourhood (Lin, personal communication), the Detroit City Council approved the sale for $1 of three-dozen unappraised, blighted parcels of Cass Corridor land to the Detroit Development Authority (DDA) to facilitate the development of the Illitch-led arena district (Reindl 2014). The Detroit Chinatown mural may not have spurred development, but it did involve youth and the community in beautifying the neighbourhood, addressing ugly aspects of Detroit's history, emphasizing the search for justice and recognizing the cultural diversity beyond what Boggs (2003, B8) calls Detroit's 'black and white binary'. While the Detroit Chinatown mural could be moved from Chung's, as it is on wooden panels, if retained in place as part of recognizing and remembering Chinatown, it may ironically be visited and viewed more in the forthcoming entertainment district.

Far from Downtown and Midtown, Artist Village has had its successes with ongoing art projects and with one of its resident businesses, Sweet Potato Sensations, that has expanded after being given additional production and exposure resulting from a contract with the new Whole Foods supermarket in Midtown. Supplementing the murals, Chazz Miller and a group of young volunteers have created butterfly installations stemming from Miller's feeling that Detroit needed a psychological readjustment. Miller explained, 'I mean, when you look at a caterpillar, you would never imagine a caterpillar is going to turn into a butterfly. And when you look at Detroit, you never imagine Detroit is going to come up off its knees.' While not technically murals, the 4–5 foot wide painted plywood butterflies affixed on abandoned buildings prevent and abate graffiti (Terek 2010).

Like the papillons, the neighbourhood-based Detroit Chinatown and Birwood Wall murals represent hope, growth and moving forward. By reflecting their neighbourhoods' attitudes and histories, as well as Detroit's racial history which continues to shape Metro Detroit today, they embody themes, a history and a narrative of a Detroit and an America that may be unsettling for some tourists. Yet, they are not confrontational like the Belfast Nationalist murals are (Nagle 2012), but are more conciliatory, like the new murals in Belfast which have been painted over 'antagonistic' sectarian murals with images emphasizing the area's industrial roots, its cultural heritage and famous literary characters (Nagle 2012) or which have a more expansive scope beyond the thesis of two opposing communities (Lisle 2006). While the Birwood Wall no longer separates whites from blacks, post-bankruptcy Detroit still faces the challenge of avoiding becoming two cities – 'one for the upwardly mobile young and white denizens of an increasingly happening downtown, and the other for the struggling and frustrated black residents trapped in neighbourhoods that are crumbling around them' (Finley 2014). As race is still part of the discourse in Metro Detroit, with predominantly black Detroit and its predominantly white suburbs, the Detroit Industry, Birwood Wall, Artist Village and Detroit Chinatown murals that stress diversity and tolerance will continue to be very relevant.

Acknowledgements

I would like to thank Jonathan Skinner and Lee Jolliffe for their constructive comments on an earlier draft of this manuscript, which clarified and strengthened this chapter. I would also like to thank Anne Gibson for cartographic assistance and Michael Kammen for pointing me to key writings on public art controversies.

References

Aguilar, Louis. 2014. "One of Last Remaining Chinatown-era Buildings Sold in Detroit." *The Detroit News*, August 7, 2014, accessed August 7, 2014, http://www.detroitnews.com/article/20140807/BIZ03/308070087/1001/BIZ/One-last-remaining-Chinatown-era-buildings-sold-Detroit.

Arreola, Daniel D. 1984. "Mexican American Exterior Murals." *The Geographical Review* 74: 409–24.

Berman, Laura. 2013. "From DIA's Formation, No One Could Have Predicted the Jeopardy It Faces." *The Detroit News*, 13 September 2013, accessed September 13, 2013, http://www.detroitnews.com/article/20130913/METRO01/309130040/From-DIA-s-formation-no-one-could-predicted-jeopardy-faces?odyssey=mod|newswe ll|text|FRONTPAGE|s.

Blake, Casey N. 1993. "An Atmosphere of Effrontery: Richard Serra, Tilted Arc, and the Crisis of Public Art." In *The Power of Culture: Critical Essays in American History*, edited by Richard Wightman Fox and T.J. Jackson Lears, 246–89. Chicago: University of Chicago Press.

Boggs, Grace Lee. 2003. "Living for Change; My Lucky 88th." *Michigan Citizen*, July 19, 2003, B8.

Breitbart, Myrna Margulies. 1995. "Banners for the Street: Reclaiming Space and Designing Change with Urban Youth." *Journal of Planning Education & Research* 15: 35–49.

Detroit Asian Youth Project. 2005. "2005 Summer Intensive Program," accessed April 4, 2007, http://www-personal.umich.edu/~hugoshi/daybrochure.doc.

Detroit Chinatown Revitalization Group. 2006. "Detroit Chinatown Revitalization Project Draft Report."

Downs, Linda Bank. 1999. *Diego Rivera: The Detroit Industry Murals.* New York: The Detroit Institute of Arts in association with W.W. Norton & Company.

Finley, Nolan. 2014. "Finley: Where Are the Black People?" *The Detroit News*, December 15, 2014, accessed December 15, 2014, http://www.detroitnews.com/story/opinion/columnists/nolan-finley/2014/12/14/black-people/20322377/.

Gill, John. 1962. "Chinese Reject Village Role, Will Rebuild Along Cass." *The Detroit News*, November 4, 1962, 6B.

Goalwin, Gregory. 2013. "The Art of War: Instability, Insecurity, and Ideological Imagery in Northern Ireland's Political Murals, 1979–1998." *International Journal of Politics, Culture, and Society* 26: 189–215.

Kammen, Michael. 2006. *Visual Shock: A History of Art Controversies in American Culture.* New York: Vintage Books.

Karoub, Jeff. 2013. "Wall That Once Divided Races in Detroit Remains, Teaches." *USA Today*, May 1, 2013, accessed May 1, 2013, http://www.usatoday.com/story/news/nation/2013/05/01/detroit-race-wall/2127165/.

Keane, Jeff. 2011. "Chazz Miller." *The South End*, April 21, 2011, accessed April 21, 2011, http://www.thesouthend.wayne.edu/archives/article_88dc034a-c894-5af3-bfc2-bf1cb116bb0c.html.

Koster, Rhonda and James E. Randall. 2005. "Indicators of Community Economic Development Through Mural-Based Tourism." *Canadian Geographer/Le Géographe Canadien* 49: 42–60.

Lange, Amy. 2006. "On the Mark: Artist Chazz Miller Teams Up with the Motor City Blight Busters." *Real Detroit Weekly*, May 10, 2006, accessed May 9, 2007, www.realdetroitweekly.com/article_1375.shtml.

Leesan, Peter, and Julian Agyeman. 1986. "A Sense of Place? A Place of Our Own." *Bulletin of Environmental Education* 183: 4–11.

Levine, Caroline. 2002. "The Paradox of Public Art: Democratic Space, the Avant-garde, and Richard Serra's 'Tilted Arc'." *Philosophy and Geography* 5: 51–68.

Lin, Judy. 2008. "Artist Paints Motown Murals; Man Inspired by Diego Rivera Envisions an Outdoor Museum in Detroit." *The Detroit News*, July 25, 2008, accessed July 25, 2008, http://www.detnews.com/2005/metro/0505/22/D03-189262.htm.

Lin, Michelle, and Soh Suzuki. n.d. "Detroit Chinatown Mural," accessed November 28, 2014, www.kuidaosumi.com/murals/mural-brochure.doc.

Lisle, Debbie. 2006. "Local Symbols, Global Networks: Rereading the Murals of Belfast." *Alternatives* 31: 27–52.

Marling, Karel Ann. 1982. *Wall-to-Wall America: A Cultural History of Post-Office Murals in the Great Depression.* Minneapolis, MN: University of Minnesota Press.

Nagle, John. 2012. "Between Trauma and Healing: Tourism and Neoliberal Peace-building in Divided Societies." In *Writings on the Dark Side of Travel,* edited by Jonathan Skinner, 29–46. New York and Oxford: Berghahn.

NBCNews. 2006. "Wall Separating Black, White Detroit Gets Mural," accessed July 13, 2013, http://www.nbcnews.com/id/12839157/ns/us_news-life/t/wall-separating-black-white-detroit-gets-mural.

Ohnuki, Emiko. 1964. "The Detroit Chinese – A Study of Socio-Cultural Changes in the Detroit Chinese Community from 1872 through 1963." MS thesis, University of Wisconsin.

Patty, Stanton H. 1992. "Canadian Town Brushed Itself Out of a Corner: Tiny Chemainus Was About to Shut Down When Artists' Murals Revitalized Business." *Los Angeles Times* June 21, 1992, 5.

Reindl, JC. 2014. "Q+A on New Red Wings Arena: Who's Paying for Entertainment District?" *Detroit Free Press*, July 21 2014, accessed July 21, 2014, http://www.freep.com/article/20140721/BUSINESS/307210149/Q-new-Red-Wings-arena-Who-s-paying-entertainment-district.

Stryker, Mark. 2014. "Fight Over DIA Value Resumes in Court Next Week." *Detroit Free Press*, September 25, 2014, accessed September 25, 2014, http://www.freep.com/story/news/local/2014/09/25/dia-art-detroit-bankruptcy-trial-valuation/16184545/.

Sugrue, Thomas J. 2005. *The Origins of the Urban Crisis: Race and Inequality in Postwar Detroit.* Princeton, NJ: Princeton University Press.

Suzuki, Soh and Michelle Lin. 2003. "Chinatown's Coming Back." *Michigan Citizen* 25 (46): B8.

Terek, Donna. 2010. "1,000 Artist-Painted Butterflies to Help Fight Detroit Blight; Artist and Volunteers to Beautify the City This Summer with 1,000 Painted Cutouts of Public Art." *The Detroit News*, May 22, 2010, accessed May 22, 2010, http://www.detnews.com/article/20100522/OPINION03/5220353/1-000-artist-painted-butterflies-to-help-fight-Detroit-blight.

The South End. 2005. "Detroit's Chinatown: Barely Surviving After Three Slices to the Heart." *The South End*, October 4, 2005, accessed September 25, 2006, http://www.southend.wayne.edu/article.php?story_id=1711.

Williams, Candice. 2014. "Rivera's 'Detroit Industry' Murals at DIA One of Four New National Landmarks." *The Detroit News*, April 23, 2014, accessed April 23, 2014, http://www.detroitnews.com/article/20140423/METRO01/304230097/1409/METRO/Rivera-s-Detroit-Industry-murals-DIA-one-four-new-national-landmarks.

11 Visiting murals and graffiti art in Brazil

Angela C. Flecha, Cristina Jönsson and D'Arcy Dornan

Introduction

Everywhere one looks, there are walls: house walls, store walls, business building walls, office walls, transportation infrastructure walls, walkway walls. Some walls have some form of expression, whether it be written, drawn or painted. Wall or mural art is a fundamental characteristic of urban art and street art as popular expression and is found in large and small cities.

This chapter will identify the role of murals in the expression of Brazilian identity, delving into their meanings as a reflection of society. It draws upon historical and contemporary sources on visibility in the expression of the art in murals painted either in inside environments or on outside walls by Brazilian artists. In addition to investigating the murals and urban art-related tourism products (cultural heritage and or art trails), key people in the world of tourism and art (murals and urban art-related tourism sectors) were interviewed. Additionally, this chapter introduces the development of tourism routes related to murals, as in the Brazilian cities of São Paulo and Rio de Janeiro, where visitors can visit and experience Brazilian urban art.

Context of Brazilian murals

Brazil is a country that has had a muralist culture since the 1940s. The mural is the opposite of the easel painting. This technique has a social character, integrating itself to the surface of a wall with decorative purpose, illustrative or even didactic. When applied directly to the wall, the mural requires the use of techniques ranging from the mosaic, the fresco and the acrylic. It is deeply linked to architecture, where the use of colour and design and the thematic treatment can radically change the perception and spatial proportions of the building. In the early twentieth century, a technique of incorporating panels and sculptures in murals was widely used and named 'muralismo'. Mexican muralismo gained international recognition, attracting attention and influencing countless painters, especially in Latin America. The large murals were directly linked to social and political context of the country, marked by the Mexican Revolution of 1910–1920. Diego

Rivera (1886–1957), one of the main exponents of Mexican murals, used art as 'a weapon', a revolutionary instrument of struggle against oppression. In the same way, Brazilian artists such as Di Cavalcanti, Cândido Portinari and Cícero Dias also distinguished themselves using this muralismo technique. Candido Portinari, the most well-known Brazilian muralist, helped to express Brazilian culture and identity. He left an extraordinary legacy of over five thousand murals, frescoes and panels, as well as paintings, drawings and prints that form a broad critical synthesis of all aspects of Brazilian identity. His most renowned piece entitled *War and Peace* was donated to the UN (1956) (as of July 19, 2014, the EXPOMUS listed on its website) and graces its walls in New York.

The baby-boomer generation, born in the post-World War II, came of age in the 1960s with a strong intolerance of social and cultural oppression. Among many other events for which this liberal era was known, a new art form of political activism begins to manifest itself with ever more vigour. If, in the early twentieth century, the burning question was nationalism due to strong political and sociocultural repression, the focus in the 1960s and 1970s became 'Group art'. The ensuing concern about having a specific and/or sole author on a work of art gained usage due to enduring social and political issues and policies. There were groups that sought a form of artistic expression that went beyond the remit of curators of museums, galleries and/or any traditional form of exposure; this was particularly noted in the Brazilian cities of São Paulo and Rio de Janeiro during this same period. These artists believed that institutions were locking up the art, restricting and limiting it to a certain social class. In the late 1970s, groups of artists and activists proliferated the world, motivated not only by political issues but also by those related to the environment: Greenpeace, Abbie Hoffmann and the Yippie group in the United States; the Provos in the Netherlands led by Grootveldt; the Situationists in Paris led by Guy Debord; and others. The 'interfering' with city spaces for different reasons and to achieve different objectives is part of the history of artist groups from the 1970s to the present day.

In São Paulo city, one sees the emergence of mural groups like Viajou Sem Passaporte (Travelled without Passport) (1978–1982), Tupinãodá (Tupi do not work), Manga Rosa (Pink Mango) (1978–1982), Gextu, d'Magrelos and 3NÓS3, among others. The latter starred in the X-Galeria action and sealed the doors of several art galleries in São Paulo with tape in the form of an 'X', and left on site a mimeographed sheet of paper with the phrase: 'What's inside is /What's outside expands' (Nichelle 2010, 15), making an allusion to censorship of the military dictatorship of the 1970s when the galleries at the time were closed not only to young artists, but literally closed, requiring you to ring a bell so the doors could be opened.

It was from the numerous derivations of murals and graffiti that the graffiti signs and signatures originated from the hip-hop movement in New York to elsewhere. Graffiti letters with elaborate designs, known in Brazil as 'grapixo', emerged and evolved from this era. The scenario of urban art in Brazil is evident in that there have never been so many talented artists, growing public interest, art collectors, researchers and media willing to give visibility and publicity to the aesthetic language of urban art. Additionally, manifestations of urban art have exploded in numbers and received much public attention, which has led to traditional art media trying to better understand the ever-evolving urban art world. Such manifestations of urban art seem to be helping to build greater appreciation for this kind of art in particular, and art in general. It is in this context that this chapter discusses the expression of the Brazilian identity through street or urban art, specifically mural and graffiti art, both indoors and outdoors.

Street or urban art

The mural is one of the two large divisions of paintings and possesses a unique social character. It is integrated itself on the surface of a wall as a decoration and/or illustration. When applied directly to the wall, the wall painting application consists of techniques such as mosaic, alfresco and/or acrylic (Leite 1988, 338). No other such art has had more community support and long-term social impact than that of murals, a uniquely democratic public art form, highly visible and sometimes collaboratively executed (Cockcroft, Weber and Cockcroft 1998, xi–xv). They are said to be 'newspapers on walls,' and a wealth of information is contained in them (Holscher 1976, 77).

This mural art form often involves the use of aerosol paint cans by artists who are commissioned by an individual, group of community residents, a business or a city. Murals frequently represent a community effort, large or small, whereas graffiti art or tagging is a more individualised effort of creative expression. 'What was once a hideous forest of concrete pillars soon became a pleasant and attractive place, a park decorated with paintings of remarkable beauty whose subject matter was critical and even subversive' (Treguer 1992, 24). They provide a 'canvas' on which to illustrate historical and or cultural heritage knowledge, as well as to articulate the struggles against oppression (Delgado and Barton 1998). The cited authors highlight the importance of location of a mural, adding a crucial perspective. There are three perspectives concerning location: (1) limited audience exposure – small public places such as alleys or infrequently travelled areas, (2) targeted audience exposure – inside select buildings such as schools and police stations, and (3) maximum audience exposure – public areas with high volume traffic.

The exit of this art from conventional spaces into public spaces – the city – was facilitated by urban architecture. Cartaxo (2009, 5) observes, generally, that art and architecture had their limits in the 1960s when their objectives and attitudes converged in a determined fashion. Mural painting has an intimate relationship with architecture. The mural painting technique and its application of colour and drawings, along with its thematic treatment, can radically alter the perception and spatial and/or architectural proportions of any construction.

The pictorial universe of Emiliano Augusto Cavalcanti de Albuquerque Melo, also known as Di Cavalcanti, includes an intense world of forms, colours, lights and spaces. His art contributed expressively to the elevation of Brazilian art during other movements in the middle of the twentieth century, with its recognisable and vibrant colours, sinuous forms and typical Brazilian themes such as carnival, mulattoes and tropicalism.

Cícero Dias, a Brazilian-born modernist painter, had his professional debut in Rio de Janeiro. His works of art generated much impact, but few understood them, as João Gabriel de Lima noted in a *Revista Veja* article on January 31, 2001. He spoke of the irrepressible irresponsible and revealed the tropical world of the sugar cane plantations, the furious passions, the dreams that were real fires of the senses.

In the same way as Di Cavalcanti and Candido Portinari, Cícero Dias had a profound influence on the Brazilian sociopolitical scene, and Cícero Dias' studio was frequently raided due to his support of the Brazilian Communist Party. He was persecuted when Getúlio Vargas installed the dictatorship in the New State of Brazil in 1937. The authorities in the state of Pernambuco called him the artist that paints images of Lenin by order of leftist students noted in a *Folha de São Paulo* article on January 28, 2003). Cícero Dias was the creator of the first abstract mural in Latin America in 1948. Despite living in Paris, he continued depicting sugar cane plantations, plantation houses, tropical abundance, the Capibaribe River and the Boa Viagem beach neighbourhood in Recife in his paintings from his imagination. (Vainsencher 2007).

Cândido Portinari was the first painter to adopt the mural painting in his general works. His oeuvres that stood out the most were the 36 mural paintings and 123 panels. He was strongly influenced by the sociopolitical reality of the country and thus developed many controversial works during a profound technological and sociocultural developmental phase through which the country was passing. Anything from the earth to man, from coffee plantations to arid lands, from sterile fields to slum dwellings inhabited by indigenous nomads, the Negro and the Portuguese were depicted by the artist. His Picasso influence helped him become a successful artist of national and international proportions, who, through murals, found an exit to the socialisation of his art. The panels and murals were a phase of Portinari's evolution that reflect the relevance of the social themes from the 1930s–1950s during the art movements of Brazil. Symbols of death, sacrifices, united families, rebellion and despair all were used on numerous panels and murals. It is notable that in the four panels found at the Hispanic Foundation of the Library of American Congress, with themes referring to the Hispanic-American history, Portinari demonstrates his concern for the human dimension as much as his concern for historic events. The artist's racial choice to dominate a composition is not the white (the European) but a black (Fabris 1990; Smith 1943). During the 1950s, a movement that supported paintings with historic themes and Brazilian art in public spaces emerged. However, the history of urban art in Brazil began during the 1960s with wall writings against the dictatorial regime. They were loaded with phrases against censorship, torture, North American imperialism and the encouragement of armed fights. These messages were painted on walls and façades on both public and private buildings. The twentieth century artists in Brazil almost had a responsibility by the current dictatorial regime to promote Brazilian culture, even serving as promoters for its dictatorial government. If the twentieth century was marked by a strong nationalist current, its end pointed to a causal disconnect with the twenty-first century and the artists that were emerging in Brazil at that time.

From Brazilian murals to Brazilian graffiti

Graffiti in Portuguese, grafito; in Italian, graffitto; in Greek, *graphein*. Graffitto means inscription or drawing of the old era, streaked with pencil or charcoal, on rocks or walls (Gitahy 1999, 20). In the singular, it is a technique (a piece of painting on the wall), while in the plural, it refers to finished drawings (the graffiti of the Palace of Pisa, for example). It is a form of visually artistic expression (plastic or not) that uses combined words and/or images in order to transmit a reflective message. Due to its strong artistic connotations, graffiti does not attempt to impose determined ideas on the observer, but allows for reflection and interpretation (Moraes 2006). In the four corners of the world, the activity (with spray paint) is recognised and represented, including in Brazil (Souza 2007, 27). Graffiti, a popular art form, is often covered by the popular press. This form of artistic expression is usually initiated by individuals rather than groups or communities. The messages contained in graffiti art generally reflect the struggles associated with urban living and issues of oppression (Ferrell 1995; Delgado and Barton 1998). They are a form of social commentary.

Graffiti, the unauthorised written, scratched, marked, sprayed or affixed defacement of public/private property, is considered by some to be a social crime, an act of youthful vandalism, which needs to be erased from urbanity because of the feelings of disgust/fear it engenders in the general populace. However, in recent years, a move has taken place to distance illegal graffiti from its legally sanctioned counterpart, urban art (such as murals on permitted structures) through the creation of a conceptual distinction between 'graffiti as crime' and 'graffiti as cultural expression' (Taylor and Marais, 2009). The classifications of tagging and graffiti have simply been poorly interpreted, due to its free form of expression. Tagging is the practise of writing/spraying one's signature on a surface, while graffiti is directly related to the plastic arts and painting. The first privileges the word and the letter, whereas the latter has to do with drawing, the plastic representation of the image (Souza 2007, 93). What changes is the aesthetics. Graffiti is an art that is subversive at its roots (Soares et al. 2005). It is important to note, then, how graffiti relates to the contemporary muralist movements and pop art.

Brazilian contemporary graffiti is a hybrid between a traditional aesthetic of street art and the murals of the twentieth century (from the muralism of Di Cavalcanti, Cândido Portinari, Picasso and Diego Rivera, and Andy Warhol's pop art) with the influence of hip-hop graffiti from New York. It has a unique aesthetic that mixes realism, fantasy and political themes, which is imitated all over the world (Schacter and Fekner 2013, 10). Graffiti is often linked to a discourse on awareness, salvation or liberation of delinquent youth through the art and the hip-hop movement (Souza 2007, 29). The practise of urban intervention has gained much force in Brazil since the end of the 1990s (Mesquita 2011, 52). However, due to the high prices of spray paint, artists have resorted to the use of latex paint and rollers in order to fill the outlines that have been spray-painted, resulting in the emergence of a singular graffiti art form known as 'Brazilian Graffiti'. Table 11.1 lists the Brazilian states with the most graffiti. Note that São Paulo is the state with the highest concentration of murals, followed by Rio de Janeiro and cities of south region of Brazil.

Table 11.1 Brazilian states with urban graffiti

State	City	Quantity
Amazonas	Manaus	85
Bahia	Lençóis	1
	Salvador	32
Distrito Federal	Brasília	97
Ceará	Fortaleza	22
Espírito Santo	Vila Velha	2
Goiás	Goiânia	35
Minas Gerais	Belo Horizonte	53
Maranhão	São Luis	23
Pará	Belém	15
Paraíba	João Pessoa	40
Paraná	Curitiba	53
	Foz do Iguaçu	20
Pernambuco	Recife	40
Rio de Janeiro	Rio de Janeiro	6591
	Nova Friburgo	5
	Petropolis	15
	Niteroi	235
	Teresopolis	15
Rio Grande do Norte	Natal	1
Rio Grande do Sul	Laguna	1
	Porto Alegre	22
Santa Catarina	Florianopolis	131
São Paulo	São Paulo	4512
	Campinas	55

Primary source, 2015.

Graffiti in São Paulo

Since the 1970s, artistic and cultural manifestations have acquired a more poetic and lucid nature. During this era, significant names in urban art emerged, such as Alex Vallauri, Carlos Matuk, John Howard, Waldemar Zaidler and Hudinilson Júnior, among others. These artists developed their works from a foundation in graffiti. In the city of São Paulo, the 3NÓS3 group, formed by Hudinilson Júnior, Mário Ramiro and Rafael França, developed eighteen interventions that caught the attention of both those passing by and the media. This group, along with Viajou Sem Passaporte and Manga Rosa (Monachesi 2003, 4–6), were looking for a form of artistic expression that was beyond museum curators, galleries and other traditional exhibition spaces. They believed that these institutions imprisoned art, restricting it and limiting the art to a determined social class. The stencil technique they used is carried out with a hollow mould that is covered with paint and forms a well-outlined drawing. This technique is widely used in urban art, either directly on the wall or on paper that is then glued onto the wall.

During the 1980s, the urban art collective, TupinãoDá, made up of Jaime Prades, Milton Sogabe, José Carratu, Carlos Delfino and Rui Amaral, carried out important happenings/actions in the city of São Paulo that became symbolic of the history of urban art in the country (Ferreira 2011). After this productive phase of graffiti in Brazil, there was a rapid influence from American hip-hop in the 1960s and 1970s. This cultural movement explored the languages of the music commanded by DJs, poetry, rap and dance, which was finally illustrated visually by the images of the graffiti artist. The most significant artists in the Brazilian urban art today are OSGEMEOS (The Twins – Otavio and Gustavo Pandolfo), Binho Ribeiro, Speto (Spit), Eduardo Kobra, Nunca (Never), Titi Freak and Presto, Alexandre Orion, Alex Senna, Andre Farkas, Zezão and Crânio (Skull).

OSGEMEOS cover topics such as family and social criticism. Their graffiti are scattered across various US cities, England, Germany, Greece, Cuba, Canada, Poland and many others countries as of February 17, 2015, the OSGEMEOS listed on its website.

The graffiti artist Paulo Cesar Silva, also known as Speto, helped shape the Brazilian graffiti style traditions of folk art and African art. He created a style reminiscent of xylographs, especially the xylography of Cordel, which are based on booklets common in northeastern Brazil containing folk poems and displayed for sale hanging from cords or twines, which gave rise to the name. Speto, the designer, illustrator and graffiti artist, has made the street his artistic platform for the last 27 years. He is one of the greatest exponents of Brazilian graffiti abroad. Speto accomplished his first works in the 1980s in his native city of São Paulo. He was influenced by hip-hop culture and also by classic movies that introduced graffiti and hip-hop to the world that had recently arrived in the city (Kalimo 2013).

Fabio Luiz Santos Ribeiro, also known as Binho Ribeiro, is one of the pioneers of street art in Brazil and Latin America. He is a journalist and magazine editor and published author with books on graffiti. He is an idealist in his dissemination of street culture and art and is today one of the mentors in the struggle to consolidate it as a driving force in the world of art. Last but not least, Eduardo Kobra began his artistic career in the suburbs of São Paulo and has been highlighted for the realism qualities of his paintings. He created the project, 'Memory Wall', that seeks to transform the urban landscape, designing everyday historical urban scenes. The project is present in cities such Athens, Lyon, London, New York, Miami and Los Angeles as of 2013, the Binho Ribeiro artist listed on his website.

Graffiti in Rio de Janeiro

Graffiti started to distinguish itself in Rio in the 1990s in São Gonçalo, in favelas (slums) and suburbs of the city. Acme and Fábio Ema are the veterans of this first generation of the favela Pavão-Pavãozinho (Sá and Almeida 2006). Another important artist is Smael or Ismael, who became interested in graffiti during the time that he frequented the Lapa neighbourhood in Rio during the 1990s. In 1999, he painted his first wall. Since he wanted to create a different 'style of writing' he started using Japanese characters to design his own style. He then moved on to Korean characters. When it came to Portuguese, his letters were so deformed that they were bordering on the abstract. Since the exposition at Haus, his work has been selected to be part of the Great Market of Contemporary Art (GMAC) in Paris. Smael continues to paint walls of the city of Rio with friends of the Santa Crew and the Nação Crew (Sá and Almeida 2006).

Besides these individual artworks by particular artists, there are also social integration projects in Rio in which graffiti can be seen, for example, in projects by NGOs such as CUFA (Central Única das Favelas) and the Afroreggae (in Vigário Geral Slum in Rio de Janeiro) and participate in programmes connected to UNESCO as Cleusa Maria noted in a *Jornal do Brasil* article on June 26, 2005. CUFA (Central Unica das Favelas) is a Brazilian organization recognised in political, social, sporting and cultural areas throughout Brazil that aims to empower slum dwellers. It was created from the union of young people from various favelas seeking spaces to express their feelings, thoughts and questions about life. The AfroReggae Cultural Group is a nongovernmental organization founded in 1993 with a mission to promote inclusion and social justice through art, Afro-Brazilian culture and education. The group aims to awaken the artistic potential of young working class people. The initiative increases the self-esteem of young slum dwellers, in addition to generating income, and helps them move away from the influence of drug trafficking. AfroReggae has developed projects in poor areas throughout its history.

The AeroSoul Carioca Team is also based in Rio de Janeiro. The word 'carioca' comes from the word 'Tupi kari'oka', which is a combination of the words 'kara'iwa' (Caraiba or white man) and 'oka' (home). The meaning of the word, therefore, was the 'house of white men', a building made of stone and lime unknown by the Indians. The first houses were Carioca calls were built in the city of Rio de Janeiro in 1503 (Bueno 2003). The AeroSoul Carioca Team, as fans of graffiti and urban cultures, have catalogued 400 pieces of art by 300 different artists. The pieces, nestled closely on the grey cement walls, are often referenced by the pieces they are next to, so if your piece is good, the artist that comes along after has to create something even better (Olivero 2012). Carioca youth, hit hardest by economic disparities, use graffiti painting to send their messages to the masses. In Rio de Janeiro, street art is ubiquitous. It exists in all corners of the city, from the favela to upper-class neighbourhoods, from residential, touristic areas to institutional areas, as Michelle Young noted in an *Untapped Cities* article on February 13, 2012. The Fleshbeck Crew pioneered the graffiti movement in Rio and still remain some of the most respected figures on the Rio scene, composed of artists Bruno Bogossian (BR), Rogério Fonseca (Krrank), Márcio Ribeiro (Piá), Marcio SWK, Leonardo Uzai (Nhôzi) and Rod. The Crew is a group of friends, artists with similar interests who intend to promote their art with the support of a united community. The Crew honed their skills in sketchbooks before transforming their work to the streets. The Fleshbeck Crew was one of the original groups working in Rio. Many of their founders, such as BR and Toz Krrank, have gained international notoriety, revealing the importance of the group quite 'literally' (Walters 2012). Other contemporary graffiti artists, the new generation of graffiti artists, are Mateu Velasco and Clivson da Silva (named Akuma). Mateu Velasco grew up in Laranjeiras neighbourhood and did a course in industrial drawing at the Pontifícia Universidade Católica (Catholic University). While at university, he became enchanted with the graffiti technique and created his own style. One of his panels was elected to decorate the wall of Casa de Saúde São José (Hospital) in the Humaitá neighbourhood. Clivson da Silva 'Akuma' is a resident of Niterói (a city located across the Guanabara Bay from Rio). He went through the tagger phase until he started tagging with Fábio Ema. He showed talent with spray cans, creating volume and three-dimensional effects. In 2001, Akuma and Fábio Ema painted the façade of the famous Brazilian singer and composer Gilberto Gil's studio in Gávea.

The Gamboa and Saúde, neighbourhoods of Rio de Janeiro city (Port Zone), are undergoing a process of rapid change. Wonderfully colourful graffiti interacts with newly excavated sites of Afro-Brazilian history, colonial houses competing with the plans of new investors. In 2013, according to the revitalization of the harbour area – Porto Maravilha (Wonderful Harbour)—Rio de Janeiro commissioned an enormous work of art: its greatest wall of graffiti created in the harbour area. This place has a profound historical importance, and it is the object of studies and excavations that brought to the forefront the historical and cultural significance of the place for understanding the process of the African diaspora and the formation of Brazilian society. Archaeological findings have motivated the creation of the Curatorial Work Group Circuit History and Archaeology of African Heritage (CDURP 2011). The mural artist, Tomaz Viana (Toz), with the participation of over eight additional artists, created this mural measuring 2,100 square metres, 30 metres high and 70 metres wide. Toz used 1,500 spray paint cans on the panel which is located on Sacadura Cabral Street at the back of the B2W company as Renata Saavedra noted in the Department of Cultura of the Rio de Janeiro State article on February, 25 2013. Guided visits/tours distribute 10 per cent of the tour cost to the Instituto de Pesquisa de História dos Negros (Research Institute of Afro-Brazilian History) as of 2013, the Rio Art Tours listed on its website. Located on a site where the old Cemetery of New Blacks (name given to newly arrived slaves in Brazil) was found, the IPN performs Interventions Project that invites artists to create works on a wall of its internal courtyard. Other cities like Petropolis, Teresópolis and Nova Friburgo, in the mountains of Rio de Janeiro, have similar mural projects as they regenerate through art.

Dates, remembrances and actualities

Graffiti day was informally created in 1988, and in São Paulo, it became municipal law in 2003. This is a tribute to Alex Vallauri, one of the pioneers of the Brazilian street art and one of the leading characters in world graffiti. Since 2006, there have been various events, with extensive programmes in São Paulo, during the celebration of Graffiti Day. There is a 12 metre by 7 metre mural that is renovated collectively and annually by various artists as of March 29, 2014, the *Rede Brasil Atual* listed on its website. In 2014, the eighth anniversary of the event presented Bixiga 70, Mc Sombra, Vai-Vai, Zebrabeat, Nomade Orquestra, Coletivo Stencil Brasil and Sarau Suburbano e Capoeiras da Bela Vista. Other initiatives that bring colour and life to the poorest part of the city are the 'Favela Bela' (Beautiful Slum), listed on as of 2013, the MUQUIFU website as of 2013, that have hundreds of community facades of houses painted, and the project of Dulux 'Tudo de cor para você' (All the colour for you) in the favela of Santa Marta in Rio de Janeiro, whose aim is far beyond leaving the beautiful walls. The meaning has a longer range, reaching the inside people as of February 19, 2015, the Dulux listed on its website. In Santa Marta, where the implementation of the pacification program by the police in 2008 practically erased the violence, the transformation also takes place through the colours, whose power has improved the daily lives of an entire community, as Joana Gontijo noted in a *Correio Braziliense* article on March 31, 2013. The final project, the 2-kilometre-long wall located on Andradas Avenue in Belo Horizonte city (in the state of Minas Gerais), was aimed to inspire people through the preservation and injection of colour that was painted on the community's houses. The activity of painting generates a change in people's habits and gives a feeling of pride and ownership of the job at hand, as the Dulux listed on their website on February 19, 2015.

Brazilian street art tourism

São Paulo, the social and cultural metropolitan centre of Brazil, can be considered an important laboratory of ideas. The number of cultural attractions found here spread throughout the city, revitalize and reinvent areas, and their connections make São Paulo a unique city, as SPTuris listed on their website as of February 17, 2015. São Paulo City Hall, with the cooperation of São Paulo Tourism, developed an urban art circuit with the intention of revealing the innovative spirit of this metropolis for visitors. Moreover, the Museu Aberto de Arte Urbana – MAAU (Urban Art Open Air Museum) in São Paulo recently added the pillars of sustenance at the Blue Line 1 metro at the Carandiru station.

The tour begins at the wall of Cambuci beyond the axis Vila Madalena Pinheiros. In this neighbourhood, the famous Pandolfo brothers live (OSGEMEOS and Nina). The idea is to start the tour on the corner of Lavapés Street and Justo Azambuja Street. At the Paulo Kobayashi Square, a huge 10 m panel attracts attention entitled 'Urban Forest'. It was inspired by the environment and is curated by Binho Ribeiro, with the collaboration of various artists. Other graffiti complete the 1,500 square metres of Brazilian and foreign artistic work.

São Paulo is one of the world capitals of graffiti, and it proves this through the transformation of a whole urban space into an open-air gallery. Tens of columns that sustain the subway at Cruzeiro do Sul Avenue, from the Tietê Station (where the main bus terminal of the city is), passing through the Carandiru Station (beside the Youth Park) and extending to Santana Station have become the First Open Urban Art Museum as of February 17, 2015, the SPTuris listed on its website. The idea was developed in April 2011, when eleven graffiti artists were arrested and processed for environmental crime for painting the metro columns along the Cruzeiro do Sul Avenue with no authorization, as Tatiane Rosset noted in a *Revista Veja* article on April 11, 2014. This act generated a graffiti class mobilization that resulted in the MAAU project developed by artists Binho Ribeiro and Chivitz. Six months later, in partnership with the public sector powers, the initiative was implemented, providing the opportunity for 70 panels to be painted by 58 artists and to be renewed annually to provide an opportunity for new names, new artists. This outside space also invests in educative actions with the local population and in the education of the public and valuing of graffiti as a popular art form.

Fading, light and shadow. A tour guide points to the paintings, draws attention to signatures and techniques. No one is in a museum, much less seeing pictures. They are looking at graffiti on Dr Arnaldo Avenue, west of São Paulo. Among car horns and noisy buses, the group of tourists walk through the Pinheiros neighbourhood towards Vila Madalena, seeking drawings to help guide the Soul Sampa travel agency that organizes themed city tours and since 2015 started to exploit the fame of São Paulo graffiti.

Five kilometres along the asphalt 'lie' works of known artists like Titi Freak and Rui Amaral, plus a new generation of names like Zito, who combines graffiti and photography in a work located under the Bridge Street João Moura. The guide talks about the gang taggers, such as Addiction and the Scares collective, and their street philosophies. They are 'grapixo' – a mix of graffiti and tagging – on the Cardinal Arcoverde, for example, letters in elaborate blue tones and contours make mystery of what, after all, was written there. Sometimes no one can understand what the graffiti artists try to say; they are intellectuals with their own creative and sometimes private language. Ironically, they can marginalize those who marginalize.

The ride lasts five hours, including one hour at the end to a spray workshop and breaks for lunch and the opportunity to take pictures – especially on the stairs of Cristiano Viana street and Beco of Batman (a long cobblestone alley in Vila Madalena), following local graffiti artists from the 1980s. Everyone wants to see OSGEMEOS. Everyone wants to see the work of OSGEMEOS, the collective Vidaloka ('crazy life') Zezão, famous for blue tubes that paints the city's underground also surprises the visitor with a mural painted on Beco of Batman, an image filled with coloured smoke clouds of spray and stencil, something only the most understood recognize. It is a different way to discover the neighbourhood, both fun and a ramble.

Rio de Janeiro is a city exuberant in nature and full of undeniably beautiful landscapes where graffiti can still stand out. Spread across all over the city, graffiti murals bring colour and transformation to the walls and buildings on screens filled with the most genuine expression of Rio's urban art. Recently, Terminal Alvorada in the Barra da Tijuca neighbourhood won six awards for local work by local artists; growing visibility given to graffiti worldwide that puts Rio at the heart of a global framework of the murals movement. The graffiti artists even turned the object of their work to the church: The Chapel San Jose, Flag Square, became the first entirely graffiti construction of Brazil.

In the state of Rio Grande do Sul, in the capital Porto Alegre, a leading newspaper of the city urged: 'Where there is urban art in Porto Alegre?' in March 24, 2015, the *Correio do Povo* listed on its website. The question was motivated by the fact that it was the two hundred and forty-first anniversary of the founding of the city. The newspaper called on readers to help put together a collaborative art map on the city walls. This gave rise to various scripts as artists and cultural agitators were called to play the role of trustees and indicate their preferred locations for the artwork. The result will be the script of an art gallery in the open.

In Brasilia, Federal District, as of May 23, 2015, the *Mapa Gentil* listed on its website, a cultural project of art and education that aims to encourage a creative look at the city (5 Pictures) and surroundings through various artistic languages has been created. Graffiti, stencil, painting, word and poetry are the tools used to create installations and performances in the different urban settings there. The design by the proposed actions seek the democratic insertion of art in everyday life, giving new meaning to the collective space, embellishing walls, streets and buildings. Thus, the Gentil Map (Kind Map) (2012) proposes a dialogue between individuals and their space, encouraging reflection on society and human relationships, raising awareness for the common good and integrating the town and art collective. This project developed a map of urban art, incorporating classes during the tours on weekdays and Saturdays. Visitors have the advantage of mediation guides that bear the name of 'gentle' properly trained experts who will explain the works and guide visitors throughout the route.

In 2015, in Belo Horizonte and Porto Alegre cities, The Santander Bank took to the streets with an art circuit design presented through contemporary art. Santander Art Circuit promotes artists and their art, giving the facades of bank agencies for artistic intervention. In this manner, it takes art to a broad and diverse audience who walks through the streets of Belo Horizonte and Porto Alegre. The proposal provides an approach to the bank's collection of artworks that served as the starting point and source of inspiration for artists. Beginning in Porto Alegre in 2013 and Belo Horizonte in 2015, ten branches of the bank agencies across the cities received artworks up to 10 metres high. The artworks are large, outdoors and serve the goal of bringing people together through art. These artworks were produced and contributes to the cultural repertoire of the population. The project created a network so that the public can go on a circuit through the urban areas with the purpose of awakening their creativity and sensitivity, thereby strengthening civic ideas and enriching cosmopolitan worldviews as the Santander Bank listed on its website on May 23, 2015.

Conclusion

Despite the large number of famous graffiti artists known through their murals and visual panels on the streets, there is an evident style shift amongst the great muralists of the twentieth century compared to those of the twenty-first century. What was once political has turned artistic (Sá and Almeida 2006). It is obvious that intentions of the current muralists differ greatly from the muralists of the last century, who used murals to reflect, tell stories and regain history and culture. The muralists of the twenty-first century use and breathe art for art's sake through the murals without abandoning culture and notions of social inclusion. The abundance of walls is what makes the large cities of Brazil an ideal urban artist's urban atelier. Despite their art being developed in Brazil, Brazilian artists became famous when they exposed or produced their art outside Brazil. Graffiti has brought new techniques and new ways of creating art to our urban landscape. What was once seen as vandalism and crime is today more accepted as urban art and cultural expression. This acceptance is reflected by the availability of courses, seminars and events about urban art. What was once a polemical urban problem is today viewed as colourful and creative; what were once words (tags) are today messages of self-confidence and beauty. The city itself is offering to its inhabitants, and to its visitors, a unique urban cultural tourism experience through development of 'graffiti tours', available to visit in person and or virtually – the latter via the São Paulo Street Art Gallery Google links. Perhaps the hoped for numbers of tourists visiting the city of Rio de Janeiro during the 2016 Olympic Games will inspire the city to structure a similar art route? The literature regarding urban art in Brazil is still very limited, but with publications such as this book, illustrated books on world graffiti, and the continued development of cultural trails (art, gastronomy and or other) becoming more common, such examples may lead to the development of other urban art routes and similar types of visits across Brazil and other countries.

References

Binho Ribeiro. 2013. Last modified, 2013, http://www.binhoribeiro.com.br/sobre/.

Bueno, Márcio. 2003. *A Origem Curiosa das Palavras*. São Paulo: Editora José Olympio.

Cartaxo, Z. 2009. "Arte nos Espaços Públicos: a cidade como realidade." O Percevejo Online. v. 1, n. 1, Jan–Jul 2009, accessed February 16, 2015. http://seer.unirio.br/index.php/opercevejoonline/index.

CDURP (Companhia de Desenvolvimento Urbano da Região do Porto do Rio de Janeiro). 2011. "Circuito Histórico E Arqueológico Da Celebração Da Herança Africana," accessed January 16, 2016. http://www.portomaravilha.com.br/circuito.

Cockcroft, Eva Sperling, John Pitman Weber and James D. Cockcroft. 1998. *Toward a People's Art: The Contemporary Mural Movement*. Albuquerque, NM: University of New Mexico Press.

Correio do Povo. 2015. "Circuito de arte invade ruas de Porto Alegre na quarta-feira." Arte & Agenda. Variedades. Exposição, last modified March 24, 2015, accessed January 16, 2016, http://www.correiodopovo.com.br/ArteAgenda/Variedades/Exposi%C3%A7%C3%A3o/2015/3/552125/Circuito-de-arte-invade-ruas-de-Porto-Alegre-na-quartafeira.

Delgado, Melvin and Keva Barton. 1998. "Murals in Latino Communities: Social Indicators of Community Strengths." *Social Work* 43 (4): 346–56.

Dulux. "Let's Colour program," last modified 2011, accessed February 19, 2015, http://www.letscolourproject.com/.

EXPOMUS (Exposições, Museus, Projetos Culturais Ltda). 2014. *Guerra e Paz*, last modified 2015, accessed July 19, 2014, http://www.expomus.com.br/projeto/guerra-e-paz.

Fabris, A. 1990. *Portinari, Pintor Social*. São Paulo: Editora Perspectiva, Universidade de São Paulo.

Ferreira, M.A. 2011. "Arte Urbana no Brasil: expressões da diversidade contemporânea." Paper Presented at the VIII Encontro Nacional de História da Mídia, April 28–30. Guarapuava, PR.

Ferrell, Jeff. 1995. "Urban Graffiti: Crime, Control, and Resistance." *Youth & Society* 27: 73–92.

Folha de São Paulo. 2003. "Pintor pernambucano Cícero Dias morre aos 95 anos, em Paris." Ilustrada. Folha Online, last modified January 28, 2003—15h52, accessed February 15, 2015, http://www1.folha.uol.com.br/folha/ilustrada/ult90u30327.shtml.

Gitahy, Celso. 1999. *O que é graffiti*. São Paulo: Editora Brasiliense.

Gontijo, Joana. 2013. "Projeto transforma favela no Rio de Janeiro pelo poder das cores." *Lugar Certo (O Popular)*, accessed January 13, 2016, http://correiobraziliense.lugarcerto.com.br/app/noticia/ultimas/2015/03/31/interna_noticias,48934/projeto-transforma-favela-no-rio-de-janeiro-pelo-poder-das-cores.shtml.

Holscher, Louis M. 1976. "Artists & Murals in East Los Angeles and Boyle Heights: A Sociological Observation." *Humboldt Journal of Social Relations* 3: 25–29.

Kalimo. 2013. Lab^k, Speto: o grafite brasileiro, last modified August 2013, accessed February 17, 2015. http://lab.kalimo.com.br/2013/08/speto-o-grafite-brasileiro/.

Leite, José Roberto Teixeira. 1988. *Dicionário Crítico da Pintura no Brasil*. Rio de Janeiro: Artlivre.

Lima, João Gabriel. 2001. "O boêmio em fase cor-de-rosa." *Revista Veja*. Edition 1685, last modified January 31, 2001, accessed February 14, 2015. http://veja.abril.com.br/310101/p_122.html.

Mapa Gentil. 2015. *O projeto*, last modified, 2015, accessed May 23, 2015, http://mapagentil.com.br/o-mapa-2/.

Maria, Cleusa. 2005. "Arte no meio da rua: Artistas que buscam humanizar as cidades, os graffiteiros não param de formar novos grupos no Rio." *Jornal do Brasil*, accessed February 12, 2015, http://memoria.bn.br/DocReader/DocReader.aspx?bib=030015_12&PagFis=136052&Pesq=

Mesquita, A. 2011. *Insurgências Poéticas: Arte Ativista e Ação Coletiva*. São Paulo: Annablume/Fapesp.

Monachesi, Juliana. 2003. "A explosão do a(r)tivismo." *Folha de São Paulo*, 4–9, last modified June 26, 2005, accessed February 13, 2015, http://memoria.bn.br/DocReader/docreader.aspx?bib=030015_12&PagFis=136052.

Moraes, Vinicius Borges. 2006. "A pichação e a grafitagem na óptica do direito penal: delito de dano ou crime ambiental?" *Jus Navigandi*, Teresina, 11(970), last modified February 27, 2006, accessed February 15, 2015, http://jus.com.br/artigos/8039.

Museu dos Quilombos e Favelas Urbanos (MUQUIFU). 2013. *Meu olha sobre a favela—Favela Bela*, last modified 2013, http://muquifu.com.br/site/exposicoes/meu-olhar-sobre-a-favela/.

Nichelle, Aracéli Cecilia. 2010. "O que está dentro fica/ o que está fora se expande, 3nós3—coletivo de arte no Brasil." Master diss., Stadual University of Santa Catarina, Florianópolis.

Olivero, Lu. 2012. "AEROSOuL Carioca: A Journey Inside Rio's Graffiti Culture." *Kickstarter*, last modified January 16, 2013, accessed February 20, 2015, https://www.kickstarter.com/projects/1840769012/aerosoul-carioca-a-journey-inside-rios-graffiti-cu.

OSGEMEOS. 2015. "Mural em homenagem à memória de Dash Snow (SACER IRAK CREW), and the Iz the Wiz," last modified 2015, accessed February 17, 2015. http://www.osgemeos.com.br/en/mural-created-by-osgemeos-in-new-york-is-unveiled/.

Rede Brasil Atual. 2014. "'Dia do Graffiti' leva arte de rua, música e poesia ao Bixiga." Redação RBA, last modified March 29, 2014, http://www.redebrasilatual.com.br/entretenimento/2014/03/dia-do-graffiti-leva-arte-de-rua-musica-e-poesia-ao-bixiga-9972.html.

Rio Art Tours. "The Most Innovative Tours in Rio de Janeiro," last modified 2015, http://rioarttours.org/pt/any-road-art-tours/#curated_tours_list_name=rioarttours.

Rosset, Tatiane. 2014. "Museu Aberto de Arte Urbana, em Santana, ganha 22 novos murais." *Revista Veja*, last modified 11 April 2014, accessed February 17, 2015. http://vejasp.abril.com.br/blogs/graffiti/page/2/.

Santander Bank. 2015. *O projeto*, last modified 2015, accessed May 23, 2015, https://www.santander.com.br/portal/wps/gcm/package/cultura/circuito_de_arte_27052015_92354.zip/projeto.html.

Saavedra, Renata. 2013. "Rio ganha mural de grafite gigante na Zona Portuária. O grafiteiro Toz fala do bom momento da arte urbana na cidade." *Secretaria de Cultura do Estadodo Rio de Janeiro*, last modified February 25, 2013, accessed February 20, 2015, http://www.cultura.rj.gov.br/entrevistas/rio-ganha-mural-de-grafite-gigante-na-zona-portuaria.

Schacter, Rafael and John Fekner. 2013. *The World Atlas of Street Art and Graffiti*. New Haven, CT: Yale University Press.

Smith, Robert Chester. 1943. *Murals by Candido Portinari: In the Hispanic Foundation of the Library of Congress*, 31–32, Washington.

Soares, Luiz Eduardo, M.V. Bill and Celso Athayde. 2005. *Cabeça de Porco*. Rio de Janeiro: Objetiva.

Souza, David da Costa Aguiar. 2007. "Pichação carioca: etnografia e uma proposta de entendimento." Master diss., Universidade Federal do Rio de Janeiro.

SPTuris (São Paulo Tourism Department). 2015. "Roteiro Cidade Criativa." Prefeitura Municipal de São Paulo, last modified 2015, accessed February 17, 2015, http://www.cidadedesaopaulo.com/sp/br/o-que-visitar/roteiros/roteiros-tematicos/roteiro-criativa.

Taylor, Myra and Ida Marais. 2009. "Does Urban Art Deter Graffiti Proliferation?" Papers from the British Criminology Conference. British Society of Criminology, www.britsoccrim.org, ISSN 1759-0043; Vol. 9, pp. 57–70, Panel Paper.

Treguer, Annick. 1992. "The Chicanos—Muralists with a Message." *UNESCO Courier* 45: 22–24.

Vainsencher, Semira Adler. 2007. *Cícero Dias*. Recife: Fundação Joaquim Nabuco, last modified 11 October 2007, accessed February 12, 2015, http://basilio.fundaj.gov.br/pesquisaescolar/index.php?option=com_content&view=article&id=563:cicero-dias&catid=38:letra-c.

Walters, Nathan M. 2012. "Fleshbeck Crew, Rio's Graffiti Originators." *The Rio Times*, last modified 5 May 2012, accessed February 20, 2015, http://riotimesonline.com/brazil-news/rio-entertainment/fleshbeck-crew-rios-graffiti-originators.

Young, Michelle. 2012. "The Legalization of Street Art in Rio de Janeiro, Brazil." *Untapped Cities: Rediscover Your City*, last modified February 13, 2012, accessed 19 February 2015, http://untappedcities.com/2012/02/13/the-legalization-of-street-art-in-rio-de-janeiro-brazil/.

12 Balancing Uruguayan identity and sustainable economic development through street art

María de Miguel Molina, Virginia Santamarina Campos, Blanca de Miguel Molina and Eva Martínez Carazo

Introduction

Uruguayan contemporary muralism refers to muralism production in the twentieth and twenty-first centuries. It comprises murals that come under the social realism, constructivism and formalist traditions of the twentieth century, as well as the most recent production from the end of the twentieth century to the present, which focuses on the social function of murals. Production is concentrated mainly in the cities of Montevideo and Colonia, where 289 murals (248 in Montevideo and 41 in Colonia) with artistic and historical qualities linked to social realism and constructivism movements from the twentieth century (de Miguel et al. 2013, 33) have been identified. These murals were painted by an exclusive minority of artists linked to 'high culture' and are generally located in enclosed spaces.

However, towards the end of the twentieth century, another kind of muralism, associated with street art, developed in other areas of Uruguay. This type of mural is in part constructed by the most vulnerable groups: those seeking access to the creation and consumption of popular culture through public open spaces (Santamarina et al. 2015, 490). Some of the characteristics of this kind of 'open art' or 'street art' are related to inclusive innovation and identity, and it is these features that we would like to analyse in this chapter in order to explain these movements and their local impact in greater depth. In these murals, the street is presented as a public space in which we can understand the history and culture of the population (Saunders 2013, 536), such as in Image 1. In the three towns we selected, we found 104 murals: 35 in Rosario del Colla, 50 in San Gregorio de Polanco and 19 in Pan de Azúcar. These towns have undergone a process of local economic regeneration in which murals have been linked to tourism without losing their popular identity.

Inclusive innovation policies mainly aim to influence the development of affordable products and services tailored to the needs of groups at risk of social exclusion who can participate in inclusive innovation, either as innovators or as users of innovations (UNCTAD 2014, 6). As Foster and Heeks (2013, 335) highlight, inclusive innovation is focused not only on poor people

Figure 12.1 Honey, if I can stretch my salary as much as I can stretch my accordion,
we'll be spending the summer in Cancun.
Source: Own photographs, Pan de Azúcar (Uruguay).

but also on other vulnerable groups, such as women, young people, disabled
people and ethnic minorities, and aims to improve their social development.
At this point, we think that 'street mural art' is a way to achieve inclusive innovation, as it can generate local development through employment, create
a sense of identity and, in some cases, boost economic growth through tourism. The three towns that we selected are examples of local development as
a result of mural art. They are not the most visited destinations in Uruguay,
but they have reached a high degree of sustainable development, thanks to
murals. Moreover, they have created a new generation of citizens who feel
connected to art, culture and their own history.

Methodology

This study consisted of a content analysis (Berg and Lune 2012, 349) of two
kinds of information: on one hand, the literature analysing the concepts of
muralism and street art in relation to identity and, on the other hand, primary data collected by our research group consisting of in-depth interviews
conducted in the Uruguayan towns of Rosario del Colla, Pan de Azúcar
and San Gregorio de Polanco. Different concepts were reviewed through a

content analysis of the literature. We then completed a qualitative analysis from several in-depth interviews in order to find the relation between this mural art, the identity of Uruguayan citizens and the economic develop-ment of these towns. The keywords that we used for our searches in the Web of Science (Thompson Reuters) and Google Scholar were 'muralism', 'street art', 'identity' and a combination of all of them.

We found 604 scientific papers that contained the term 'street art' and 81 papers matching the words 'street art + identity' and 'muralism + identity'. We narrowed this search down to 44 core papers.

We conducted a qualitative analysis study for the in-depth interviews. From June 14 to July 17, 2013, the research group conducted 38 in-depth, in-person interviews in these three towns as part of a research project about the social implications of Uruguayan muralism, supported by the Spanish government. The sample consisted of artists and people involved in the con-servation and promotion of Uruguayan muralism in the towns of Rosario del Colla, Pan de Azúcar and San Gregorio de Polanco. All the interviews were conducted using the same scripted set of questions, which included minor changes depending on the particular town and respondent and were based on a semi-structured format. This format was chosen to allow re-spondents to express themselves freely and provide as much information as possible (Bernard 2000, 182).

We only selected the interviews of people who had some kind of link to mural conservation and were aware of the tourist impact of murals, i.e. those who were related to local tourism in the Uruguayan towns of San Gregorio de Polanco, Pan de Azúcar and Rosario del Colla. The selected interviews (11 out of 38) were used to identify the links between Uruguayan identity, tourism and muralism through a content analysis (Weber 1990, 44; Sierra 2001, 286–9). The selected keywords were 'identity', 'mural', 'open museum' and 'tourism'.

We conducted more interviews at San Gregorio de Polanco because its tourist industry is more highly developed, thanks to muralism, in compar-ison with Pan de Azúcar or Rosario del Colla (35 murals in Rosario del Colla, 50 in San Gregorio de Polanco and 19 in Pan de Azúcar). However, all three towns have had good experiences in using murals to enhance identity and attract tourism.

Literature review

The concept of local identity has been studied by literature since the 1990s. The importance of local identity became a trend in marketing locations as a way to differentiate them (Erickson and Roberts 1997, 35; Batista, Kovacs and Lesky 2013, 103). Moreover, as globalization threatened to lead to changes in or loss of identity, this became especially common in the street art of the biggest cities of the world where there was a solid ethnic mix, such as New York (Strong 1998, 9). At the start of the twenty-first century, some places started to use street art as a way to achieve regeneration (Zorach

2011, 66) and enhance local identity, whilst promoting the image of the town or city at the same time (McCarthy 2006, 245).

Nevertheless, from a political point of view, this way of defending identity had begun beforehand at the end of the twentieth century. This can be seen in some examples of mural paintings in different countries, such as:

Brazil (Aldana 2013, 229), expressing the 'abertura' or 'democratization' period of Brazilian history, when the military regime, in power since 1964, made a slow transition to democracy.

El Salvador (Heidenry 2014, 122), reflecting the brutal post-civil war period (1980–1992).

Mexico (Coffey 2012, 25), focusing on the post-revolutionary state when mestizo identity was enhanced.

Berlin (Colomb 2012, 142), whose public policies show the 'creative side' of post-wall subculture expressions that had previously been illegitimate (like street art and graffiti).

Spain (Garcia 2014, 296), symbolizing freedom during the transition from dictatorship to democracy.

Algiers (Grabar 2014, 389), showing postcolonial discourse after 1962 to reclaim nationalism.

Northern Ireland (Rolston 2012, 447), helping the peace process between Unionists and Republicans.

Egypt (Abaza 2013, 126), where street art mirrors the protests and violent confrontations of 2011 in Cairo.

At present, both views can represent and construct shared local identities: political, economic (linked to creative industry and tourism) and social. However, it is important not to lose authenticity, that is, original local values (Taylor 2001), when using cultural art for marketing and branding places (McClinchey 2008, 252; Banet-Weiser 2011, 644).

Street art covers a wide range of disciplines like 'hybrid art' (Irvine 2011, 235) and 'democratic art' (Riggle 2010, 255; Jagodzinska 2011, 3). In the case of mural art, we should distinguish between outdoor muralism (muralism can also be indoors) with its long history and graffiti, which started to develop in the late 1960s and early 1970s in North America (Young 2010, 100). The origins of graffiti are related to the response of young Americans to the social and political crisis taking place in the country at the time. Modern graffiti has developed into a hip-hop subculture that combines rap, break-dancing and graffiti, making it a global practise (McAuliffe 2012, 192). According to Crosier (2010, 21), murals and graffiti have a social base and are large paintings whose environment is a public space. Conversely, muralism follows a traditional process of production where the aim is to build a message, and a political or social narrative, of the place (Image 2). In addition, graffiti usually appears without permission (Young 2010, 100; 2012, 297; Monto, Machalek and Anderson 2013, 280) and is intentionally ephemeral, although this has changed in recent times (Irvine 2011, 28).

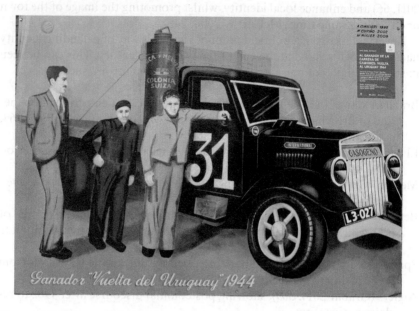

Figure 12.2 Winner of the Uruguay trucks race, 1944.
Source: Own photographs. Rosario del Colla (Uruguay).

Recently, some researchers have shown that, in some cases, graffiti can be understood as a sophisticated form of creative industry (Dickens 2010, 63; McAuliffe 2012, 193–4) and is nowadays a recognized art movement (Irvine 2011, 235; Bengtsen 2013, 67; Gartus and Leder 2014, 311). In fact, 'legal' graffiti is being used to promote creative cities (McAuliffe 2012, 190). However, the development of this kind of public urban strategy should be 'focused upon notions of "negotiated consent" to the presence of graffiti and "zones of tolerance" with varying degrees of self-regulation by graffiti writers or external regulation by police and council authorities' (Young 2010, 99). If cities want to create a sense of local identity, the negotiation with their citizens is fundamental (Atkinson 2007, 537; Moctezuma 2001, 126; Metaxas 2009, 1372; Visconti et al. 2010, 511; Iveson 2013, 955). In some cases, to attract tourism, cities deliberately showcase the identity of minority cultures and their traditional cultural heritage (fine art, dance, food and so on), often overshadowing the youth in the areas and their new urban interests like graffiti art (Morgan 2012, 207, 216).

To give an example of this, New Orleans successfully managed a new graffiti movement after the 2005 Hurricane Katrina catastrophe, negotiating with street artists (locals and non-locals), anti-graffiti activists and property owners to have their work represented through regeneration projects (Ehrenfeucht 2014, 965). In a different environment, at the Edinburgh Fringe Festival, artists successfully negotiate the use of public spaces with other users of the space (Munro and Jordan 2013, 1497). Lastly, since the end of the twentieth century, San Gregorio de Polanco in Uruguay has explicitly focused its tourism planning on the showcasing of murals. Accordingly, we have decided to use the expression 'street mural art' because we think that legal and professional graffiti could be included in the wider concept of muralism. It can also be used for other purposes served by murals, such as advertising (Borghini et al. 2010, 116, 123) and beautification (Koster 2008, 180, 275).

In a clear research strategy, we can also add a sense of social identity to this concept of muralism, as well as seeing it as a way to improve local development using murals as a tourist attraction. Such a strategy should follow an integrated process because if it narrows place branding too much, it could limit investments in other types of economic local development (Stern and Hall 2010, 4–5). Koster (2008, 170) has studied the opportunities of marketing murals, whilst other authors have also assessed other kinds of street art. For example, Figini and Vici (2012, 825) and Herrero, Sanz and Devesa (2011, 651) studied the potential of cultural art and other related activities as a tool for reducing seasonality. In addition, Plaza (2008, 514) studied how a heritage investment can become an effective employment creator if it becomes an effective tourist attraction.

The way of marketing street art murals has been normally to exhibit them as 'outdoor museums' as opposed to enclosed museums. They are one of three kinds of museums: open-air museums, ecomuseums and museum networks (Pressenda and Sturani 2007, 332). In our study, we observed that the term 'open-air museum' is the most commonly used name, although sometimes the name ecomuseum could be applied, as this follows a specific topic in a precise landscape and environment (some museums use the wrong name). Outdoor museums allow a broader audience to experience art directly, and both open-air museums and ecomuseums try to connect with the local community in some way (deeply in the second case). The main difference is that in an open-air museum, not all the murals have a common 'history' with the environment, even though different topics are developed, while in the case of ecomuseums, the murals have a coherence about them, i.e. they are an integrated set of works (Pressenda and Sturani 2007, 335).

In the next section, we assess the implications of the muralism movement in the Uruguayan towns of Rosario del Colla, San Gregorio de Polanco and Pan de Azúcar through the content analysis of primary data collected by in-person, in-depth interviews.

Case study: Uruguayan towns (Rosario del Colla, San Gregorio de Polanco and Pan de Azúcar)

Rosario del Colla, San Gregorio de Polanco and Pan de Azúcar are all towns in Uruguay that have some common characteristics. At the end of the twentieth century, they went through a social and economic crisis, for different reasons, that forced them to implement new ways of developing their economies and reinforcing their local sense of identity. All three towns tried to enhance a specific type of tourism: cultural in Rosario, rural in San Gregorio and sun and sand in Pan de Azúcar (de Miguel et al. 2013, 33). Although the period from 2008 to 2011 was very positive in terms of recovering tourism in Uruguay, in the last few years, tourism has decreased slightly as a whole, except for some select destinations (Uruguayan Ministry of Tourism and Transport 2014, 14).

To give some examples, Rosario del Colla was a flourishing town until the construction of the railway to Montevideo at the end of the nineteenth century, which took away the majority of the investments. San Gregorio de Polanco was an inland rural town with some tourism concentrated in the summer at its river beach. Pan de Azúcar, as a coastal town, was focused on sun and sand tourism and wanted to diversify both its summer tourism as well as its tourism during the rest of the year. All of their development occurred at the same time in the 1990s with the creation of open-air museums based on mural art. Uruguay has a long mural tradition, yet each of these cities sought not to develop elitist muralism as before but to combine works of recognized artists with others designed by young artists or even local people.

In 1993, San Gregorio de Polanco, in the Tacuarembó department, imitated the idea of an open-air museum based on murals from the Spanish town of Escariche (Guadalajara) but in a more ambitious way, i.e. by allowing the murals to feature free content yet attracting recognized national and international artists to the town. Similarly, in 1994, the first town that decided to create a historic open-air museum to mural art was Rosario del Colla, a town with approximately 10,000 inhabitants that belongs to the Colonia department. In this case, the concept of the ecomuseum could be applied, as the aim was to offer a coherent and integrated set of murals (Pressenda and Sturani 2007, 335). The town's objective was to showcase the identity and values of local people with murals that reflected the town's history, its important people and events (Image 2).

Finally, Pan de Azúcar, in the Maldonado department, wanted to enhance its cultural image through the creation of an open-air museum with murals focused on the 'tango' dance from a comic perspective (Image 1). The mural museum was started in 1998, making it the last town in this study to develop a mural tourism approach. The initiative was supported by the company RG y Asociados Emprendimientos Culturales and by some internationally recognized Uruguayan and Argentinian artists such as Carlos Páez Vilaró and Tabaré. With its focus on humour and tango (a traditional dance in Uruguay and Argentina), it can also be classified as an ecomuseum due to its specific focus on an original cultural asset.

We would suggest that all three towns have used street mural art in a similar fashion, following a planned method and making room for both recognized and novel artists.

Results: in-depth interviews

We analysed the opinions and evidence given by some interviewees located in the three Uruguayan towns. We selected 11 interviewees, the majority of whom were from San Gregorio de Polanco, as it was the town where the muralism strategy had developed the furthest and the number of murals was higher: 35 in Rosario del Colla, 50 in San Gregorio de Polanco and 19 in Pan de Azúcar (all of them registered by our research team).

We found two kinds of stakeholders amongst the interviewees: those related to local or regional government and those related to private organizations or citizens. In general, we focused on the social and economic views expressed by the respondents. For all of the interviewees, identity and tourism had improved due to the new murals around the towns and both were important because, as one insightful respondent noted, 'a place without culture has no future' [Interviewee].[1]

Pan de Azúcar

The idea at the start of the murals project was to generate an open museum to create a touristic and cultural itinerary for the town of Piriápolis (close to Pan de Azúcar). Private investors promoted the muralism movement to create this itinerary in the Maldonado department as a complement to the sun and sand tourism marketing for Piriápolis, a well-known coastal destination 11.5 km from Pan de Azúcar. The commissioned Argentinian and Uruguayan artists painted some of these murals as caricatures because the main theme of murals was humour and the tango, a traditional dance in both countries.

In Pan de Azúcar, we perceived a lack of planning for the open museum. An interviewee indicated: 'This caused several problems ... The mural tours do not cover all the artworks, selectively discriminating what counts as a "good" mural for the tourist to see ... The museum does not receive public investment for street murals (only for indoor murals) and some of them need to be urgently restored ... Accordingly, the original goal of the murals, as a way to recover local identity, has been lost while other kinds of ambition have emerged'.[2]

In this case, this is where the concept of the ecomuseum would have arisen. However, the lack of a long-term strategy to develop this has eroded this option. Furthermore, the general policy on restoration is not clear and has divided opinion: for some people, murals are ephemeral and should not be restored, while for others, it is the way to conserve local identity. In sum, the final valuation of the open museum is positive overall, as it has helped the town to establish itself as a cultural destination and not just as a beach resort for sun and sand tourism. The same has happened in other nearby towns such as Punta del Este. According to a spokesperson at the open museum [Interviewee],[3] 'at present, the museum is being visited by over 1000 tourists per year'.

According to the Uruguayan Ministry of Tourism and Transport (2014, 82), in 2013, Piriápolis received 107,607 visitors (3.8 per cent of all visitors to Uruguay), with tourist numbers increasing by 63 per cent in the last decade. This is on top of the large number of overnight stays it has as a sun and sand destination. Now it is a destination combining a beach resort and culture. Despite their success in attracting tourists, the murals need to be better conserved. If not, this kind of cultural tourism will be lost.

Rosario del Colla

In 1994, a group of people from the fine arts and tourism sectors decided to create the first Uruguayan history museum to attract visitors to the town of Rosario from Colonia de Sacramento – a city that had been declared a World Heritage site in 1995 by the United Nations Organization for Education, Science and Culture (UNESCO).

Rosario was mainly constructed by the Spanish in the nineteenth century and therefore does not have a long history. The objective of creating an open-air museum was to counteract the social and economic crisis of the 1990s. The main goal of the museum was to enhance local values and remind visitors of the historical events that had taken place in the town. In the case of Rosario, the concept of an ecomuseum would appear to be more apt than that of an open-air museum (Pressenda and Sturani 2007, 335). However, they decided to use the latter.

An interviewee indicated: 'In Rosario del Colla the situation is unique ... Initially, the project was not centred on murals. This idea was conceived by young local artists such as Andrés Quagliotti, Digna Velázquez de Garat and Mario Cuitiño. Few of the muralists were professional. The artists even had to bring their own materials. They created 54 murals but their excessively local focus reduced the museum's national and international impact, and relegated it to provincial status ... The starting idea for the murals only focused on history and identity ... Artists were free to express their history through different types of materials, and either abstract or realistic artwork ... The most important thing was to show young people the unknown history of the town and to rekindle interest in its heritage using mural art as a tool to recover identity. Not only images but also sentences, from books or invented ones, are present ... The citizens did not accept all the murals because elderly people had different ideas about the most important local events ... Sometimes the owners of the town's buildings did not agree to the murals being painted on their property'.[4]

The department of Colonia is the fourth most visited region in Uruguay, accounting for 10 per cent of the visitors to Uruguay in 2013 (almost 287,000) (Uruguayan Ministry of Tourism and Transport 2014, 37). In 2009, the Colonia Department Tourism Association presented the project 'Tourist Route: the Mural Art Museum of Rosario', proposing Rosario as part of Colonia's marketing strategy. The first step was to restore some murals and to finish others. In addition, different marketing and outreach activities were carried out, such as open workshops for local team groups (PNUMA et al. 2011: 28).

Out of these three cases, Rosario is the only one that grew in terms of visitors during 2014, even though the number of overnight stays per visitor was lower than in the coastal destinations (Uruguayan Ministry of Tourism and Transport, 2014). With appropriate action guidelines, there is a good chance of attracting more tourism to Rosario.

The town normally receives visitors during the morning, and its principal local attractions are the Mural Art Museum and the seasonal Carnival festivals. The difficulty lies in attracting visitors for several days because there is a lack of tourist services, hotels and restaurants in Rosario (PNUMA et al. 2011: 25).

From an economic point of view, if murals are considered to be a tourist attraction, then the conservation and restoration of murals must be a permanent feature. Clearly, citizens respect murals because they are part of their history, and some murals are well conserved, but others need to be restored. The problem is that the original artist cannot always carry out the restoration, so the town asks young artists with fewer resources to work on them. In 2011, some restoration work was carried out with the support of local government and businesses. First, a photographic record was made of the murals. Then, the Rosario local business association assessed the process and sent the records to the Colonia department. For their services, artists received 80 per cent of their fees from the Department. Normally, such conservation initiatives have tended to be private rather than public. The museum's intention is to conserve the best wall murals because the mural route is now well known (Figure 12.3).

However, it is difficult to add new murals because the town is too small. Some murals are not of a particularly high quality, but they have great symbolic value, such as those representing the Carnival festival, for example, 'Homenaje al Carnaval' painted by Metzen and Malán. The problem is that there is no signed agreement with building owners to conserve murals and some murals have been destroyed in order to build or renovate new buildings. This was the case of the mural 'A la gran patona', painted by the aforementioned artists, which now has a window in the middle of it. Negotiations are normally verbal, and when there is a change of ownership, the new owners do not always respect the agreement.

Conserving murals can be a contentious matter. Some people want to conserve them (especially murals with greater historic value), whilst other experts think of murals as an ephemeral art, always alive and in transition. Murals can be restored, repainted or left to perish; it depends on the point of view of the viewer. At present, restoring murals in Rosario del Colla is considered to be essential, and between 2013 and 2014, seven murals were restored. This is because of the city's approach to using them as advertising and educational tools, working together with schools and universities to

Figure 12.3 First Uruguayan historic mural art museum.
Source: Intendancy of Colonia, 2013.

showcase the history of the town. For instance, teachers at primary schools use murals to show students their local history. This also helps to reinforce a sense of local identity. In addition to this, secondary schools and the Labour University of Uruguay (UTU) use murals as a learning activity. They select particular students to receive lessons on how to produce a mural. This means more murals will be created in the future.

San Gregorio de Polanco

The third case we studied, San Gregorio de Polanco, is the most successful in terms of local economic and cultural development based on murals. 'San Gregorio was a rural town where people worked in farming and in tourism during the summer … However, the local government thought that this was not lucrative enough and that a change was needed … We are used to reinventing ourselves every day to stay alive … creating new ways to continue to be a cultural focus through murals' [Interviewee].[5]

Mural art has been used in the past to attract tourists. However, in Uruguay, this idea was new. In the mid-twentieth century, the mural movement experienced a golden period with Torres García in Montevideo and other artists but, in the 1970 and 1980s, these art expressions came to be dismissed. The Uruguayan dictatorship between 1973 and 1982 resulted in the closure of the National Fine Arts School and the exile of many artists. In this period, mural production and quality dropped drastically, except in Montevideo, where Eloy Boschi put together a group of murals at the National Harbour Administration (Martínez, Campos and Molina 2014, 1007).

The San Gregorio local government revived the movement in 1993. 'With the support of the civil society the first Open Museum of Ibero-American Art (MAAIS) was created … This had a huge media impact … Around 300 artists have participated in the San Gregorio project … Central Government, however, has never supported the project' [Interviewee].[6]

In this case, subject matter was open and the mural project grew very quickly. It started with 27 murals by local artists followed by invitations for international artists. A first national call led to the participation of 47 well-known artists in Uruguay: for example, Tola Invernizzi, Dutra Gallego, Augusto Esolk, Tomás Blezio, Gustavo Alamón, Gustavo Alsó, and the workshops of MxM, Clever Lara, Arte Mayor and Dumas Oroño. Later participation brought in international artists from different countries: Felipe Ehremberg from Mexico, Carlos Guzmán from Bolivia, Carlos Colombino from Uruguay and Marilyn Lindstrom from the United States, among others (Martínez, Campos and Molina 2014, 1008).

'The first visitors and tourists were locals: they found that the murals transformed the culture of the citizens – the colour of the town changed … The entire community got involved in the project. Local development was reflected in the increase in room rentals, food stores and laundries for visiting tourists and artists … Artists needed the support of local business for accommodation and meals … They were generally not paid for their services … Some artists offered their services to San Gregorio … It demonstrated how a cultural event can change the life of a town' [Interviewee].[7]

Nevertheless, agreements must be drawn up with house owners through a project approved by a commission, even if the owner agrees. 'There is an NGO, 'Amigos del Arte y la Cultura' (Friends of Art and Culture), that started more than 20 years ago to protect the murals … Now the open museum has around 70–80 works, not only murals but also sculptures' [Interviewee].[8] 'They also keep up the artistic quality of the museum … It is considered an honour to be invited to paint a mural' [Interviewee].[9]

The town developed considerably from a tourist and commercial (economic) point of view thanks to the open museum. In 2013, the Department of Tacuarembó received 115,946 visitors, accounting for 2.9 per cent of Uruguay's tourism (Uruguayan Ministry of Tourism and Transport 2014, 114). 'The town has a population of 3500 inhabitants but, in summer, it caters for the arrival of up to 15,000 people [Interviewee].[10] 'Tourism seasonality has changed because some tourists now visit the town in winter … In addition, the value of property has gone up because the town is a peninsula and there are a limited number of areas that can be built upon … Hotel capacity is limited (around 1200 beds) … If you have tourists, you need infrastructure to support services and San Gregorio does not have an effective Tourist Board. It takes 2 days to visit the town and the open museum…. This means there is scope to offer services like shops, hotels and restaurants' [Interviewee].[11]

In 2013, citizens and local government, with the help of the INCA Paints Company, used the twentieth anniversary of the museum (MAAIS) to develop the project 'Alfombra Integradora' (Integration Carpet) that generated considerable interest outside Uruguay, mainly in Spain. This project was only for local citizens and was a participative and colourful ground mural made by the citizens with the help of artists (each prepared a different part of the mural). It was also an inclusive initiative with some people coming from marginal backgrounds, thus creating a new experience for them and helping them to value art and respect and conserve the murals. It also reinforced their sense of identity.

Other activities took place to mark this anniversary, such as tango dancing shows in front of the mural to Gardel. In addition, 20 new murals were painted, not only by recognized artists but also by new local artists. The idea is to continue with the activity in the future, making it important to give local people space for them to express their local identity. Some artists allowed people to help them, which generated a wonderful experience for children and young people. However, the murals will need more promotional activity. There is a lack of internet promotion, for example.

The town participated in a state agreement (Uruguay Integra second phase 2012–2015) that supported the printing of some maps of the town and the open museum. Nevertheless, 'the ephemeral works will need to be recorded in some kind of publication in order to keep them in the civic memory' [Interviewee].[12] 'New generations should keep and improve the open museum to preserve their identity' [Interviewees].[13]

Conclusions

In this study, we have analysed Uruguayan murals from a different point of view than the Colonia and Montevideo examples (de Miguel et al., 2013, 33) where murals are given greater artistic value but are not always related to the identity of the Uruguayan population. It has been observed that mural art has acted as a driver for constructing identity and attracting more visitors (McCarthy, 2006, 245; Koster, 2008, 170; McAuliffe, 2012, 190). We found that in these towns, mural art has become a driver of different types of local development. From a social point of view, it has also been one of the best ways to gain a sense of identity: young people and children have got to know their culture and history thanks to mural art. From the political perspective, mural art has reflected and conserved some of the historical events of these towns. Finally, as an economic driver, murals have attracted more tourism to the area, breaking the seasonality of these places and enabling the tourism and hospitality sector to expand. However, the limited capacity of these towns only allows them to cater for the tourist demand generated by the murals. In the future, more promotion will be necessary to improve the image of these locations.

In the three towns studied, many social groups have benefited from the street muralism movement. Young people and children have had the chance to learn about their history and recognize their identity. Unemployed people have found new ways to obtain employment, and the creative sector has become a new career path for them. According to the Uruguayan Ministry of Tourism and Transport (2014, 121), in 2013, employment in the tourism sector increased by 1.7 per cent. Murals bring beauty to a location that ultimately attracts more visitors and tourists. Businesses (hotels, restaurants, shops) can generate a market not only in summer but also in winter, breaking seasonality. Schools and universities can teach their students different disciplines, from history and art to restoration, and all outdoors. As such, muralism has led to positive development of these towns.

Nevertheless, some challenges have arisen. The first one is how to give continuity to these open museums. Although, Pan de Azúcar and Rosario started as ecomuseums, they are currently exploring different themes, which could lead to a loss of identity and distinctiveness. It seems that depending on local government and the support of civil society means that the museums have little control over their activities. There is no funding from the central government. Artists give their work free, but this situation could change if other places start to offer remunerated work. The towns of Pan de Azúcar and Rosario del Colla have other natural attractions (sun and sand, cultural), but San Gregorio de Polanco is an inland town. Another important trend to note concerns the conservation and restoration of mural art. On one hand, there are a lack of professionals working on the conservation and restoration of murals. On the other, artists have different ways of conserving street art (ephemeral or permanent).

These two differing views can affect all of the mural process (which materials to select, which murals to conserve, the digitalization and registration of the murals and so on). We also observed a shortage of promotion of the open museums, particularly on the internet. As an anecdote, our research group has catalogued 514 murals in Uruguay, more than the Uruguayan government. Some murals have disappeared, and there is no registration or public recognition of them. This is despite Uruguay being one of the countries with one of the most active muralism movements. It is true that the three towns studied need sustainable development and should not force their capacity, but an appropriate promotion package still needs to be put in place to continue to develop economic activity. These towns are working with very interesting strategic plans to attract foreign visitors and tourists in a sustainable way with the support of the United Nations Program for the Environment (PNUMA et al. 2011).

To conclude, we have learned several lessons from this study: mural street art is an attractive way to show the history of a town or city in an easy and visual fashion. As public art, it is accessible to everybody, including citizens and visitors. Policymakers and governments should therefore give value to their mural art in order to enhance their tourist attractions, conserve their towns' identities, construct a sense of community and explore new sectors such as the creative industry. Negotiation with the community, and especially building owners, is crucial. Open museums will need to develop a specific strategy which has been agreed upon within the community (Young 2010, 106) and which finds ways to participate with the different stakeholders in policymaking and provide negotiated solutions. Inclusive policies could use street art to link the community to young people. While traditional arts are not so attractive to young people, street art seems to be more engaging. Through murals, schools and children have new ways to visit their city and to study different disciplines – not only in terms of history but also in terms of art.

Finally, in our case study, these murals should serve to further the promotion of Uruguay. On many occasions, this country's cultural heritage is unknown, although it has a great variety of artistic and social murals, many of which are of very high quality. Although some efforts have been made, the country is still better known for its sun and sand tourism and the UNESCO heritage town of Colonia than it is for its mural heritage.

Notes

1 Local Government, San Gregorio de Polanco, June 16, 2013.
2 Maldonado Cultural Department, Pan de Azúcar, June 14, 2013.
3 Open Museum, Pan de Azúcar, November 27, 2015.
4 Tourism Agency, Rosario del Colla, June 18, 2013.
5 Head of the Restoration Program, 25th October Cooperative (Social Development Ministry), San Gregorio de Polanco, June 16, 2013.
6 Head of the Restoration Program.
7 MAAIS Curator, San Gregorio de Polanco, June 17, 2013.
8 Festival Commission Twentieth Anniversary MAAIS (Open Museum of Ibero-American Art, San Gregorio de Polanco), San Gregorio de Polanco, June 17, 2013.
9 MAAIS Curator.
10 Head of the Restoration Programme.
11 Local Government.
12 Festival-commission Twentieth Anniversary MAAIS.
13 Social Cooperative of Women "Polanquenyas Contigo", San Gregorio de Polanco, June 16, 2013.

References

Abaza, Mona. 2013. "Walls, Segregating Downtown Cairo and the Mohammed Mahmud Street Graffiti." *Theory Culture & Society* 30: 122–39. doi: 10.1177/0263276412460062.

Aldana, Erin. 2013. "The Independent Aesthetic Urban Interventions and Other Forms of Marginal Art in Abertura Period Sao Paulo." *Third Text* 27: 229–41. doi: 10.1080/09528822.2013.772346.

Atkinson, David. 2007. "Kitsch Geographies and the Everyday Spaces of Social Memory." *Environment and Planning A* 39: 521–40. doi: 10.1068/a3866.

Banet-Weiser, Sarah. 2011. "Convergence on the Street. Rethinking the Authentic/ Commercial Binary." *Cultural Studies* 25: 641–58. doi: 10.1080/09502386.2011. 600553.

Batista, Anamarija, Szilvia Kovacs and Carina Lesky. 2013. "Planning Realities of Public Space: At Ground Level with Artistic Practice." *Zivot Umjetnosti* 92: 94–105.

Bengtsen, Peter. 2013. "Beyond the Public Art Machine: A Critical Examination of Street Art as Public Art." *Konsthistorisk Tidskrift* 82: 63–80. doi: 10.1080/00233609.2012.762804.

Berg, Bruce L. and Howard Lune. 2012. *Qualitative Research Methods for the Social Sciences*. New York: Pearson.

Bernard, Harvey Russell. 2000. *Social Research Methods: Qualitative and Quantitative Approaches*. London: Sage Publications.

Borghini, Stefania, Luca Visconti, Massimiliano Anderson and John F. Sherry Jr. 2010. "Symbiotic Postures of Commercial Advertising and Street Art." *Journal of Advertising* 39: 113–26. doi: 10.2753/joa0091-3367390308.

Coffey, Mary K. 2012. *How a Revolutionary Art Became Official Culture: Murals, Museums, and the Mexican State*. Durham, NC: Duke University Press.

Colomb, Claire. 2012. "Pushing the Urban Frontier: Temporary Uses of Space, City Marketing, and the Creative City Discourse in 2000s Berlin." *Journal of Urban Affairs* 34: 131–52. doi: 10.1111/j.1467-9906.2012.00607.x.

Crosier, Loren. 2010. *El Muralismo: El Papel de los Murales en la Lucha de los Organismos Sociales en la Ciudad de Buenos Aires*. Independent Study Project (ISP) Collection, Paper 879.

de Miguel Molina, María, Virginia Santamarina-Campos, Blanca de Miguel Molina and María del Val Segarra-Oña. 2013. "Creative Cities and Sustainable Development: Mural-Based Tourism as a Local Public Strategy." *Dirección y Organización* 50: 31–6.

Dickens, Lucke. 2010. "Pictures on Walls? Producing, Pricing and Collecting the Street Art Screen Print." *City* 14: 63–81.

Ehrenfeucht, Renia. 2014. "Art, Public Spaces, and Private Property along the Streets of New Orleans." *Urban Geography* 35: 965–79. doi: 10.1080/02723638.2014.945260.

Erickson, Bill and Marion Roberts. 1997. "Marketing Local Identity." *Journal of Urban Design* 2: 35–59.

Figini, Paolo and Laura Vici. 2012. "Off-Season Tourists and the Cultural Offer of a Mass-Tourism Destination: The Case of Rimini." *Tourism Management* 33: 825–39. doi: 10.1016/j.tourman.2011.09.005.

Foster, Christopher and Richard Heeks. 2013. "Conceptualising Inclusive Innovation: Modifying Systems of Innovation Frameworks to Understand Diffusion of

New Technology to Low-Income Consumers." *European Journal of Development Research* 25: 333–55. doi: 10.1057/ejdr.2013.7.

Garcia, Isabel. 2014. "Guernica on the Street during the Transition and First Years of Democracy." *Archivo Español De Arte* 87: 281–96. doi: 10.3989/aearte.2014.18.

Gartus, Andreas and Helmut Leder. 2014. "The White Cube of the Museum versus the Gray Cube of the Street: The Role of Context in Aesthetic Evaluations." *Psychology of Aesthetics Creativity and the Arts* 8: 311–20. doi: 10.1037/a0036847.

Grabar, Henry S. 2014. "Reclaiming the City: Changing Urban Meaning in Algiers after 1962." *Cultural Geographies* 21: 389–409. doi: 10.1177/1474474013506361.

Heidenry, Rachel. 2014. "The Murals of El Salvador: Reconstruction, Historical Memory and Whitewashing." *Public Art Dialogue* 4: 122–45.

Herrero, Luis César, José Ángel Sanz and María Devesa. 2011. "Measuring the Economic Value and Social Viability of a Cultural Festival as a Tourism Prototype." *Tourism Economics* 17: 639–53. doi: 10.5367/te.2011.0057.

Image 1. 2013. Research Project 'Social Function of the Uruguayan Muralism of the 20th Century' 2013. Artist: Pablo Parisse.

Image 2. 1998. Research Project 'Social Function of the Uruguayan Muralism of the 20th Century' 2013. Artist: Andrés Quagliotti.

Irvine, Martin. 2011. *The Work on the Street: Street Art and Visual Culture. Handbook of Visual Culture.* London: Palgrave Macmillan.

Iveson, Kurt. 2013. "Cities within the City: Do-It-Yourself Urbanism and the Right to the City." *International Journal of Urban and Regional Research* 37: 941–56. doi: 10.1111/1468-2427.12053.

Jagodzinska, Katarzyna. 2011. "A Museum Open to the Street." *Riha Journal* 24: 1–19.

Koster, Rhonda L.P. 2008. "Mural-Based Tourism as a Strategy for Rural Community Economic Development." In *Advances in Culture, Tourism and Hospitality Research*, edited by Arch G. Woodside, 153–292. Bingley: Emerald.

Martínez Carazo, Eva, Virginia Santamarina Campos and María de Miguel Molina. 2014. "Los procesos de regionalización del muralismo uruguayo como agente generador de turismo cultural sostenible." In *Emerge 2014 Jornada de Investigación Emergente de Conservación y Restauración del Patrimonio*, edited by Victoria Vivancos Ramón, M. Teresa Doménech Carbo, Mercedes Sánchez Pons and M. Julia Osca Pons, 1005–14. Valencia: Editorial Universidad Politécnica de Valencia.

McAuliffe, Cameron. 2012. "Graffiti or Street Art? Negotiating the Moral Geographies of the Creative City." *Journal of Urban Affairs* 34: 189–206. doi: 10.1111/j.1467-9906.2012.00610.x.

McCarthy, John. 2006. "Regeneration of Cultural Quarters: Public Art for Place Image or Place Identity?" *Journal of Urban Design* 11: 243–62.

McClinchey, Kelley A. 2008. "Urban Ethnic Festivals, Neighborhoods, and the Multiple Realities of Marketing Place." *Journal of Travel & Tourism Marketing* 25: 251–64. doi: 10.1080/10548400802508309.

Metaxas, Theodore. 2009. "Place Marketing, Strategic Planning and Competitiveness: The Case of Malta." *European Planning Studies* 17: 1357–78. doi: 10.1080/09654310903053539.

Moctezuma, Pedro. 2001. "Community-Based Organization and Participatory Planning in South-East Mexico City." *Environment and Urbanization* 13: 117–33. doi: 10.1177/095624780101300209.

Monto, Martin A., Janna Machalek and Terri L. Anderson. 2013. "Boys Doing Art: The Construction of Outlaw Masculinity in a Portland, Oregon, Graffiti Crew." *Journal of Contemporary Ethnography* 42: 259–90. doi: 10.1177/0891241612465981.

Morgan, George. 2012. "Urban Renewal and the Creative Underclass: Aboriginal Youth Subcultures in Sydney's Redfern-Waterloo." *Journal of Urban Affairs* 34: 207–22. doi: 10.1111/j.1467-9906.2012.00611.x.

Munro, Iain and Silvia Jordan. 2013. "'Living Space' at the Edinburgh Festival Fringe: Spatial Tactics and the Politics of Smooth Space." *Human Relations* 66: 1497–525. doi: 10.1177/0018726713480411.

Plaza, Beatriz. 2008. "On Some Challenges and Conditions for the Guggenheim Museum Bilbao to be an Effective Economic Re-activator." *International Journal of Urban and Regional Research* 32: 506–17. doi: 10.1111/j.1468-2427.2008.00796.x.

PNUMA, Intendencia de Colonia, and Centro Interdisciplinario de Estudios sobre el Desarrollo, Uruguay (CIEDUR). 2011. *Global Environment Outlook: GEO Rosario*. Montevideo.

Pressenda, Paola and Maria Luisa Sturani. 2007. "Open-Air Museums and Eco-museums as Tools for Landscape Management: Some Italian Experience." In *European Landscapes and Lifestyles: The Mediterranean and Beyond*, edited by Zoran Roca, 331–44. Lisboa: Ediçoes Universitarias Lusofonas.

Riggle, Nicholas Alden. 2010. "Street Art: The Transfiguration of the Common-places." *Journal of Aesthetics and Art Criticism* 68: 243–57.

Rolston, Bill. 2012. "Re-imaging: Mural Painting and the State in Northern Ireland." *International Journal of Cultural Studies* 15: 447–66. doi: 10.1177/1367877912451810.

Santamarina Campos, Virginia, Ángela Carabal Montagud, María de Miguel Molina and M.L. Martínez Bazán. 2015. "Societal and Environmental Sustainable Tourism Development. New Ways of Activation, Delivery and Diffusion of the Contemporary Uruguayan Muralism." In *Conservation Issues in Modern and Contemporary Murals*, edited by Mercedes Sánchez, Will Shank and Laura Fuster, 489–512. Newcastle upon Tyne: Cambridge Scholars Publishing.

Saunders, Angharad. 2013. "Recovering the Street: Relocalising Urban Geography." *Journal of Geography in Higher Education* 37: 536–46. doi: 10.1080/03098265.2013.801069.

Sierra Bravo, Restituto. 2001. *Técnicas de Investigación Social*. Madrid: Thomson.

Stern, Pamela and Peter V. Hall. 2010. "Historical Limits: Narrowing Possibilities in 'Ontario's Most Historic Town'." *Canadian Geographer-Geographe Canadien* 54: 209–27. doi: 10.1111/j.1541-0064.2009.00296.x.

Strong, Mary. 1998. "Big Pictures: Ethnic Identity as a Mutable Concept in New York City Street Murals." *Visual Anthropology* 11: 9–54.

Taylor, John P. 2001. "Authenticity and Sincerity in Tourism." *Annals of Tourism Research* 28: 7–26.

UNCTAD. 2014. "Innovation Policy Tools for Inclusive Development." Note by the United Nations Conference on Trade and Development Secretariat, Trade and Development Board Investment, Enterprise and Development Commission, Sixth session, Geneva, 28 April to 2 May 2014, Item 5 of the provisional agenda.

Uruguayan Ministry of Tourism and Transport. 2014. *Anuario 2014. Estadísticas de Turismo*. Montevideo: Uruguay Natural.

Visconti, Luca M., John F. Sherry, Stefania Borghini and Laurel Anderson. 2010. "Street Art, Sweet Art? Reclaiming the 'Public' in Public Place." *Journal of Consumer Research* 37: 511–29. doi: 10.1086/652731.

Weber, Robert Philip. 1990. *Basic Content Analysis.* Newbury Park, CA: Sage University Paper.

Young, Alison. 2010. "Negotiated Consent or Zero Tolerance? Responding to Graffiti and Street Art in Melbourne." *City* 14: 99–114.

———. 2012. "Criminal Images: The Affective Judgment of Graffiti and Street Art." *Crime Media Culture* 8: 297–314. doi: 10.1177/1741659012443232.

Zorach, Rebecca. 2011. "Art & Soul: An Experimental Friendship between the Street and a Museum." *Art Journal* 70: 66–87.

Part V
Northern Ireland

Part V

Northern Ireland

13 State intervention in re-imaging Northern Ireland's political murals

Implications for tourism and the communities

Maria T. Simone-Charteris

Introduction

The Troubles refers to the 30-year-long political conflict in Northern Ireland that started in 1968 and ended with the Good Friday Agreement in 1998. At the heart of the conflict lay two mutually exclusive visions of national identity and national belonging: that of Loyalists, whose goal was to remain part of the United Kingdom, and that of Nationalists, whose goal was to become part of the Republic of Ireland. During the Troubles, over 3,600 people were killed and circa 50,000 were injured (BBC 2015b). The Troubles are well documented by political murals and other visual displays. Murals have long occupied a unique place in Northern Ireland's cultural landscape. Mural painting in the Loyalist community dates back to a century ago when the first mural representing William of Orange, or 'King Billy' as he was popularly known, was painted in 1908, celebrating his defeat of the Catholic King James II at the Battle of the Boyne in 1690. It was not until the Anglo-Irish Agreement of 1985, which gave Dublin an input into Northern Irish affairs and legalized the tricolour flag as well as the Irish language, that murals became increasingly filled with paramilitary emblems and imagery. For many years, Republicans did not paint murals partly due to legislation that prevented any ostensible representations of Nationalist politics and culture. This, however, changed with the hunger strike of 1981, when many images appeared on walls in Nationalist areas in support of the hunger strikers' demand for political status. Republican mural painting later expanded to address a wide range of political issues and themes including Ireland's Celtic heritage and comparisons with other divided societies, such as the anti-Apartheid movement in South Africa (White 2011).

According to Jarman (1997, 1998), murals have been and continue to be used by the two main communities, Unionist and Republican, forming the Northern Ireland society as self-reinforcing layers of identity and declarations of territoriality. This view is supported by White (2011), who argues that murals are instrumentalized by political and paramilitary groups as propaganda tools with the aim of gaining legitimacy and winning support by expressing aspirations in a way that resonates with the communities, thus becoming markers of cultural identity. Numerous murals are deeply embedded within communities. This allows for a degree of control over the image and its meaning with access to murals being of a restricted spatial nature, indicating they were primarily aimed at a local audience.

Murals have become popular with the media that use them to convey a sense of distinctiveness, place and authenticity. However, they have become even more popular with tourists, especially since Simon Calder (a well-recognized travel writer) who, writing in *The Independent* back in 2007, referred to them as the UK's top attraction (Simone-Charteris and Boyd 2010). Lisle argues that murals in Northern Ireland have become part of a global tourist circuit that 'creates the greatest scope for disrupting the notion that the murals simply reinforce an "ideological struggle" between two homogeneous communities' (2006, 43). Indeed, the fact that tourists constitute a third audience for murals in Northern Ireland and that tourists transcend the local territoriality that murals have been used for in the past is particularly relevant with regard to the cross-community potential of tourism in the Province (Simone-Charteris and Boyd 2010; Wiedenhoft Murphy 2010).

Despite the increasing popularity of murals, their potential for cross-community collaboration and the contribution of political tourism towards Northern Ireland's economy, various government-funded initiatives have been launched – especially since 2007 – aimed at re-imaging the Province. The murals re-imaging initiatives involve the replacement of the most political murals with more neutral and non-contentious paintings or, in some cases, images printed on Perspex or aluminum and attached to walls (Rolston 2010, 2012). This is a dangerous process. What has kept murals alive for decades has been the desire of local people to articulate their politics and identity on the walls. The sanitization of murals could remove that function, taking away with it the burning incentive for local communities to paint murals. Political murals allow the working-class communities to express their culture and ethos and to remember the past. Moreover, political murals are Northern Ireland's unique selling point and the reason why a percentage of tourists visit the region, especially Belfast and Londonderry/Derry (L/Derry), whose name changes according to the interlocutor's own identity and politics. Hence, the de-politicization of murals could have serious consequences for the Province. This chapter investigates the intervention of the State to reimage political murals in Northern Ireland and explores the implications this can have on the working-class communities as well as tourism in the Province.

The State's attitude towards murals over time

The government agencies in Northern Ireland (hereafter referred to as the State and the statutory authorities) have always opposed the representation of politics through art. According to Rolston (2012), artists who made reference to the political scene in their works during the Troubles were seen to be siding with one or the other terrorist groups and engaging in propaganda. This view dominated the art establishment represented by the Arts Council, the Ulster Museum, and the Arts College. The art establishment did not consider muralists as artists and because art denied the conflict, muralists did not want to be referred to as artists either, seeing themselves as political activists instead, who used the paintbrush in the same way as others marched, picketed or carried weapons (Conway 2010). Interestingly, while the Loyalist paramilitary groups saw themselves as an extension of the British army due to their shared fight against Nationalists, and imitated the British army in their structures of battalions and companies, the British security forces did not see them this way and merely used Loyalists in their war against Republicans and Nationalists (Rolston 2005). As a consequence, the British security forces did not consider the Loyalist murals as an expression of civic responsibility as believed by the Loyalist paramilitary groups; however, they did not oppose them as harshly as they did Nationalist murals as they believed that the main political threat emanated from Republicans. It was Republican murals that the State's forces paint-bombed at night. And it was a Republican teenager, Michael McCartan, who was shot dead while he painted a Republican slogan on a wall in Belfast in 1980 (apparently the policeman who shot the teenager mistook the paintbrush the teenager was holding for a gun) (Rolston 2012).

The State had launched two initiatives, 'Spruce Up' Belfast in 1977 and 'Brighten Up Belfast' in the late 1980s, aimed at transforming the murals into an anti-violent urban landscape. 'Spruce Up' Belfast was the product of collaboration between the Northern Ireland Office (NIO), local arts councils and students from the Belfast College of Art and Design. The students were to produce politically neutral murals that were reflective of local identity (Romens 2007) and had to avoid 'hot topics' that could 'ignite sectarian division [or] prompt demands for increased social services' (Lisle 2006, 38). Most murals created under this programme did not reflect the communities and their identities. Some, for example, depicted circus and jungle scenes that were even considered insulting by the communities. By 1981, the communities had stopped applying for the programme. Similar mistakes were made with the 'Brighten Up Belfast' campaign. Many of the murals in this campaign represented images of children playing, cartoon characters and scenes of rural bliss in the middle of urban decay: they did not represent the sentiments of the communities. Needless to say, most of the murals produced by the two projects no longer exist as they were considered irrelevant to the communities and therefore not worthy of preservation (Romens 2007).

State opposition to the murals increased even more with the ensuing Peace Process after the Good Friday Agreement of 1998. After the signing of the Agreement, on their own initiative and without government funding, Republicans removed the guns and hooded men from their murals. The Loyalist murals, however, did not undergo the same transformation and continued to display belligerent themes. There were several reasons for this. Soon after the hunger strikes of the mid-1970s, Republicans had started to incorporate other themes in their murals linked to the Irish culture such as the Catholic Church, Gaelic sport music and dancing and support for other divided societies (Jarman 1997). Loyalists, unlike Republicans, did not have a wide range of themes to choose from. Secondly, Loyalists saw the agreement almost as a betrayal on behalf of the State that they had considered themselves an extension of. Therefore, for a while they were ambivalent towards the Peace Process (Rolston 2010, 2012) and this was reflected in the themes of their murals. Loyalists' unwillingness to remove bellicose symbols from their murals was seen as anachronistic by the statutory authorities as well as dangerous as, to a certain extent, it displayed a lack of commitment to the Peace Process. Hence, between 2002 and 2007, a number of initiatives were launched aimed at replacing the most offensive murals and symbols. The initiatives included:

- the 2004 Community Cohesion Unit's (CCU) work with local groups to remove contentious flags and murals (the Unit was established by the first power-sharing Executive as a means to achieve 'A Shared Future' strategy);
- the 2004 Arts Council of Northern Ireland's Private Mural project that led to the painting of 15 new murals across Belfast;
- the 2006 Belfast City Council's Greatest Belfast Mural Project (part of the 'Creating a Brighter Belfast' priority contained in the council's corporate plan for 2006/2007), set up to negotiate mural replacement with the communities (Belfast City Council 2006; Rolston 2012);
- the 2007 'Re-imaging Communities Programme', a £3.3 million government scheme designed to tackle 'the visible signs of sectarianism and racism in Northern Ireland communities, with a particular emphasis on the replacement of existing paramilitary murals and other items with new and more positive imagery' (Independent Research Solutions 2009, 2).

The 2007 'Re-imaging Communities Programme' was the most widespread of the initiatives. According to Rolston (2010, 298), one of the main criticisms directed at the programme is that '... the purpose of the programme is not just the replacement of the most offensive murals with other murals but the removal of politics from the murals altogether'. Rolston's (2010) view is echoed by the muralists themselves. For instance, according to Tom Kelly, one of the Bogside artists from L/Derry, the programme is 'a ploy to take politics out of the murals' and to build another artificial space to cover the ongoing distrust between the two communities while, according to Republican and former IRA member Danny Devenny, the statutory authorities 'try to paint over the dirty scars of war by fading down the political desires of the communities and their identity as well' (Rapp and Rhomberg 2012, 474).

The latest re-imaging initiative, 'Building Peace through the Arts – Re-Imaging Communities' was launched in 2013. The £3.125 million programme followed on from the 'Re-imaging Communities Programme (2007–2009)'. It was launched to support the delivery of 80–100 community-based projects across Northern Ireland and the southern border counties over two years, offering grants of up to £15,000 for small projects and up to £50,000 for larger-scale projects. The aim of the programme, funded by the European Union's PEACE III Programme, the Arts Council of Northern Ireland and the International Fund for Ireland, was to enable artists to work with local groups to create vibrant and attractive public spaces through the use of creative arts (Arts Council of Northern Ireland 2013). It is still too early to measure the success of this initiative as the programme has only recently ended (2015). In the near future, it will be interesting to appraise whether it has been more effective in gaining the support of the communities whose quality of life it was supposed to improve and whether 'renewal' and 'regeneration' has translated once again in the total removal of politics and community storytelling from public spaces.

The statutory authorities' commitment to create a neutral social space, which is neither Catholic nor Protestant, a sort of 'Third Space' that could be interpreted as being parallel to the desire to cater to the third audience (tourists), is evident in the total lack of references to the Troubles in the form of political murals or memorials to the dead in Belfast's city centre – the theatre of many tragic incidents between 1971 and 1998 such as Bloody Friday when 23 car bombs were driven into the city resulting in a huge loss of life on July 21, 1972 (BBC 2015a). Instead, the focus has been on developing the Titanic Quarter Project in East Belfast to commemorate the Titanic and the city's famous shipbuilding past. At the time of its construction at the Harland and Wolff shipyard, RMS Titanic was the biggest ship on earth. Unfortunately though, four days into its maiden voyage from Southampton, England to New York, USA on April 14, 1912, the 'unsinkable' ship hit an iceberg and sunk to the bottom of the Atlantic Ocean taking the lives of 1,500 people (History of the Titanic 2015). The Titanic is seen by the statutory authorities as a new brand that has the potential to bridge the gap between Catholics and Protestants (although this is questionable as the majority of shipyards workers were Protestant and the shipyard itself is located on the edge of a Protestant area, the Woodstock neighborhood). To this end, a completely new district has been built in East Belfast where hundreds of new apartments and offices have been erected as new 'shared space' named Titanic Quarter (Rapp and Rhomberg 2012). In a bid to conceal the capital city's dark past, the State has also prioritized the development of 'literary Belfast', 'factory Belfast' and 'luxury Belfast' in and around the city centre. Luxury Belfast, in particular, focuses upon the development of a strong evening economy based on upscale restaurants, clubs and boutiques that come to life after the workday (Wiedenhoft Murphy 2010).

Public sector tourism agencies adopted a similar strategy. Up to 7 to 8 years ago, Tourism Northern Ireland (Tourism NI), the official tourism organization, did not mention the political murals or the political tours offered by several private sector companies on its visitor website (discovernorthernireland.com) or on any official tourism promotional material. However, it now devotes a section of the website to murals that starts with the sentence:

> The Murals of Belfast and Londonderry are fast becoming a must-see experience for visitors. These pieces of public art ... provide the visitor with an insight into the culture and traditions of Northern Ireland. ... Many visitors come to Northern Ireland to view the Political Murals which are a big part of our history.
>
> (Discover Northern Ireland 2014)

Despite finally acknowledging that murals are a draw for tourists, most of the images of murals on the website avoid direct reference to politico-sectarian themes and paramilitary groups and instead focus on the broader history of Northern Ireland with reference to figures such as CS Lewis, George Best, and Ulster's contribution to World War I (Hill and White 2011) (see Figure 13.1).

It took the Art Council until the end of the first decade of the new millennium to belatedly recognize the contribution of artists who had addressed the Troubles in their works to the art scene in Northern Ireland and to gather some of their work together in a 'Troubles Archive' (Rolston 2012). The fact that government agencies are finally recognizing the value and potential of political murals and other political symbols obviously denotes a sea change in the official attitude towards this peculiar manifestation of cultural identity and beliefs. However, some politicians and other public figures are still firmly opposed to murals. For instance, before the Giro d'Italia was held in Northern Ireland in May 2014, the main political parties had agreed to take down election posters. However, Alliance MLA Anna Lo went one step further by stating the following: 'The very same arguments that politicians have been making about taking down election posters to showcase Northern Ireland and our beautiful scenery, also apply to flags and paramilitary murals' (BBC 2014). She added:

> Funding will be made available in towns along the route to improve the image of eyesores such as derelict buildings but I have a bigger problem with images of paramilitary gunmen. Do we really want these images to be visible on the route when millions of people will be watching the race on television?
>
> (BBC 2014)

Anna Lo's comments generated racist insults by Loyalists and criticism by senior Democratic Unionist Party (DUP) members. This goes to show just how important political symbols are to the communities that they represent.

Figure 13.1 Mural of C S Lewis on East Belfast's Ballymacarrett Road.
Source: Simone-Charteris and Boyd (2010).

The effects of re-imaging initiatives on the communities

Mural painting was a spontaneous process that grew out of the communities from 1908 onwards and served a political purpose: it articulated the hopes and fears, the political identity and ideology of people in those communities (Rolston 2012). According to Jarman (1998), all murals create a new type of space: they redefine ordinary public space as politicized space and help to reclaim it for the community. As a consequence, murals are often revered as a source of community pride and offer a sense of inclusion and membership to the locals. Together with flags and curbstones painted in either the colours of the British Union flag or the Irish tricolor, they are declarations of territoriality that reinforce the sectarian division of space (Romens 2007).

To their respective communities, murals, flags and other symbols are expressions of and creators of community solidarity, but at the same time they send messages of exclusion and intimidation to outsiders (Lisle 2006). These are symbols that speak to the community about what they have experienced. They tell the world, as well as the communities, that although they are, in the words of one mural, 'under siege', they are defiant and determined to remain true to their identities. To suggest or, even worse, to demand that the Catholics who live in Republican areas remove all the tricolours and Celtic crosses, or the Protestants who live in Loyalist areas remove all their

Union flags and crowns would be not only to call into question the identity of the living, but would also be considered as an insult to the memory of their dead and a denial of the suffering experienced by the communities over circa 30 years of conflict. The forceful removal of symbols before the community is ready to have them removed is, according to Rolston (2010), an act of violence against the identity and memory of the community and a possible source of trauma to that community.

During and in the aftermath of the Peace Process, the State authorities have advocated the transformation and even the removal of the most politically oriented murals because the paintings have been judged to be anachronistic; they are believed to be a constant reminder of the past which fans the flames of hatred, thus perpetuating an endless struggle. To some political commentators, murals, banners and slogans are not simply a cultural expression of identity but a form of recruitment to conflict. However, to hold this view is to miss the dynamic nature of symbolism (Rolston 2010). According to Rolston (2010, 291):

> [I]t is the need for current meaning and identity which creates the symbol and the ritual, not the symbol or ritual which of itself automatically engenders meaning. Thus, despite their apparent rigidity, the symbols which represent the past can be interpreted in different ways by different groups, or reinterpreted differently by the same group at different times.

This view is shared by Long (2015, 161) who states that 'symbols are dynamic and fluid, with changing meanings, functions, and impacts'. For example, the image of the best-known Republican hunger striker, Bobby Sands, continues to be used in Sinn Féin's promotional literature and representations, and a larger-than-life mural of the political prisoner dominates the side of the Sinn Féin headquarters in Belfast (see Figure 13.2). Sinn Féin is a nationalist political party present in both Northern Ireland and the Republic of Ireland (ROI), representing Republicans/Roman Catholics who want to achieve a united Ireland. The party, led by Gerry Adams since 1983, is commonly regarded as the political wing of the Irish Republican Army (IRA). The IRA formed to defend the Roman Catholic communities living in Northern Ireland who were being the victims of increased sectarian violence in the late 1960s following the Anglo-Irish Treaty of 1921 that partitioned the Island of Ireland in two: the Irish Free State (that later became the ROI) (comprising 26 counties) and Northern Ireland, also referred to as the Province of Ulster (comprising 6 counties), that continued to be part of the United Kingdom (Britannica 2016). The party that portrays Bobby Sands' image is very different from the one Bobby Sands knew when he died in 1981. In actual fact, his election as a Westminster MP at the height of his hunger strike was instrumental to the transformation of the party, along with the Peace Process, and the consequent disbandment of the party's former armed ally, the IRA. Some may see the use of Bobby Sands' image not only as anachronistic but even as opportunistic and as a betrayal of the ideals for which he fought and died for; it is highly unlikely that he would have taken a seat in a devolved parliament. The reference to Bobby Sands, however, plays a crucial role as it allows the Republican movement to link its present political stance to the past. The traditional symbolism helps 'to steady nerves'; it says to the community 'trust us; we have not given up on our ideals despite the peace process' (Rolston 2010). In addition, according to Long (2015, 161), it is important to consider that 'the intended meaning by the user of [the] symbol is not necessarily understood by the receiver, resulting in 'misinterpretation'; the author adds that 'the meaning depends on what is going on around it, its social, historical, and cultural context'. It follows that some symbols may appear anachronistic and unchanged but, in reality, they speak to identities that have changed or are changing in the transition from conflict to post-conflict Province. Thus, symbols can be the bridge between the past and the future that makes the present tolerable (Rolston 2010); they aid change in a way that no outside organization or government-funded re-imaging initiative could ever do. On the other hand, 'symbols are political in that who gets to do the constructing and interpreting of meaning is a matter of power' (Long 2015, 161). For instance, The Harland and Wolff shipyard in Belfast where RMS Titanic was built is located in East Belfast, an area known as a stronghold of loyalism as mentioned earlier on in the chapter. However, the planners of the new Titanic Quarter located in this area of the city have gone to great lengths to convey an identity which differs from the traditional unionist identity. They have chosen to convey a new and neutral identity in an effort to attract outside visitors. This approach ignores community needs and tensions. On the one hand, the negative perception of the Nationalist communities towards the shipyard's history of discrimination is ignored. On the other hand, the link to the Loyalist community is truncated. This policy of 'neutrality' can stir the feeling of alienation and marginalization among the local communities (Etchart 2008). It follows that it is essential that communities change their symbolism at their own pace for the changes to be durable and meaningful as opposed to being superficial attempts to 'aestheticize' an area or site (Hill and White 2011).

Another aspect that needs to be taken into consideration when discussing the effects of political murals' re-imaging on the communities is that of collective memory and how history is narrated. According to Skinner (2014, 86) 'telling a story also means not telling other stories'; the author goes on to say that 'storytelling is a political act depending upon who tells the story, whose story it is and what words and terms are used' (2014, 87). History is adapted to the needs of select groups in society and 'becomes an object of appropriation' (Etchart 2008, 34). The issue of storytelling is also discussed by Rolston (2010), who believes that some 'memory entrepreneurs' are more influential than others in determining official memory and denying subaltern memories. Simply put, history tends to be told from the perspective

Figure 13.2 Mural of Bobby Sands on Belfast's Republican Falls Road.
Source: Simone-Charteris and Boyd (2010).

of people in positions of power. This results in a dialectical struggle between the official memories of the powerful who try to be hegemonic, and the alternative narratives of other groups in society, particularly those who have been marginalized and oppressed. The end of conflict, though, is an opportunity for less powerful groups to affirm their memories too. At this stage, they are even less reluctant to let go of their old beliefs and symbols as these were the resource they drew upon to survive psychologically during the conflict. Therefore, government-funded re-imaging initiatives can be seen as seeking to assert the authority of the government over the visual environment of the communities (Hill and White 2011); they are a top-down approach that once again tries to impose a certain version of history. The importance for the communities to finally be able to narrate their version of history was highlighted by Séamus Creagh, the Coordinator for Coiste, an ex-prisoners organization that delivers Republican political walking tours in Belfast who was interviewed by the author. Creagh stated that:

> They [ex-prisoners] are telling their story, which is very important to us. Everyone's told our story. We can hopefully get people from other parts of the world to understand where we come from, that we don't all have horns, that we are just ordinary people who have a commitment to a political cause. And we need not apologize for that.
>
> (Séamus Creagh, Belfast, 2008, personal communication)

He also added that ex-prisoners were willing to collaborate with other organizations from both the public and private sectors in order to develop political tourism in Northern Ireland; however, as another tour guide from Coiste, Seamus Kelly, stated: 'no-one will tell us how to deliver that story. We have our side of it and we will stick to it' (Seamus Kelly, Belfast, 2008, personal communication).

The effects of re-imaging initiatives on tourism

Not only can government-funded re-imaging initiatives affect the communities' sense of identity and belonging, but they can also have serious implications for tourism. A particular form of niche tourism that has grown significantly in the last ten to fifteen years is 'dark tourism' which is the tourism of sites of death and tragedy. Different definitions of dark tourism exist depending on whether the focus is on motivation (demand) or attractions and sites (supply). According to Foley and Lennon (1996, 198) 'dark tourism' relates to 'the presentation and consumption (by visitors) of real and commodified death and disaster sites'. Tarlow adds a temporal dimension to Foley and Lennon's definition and identifies dark tourism as 'visitations to places where tragedies or historically noteworthy death has occurred and that continue to impact our lives' (2005, 48). Both definitions are quite general and lack attention to motivation. In contrast, Seaton (1999, 240) defines thanatourism, which is another word for dark tourism, as 'travel to a location wholly, or partially, motivated by the desire for actual or symbolic encounters with death, particularly, but not exclusively, violent death'. Because dark tourism is a broad concept encompassing numerous types of attractions and exhibitions, some authors have attempted to divide it into smaller more specific subcategories including battlefield tourism, cemetery tourism, disaster tourism, ghost tourism, holocaust tourism, prison tourism, suicide tourism and doomsday tourism (visits to places which are under threat) (Trotta 2006). This author considers 'political tourism' as a further subcategory of dark tourism and defines it as the tourism of places, people, and events associated with the politics of a destination. Interestingly, murals tourism, which is the topic of this book, could be regarded either as a micro niche of political tourism (if the content of the murals was political) or as a form of niche tourism per se, as murals can convey many different topics and contents. Increasingly, several post-conflict destinations and even destinations where conflict is still ongoing such as Cyprus, South Africa, Germany, the Basque Country, Israel and Palestine are offering political tourism as part of their tourism product portfolio (Alternative Tours 2016; Anglia Tours 2016; Political Tours 2016). Northern Ireland is no exception. Political tourism attractions which are popular with visitors to Northern Ireland include:

- the murals in Belfast and L/Derry;
- the Museum of Free Derry in L/Derry that focuses on the civil rights era of the 1960s and the early Troubles era of the 1970s;

- the Apprentice Boys of Derry Memorial Hall that commemorates the siege of L/Derry that took place in 1688–1689;
- the Hands Across the Divide Monument in L/Derry that symbolizes the spirit of reconciliation between the Loyalist and Republican communities;
- the Peace Walls in Belfast that separate Loyalist and Republican neighborhoods;
- the Orange Order Parades that take place across Northern Ireland in July and celebrate the victory of Protestant William III over Catholic King James II at the Battle of the Boyne in 1690;
- and numerous small memorials and gardens cemeteries found in and around Belfast and L/Derry that are tied to certain events and people such as Milltown Cemetery where Bobby Sands and other hunger strikers are buried who died in the early 1980s trying to be recognized as political prisoners.

Even churches in Northern Ireland often echo political views and have become popular with political tourists:

- St. Columb's Cathedral in L/Derry that contains relics from the Great Siege of Derry;
- St. Anne's Cathedral in Belfast that contains the tomb of Sir Edward Carson, leader of the Ulster Unionist Party (UUP);
- the Chapel of Unity inside St Anne's Cathedral where a weekly healing service is held for groups of individuals from across the sectarian divide, who meet and pray together for more mutual understanding (Simone-Charteris, Boyd and Burns 2013).

Political murals in Belfast and L/Derry, in particular, have become popular not only with the media, which use them to convey a sense of distinctiveness, place and authenticity, but also with tourists who see them as a *metériel* remnant of the conflict, a legacy of the last thirty years, a reminder of a past that should not be forgotten or concealed (McCormick and Jarman 2005; Tripwolf 2014). The popularity of murals with visitors to Northern Ireland is confirmed by TripAdvisor where West Belfast Mural Tours ranked second out of 89 tours and activities in Belfast on February, 7th 2016. The reviews of the tours were very positive, with 648 reviewers ranking them as 'excellent' and 28 as 'very good' (TripAdvisor 2016).

The popularity of murals with tourists could be explained in terms of shared identity among an imagined community, a concept discussed by Jarman (1998), Chronis (2005) and Lisle (2006). According to Jarman (1998), once a mural has been painted, neither community can control its subsequent interpretations. Therefore, murals go beyond their context in time and space. Jarman's (1998) view is shared by Lisle (2006), who believes that murals activate meanings that transcend community boundaries. Jarman's

(1998) and Lisle's (2006) views are in line with Chronis' (2005) theory that visitors at dark heritage attractions become linked to known and unknown individuals and their stories of human suffering through empathy, not only through family ties and state identification. This way, isolated accounts of death and destruction are transformed into a community story: a story that belongs to a group rather than to a person, a sort of imagined community.

Richter (1983) has suggested that specific tours and itineraries might be viewed as representing the ideological values of tourists and their political beliefs and convictions. In her view, people visiting countries experiencing political instability are themselves 'politically natured'. If the reason of their visit is empathy with one of the sides involved in the conflict, this might turn into a chance to reflect about one's beliefs and the situation back home and might generate new insights or even a change of viewpoint. An example of an attraction in Northern Ireland where this process of internal transformation happens is the Museum of Free Derry in L/Derry mentioned earlier, which is located in Glenfada Park, a run-down working class estate in the Bogside area. The Museum's location is strategic as it is central to most of the events covered by the displays. The Battle of the Bogside, a very large riot that took place during August 12 14, 1969, took place only yards away. The fighting was between the Apprentice Boys, a L/Derry-based Protestant group that ignored police warnings and marched dangerously close to the Bogside, a Catholic stronghold, the Bogside residents and the Royal Ulster Constabulary (RUC) (the police) that had been called to break up the fight. The fight resulted in 43 injured policemen, and many young, elderly and infirm residents being badly affected by tear gas (Poole and Llewellyn 2016). In addition, the civilians who were injured or killed during Bloody Sunday did so in front of the building which houses the museum (The Museum of Free Derry 2005). Bloody Sunday took place on January 30, 1972 when a civil rights demonstration ended with the shooting dead of 13 civilians by the British Army. The protesters were prevented from entering the city centre by the British Army so moved to the Bogside to attend a rally. Some young men began throwing stones at soldiers who moved into the Bogside in an arrest operation. During the next 30 minutes, the soldiers shot dead 13 men and injured a further 13 people mainly by single shots to the head and trunk. Bloody Sunday increased nationalist hostility towards the British Army and exacerbated the conflict, especially since many of the victims were shot while fleeing from the soldiers or while trying to help the wounded (CAIN 2015). The museum is staffed by community members who participated in various civil rights demonstrations and whose relatives were killed on Bloody Sunday and political tours depart from the museum conducted by former prisoners who have first-hand knowledge of the events. In addition, the museum is surrounded by the Bogside artists' political murals that are attracting large numbers of tourists. It follows that the Museum of Free Derry is instrumental in reaffirming its domestic visitors' national identity as well as its international visitors' identity as they identify themselves with the victims of the conflict and see themselves as part of an imagined community through an emphatic process. This emphatic process allows the visitors to become absorbed in the stories of the victims, make the victims' experiences their own, associate the victims' experiences with their own and ultimately fully understand through a cognitive process the victims' stories (Marcia 1990). This explains the Museum's engagement in collaborative projects with Robben Island Museum in South Africa, with a number of concentration camps in Poland and the Czech Republic, and the fact that visitors regularly come from the Basque Country, Catalonia and Palestine due to parallels being drawn by the politics of these international communities (Simone-Charteris and Boyd 2010).

A further factor that should not be underestimated when discussing political murals and tourism in the Province is their contribution towards the Peace Process. In fact, far from being anachronistic and contributing to the perpetuation of hatred and violence among the communities as maintained by some political commentators, political tours are providing an incentive for members of the two main communities forming the Northern Ireland society to work together. For example, Republican ex-prisoners' organization Coiste and Loyalist ex-prisoners' organization Epic are coordinating their political walking tours of Belfast with Epic Tours' of the Protestant Shankill Road starting at 09.30am and Coiste's tours of the Catholic Falls Road taking over at 11.00 am (Coiste 2014); the Museum of Free Derry (Republican) is managed by a cross-community board and is collaborating with the Apprentice Boys Memorial Hall (Unionist); and Kabosh, an independent theatre company resident in the Cathedral Quarter of Belfast, is involved in a number of projects with both Republican organizations (e.g. Coiste and Taxi-Trax) and Unionist organizations (e.g. the Spectrum Centre; Shankill Area Social History group (SASH)) in Belfast such as:

- 'The West Awakes' involving actors dressed in period costume meeting tour groups at different locations on the Falls Road and recounting their experience of life in the past;
- 'Shankill Stories', a social history tour with short theatre pieces inspired by stories and locations along this historic road;
- and 'Those You Pass on the Street', a drama that explores the complexities of dealing with the legacy of the conflict staged in the Skainos (in Protestant East Belfast), Culturlainn (in Catholic West Belfast) and the Mac in the city centre (McFetridge 2014).

Moreover, several taxi companies in Belfast, as well as organizations offering political walking tours in L/Derry, are planning to collaborate with their former foes to provide visitors with a more comprehensive view of the conflict (Simone-Charteris and Boyd 2010). It follows that political tourism contributes towards the Peace Process and, in so doing, also benefits the local economy and especially the communities that are most affected by the legacy of the Troubles. The most political areas in Northern Ireland, in fact, also tend to be the most economically deprived ones; in addition, many tours guides' ex-prisoner status prevents them from gaining employment in the public sector (Simone-Charteris and Boyd 2010; Wiedenhoft Murphy 2010).

However, if murals become apolitical, they will lose their authenticity and they will stop serving their original purpose which, as was discussed before, was to articulate the beliefs, fears and hopes of the communities depicted on the walls. The depoliticization of murals could result in potential visitors losing interest in visiting them. Their sanitization could prevent visitors from identifying themselves with the local community. If the politics were pulled out of images on the walls, the locals would not feel reassured that the original values and ideals their friends and family fought and died for have not been lost. If the murals were 'toned down', the working-class people would not be able to tell their side of the story. Further, if visitors stopped spending their money in the most deprived areas of Northern Ireland, these areas would lose a much-needed source of income. It is evident that the depoliticization of murals could hinder the healing process that the communities are undergoing in the aftermath of the conflict and could also lead to Northern Ireland losing the distinctiveness and authenticity that visitors interested in niche forms of tourism are after.

Conclusion

This chapter set out to investigate the effects of the State's intervention to depoliticize and sanitize political murals on the two main communities, Protestant and Catholic, that form Northern Ireland society and the possible implications of these initiatives on tourism, in particular political tourism. The rationale provided by the statutory authorities for programmes such as 'Spruce Up' Belfast in 1977, 'Brighten Up Belfast' in the late 1980s and 'Re-imaging Communities' in 2006 and 2013 is that, in the aftermath of the Troubles, political murals are anachronistic, feed a vicious circle of hatred and resentment among the communities, and therefore are not conducive to healing and moving on from a conflict to a post-conflict society (Rolston 2012). The results of this investigation, however, tell a different story; they demonstrate that enforced re-imaging would have far more negative consequences than it would positive outcomes as it would truncate the ongoing 'dialogue' between the communities that is necessary to metabolize the past in order to accept the present and move forward towards a shared future.

Since the beginning of industrial growth in the nineteenth century, Belfast has been a divided city with Catholic and Protestant families settling down in separate areas. The geographical divisions were further consolidated during the Troubles along the various peace-lines, many of which still exist today. There has always been the assumption among decision makers in Northern Ireland that economic development will improve community relations and will contribute to the resolution of the conflict (Etchart 2008). This ideology is reflected in the State's re-imagining initiatives, the development of the

232 Maria T. Simone-Charteris

Titanic Quarter and the alternative plans for the regeneration of the Maze, a prison built on the outskirts of Belfast to house Loyalist and Republican paramilitary prisoners between 1971 and 2000 (Skinner 2014), which are all aimed at improving 'the look' of Belfast in order to attract inward investment and tourism. However, international examples demonstrate the inefficiency of this modus operandi. For example, in the 1980s, local political and economic leaders launched an ambitious plan to regenerate the centre of Bilbao in the Basque Country in Spain, which was affected by civil tensions between Nationalists and the police. To do so, they closed one of the main shipyards after days of violent clashes between the workers and the police. The regeneration plan has resulted in the opening of the Guggenheim Museum and a new conference, arts and entertainment centre; the plan has been successful in improving the image of the city, however, it has not helped to solve the conflict and has created an even more bitter feeling between nationalists and working classes, who were excluded from the project and the State and its local representatives (Etchart 2008). The Bilbao example demonstrates that the physical remnants of any conflict not only need renovating physically, but most importantly they need to be processed cognitively and affectively (Skinner 2014).

As Grayson Perry, an English artist who won the 2003 Turner Prize, expresses it:

> One of the invigorating aspects of the Ulster murals was that, as well as asserting the territory, traditions, history and political messages of the conflict, they are not afraid of winding up the opposition ... to suppress the lingering bitterness under a coating of paint could be counterproductive. Better another mural than more bullets ... The artist in me thinks it would be good to let the communities continue to wear their feelings on their sleeve. Maybe one day the murals will be cherished pieces of history, old pictures of faded feelings.
>
> (Perry 2006 as cited in Rolston 2012, 17)

For this to happen, the natural evolvement of history and memorialization are essential. In short, 'the way to the future is through remembering rather than enforced forgetting, through display rather than whitewashing, through mature contestation rather than reconciliation' (Rolston 2010, 304). According to Frew and White (2011), with the advance of globalization and its homogenizing effect on culture as well as increasing competition in the tourism industry, world-wide destinations need to concentrate their efforts on the offer of a distinctive product to be successful. Political tourism attractions and sites, and political murals in particular, are Northern Ireland's most distinctive resource – one that is becoming increasingly popular with tourists. Trying to ignore or forget what has taken place through the depoliticization of murals would be a folly.

References

Alternative Tours. 2016. "Political Tours," accessed February 6, 2016. http://alternativetours-jerusalem.com/tourcats/political-tours/.

Anglia Tours. 2016. "The Quest for Political Stability in Germany After 1945: Winning the Peace," accessed February 6, 2016. http://www.angliatours.co.uk/tours/political-stability-in-germany.html.

Arts Council of Northern Ireland. 2013. "Programme Worth Over £3.1m Launched to Help Build Peace Through the Arts," accessed December 21, 2015. http://www.artscouncil-ni.org/news/programme-worth-over-3.1m-launched-to-help-build-peace-through-the-arts.

BBC. 2014. "Giro d'Italia: Call to Remove Murals and Flags from NI Route," accessed December 20, 2014. http://www.bbc.co.uk/news/uk-northern-ireland-26223060.

———. 2015a. "Bloody Friday, Belfast," accessed December 30. http://www.bbc.co.uk/history/events/bloody_friday_belfast.

———. 2015b. "The Troubles: Thirty Years of Conflict in Northern Ireland, 1968–1998," accessed December 29. http://www.bbc.co.uk/history/troubles.

Belfast City Council. 2006. *Belfast City Council Corporate Plan: Year 4 Review and Update 2006–2007*. Belfast: Belfast City Council.

Britannica. 2016. "Sinn Féin: Political Party, Ireland and United Kingdom," accessed February 6, 2016. http://www.britannica.com/topic/Sinn-Fein.

CAIN. 2015. "'Bloody Sunday', January 30, 1972—Summary of Main Events," accessed February 14, 2016. http://cain.ulst.ac.uk/events/bsunday/sum.htm.

Chronis, Athinodoros. 2005. "Coconstructing Heritage at the Gettysburg Storyscape." *Annals of Tourism Research* 32 (2): 386–406.

Coiste. 2014. "Coiste—Irish Political Tours," accessed December 24, 2014. http://www.coiste.ie/.

Conway, Jack. 2010. "Unbowed and Unbroken: A Conversation with Irish Republican Visual Artist Danny Devenny." *Radical History Review* 106: 162–70.

Discover Northern Ireland. 2014. "Murals in Belfast," accessed December 20, 2014. http://www.discovernorthernireland.com/Murals-in-Belfast-Belfast-P32135.

Etchart, Joana. 2008. "The Titanic Quarter in Belfast: Building a New Place in a Divided City." *Nordic Irish Studies* 7: 31–40.

Foley, Malcolm and John Lennon. 1996. "JFK and Dark Tourism: A Fascination with Assassination." *International Journal of Heritage Studies* 2 (4): 198–211.

Frew, Elspeth and Leanne White. 2011. "Research Directions for Tourism and National Identities." In *Tourism and National Identities: An International Perspective*, edited by Elspeth Frew and Leanne White, 215–8. London: Routledge.

Hill, Andrew and Andrew White. 2011. "Painting Peace? Murals and the Northern Ireland Peace Process." *Irish Political Studies* 27 (1): 71–88.

History of the Titanic. 2015. "History of the Titanic," accessed December 30, 2015. http://www.historyofthetitanic.org/history-of-the-titanic.html.

Independent Research Solutions (IRS). 2009. "Evaluation of the Re-imaging Communities Programme: A Report to the Arts Council of Northern Ireland," accessed December 20, 2014. http://www.artscouncil-ni.org/images/uploads/publications-documents/Re-Imaging_Final_Evaluation.pdf.

Jarman, Neil. 1997. *Material Conflicts: Parades and Visual Displays in Northern Ireland*. Oxford: Berg Publishers.

————. 1998. "Painting Landscapes: The Place of Murals in the Symbolic Construction of Urban Space." In *Symbols in Northern Ireland*, edited by Anthony Buckley, 81–97. Belfast: The Institute of Irish Studies, Queen's University Belfast.

Lisle, Debbie. 2006. "Local Symbols, Global Networks: Rereading the Murals of Belfast." *Alternatives: Global, Local, Political* 31 (1): 27–52.

Long, Lucy M. 2015. "Introduction to Part Three." In *The Food and Folklore Reader*, edited by Lucy M. Long, 159–68. London and New York: Bloomsbury Academic.

Marcia, James. 1990. "Empathy and Psychotherapy." In *Empathy and Its Development*, edited by Nancy Eisenberg and Janet Strayer, 81–102. Cambridge: The Press Syndicate of the University of Cambridge.

McCormick, Jonathan, and Neil Jarman. 2005. "Death of a Mural." *Journal of Material Culture* 10 (1): 49–71.

McFetridge, Paula. 2014. "A Response from Kabosh to the Committee for Culture, Arts and Leisure Inquiry into Inclusion in the Arts of Working Class Communities March 2014," accessed December 19, 2015. http://www.niassembly.gov.uk/globalassets/documents/environment/arts-of-working-class-communities/kabosh.pdf.

Political Tours. 2016. "Tours for 2016," accessed February 6, 2016. http://www.politicaltours.com/news-articles/travel-tours-for-2016/

Poole, Rebekah and Jennifer Llewellyn. 2016. "The Battle of the Bogside," accessed February 14, 2016. http://alphahistory.com/northernireland/battle-of-the-bogside/

Rapp, Maximilian and Markus Rhomberg. 2012. "Seeking a Neutral Identity in Northern Ireland's Political Wall Paintings." *Peace Review: A Journal of Social Justice* 24 (4): 470–7.

Richter, Linda K. 1983. "Tourism Politics and Political Science: A Case of Not so Benign Neglect." *Annals of Tourism Research* 10 (3): 313–5.

Rolston, Bill. 2005. "'An Effective Mask for Terror': Democracy, Death Squads and Northern Ireland." *Crime, Law and Social Change* 44 (2): 181–203.

————. 2010. "'Trying to Reach the Future Through the Past': Murals and Memory in Northern Ireland." *Crime Media Culture: An International Journal* 6 (3): 285–307.

————. 2012. "Re-imaging: Mural Painting and the State in Northern Ireland." *International Journal of Cultural Studies* 15 (5): 447–66.

Romens, Anne M. 2007 "Re-imaging Communities or Re-imaging Heritage? A Look at Northern Ireland's Latest Transformation Program," accessed December 20, 2014. http://ibrarian.net/navon/page.jsp?paperid=13981702&search Term=re-imaging+communities.

Seaton, Anthony V. 1999. "War and Thanatourism: Waterloo 1815–1914." *Annals of Tourism Research* 26 (1): 130–58.

Simone-Charteris, Maria T. and Stephen W. Boyd. 2010. "Northern Ireland Reemerges from the Ashes: The Contribution of Political Tourism towards a More Visited and Peaceful Environment." In *Tourism, Progress and Peace*, edited by Omar Moufakkir and Ian Kelly, 179–98. Wallingford: CABI.

Simone-Charteris, Maria. T., Stephen W. Boyd and Amy Burns. 2013. "The Contribution of Dark Tourism to Place Identity in Northern Ireland." In *Dark Tourism and Place Identity: Managing and Interpreting Dark Place*, edited by Leanne White and Elspeth Frew, 60–78. London: Routledge.

Skinner, Jonathan. 2014. "Maze Breaks in Northern Ireland: Terrorism, Tourism and Storytelling in the Shadows of Modernity." In *Displaced Heritage: Responses* to *Disaster, Trauma, and Loss*, edited by Ian Convery, Gerard Corsane and Peter Davis, 85–93. Woodbridge: The Boydell Press.

Tarlow, Peter E. 2005. "Dark Tourism: The Appealing 'Dark' Side of Tourism and More." In *Niche Tourism: Contemporary Issues, Trends and Case*, edited by Marina Novelli, 47–57. Oxford: Elsevier.

The Museum of Free Derry. 2005. "Glenfada Park," accessed December 24, 2014. http://www.museumoffreederry.org/location.html.

TripAdvisor. 2016. "West Belfast Mural Tours," accessed February 7, 2016. https://www.tripadvisor.co.uk/Attraction_Review-g186470-d3902162-Reviews-West_Belfast_Mural_Tours-Belfast_Northern_Ireland.html.

Tripwolf. 2014. "Peace Lines," accessed December 23, 2014. http://www.tripwolf.com/en/guide/show/17634/Northern-Ireland/Belfast/Peace-Lines.

Trotta, James. 2013. "Grief Tourism," accessed December 23, 2014. http://www.grief-tourism.com/

White, Beatrice. 2011. "The Writing on the Wall: the Significance of Murals in the Northern Ireland Conflict." In *Walking the Tightrope: Europe between Europeanisation and Globalisation: Selected Papers Presented at European Studies Intensive Programme 2010, University of Groningen*, edited by Janny de Jong, Ine Megens and Margriet van der Waal, 307–25. Groningen: Groningen University Press.

Wiedenhoft Murphy, Wendy Ann. 2010. "Touring the Troubles in West Belfast: Building Peace or Reproducing Conflict? *Peace & Change* 35 (4): 537–60.

14 The Gaeltacht Quarter of Mural City

Irish in Falls Road murals

Siun Carden

The Falls Road area in West Belfast, an established destination for so-called 'Troubles tourism', has in recent years been marketed as the 'Gaeltacht Quarter', an Irish-language-themed cultural quarter. The 'linguistic land-scape' (Landry and Bourhis 1997) of this cultural quarter includes not only bilingual signage and advertisements but also the murals that emerged dur-ing the conflict. These provide a high-profile and politically charged canvas for a multilingual 'mosaic of different texts' (Jaworski and Thurlow 2010, 32) that convey complex messages about the place of different languages and different people within Belfast and beyond. Languages act as 'emblems of ethnicity' (McCoy 1997, 117) and can be 'potent resources in the arenas of politics and identity' (Cohen 1998, 23), quite apart from what is said in them. While the Gaeltacht Quarter casts Irish as an economic resource rather than a political one, aiming to turn an emblem of ethnicity into a Unique Selling Point, the language never loses its symbolic significance. As Shohamy and Gorter (2009, 14) suggest, 'Writing on open display ... is a genie let out of the bottle', open to multiple readings. Although Belfast has been called 'an open-air gallery – a spectacle that is consumed' (Lisle 2006, 33), no city is only that. Urban division provides sites of spectacle for visitors, but contin-ues to shape local lives: the 'peace lines in Belfast were not created as a tour-ist attraction' (Leonard 2011, 123). Tourism is one way in which residents 'contend for visibility and for economic and political survival' (Jaworski and Thurlow 2010, 32). This chapter examines the evolving uses of Irish in Falls Road murals as the latest plan for the Gaeltacht Quarter aspires to double their number.

The Falls Road and the Gaeltacht Quarter

Catholic West Belfast has always had a strong and distinct place identity. The Falls Road, which forms an arterial route between sprawling Catholic resi-dential areas and the city centre, is perhaps the most famous Catholic place-name within Belfast's largely segregated working-class landscape. A Republican heartland that experienced some of the most intense conflict between 1969 and 1998, and acted as 'the cockpit of the North' (Livingstone

1998, 24) during decades of violence, it remains part of what O'Dowd and Komarova (2009, 10) call 'Troubles Belfast' rather than the 'Consumerist Belfast' that has emerged in more prosperous areas in the years of peace. The area's discrete identity finds its most concrete expression in the 'peace-walls' that separate it from the neighbouring Protestant Shankill Road. Less spectacular distinctions between Catholic West Belfast and the city as a whole are, however, at least as important as this crude sectarian territoriality in creating the conditions for a distinct place identity to emerge. These include multiple deprivation and planning decisions taken with more of a view to crowd control than livability. Within the relative isolation of this 'city within a city' (Boal and Livingstone 1984, 168), forms of 'cultural expression' connected to Irishness 'went on without impinging much upon the daily lives of unionists ... safely hidden away in the ghetto' (Rolston 1991,71). The Gaeltacht Quarter project builds on the Irish language initiatives and (later) tourist infrastructure that developed within this densely interconnected neighbourhood.

In the 1960s, a small community of Irish language speakers and learners, socially centred on the Cumann Chluain Árd Irish language club, established an urban neo-gaeltacht on the Shaws Road, about four miles from the city centre. A 'gaeltacht' is a place or community where Irish is spoken, and the word usually refers to the areas designated as 'gaeltachts' in the Republic of Ireland, where government policy has official aims to protect the language in daily use. In the newly established, self-declared urban gaeltacht on the Shaw's Road, families who wished to raise their children with Irish could live side by side. The first Irish-medium school in the north, Bunscoil Phobail Feirste, was created by this group. West Belfast is now home to Northern Ireland's only Irish-medium second-level school, Coláiste Feirste, and many primary and nursery schools. The Shaw's Road community acquired a disused Presbyterian church on the main Falls Road itself, about two miles from the city centre, where Coláiste Feirste first opened. This building then became an Irish-language arts centre, the Cultúrann MacAdam Ó Fiaich that, as well as a café, bookshop, radio station (Raidió Fáilte) and theatre, provided initial office space for initiatives such as the local tourism organization Fáilte Feirste Thiar and the development organization Forbairt Feirste. Eventually, the Cultúrlann became the nucleus of the Gaeltacht Quarter. The novelty of the Gaeltacht Quarter designation is that it attempts to connect this very localized infrastructure with the governance, economy and public image of Belfast as a whole, using tourism as the linking mechanism.

The Gaeltacht Quarter uses the Irish language as a theme to mark the area out as a distinctive tourist attraction. The West Belfast and Greater Shankill Task Force, set up to consider solutions to the long-term economic problems of the area, suggested that the Irish language could be used as a local USP for cultural tourism (2002, 48). Forbairt Feirste and Fáilte Feirste Thiar/Visit West Belfast drove the project forward. The Gaeltacht Quarter officially emerged in the early 2000s as part of a city-wide process in which Belfast City Council identified seven nascent 'Quarters', Cathedral Quarter, Titanic Quarter, Queen's Quarter, Linen Quarter, Library Quarter and Market Quarter. Clive Dutton, an English regeneration expert, produced a report setting out what a Gaeltacht Quarter might look like (Dutton 2004). Some of Belfast's new Quarters, such as the Linen and Library Quarters, have hitherto had little impact beyond discreet street signage. Belfast City Council has since moved away from the cultural quarters' model towards a 'destination-led' approach to tourism (Integrated Strategic Framework for Belfast Tourism 2010–2014, 13). The Gaeltacht Quarter, however, has survived to become one of the Northern Ireland Tourist Board and Belfast City Council's current priority destinations.

In 2013, the 'Big Gaeltacht Quarter Plan' (Dutton 2013) was published, laying out an ambitious 20-year action plan for the area in which murals tourism plays a central role. The plan identifies 'the multitude of murals' as 'the most visually distinctive characteristic' of the Quarter area (Dutton 2013, 36). Alongside the Gaeltacht Quarter, it suggests that a 'complementary brand of Mural City should be vigorously championed'. The first action point in the 'Identity' section of the plan is that 'by 31 December 2015 the number of murals in the Gaeltacht Quarter will have doubled and Mural City will be an internationally recognised brand' (Dutton 2013, 36). Doubling the number of murals in this area does not mean creating more of the same. In a 2014 video interview for the World Cities Network, Dutton elaborates on the change that is envisioned,

> the Gaeltacht Quarter, it's [...] a modest kind of cityscape. But what are very distinctive are the murals that are there. [...] The majority of those are actually commemorating, allowing people to remember people, events, incidents of the past. [...] Why don't we double the number? 200 more [...] the next 200 will look to the future and celebrating the future, because there's enough that commemorate the past.
>
> (Kilkelly 2014)

This impetus towards more murals, but different ones, reflects political, ethical and commercial dilemmas around the promotion of so-called 'troubles tourism' (Brown, McDonagh and Shultz 2013, 1262). While the 'troubles' were ongoing, the tourist industry in Northern Ireland suffered from the practical effects and public relations challenges of conflict, combined with a changing global marketplace in international tourism (Boyd 2000, 151–2). The impact of political violence on tourism is most evident in the early years of the 'troubles', with the number of staying visitors falling from 1,197,000 in 1968 to 407,000 in 1972 (Boyd 2000, 154; NITB 2008, 12, 15). There was some growth in the tourism industry during the 1980s, reflecting international trends towards a greater focus on travel and leisure, and visitor numbers rose as the peace process progressed in the 1990s (O'Neill and Fitz 1996, 161). However, the British holiday-makers who had been pre-conflict Northern Ireland's 'primary domestic market' were gone, the industry was slow to adapt to changing market conditions, and Northern Ireland was 'left behind' in terms of tourism development (Leslie 1999, 37).

Since the 1998 Good Friday Agreement, tourism to Northern Ireland has been promoted as a driver of progress towards economic and political 'normality', although the management and promotion of tourism continue to present conflict-related challenges for local government and planning authorities (Simone-Charteris and Boyd 2010, 184, 189). Politically, public bodies such as the Northern Ireland Tourist Board, and local government structures such as Belfast City Council, have steered as clear as possible of 'Troubles Belfast' (O'Dowd and Komarova 2009, 10), leaving the private sector and neighbourhood-level organizations to provide for tourists interested in the conflict as they see fit (Simone-Charteris and Boyd 2010, 184, 189). It is not possible for Belfast City Council to avoid the matter entirely. For example, in an interview I conducted in 2013, a BCC employee recalled that their tourism division had received so many complaints from members of the public who objected to one element or another of private bus tour commentaries, imagining that the council must have some responsibility for their content, that they had eventually issued advisory suggestions for the guides. Ethically, there is a wariness on the part of some commentators (eg Wiedenhoft Murphy 2010) and indeed some tourists (Murtagh and Michael, forthcoming) about the effects of such tourism and whether, even in inviting visitors to share in celebrating peace, it might lead 'to the international legitimization of sectarian politics and sectarian landscapes' (McDowell 2008, 406). Commercially, the continuing interest of international publics in a conflict that has long faded from international media cannot be assured. The drive to cater for those that are here is therefore balanced with a need to broaden the appeal of destinations reliant on conflict-related visitors. At a neighbourhood level, the presence of tourists is sought after first because of their spending power, and second because they function as an audience for the competing narratives local actors wish to disseminate, providing a way of reaching over the heads of local antagonists towards a broader legitimacy. Third, in a regional context where economic competitiveness is prized almost as much as political conflict is feared, tourists – whether real or hypothesized – offer local interest groups a useful form of leverage in negotiations around how the city's past is represented and its future is planned.

Conflict, the quotidian and the commercial in the linguistic landscape of the Falls Road

A crucial way in which the Gaeltacht Quarter is distinguished from its surroundings and promoted as a unique tourism product is through the creation of a particular kind of multilingual 'linguistic landscape' (Landry and Bourhis 1997; Shohamy and Gorter 2009). Using the Irish language as a theme means making it visible and, while conversing in Irish is not something many tourists, or indeed most local residents, can take part in, Irish as a visual symbol can be consumed by everyone. Through the part-funding of bilingual or completely Irish shop signs, Forbairt Feirste has both greatly increased the amount of Irish that is visible in the Gaeltacht Quarter and shifted the contexts in which it is seen towards the quotidian and the commercial. Writing about Irish in West Belfast around the time of the 1998 Good Friday Agreement, O'Reilly (1998, 54) reported that 'Republican influence on the Irish language revival has been disproportionately visible in the form of murals, banners, slogans, and high profile political activity'; while such influence is still strong, it no longer dominates the linguistic landscape of the area. Without any nationalist references in terms of graphics or textual content, with the arguable exception of the occasional use of an 'Gaelic' typeface (Staunton 2005, 22), the use of Irish in bilingual signage and advertisements positions it as part of the contemporary commercial world – a world in which Irish speakers use *'leabaí ghreine'* (sunbeds), where a UK supermarket chain welcomes shoppers with *'Fáilte go Sainsburys, Iarthar Bhéal Feirste'* ('Welcome to Sainsburys, West Belfast'), and where even the Ladbrokes betting shop invites passers-by to *'lig do chroí chun rásaí!'* ('let your heart go to the races!/'let your heart race!'). As Shohamy and Gorter (2009, 23) argue, every inscription, however banal the context, 'conveys a message about itself that refers to the language in which it is redacted: 'There is someone out there who reads Language X'. The use of Irish, historically associated with poverty, rurality and the archaic (McCoy 1997, 118) in such commercial contexts, also conveys the message that the people 'out there' who read Irish are modern, urban actors in the market economy. This makes such signage far from apolitical. However, the linguistic landscape of the Gaeltacht Quarter also includes a more overtly political element in the form of murals.

The local mural tradition offers a unique context for language as spectacle with its own political and aesthetic qualities enacted with a particular consciousness of spatial territory. While mural painting was an established tradition in some Protestant neighbourhoods long before the 'Troubles' (Hill and White 2012, 72), murals in Catholic areas emerged directly out of political conflict. Murals have been a feature of the area around the Falls Road since the 'murals boom' (Sluka 1992, 195) of the early 1980s when the horror of the hunger strikes among Republican prisoners contributed to a period of 'intense politicization' (Mac Ionnrachtaigh 2013, 150) among the general Catholic and nationalist population. Sluka (1992, 195) identifies four stages in the development of murals in these areas: pre-1981, when very few murals existed; the 'hunger strike period', 1981–1982, when political graffiti in support of Republican prisoners was elaborated and formalized into wall-sized murals; the 'armed struggle period', 1983–1984, when murals were used to advertise and encourage local support for the IRA's intensified campaign of violence; and the 'party-political period' from 1985 on, with mural painting in nationalist areas increasingly organized and directed by Sinn Féin. During the 1980s, murals in Catholic neighbourhoods offered an informal political platform for nationalist residents and interest groups who had relatively little sway within the formal political system.

By contrast, in some Protestant areas of Belfast, mural painting was part of the annual Unionist commemoration of the 1690 Battle of the Boyne even before the partition of Ireland. Celebrating this historic victory and opposing contemporary Irish Nationalism, 'Unionist murals [...] were pro-state murals' (Rolston 2012, 448). The Loyalist paramilitary murals which emerged during the 1980s had a more complex relationship to the political establishment, expressing a sense of betrayal by both the UK government and mainstream Unionism (Hill and White 2012, 73). With their co-option of British military symbolism and promise of armed opposition to Irish Republicanism with or without their unreliable allies, Loyalist murals expressed an uncompromising commitment to the Northern Irish state (Rolston 2012, 450).

Murals in Republican areas challenged the idea of Northern Ireland as a functioning, integral part of the United Kingdom, while presenting Republican paramilitarism as justifiable, even inevitable, resistance to oppression. While unionist authorities were keen to downplay and delegitimize opposition to the Northern Irish state, these murals were 'a step toward countering the image of stability and acceptance generated by the "normal" appearance of much of the urban landscape in Belfast' (Sluka 1992, 214). More than just reflections of the conflict, they became tools in it; Republican murals 'were now intimately implicated in the war, mobilizing local support, reaffirming beleaguered ideologies and railing against the state and its forces' (Rolston 2012, 450). Given this, the mural itself as a locus of expression has a continuing symbolic link to conflict, regardless of changes to the content. The 'mosaic of different texts' (Jaworski and Thurlow 2010, 32) that conveys complex messages about the place of different languages and different people within cities is endowed with a lingering sense of territoriality for local audiences when framed within this mural tradition.

The highly visible role of Belfast murals in representing cultural identities, territorial claims and the antagonism of conflict makes each of them a potential canvas for the negotiation and ideological work of reimagining post-conflict communities. In fact, this is by no means just a 'post-conflict' process; murals have been subject to forces of change and 're-imaging' from within and outside their working-class neighbourhoods since the early years of the so-called 'Troubles' (see Chapters 13 and 15 in this volume). Early 're-imaging' schemes, backed by Belfast City Council between 1976 and 1981, drew criticism for the shallow nature of engagement between painters and residents, and the irrelevance or inappropriateness of the resulting artworks (Rolston 1991, 67). More recently, some loyalist paramilitary murals have been replaced with less threatening images agreed on through long and difficult negotiation (Hill and White 2012, 73–4). While Catholic areas have entered into official re-imaging schemes less frequently than Protestant ones (Hill and White 2012, 77), this is not to say that murals in these areas have not changed. Rather, the content of murals in Republican areas has shifted away from paramilitary slogans and imagery and towards 'community activism in response to state violence', with increased use of 'political, historical, and heritage motifs' in a more organic fashion, as the peace process took hold (McCormick and Jarman 2005, 52; Hartnett 2011, 85; see also Rolston 2013, ii).

The international publics, which have always been among intended audiences of murals in Republican areas, are now physically present in Belfast streets rather than in front of televisions or at diasporic gatherings around the world. In 2012, 8 per cent of 1.75 million out-of-state overnight visitors to Belfast reported visiting political murals, and 24 per cent reported visiting 'Areas associated with troubles' (Belfast City Council 2012, 13–4). The immediacy of these encounters changes the nature of a mural's appeal to sympathy, credulity, political and financial support. Whereas a mural used as a backdrop to a news report might persuade a distant viewer to engage with a particular message, whether by exerting political pressure in their own country, donating money to a cause or simply thinking about the subject, the same viewer consuming the mural in person is already an actor in the evolving political situation in Northern Ireland. Tourists 'become propagators of messages and their own experiences to their friends and relatives' (Simone-Charteris and Boyd 2010, 183) and, in the age of social media, holiday photos and travellers' tales reach wider audiences than ever before. While the mural's role as a tool of conflict has faded, its potential as a post-conflict propaganda tool has not. The use of multiple languages offers a way of representing evolving intercommunal relationships to diverse audiences.

The changing place of Irish in Falls Road murals

Historically, murals taking the Irish language as their subject have focused squarely on the relationship between Irish and English, exhorting local people to use the minoritized language as a form of resistance to Anglophone hegemony and, by extension, to British cultural influence and political control in Northern Ireland. This 'oppositional' (Kachuk 1993) positioning of the two languages is clear in phrases like '*Is Fearr Gaeilge Briste ná Béarla Cliste*' ('Broken Irish is Better than Clever English') painted until a few years ago on a wall at Whiterock Road off the Falls. During the conflict, where Irish was used in murals addressing themes other than the language itself, it was most often used to convey this oppositional position. The use of Irish in explicitly Republican murals can embody a territorial claim based on the idea of indigeneity. For example, a well-known mural painted in 1981, also on the Whiterock Road at the boundary of the Ballymurphy estate (where eleven civilians were shot dead by the Parachute Regiment over 2 days in 1971), depicted a British soldier surrounded by the slogan

'*Slán Abhaile – Fág Ar Sraideanna*' ('Safe Home – Leave Our Streets'). These words, implicitly addressed to the British army in a language very few British soldiers could be expected to understand, demonstrate the multiple levels of communication involved in such public texts. Unintelligibility is itself symbolic, the exclusionary potential of any language is a powerful way of enforcing social boundaries. The use of Irish did not create any risk of the mural's message being misunderstood. The central image was fringed with smaller paintings, illustrating specific political demands with captions in English, 'End collusion', 'Release POWs', 'Disband the RUC' and 'End Unionist veto'. The choice of Irish for the central slogan, with the contextually sinister Irish farewell blessing to visitors, 'slán abhaile', sets up an implied audience for the mural that consists of insiders, people who belong, understand the simple Irish of the mural and are in on the joke, and outsiders represented by the painted British soldier who are unwelcome, uncomprehending and out of place. It does not work, of course, if the message is really lost on outsiders. The wider audience for this performance of linguistic boundary-making – such as passing motorists, TV viewers, groups of tourists led by Republican ex-prisoners, and those who have consumed and reproduced their photographs – is essential to the success of the mural in furthering the political demands it makes, regardless of any individual viewer's knowledge of Irish. In Barth's (1969, 14–5) formulation, it is 'the ethnic boundary that defines the group, not the cultural stuff that it encloses' (see also May 2011, 33). The partial use of untranslated Irish is no barrier to this mural's message, even though this is nominally directed at Anglophone Britain, because its message is that this place and its people possess a quality that is incommensurate with Britishness.

This message can also be packaged in much less antagonistic ways. The previously mentioned '*Is Fearr Gaeilge Briste ná Béarla Cliste*' ('Broken Irish is Better than Clever English') mural consisted of simple and roughly painted letters, visually not far removed from graffiti on a plain background. It was replaced in 2009 by two new murals organized by Glór na Móna (a local Irish language organization) and the Upper Springfield Development Trust, funded by the Re-imaging Communities, Shared Communities Consortium and the Belfast Regeneration Office's Neighbourhood Renewal programme, and designed by artists Frankie Maher and Risteard O'Murchú with young people from nearby Irish-medium primary and nursery schools. These murals show the continuing local association between language revitalization and Republican political goals, as well as the new emphasis on language as a cultural resource with economic benefits. The left-hand mural on a green background shows the words '*Sí Athghabháil na Gaeilge*' ('The repossession of Irish is …') on one side and '*Athghabháil na hÉireann*' ('the repossession of Ireland') on the other. This is based on a quote from Máirtín Ó Cadhain, an author born in the Connemara gaeltacht in 1909 who was interned during World War II as an IRA member, '*Sí an ghaeilge athghabháil na hÉireann agus is í athghabháil na hÉireann slánú na gaeilge*' which can be translated as 'the Irish language entails the repossession of Ireland and the repossession of Ireland is the salvation of the Irish language' (Blake 2011, 119). The name of a local Irish-medium primary school, Gaelscoil na Móna, is painted inside a Celtic knotwork design at one end and the logo of Glór na Móna at the other. The right-hand mural is dominated by the words *'Gabh Gaelach!'* in bright yellow on a red background. This phrase has been adopted as a campaign slogan in recent years by local Irish language activists and is effectively interlingual, pronounced as something close to 'Go Gaelic!' and used to mean 'Go Irish!' The mural shows two older slogans in much smaller letters, *'Is Fearr Gaeilge Briste ná Béarla Cliste'* ('Broken Irish is better than Clever English'), and *'tír gan teanga, tír gan ainm'*/('a country without a language is a country without a soul'). The words *'ceol'* ('music'), *'damhsa sean-nós'* ('old-style dancing'), and *'spóirt'* ('sports') are also shown, each with an illustration along with the name of the Irish-medium primary school that worked with the artist, *'Bunscoil an tsléibh dhuibh'* ('Black Mountain Primary School'). At the launch of these two murals, during *Féile an Phobail* (the West Belfast Festival) in 2009, Feargal MacIonnractaigh (a project officer with Forbairt Feirste) spoke about the historical links between Irish and Republicanism, the growth of the Irish-medium education sector, and the idea of Irish as an economic driver, saying that "it's about seeing the Irish language as a resource, as a resource of ours that can be used to aid the regeneration of our community". The metalinguistic discourses that Heller and Duchêne (2012, 5) call 'pride' (language understood in terms of rooted communal identities and romantic nationalism) and 'profit' (language deployed as a competitive instrumental skillset in the global marketplace) are intertwined here. The professionalization and prettification of Irish language murals, with bright colours, crisp fonts and innocuous illustrations, is not just about making them less threatening, but about making them more 'official' (Gorter 2006, 68) with the assertion of authority that comes with that (Kallen 2009, 273).

The fonts that are now used to signal Irishness are based on the typefaces that were used to represent the Irish language until the mid-twentieth century. Although these were phased out for printing in Irish by 1965, thanks to their continuing association with Ireland and adaptability to languages other than Irish, they have 'become a means to sell all things Irish on the international market', pressed into branding efforts like other 'characteristic scripts' (Staunton 2005, 22; Heller and Duchêne 2012, 10). While Staunton (2005, 28) suggests that the shift in these fonts' usage from official Irish language text towards private sector English language text represents a move from 'propaganda' to 'advertising', their use in Falls Road murals demonstrates that the two are far from mutually exclusive. By suggesting the existence of an Irish linguistic identity without demanding any multi-linguistic competence from the Anglophone reader, the use of these fonts in such murals produces a sense of Irishness that is decorative and accessible (especially where they are used for text in English), offering the tourist 'the opportunity to experience

Irish authenticity at minimal linguistic cost' (Kallen 2009, 278). Branding the Falls Road as 'authentically Irish' is more than a commercial matter given the significance of this area as a famously Irish Republican neighbourhood historically antagonistic to the Northern Irish state.

In the heart of the Gaeltacht Quarter, opposite the Cultúrlann, the Irish language umbrella group Pobal has commissioned a series of murals over recent years as part of its campaign for an Irish Language Act in Northern Ireland. While the Good Friday Agreement includes a commitment to 'take resolute action to promote the (Irish) language', and so opens the way for an unprecedented level of state support for the language in the north, the Irish language does not have the kind of legislative protection within Northern Ireland that Scots Gaelic has in Scotland, or Welsh has in Wales (ILA, Pobal 2006). Pobal's murals reflect its campaigning stance that 'language rights are human rights' – *'cearta teanga, cearta daonna'*, as one of its previous murals proclaimed – and stress the idea of Irish speakers as a community whose legal rights are in need of protection. The latest Pobal mural plays on the Irish term for umbrella, *'scáth fearthainne'*, within which the word *'scáth'* means 'shelter'. It features the Irish proverb *'Ar scáth a chéile a mhaireann na daoine'* ('people live in each other's shelter/shadows') and depicts a crowd of people marching beneath umbrellas as if on a political demonstration, holding a large banner with the Pobal logo and 'Advocacy for the Irish Language' and a smaller banner above them with 'Abhcóideacht ar son na gaeilge' ('Advocacy on behalf of Irish'). Both of these phrases are in an Irish-looking font. The colourful umbrellas are decorated with Irish and English words for terms like 'advocacy', 'community development', 'research', 'monitoring', 'strategy', 'rights', 'revelry', 'arts' and 'legislation' (Figure 14.1).

Pobal's approach positions the Irish language with reference to other minority languages rather than in opposition to Britishness. The linguistic ideology that sees the speakers of lesser-used languages as threatened communities entitled to similar legal protection as members of any other beleaguered minority group fits comfortably within the political landscape of the Falls Road with its valorizing of communal action and the discourse of human rights but is much less concerned with national identity than linguistic vitality.

The most visited mural site on the Falls is known as the 'international wall'. Situated at the junction of Divis Street and Northumberland Street, close to where Catholic West Belfast is divided from the city centre by the motorway's 'tarmac moat' (Emerson 2008), this long stretch of brick wall is a highly desirable location exemplifying the 'situation, ownership, composition and artistic merit' that produce successful murals (McCormick and Jarman 2005, 60). The many murals painted on it are therefore subject to a very high rate of turnover (McCormick and Jarman 2005, 60; see Extramural Activity 2013 for a photographic record of changes at this site between 2000 and 2013). Pressure on this precious real estate has resulted in the space given over to murals extending from the main roughly 100-metre-long stretch of

Figure 14.1 Pobal mural, Brighton Street.
Source: Siún Carden.

wall on Divis Street ever further around the corner along Northumberland Street where an equally large area is now occupied by murals, ending only at the 'peace-line' with the Protestant Shankill. The short-lived nature of individual murals at this site is not an example of the 'temporal frailty' (McCormick and Jarman 2005, 53) of the medium whereby murals demand constant protection and maintenance. Rather, in its topicality, this wall has come to resemble a breaking news ticker tape of broadly Republican views on everything from Gaza to climate change. A convenient stop for walking, taxi and bus tours, some of its murals address tourists directly, urging them to 'Get the real story, local history from local people' with a West Belfast Taxi Association tour, or by visiting the Republican History Museum at Conway Mill. As well as Sinn Fein, other Republican groups like the Republican Network for Unity, Éirigí, the Workers' Party and the IRSP/INLA are represented, and some murals are devoted to non-Republican organizations with overlapping aims such as Amnesty International and Unite, the public-sector workers' union, the local Travellers group, An Munia Tober, and the West Anti-Racism Network. While there is no official procedure for allotting time on the wall to different groups and causes, the competition for mural space is tempered by the political dominance of Sinn Féin in this area of Belfast that gives them an effective veto over what appears on the wall. The mainstream Republicanism of Sinn Féin and causes dear to it occupies the Divis Street section of the wall, which is the most prominently visible to passing traffic. Smaller Republican groups and those opposed to the peace process are located around the corner on Northumberland Street. Given its visibility, this junction is desirable not only to muralists but also to advertisers. In 2014, the double billboard at the corner of Northumberland street advertised McDonalds and tours of 'Belfast's Infamous Prison', Crumlin Road Gaol, juxtaposed by celebrations of socialism and militant Republicanism and expressions of support for 'political prisoners' in Northern Ireland and around the world (see related chapters in this volume). That these murals are themselves tourist products only makes the combination of protest and theme park odder.

As its nickname suggests, many of the murals on the international wall reference other parts of the world. Republican murals 'have always made explicit connections to anti-imperial struggles, revolutionary movements, and other groups whose civil rights have been denied by ruling structures' (Lisle 2006, 40; see also Leonard 2011, 123). As of April 2015, for example, murals at this site include references to the nineteenth-century anti-slavery campaigner Frederick Douglass, South Africa's Nelson Mandela, socialist president of Chile Salvadore Allende, Native American activist Leonard Peltier and Basque separatist Arnaldo Otegi, as well as no fewer than five separate murals expressing support for Gaza. Positioning Irish Republicanism within this type of pluralistic worldview for tourism is in itself a way of pressing the cause at home, as 'Republican discourses to a "neutral" outsider may prove more effective given the international framework in which such discourses are rationalized and validated' (Leonard 2011, 122). The use of multiple languages at this high profile site is a powerful way of constructing this international framework. Placing Irish amongst other languages (currently Arabic, Spanish and Basque), as well as the ubiquitous English, enacts openness to cultural diversity while positioning Irish as equal to world languages in status, and part of the global family of threatened minority languages. The inscription of resonant phrases like '*¡No Pasarán!*' ('They shall not pass', used by anti-fascists) or '*La Historia es nuestra y la hacen los pueblos*' ('History is ours and it is made by the people', part of Salvador Allende's last speech), alongside quotes from Bobby Sands or Pádraig Pearse, sets up flattering equivalences for the Republican movement but also builds up a continually changing multilingual landscape and, as Gal (2012, 34) points out, multilingualism 'itself is an iconic sign' which has historically been 'an image of wavering, it provoked doubts about the speaker's national loyalty. In the new framework, it is iconic of flexibility and the "cosmopolitan"' (see also Hannerz 1996, 21).

Within this political nexus, Irish is deployed in various ways: to convey everything from Republican struggle to global economic competitiveness and, ultimately, to link the two. In the names of Republican political organizations like *Sinn Féin* and *Éirigí*, it is fundamentally connected to Republican ideology. *Scairt Amach* ('the voice of Republican prisoners') invokes the influence of Republican prisoners on the revival of the language in west Belfast. Irish is used, gaelic script and all, in the common memorial phrase 'I nDíl Chuimhne' ('in memory of') on a mural marking the twenty-fifth anniversary of the attack on a funeral at Milltown cemetery. A memorial to Father Alec Reid describes him as 'The *Sagart'* ('Priest') and 'the peacemaker', reflecting and showing support for his role in the peace process (Figure 14.2).

A mural in support of Basque separatists combines English, Irish and Basque, reading 'The Pathway to Peace'/'*Pake Bidean'*, and 'Free them all!'/'*Scaoiltear saor uilig iad'*. This conflates the violent campaigns, experiences of imprisonment and movements towards peace of Basque and Irish nationalists while emphasizing the parallels between Irish and other minoritized languages, particularly those associated with unfulfilled nationalist aspirations. A November 2014 addition to the international wall calls for a referendum on Catalan independence; classes in Basque, Catalan, Scots Gaelic and Manx are occasionally available in the Gaeltacht Quarter; and there is a small minority language tourism circuit – the Republican tour company Coiste offer tours in Basque, for example, and I accompanied a tour group of Welsh-medium school teachers in 2008.

Pobal represent their campaign for an Irish Language Act at the international wall with a mural depicting realistic demonstration scenes using phrases like 'Is Gaeil Sinn' ('We Are Gaels') surrounded with the same bilingual terms – advocacy, community development etc. – as their other

Figure 14.2 Part of the International Wall, Divis Street.
Source: Siún Carden.

mural further up the road. As Urla (2012, 84) argues, the use of languages like Irish to produce management-speak 'reverses the long-standing association of minority languages and language diversity with backwardness and the antithesis of innovation'. The height of this approach to the Irish language appears in the latest international wall mural devoted to the Gaeltacht Quarter itself, launched in 2013 to coincide with the publication of the new 20-year strategy. Replacing a previous Gaeltacht Quarter mural which read *'Ag Fíorú na Ceathrún Gaeltachta'*, 'Delivering on the Gaeltacht Quarter', this depicts a brightly-coloured diagram representing The Big Gaeltacht Quarter Plan. The word *'GAELTACHT'* arches over a network of terms like *'teanga*/language', *'spórt*/sport', *cultúr*/culture', *'oidhreacht*/heritage', *oideachas*/education', and even *'draíocht*/magic', all interlinked with lines marked *'póist*/jobs' and with *'turascóireacht*/tourism' at the very centre. Arrows point out from this network towards 'THE WORLD, *AN DOMHAN'* and 'THE CITY, *AN CHATHAIR'*, propped up by 'CELEBRATION, *CEILIUIR'* and 'PROFILE, *PROIFIL'*. The foundation of the diagram is formed by 'RESILIENT, *ATHLEIMNEACH'* and 'DISTINCTIVE/AUTHENTIC, *SAINIUIL/UDARACH'* (Figure 14.3).

Silverstein and Urban (1996, 11) argue that 'Politics can be seen [...] as the struggle to entextualise authoritatively, and hence [...] to fix certain metadiscursive perspectives on texts and discourse practices'. In the international

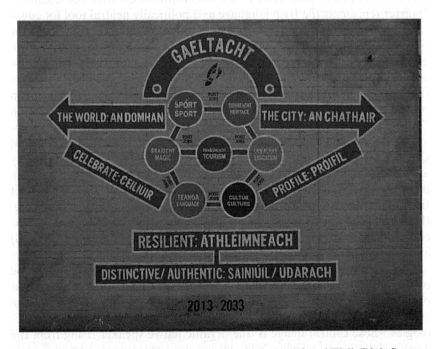

Figure 14.3 The Gaeltacht Quarter mural on the International Wall, Divis Street.
Source: Siún Carden.

wall, the viewer is presented with not only a constant multilingual 'struggle to entextualise' the position of Irishness in Belfast authoritatively but, here, directions on how to read it. (NB: Clive Dutton died on June 8, 2015. A memorial mural proclaiming him 'Gaeltacht Quarter Champion' with the phrase '*Ar Aghaidh Linn*/Onwards' has since replaced the previous Gaeltacht Quarter mural on the International Wall.)

Conclusion

The use of Irish in the Gaeltacht Quarter murals demonstrates a tension between exoticization, creating a spectacle of cultural difference, and normalization, presenting Irish as part of an integrated global economy. This tension reflects those between 'pride and profit' (Heller and Duchêne 2012, 16) and between 'the value of the pure and the hybrid' (Heller 2006, ix) that characterize many minority language movements in the twenty-first century, emerging as they do from the unreconciled forces of romantic nationalism and modernity (Eriksen 1992, 313). The tourism industry operates at the crux of this paradox, commodifying linguistic expertise and creating commercial products from linguistic attributes that also function as ethnonational boundary markers or rallying points. While the Irish featured in brightly painted murals offers an accessible visual cue to non-Irish speakers that they are in a distinct place called the Gaeltacht Quarter, the Gaeltacht Quarter represents the Irish language as a politically neutral tool for countering the deprivation, poor infrastructure and communal trauma of the post-conflict period, as an aspirational path towards an exalted form of 'normality'. Just like their more adversarial predecessors, the latest wave of murals around the Falls Road are intended to mark the place out from the 'normal' Belfast urban landscape, but the aim of this distinction is a recognizable USP (Unique Selling Point) for tourists within what Dutton (2013) calls a 'modest kind of cityscape', rather than to destabilize the image of Belfast as a consensual and peaceful society. Indeed, the Gaeltacht Quarter's current vision of 'Mural City', where murals multiply furiously as the city's central conflict fades away, is in itself a kind of 'normalization' process with the stated aim to 'look to the future' (Dutton 2013). The use of Irish in murals to provide an accessible 'transcendence from the mundane' (Kallen 2009, 271) for tourists means moving away from performances of exclusivity (as in the previously mentioned '*Slán Abhaile*', 'Safe Home' mural) and towards performances of the welcomingly multilingual.

The shifting interplay of English and Irish in the linguistic landscape of the Falls Road demonstrates the 'co-constituent' nature of pride and profit as 'discursive tropes' (Heller and Duchêne 2012, 16) which frame the evolving relationship between language and nationalism. Language ideologies whose central image is 'the organic native speaker rising from the earth' (Heller and Duchêne 2012, 13) are now accompanied by visions of the ideal speaker as someone who is technically accomplished, culturally fluid, geographically mobile and not so much rising from the earth as built from concrete. This does not mean that older understandings of the relationship between language and nationhood have gone away. The repositioning of the Irish language in the linguistic landscape of the Falls Road as 'official' or 'central' (Jaworski and Thurlow 2010, 10), after its long exclusion from the official realm in Northern Ireland (McCoy 1997, 120, Kallen 2009, 275), is profoundly connected to the changing place of Irishness within the Northern Irish state. While it is true that 'it matters little to the tourist what language the local schools use or what language is used at meetings of a residents' association' (Kallen 2009, 272), the presence of tourists does matter for the status of Irish in Belfast because tourism provides a way to frame the language as a cultural resource for the whole city rather than a territorial claim to it. Given its links with conflict transformation and tourism, the evolving mural tradition of the Falls Road is a powerful way for the changing place of Irish in Belfast to be written into the culture of the city.

References

Barth, Fredrik. 1969. "Introduction." In *Ethnic Groups and Boundaries: The Social Organization of Culture Difference*, edited by Fredrik Barth, 9–38. Oslo: Universitetsforlaget.

Belfast City Council. 2010. *Integrated Strategic Framework for Belfast Tourism 2010–2014*. Belfast: Belfast City Council.

———. 2012. *Belfast Tourism Monitor 2012*. Belfast: Millward Brown Belfast.

Blake, Séamus. 2011. "Seán Ó Tuama and Irish Gaelic in the Twentieth Century." *American Journal of Irish Studies* 8: 117–36.

Boal, Frederick W. and David N. Livingstone. 1984. "The Frontier in the City: Ethnonationalism in Belfast." *International Political Science Review* 5 (2): 61–179.

Boyd, Stephen W. 2000. "'Heritage' Tourism in Northern Ireland: Opportunity under Peace." *Current Issues in Tourism* 3 (2): 150–74.

Brown, Stephen, Pierre McDonagh and Clifford J. Shultz II. 2013. "A Brand so Bad It's Good: The Paradoxical Place Marketing of Belfast." *Journal of Marketing Management* 29 (11–12): 1251–76.

Cohen, Anthony P. 1998. "Boundary, Culture, Identity." In *The Frontiers of Europe*, edited by Malcolm Anderson and Eberhard Bort, 22–35. London: Continuum International Publishing Group.

Dutton, Clive. 2004. "Gaeltacht Quarter: The establishment of a development board and related issues." *Final report to the Department of Culture, Art and Leisure, the Department of Social Development and the Department of Enterprise, Trade and Investment. Belfast.*

———. 2013. *The Big Gaeltacht Quarter Plan 2013–2033*. Belfast: Forbairt Feirste.

Emerson, Newton. 2008. "Siege Mentalities and the Fetishisation of West Belfast.' *Irish News*, May 15.

Eriksen, Thomas H. 1992. "Linguistic Hegemony and Minority Resistance." *Journal of Peace Research* 29 (3): 313–32.

Extramural Activity. 2013. "For the Record: International Wall." *Extra Mural Activity*, accessed February 28, 2014. http://extramuralactivity.com/2013/02/28/for-the-record-international-wall-2013-02/.

Gal, Susan. 2012. "Sociolinguistic Regimes and the Management of 'Diversity'." In *Language in Late Capitalism: Pride and Profit*, edited by Alexandre Duchêne and Monica Heller, 22–42. London: Routledge.

Gorter, Durk, ed. 2006. *Linguistic landscape: A new approach to multilingualism.* Clevedon: Multilingual Matters.

Hannerz, Ulf. 1996. *Transnational Connections: Culture, People, Places.* 1st ed. London: Routledge.

Hartnett, Alexandra. 2011. "Aestheticized Geographies of Conflict: The Politicization of Culture and the Culture of Politics in Belfast's Mural Tradition." In *Contested Cultural Heritage*, edited by Helaine Silverman, 69–107. New York: Springer.

Heller, Monica. 2006. *Linguistic Minorities and Modernity: A Sociolinguistic Ethnography.* London: Continuum.

Heller, Monica and Alexandre Duchêne. 2012. "Pride and Profit, Changing Discourses of Language, Capital and Nation-State." In *Language in Late Capitalism: Pride and Profit*, edited by Alexandre Duchêne and Monica Heller, 1–22. London: Routledge.

Hill, Andrew and Andrew White. 2012. "Painting Peace? Murals and the Northern Ireland Peace Process." *Irish Political Studies* 27 (1): 71–88.

Jaworski, Adam and Crispin Thurlow. 2010. *Semiotic Landscapes: Language, Image, Space.* London: Continuum International Publishing Group.

Kachuk, Patricia. 1993. "Irish Language Activism in West Belfast, a Resistance to British Cultural Hegemony." PhD diss., University of British Columbia.

Kallen, Jeffrey L. 2014. "The Political Border and Linguistic Identities in Ireland: What Can the Linguistic Landscape Tell Us?" *In Language, Borders and Identity* edited by Dominic Watt, 154–168. Edinburgh: Edinburgh University Press.

Kilkelly, Brian. 2014. "Clive Dutton Shares His Thoughts About One of the Most Resilient Places in the World." *World Cities Network*, accessed January 27, 2014. http://www.worldcitiesnetwork.org/knowledge-hub/article/clive-dutton-shares-his-thoughts-on-one-of-the-most-resilient-place-in-the-world-222/.

Landry, Rodrigue and Richard Y. Bourhis. 1997. "Linguistic Landscape and Ethnolinguistic Vitality." *Journal of Language and Social Psychology* 16 (1): 23–49.

Leonard, Madeleine. 2011. "A Tale of Two Cities: 'Authentic' Tourism in Belfast." *Irish Journal of Sociology* 19 (2): 111–26.

Leslie, David. 1999. "Terrorism and Tourism: The Northern Ireland Situation—A Look behind the Veil of Certainty." *Journal of Travel Research* 38 (1): 37–40.

Lisle, Debbie. 2006. "Local Symbols, Global Networks, Rereading the Murals of Belfast." *Alternatives, Global, Local, Political* 31 (1): 27–52.

Livingstone, Robin. 1998. *The Road: Memories of the Falls.* Belfast: Blackstaff Press.

Mac Ionnrachtaigh, Feargal. 2013. *Language, Resistance and Revival, Republican Prisoners and the Irish Language in the North of Ireland.* London: Pluto Press.

McCormick, Jonathan and Neil Jarman. 2005. "Death of a Mural." *Journal of Material Culture* 10 (1): 49–71.

McCoy, Gordon. 1997. "Protestant Learners of Irish in Northern Ireland." PhD diss., Queen's University Belfast.

McDowell, Sara. 2008. "Selling Conflict Heritage through Tourism in Peacetime Northern Ireland: Transforming Conflict or Exacerbating Difference." *International Journal of Heritage Studies* 14 (5): 405–21.

May, Stephen. 2011. *Language and Minority Rights: Ethnicity, Nationalism and the Politics of Language*. New York: Routledge.

Northern Ireland Tourist Board. 2008. *Northern Ireland Tourism 1948–2008: Past Achievements and Future Growth*. Belfast.

O'Dowd, Liam, and Milena Komarova. 2009. "Regeneration in a Contested City: A Belfast case study." *Conflict in Cities*.

O'Neill, Martin A. and Frank Fitz. 1996. "Northern Ireland Tourism: What Chance Now?" *Tourism Management* 17 (3): 161–3.

O'Reilly, Camille. 1998. *The Irish Language in Northern Ireland: The Politics of Culture*. Basingstoke: Macmillan.

Rolston, Bill. 1991. *Politics and Painting, Murals and Conflict in Northern Ireland*. Cranbury, NJ: Associated Universities Press.

———. 2012. "Re-imaging, Mural Painting and the State in Northern Ireland." *International Journal of Cultural Studies* 15 (5): 447–66.

———. 2013. *Drawing support 4: Murals and conflict transformation in Northern Ireland*.

Shohamy, Elana G. and Durk Gorter. 2009. *Linguistic Landscape, Expanding the Scenery*. London: Routledge.

Silverstein, Michael and Greg Urban. 1996. *Natural histories of discourse*. Chicago: University of Chicago Press.

Simone-Charteris, Maria and Stephen W. Boyd. 2010. "Northern Ireland Re-emerges from the Ashes, the Contribution of Political Tourism towards a More Visited and Peaceful Environment." In *Tourism, Progress, and Peace*, edited by Omar Moufakkir and Ian Kelly, 179–98. Wallingford: CABI.

Sluka, Jeffrey. 1992. "The Politics of Painting, Political Murals in Northern Ireland." In *The Paths to Domination, Resistance, and Terror*, edited by Caroline Nordstrom and JoAnn Martin, 190–216. Oxford: University of California Press.

Staunton, Mathew D. 2005. "Trojan Horses and Friendly Faces: Irish Gaelic Typography as Propaganda." *Revue LISA/LISA E-Journal. Littératures, Histoire Des Idées, Images, Sociétés Du Monde Anglophone—Literature, History of Ideas, Images and Societies of the English-Speaking World*, 3 (1): 85–98.

Urla, Jacqueline. 2012. *Reclaiming Basque: Language, nation and cultural activism*. Reno, NV: University of Nevada Press.

Wiedenhoft Murphy, Wendy Ann. 2010. "Touring the Troubles in West Belfast: Building Peace or Reproducing Conflict?" *Peace & Change* 35 (4): 537–60.

15 Extra-mural activities and trauma tourism

Public and community sector re-imaging of street art in Belfast

Katy Radford

This chapter examines the creation, removal and reception of murals on a small housing estate in West Belfast and the complexities as to how these processes can be interpreted, misinterpreted and reinterpreted. To do so, I draw on three broad perspectives: that of the tourist and the taxi company ferrying them to and from the mural sites; that of those involved in the creation of the mural; and my authorial reflections as someone who has been working as a practitioner and action-researcher on conflict transformation programmes on that estate for the past seventeen years.

Mural watching has been growing as a subject for examination in Northern Ireland since the early 1990s (Jarman, 1992, 1993, 1996a, b, 1998; McCormick and Jarman 2005; Rolston 2012). More recently, visiting murals has developed as a low-cost, high-drama tourist activity which Skinner (2015) recognizes as having potential to bring revenue and regeneration to deprived areas. Contrary to others who consider this a process of honourable 'political' tourism worthy of governmental marketing support, I consider much of this practice to be a continuation of predominantly sectarian, often party political, propaganda. To that end, I prefer to draw on Clarke's term, "trauma tourism" (2010). And while there is invariably a connection to Politics with both a small and a large 'p', there is an even more impactful one to the health and well-being of individuals and communities who live in the shadow of murals where traumatic loss and growth are ever present.

Here, my intention is to consider the impact murals, as a part of trauma-tourism on the Lower Shankill estate (and in surrounding areas), can have on the formation and sustaining of cultural heritage and identity, and also on the choreography of structural and relational dynamics between those who are 'stakeholders' in the re-imaging of areas. In so doing, I avoid an analysis of the tourist-trapping 'schtick tricks' of the tour guide as a performer (Feldman 2007 in Skinner 2014), whose sleight of hand between 'terrorist' versus 'freedom fighter', state 'oppressor' or 'defender' is undertaken specifically to leave the tourist reflecting through his (note the predominantly male domain) carefully planted smoke and mirrors. Rather, I prefer to consider the trans-generational impact of conflict-related trauma that can occur within communities who live with murals that are a staple of the emerging 'dark' and trauma tourism markets. I further suggest that murals act as a magnet for conflict-hungry tourists, for whom those with the lure of spent bullets, *l'air du cordite*, and pithy mantras are often of more interest than other more artistically complex interpretations or which point to the plurality of socio-economic struggles between otherwise segregated communities. Furthermore, I suggest that the murals do not provide any meaningful tourism with advantages to the area generally. While they may be of primary benefit to male former combatants or the taxi drivers and other political activists who wish to advance a particular ideology, they are of little or minimal economic benefit to the communities in which they are sited and are used to embed a sense of victimhood within the locale.

Mural watching one

February, 2015. It's raining in Denmark Street on the Lower Shankill Estate in Belfast. Horrible, sideways fast-falling rain, the relentless kind that creeps into loose cuffs and collars and leaves you damp for a day. The kind that bounces off anything flat, creating doubly wet surfaces as it lands a second time. West Belfast Sunday morning February rain. The Estate is in the Shankill area of Belfast, a small Protestant, Unionist and Loyalist enclave in the mainly Catholic, Nationalist Republican West Belfast.

The Shankill is bound on the West side by one of the many walls throughout the city (and other areas of Northern Ireland) that are known indiscriminately as both Peace Walls and Interface Barriers. They were erected by the Department of Justice to separate Catholic Nationalist Republicans from Protestant Unionist Loyalists, in the main in working class areas and, despite a governmental commitment to ensuring they will all be removed by 2023, they are maintained by the Government as community consultations indicate a desire by residents for their presence. Running up to and into the West side of the interface is the Falls Road. The collective name given to murals that appear there is referred to as the 'International Wall', and it is the first stop on the agenda of any self-respecting cab driver's dark-tourism tour. Perhaps unsurprisingly, that is not just because of the frequently changing content and artistic diversity of the murals, but because one of the enduring murals on the wall indicates the centrality of the West Belfast Taxi Association to the mural's tourism. The majority of drivers within the Association are interconnected through their overarching Republican heritage and commitment to the many factions who have taken to both armed and political struggle for autonomy from Britain.

Over the past decades, the International Wall has been a beacon of imagery that draws attention to universally recognizable global injustices and conflicts that highlight victims of international colonial oppression and state force. *No imperialist intervention in Iran* (2006). *Support the Hunger Strikers in Turkey* (2004). Murals here are painted and maintained by those connected to the Republican movement, and consequently, references to British and state rights and other abuses are a key focal point – 'Collusion was not only not an illusion'. Images are frequently replaced and often aligned by visual design or the use of graphics and language, one geographical situation with another. *Where in the World?* (2014) is a mural that depicts terrified Palestinian children fleeing from smiling Israeli soldiers with the message 'Immediate expulsion of All Israeli Diplomats from Eire' found at the bottom. The image makes a direct visual equation of the Israeli Operation 'Protective Edge' in Gaza with Nick Ut's 1971 Associated Press Pulitzer-winning image of the Vietnam War. As with the murals and other pictorial art on the walls in the West Bank and Gaza, the language is predominantly English, but with some key words in Irish, Basque and Arabic. *Palestine: We will return Barbarian Israeli Aggression* (2009), *Askatasuna* (2009), *Cuba 50 years* (2009), *Saoirse do Peltier* (2006). These, with their distinct international focus, sit alongside murals with commentary on changing local matters, with some memorializing key historical injustices and icons relevant to a range of Republican parties and ideological movements both historical and contemporary, including the H-block Hunger Strikers, the 32 County Sovereignty Movement, the Police use of Plastic bullets on children and the West Belfast Taxi Association. The relevance of the Taxi Association's role servicing tourists and its motivation as a key interest group in the retention of politically motivated murals, particularly those marking division between the two majority communities in West Belfast, will be built on as the interwoven narratives within this chapter unfold.

Through the interface barrier, an extension of the wall marks the perimeter of the Loyalist heartland at Cupar Way. There, images are no longer easy or clear to see. Drivers from the West Belfast Taxi Association are key amongst those mural tour providers who provide their fares with black markers to sign their names on murals on the Loyalist side. Consequently, works by a range of muralists that are sited on the Loyalist side have been defaced. This includes that of the eminent Irish artist, Rita Duffy RUA (Member of the Royal Ulster Academy). Murals were traditionally painted onto walls. This practice has been developed over the years so that murals are now created in a range of materials, including photographs onto Perspex (acrylic glass), painting onto plywood. Her mural "Banquet", a 30-feet-long photographic panelled mural tribute to Women's Suffrage, is a bright, colourful piece featuring an image of many women dressed to represent the historical and contemporary contribution made by women in Northern Ireland to equality in education, employment and to achieving democratic voting rights in 1928. It was funded by the Arts Council of Northern Ireland and originally launched on the Shankill Road to mark the centenary of International Women's Day on April 8, 2011. Its social significance and artistic value was reported extensively in the broadcast and print media, not least because of the artist's reputation, but also because of its significant recalibration of the gendered nature of the subject of and those artists who are creating murals within the area. It was not long before 'the boys' – the term of ironic endearment applied to loyalist community activists who have close connections to paramilitaries – had negotiated a permanent place for it on the Cupar Way wall (to replace a 2002 board mural celebrating the 50th Anniversary of Queen Elizabeth II's coronation), and even less time before it's deterioration began to be orchestrated: at the end of 2015, Duffy's work had been extensively scrawled over by hundreds of visiting tourists.

Thus, it can be seen that tourists' experiences of visiting murals in West Belfast are significantly different on each side of the interface. On the Republican side, tourists are invited to stand with respect in reverential solidarity with community artists' interpretations of those who have been oppressed, more often than not with links back to British imperialism and colonialism. The imagery is deeply political and personalized with grief and isolation, and the violence and brutality of imposed regimes is the principal *leit motif*. On the Loyalist side, taxi drivers invite their fares to participate in the degeneration of the mural Berlin-Wall-graffiti-style, thus negating, and, signature-by-signature, removing the artistry or craftsmanship in the murals, a number of which have been publically funded as part of a series of regeneration programmes. Signs put up by those responsible for the murals remain ignored. The images on the Loyalist side range from those such as work of Duffy – providing a classically art-school trained vision – to those which are often misspelt, heartfelt graffiti relating to perceived betrayals and political chicanery aimed at naming and shaming perpetrators both from within and outside the community.

A black taxi is parked by the one commercial outlet on the Lower Shankill Estate, a small newsagent and sweetshop. The estate has approximately 450 public housing and privately owned homes, a primary school and a health centre. It's red, white and blue painted kerbstones mark the estate out as Loyalist. During the year 2000, a loyalist feud on the estate saw the UDA displace scores of individuals and families who had allegiance to rival loyalist group, the Ulster Volunteer Force (UVF).

A young woman leaves the shop carrying a pint of milk and hurries through the rain past the cab. She avoids any eye contact with the taxi driver and 'tuts' at the cab's occupants – who are grappling with cameras and clearly there to photograph the mural at the end of her street – as she is forced to walk around them and step through a puddle to enter her home. The small 1970s-built double-storey terraced houses has a flowerless front garden paved over to secure a safe space for an aspired-for car and plastic-sit-upon toy trucks. The small porch recently built onto the house next door to hers sets that apart from other more uniform houses, indicating that it is now owner-occupied rather than retained as public housing. The impact of private ownership extends past the individual upward mobility of former tenants, who became owner-occupiers after purchasing public housing stock at discount. Rather, it means that when those properties are resold on the open market, they are of interest to those from outside the area hungry for commercial investment on the demonized estate with its immediate proximity to the city centre. This steady increase of external ownership is an issue that is bubbling under the surface for community activists in the area who are fearful of how this might destabilize any balance of power and the local allegiances on the estates.

The gable wall on the end of the street displays the image of a moustached man with paramilitary symbols. The taxi's Catalan occupants, Yanhira and Amadeu, are now photographing it. They stand out as 'foreign' in belted puffa jackets in bold primary colours. They are enthralled by the driver's well-rehearsed stories of his youth in 1970s Belfast, which he paints red in tooth and claw (to paraphrase Tennyson) with tales of bullets, blood and bombings and shades with hints of involvement in a world of state and security collusion, internment and betrayals. The Catalans, like the taxi driver – who gives them barely any information on the mural and only a very generalized overview of the body of work on the estate – are oblivious to the microdynamics of the estate and the nuances of the lives of those who live there. They have been living in Republican West Belfast for six months and have a keen interest in murals. In preparation for the November 9th, 2014, non-binding vote on Catalonian independence, they painted a bright yellow mural with red and black lettering with the date and a plea for their countrymen to "Say Yes to the Referendum for Independence for Catalan Countries". Sponsoring and executing the mural on the International Wall necessitated their painting over of a mural dedicated to the first Irish Republican Army (IRA) blanketman/hunger striker, Kieran Nugent. (The Catalans add comedic insult to injury by pronouncing Nugent's name with a hard 'g'). The consternation this created within Republican circles was not without note and took some smoothing over by a range of intermediaries with the Catalans left feeling taken advantage of by the whole process: "I think it was something to do with inter-Republican rivalries – someone else wanted that mural down so we were encouraged to paint over it and then it was gone and we got the blame" came their explanation. After the vote, Danny Devaney, the veteran and well-respected Republican muralist, repainted the image of Kieran Nugent over the Catalan's mural. The second version differs from the first in that there is an inclusion of a reference to the women's protest in Armagh prison; one of the figures standing holds a poster reading 'Thatcher – Wanted for murder and torture of Irish prisoners' poster that previously filled the top-left corner.

This is the first time the Catalans have ventured into the Loyalist area to consider the murals there. They look up at the moustached face and the banner above his head, which reads 'Lt. Co. William 'Bucky' McCollough'. A Shankill-born man, Bucky McCollough was ascribed the moniker Lieutenant Colonel as a leading figure with the Inner Circle of the West Belfast paramilitary Ulster Defence Association (UDA). He joined the UDA in 1971 and his alleged involvement in sectarian killings and racketeering to fund the Ulster Freedom Fighters (UFF) (its military wing) saw him frequently questioned but never charged by the police force, the then

Royal Ulster Constabulary. A Loyalist 'icon' (Lister and Jordan 2004, 335), on October 16, 1981, he was shot 12 times at the door of his house on the Shankill Estate where he lived with his wife and children, the youngest of whom, Alan, was 3 months old at the time of his father's death. His widow still continues to live on the street close to the mural where she raised the children under his painted vigilance. Many within the UDA consider that he had been set up by another UDA extortionist (James Craig, later killed by the UFF for his alleged collusion with both the IRA and INLA), but his killing was, in fact, carried out by the INLA. The mural erected as McCullough's memorial remains, despite the majority of others in the area being regularly removed or replaced. Thirty years after it was first painted, 'the Belfast fresco', as some sardonically refer to it, is 'touched up' every few years. It remains a constant reminder to his family, other residents and visitors to that community that the area's history continues to be deeply connected to the loyalist paramilitary grouping, the UDA, irrespective of any other messages of the day being transmitted.

On a pale blue background, the mural has several key components. A tondo with a frame of red flowers encircles McCullough's face with the dates of his life on it (1949–1981). They look surprisingly poppy-like but, as those flowers are normally associated with the rivalry loyalist paramilitary grouping the Ulster Volunteer Force (UVF), the artist may well have intended them to be roses or camellia. At the bottom of the mural, the message 'In loving memory of all our fallen comrades from A Coy, B Coy, C Coy from 2 Batt UFF West Belfast Brigade. Murdered by the Enemies of Ulster' is inscribed on a cartouche in the form of an unfurling scroll. The silhouettes of two men in combat fatigues and carrying rifles flank McCullough, who wears a green army-style jumper. To the side of McCullough's face are two shields – one representing the UDA and the other, its military with the UFF – and to the left and right of the shields are two pillars resting on plinths inscribed 'Always Remembered' and '*Quis Separabit*' (the motto of the UDA) (Figure 15.1).

Mural watching two

October 2, 2015. There is an unusual amount of activity outside the Living Hope Church on Shankill Parade. Photographers from a news agency and the local paper are arranging into poses local Councillors and MLAs, workers from the Northern Ireland Housing Executive and from the Arts Council for Northern Ireland, and the Belfast artist Leslie Cherry, who has been responsible for realizing the vision of the Lower Shankill Community Association (LSCA). The LSCA is the body working for the regeneration of the area and is closely connected to the UDA. Three white police Land Rovers are parked along the road and a number of middle-ranking officers stand chatting to a number of middle-ranking community and voluntary workers who are providing 'security and bodyguard' to members of the

Figure 15.1 Title: William 'Bucky' McCollough Lower Shankill Estate, Belfast.
Source: Neil Jarman.

LSCA. Today marks the official launch of five new murals. After a series of negotiations with community activists, the LSCA are unveiling a range of murals to replace former images. In an unusual departure for murals supplanting others, reproductions of the replaced images now appear below the new panels in small frames with explanations as to their content. This provides both a continuity with the past and the continuation of a tradition of paramilitary murals remaining on the wall as subordinates to the new non-paramilitary mural. The speeches are over, and a photo-op tour of the new murals is about to begin. Ian McLaughlin, the spokesman for the LSCA, suggests that they indicate a move forward in how the community wishes to present itself to itself and to wider society. In response to the terms of reference for the tender for the work that McLaughlin was involved in drawing up and appointing the artist on, Cherry committed to undertake a series of consultations with local residents, hence the presence in the hall of a excited bunch of primary school children, a women's group and elderly residents from a local sheltered-housing 'fold', all vying with each other, and the police, press and 'the boys' in the back of the room for the chicken goujons and cocktail sausages laid on as both an incentive and thank you for their attendance at the event.

The main group members of the tour are standing on Denmark Street underneath a large-scale representation of the old disability activists' slogan 'Nothing about us without us is for us'. The text is superimposed over hundreds of photographs of local people and places brought by some of those that Cherry has consulted with in a skilled and successful facilitation process that ensured buy-in by those consulted with the consultees – it replaces the Malvern Street Orange Arch mural. At the photo line-up, there is a degree of good-natured jockeying for position, and elected representatives from the DUP and SDLP tweet their presence at and approval of the images and re-imaging.

Many in this new tranche of murals draws on aspirational political rhetoric and comprise of single or composite photographs overlaid with text with a heavy use of graphic design onto plastic and board. Gone are the visually representational and more aesthetically painterly murals painted onto whitewashed walls. No more like the 'Cromwell and the Protestant martyrs' with historical, metanarrative-perpetuating sectarian division and supremacy. In place of a Scotland/Ulster mural comprising flags and red hands alongside an Ulster Freedom Fights (UFF) emblem, and one for a defunct company within the UFF masked men, a new mural featuring a quotation from the anthropologist Margaret Mead also makes the cut. Mead, however, is cited not as an anthropologist, but as an American author. Laid over a map of the Shankill is the quotation: 'Never Doubt that a small group of thoughtful, concerned citizens can CHANGE THE WORLD' (the capitals indicating a desire for direct action). I wander off and find the artist and Sam Hinton, who I first met when he was preparing a wall by painting it white for new murals during the Loyalist Feud of 2000 on the estate. They are standing beneath one of Leslie's new text-led creations *Don't call me Resilient* (Figure 15.2).

Policy

Northern Ireland is a region that remains a segregated and divided society 20 years after the IRA ceasefire and 15 years after the signing of the Good Friday (Belfast) Agreement. This event in 1998 heralded, amongst other seismic shifts by powerful armed groups to address previous inequalities, the decommissioning of weapons held by paramilitaries and the normalization of security arrangements, including a remodelling of the police service. It might have been anticipated that gable walls with images of paramilitaries might also have been decommissioned at that time, but yet images of masked men, paramilitary insignia and weaponry remain a familiar feature of public life and news. They continue to be a barometer by which to gauge territorial allegiance, public opinion and local dynamics as directed by those purporting to speak on behalf of communities in which they operate.

The latest round of internationally mediated 'peace' initiatives, the Haas O'Suillivan talks designed to address stalemates within the Peace Process, resulted in the 2014 Stormont House Agreement. Within this, the concept of 'Dealing with the Past' was identified as a key priority for all political parties. The re-imaging of Estates like the Lower Shankill are in keeping with progressing both this and the aims of the Programme for Government

Figure 15.2 "Don't Call Me Resilient": justifying victim-status overseen by para-
          military flags.
Source: Neil Jarman.

strategy in relation to both social and economic regeneration, as well as the Office of the First Minister and Deputy First Minister's overarching community cohesion strategy 'Together Building a United Community' (2013). Within that strategy, the aim of addressing the bipolarity of society by building a united community based on equality of opportunity, the desirability of good relations and reconciliation is aspirational and aligned to one 'where cultural expression is celebrated and embraced'. Accompanying these overarching strategies are a series of departmental and localized policies and protocols that address how social regeneration can be aided by the use of a range of art forms, and the use of symbols and emblems in the design and use of public spaces. This includes the Arts Council of Northern Ireland (2013a) Five Year Strategic Plan (2013–2018), 'Ambitions for the Arts', which incorporates the need to engage the most marginalized and to target social exclusion and the Northern Ireland Housing Executive's (NIHE) internal Social Investment Plan. The Building Peace through the Arts initiative which builds on the Arts Council for Northern Ireland (ACNI) (2013b) Art of Regeneration and Re-Imaging Communities Programmes is supported by both the NIHE and ACNI. It operates at a budget of just under 2.5K Sterling and is a grant-based programme 'to enable communities to positively, collaboratively and artistically express who they are, through localized public art projects' (Wallace 2014, 6). Wallace's review of the Re-Imaging programme concluded that the removal of mural and emblems were locally contentious and as 'projects were encouraged to move at their own pace. [...] [t]he work often involved lengthy discussion, negotiations and protracted timescales' which were further stalled by the political situation and external events or tensions that impacted the programme and consequently resulted in 'a few of the projects stalling because of statements made by political representatives and others' (Wallace 2014, 6).

Politics of memory and identity

Clearly, then, it can be seen that murals and the components within them that address memorialization are facets that embody the challenges faced by government and communities as they commit to moving forward and engaging in conflict transformation and de facto preparing Northern Ireland for normalization as a site for economic and tourist regeneration. The murals, however, whilst attractive to some tourists, have a greater imperative in that they epitomize and are explicitly used to consolidate forms and expressions of identity that impact on both state and community norms of authority and de facto governance within communities. This is often reflected in responses to aggressive, predominantly male (both subject and creators) and militaristic models. David Rieff (2011, 55–56) suggests that 'historical memory is rarely as hospitable to peace and reconciliation as it is to grudges and martyrdom', and in this instance, it is clearly eminent in traditional murals. Memory and identity are clearly being imprinted onto the physical environment through murals, and this in turn has an impact on the type of tourism that is both being sought out by and for whom it is being proffered.

The politics of identity and political memory are complex and interlinked concepts that can be split into two spheres: the first, the big meta-camp, which has political rhetoric and collective certainty at the fore; and the second, a small space where the personal and individual relational interactions with events occur. Each of these has the potential to challenge critics of plural narratives by imposing fixed meaning. And, in so doing, the democracy of memory and identity can become a casualty of historical and territorial recontextualising. Imposing such partial narratives creates an unbalanced relationship between communities and their past that lies on a rather lumpy double mattress of memory creation and sustenance. By sustenance, I consider the way in which the commodification of memory is played out to fuel the needs of the viewer, both internal (residents and community activists) and external (tourists' and their tour guides). And it would seem that while there is little to be gained ethically and economically by 'trauma' murals, there is much to be gained ideologically and, more specifically, in terms of advancing sectarian politics by painting it into the landscape.

It is also noteworthy that mural artists grapple with how to bring novelty to murals, painting in their practice through form, graphics, subject and materials. This struggle is not just impacted by the availability of material resources but also in the readiness and capacity of the communities and their funders to engage with new concepts that move away from trauma and victimhood, either directly or indirectly. In the following section, I endeavour to illustrate this with reference to the murals *Lt. Col. Bucky McCullough* and *Resilience*, both subjects of which can be seen to have impacted significantly on conflict transformation processes, throwing into relief some people's hopes of and aspirations for a shared future.

Lt. Col. Bucky McCullough

Paul Ricouer (2004) problematizes the hierarchy in which some commemoration and memorialization confers a hierarchy in afterlife, refusing to let the dead be erased. This problematic is clearly bestowed through political and ideological murals in public arenas that see the military and paramilitary dead elevated from the rank and file to achieve iconic eminence, status and principal identity as political heroes and martyrs. Bucky McCullough has, for 30 years, been casting a watchful eye over those who pass by the Denmark Street on which he resided. Bucky's son, Alan – the baby of 3 months at the time of his father's death – was a key contributor to a research project that I was conducting the interviews for with participants from Northern Ireland discussing the recruitment of Young Soldiers to paramilitary organizations for the International Labour Organisation and the Quaker Office at the UN in Geneva (Brett and Specht 2004). When we first met, he was a 17-year-old on the estate and a member of the Ulster Young

Militants, the youth wing associated with the UDA. He wore an image of his dead father around his neck. He was immensely proud to be connected to, and both running drugs to and from, 'the flats on the estate' and carrying out other illegal errands for the paramilitary leader/gangster Johnny Adair, who was a significant controlling element within the UDA in West Belfast and living on the estate at that time. By the age of 21, Alan had allegedly become the military commander for Adair's West Belfast 'C' Company and, together with Adair and other associates, had been expelled from Northern Ireland by other factions within the UDA; Adair's rogue criminality had grown after a bloody coup on the estate in 2000. Alan had grown up with his father's image painted 30 feet high on the gable wall of the house where he lived. The mural was a constant reminder of his family and community history valorizing his father's role as a paramilitary leader. Irrespective of the choices Alan made in terms of his loyalty to Adair, it could be suggested that Bucky's Lt. Col. mural persona was a created memory, an absent presence in his son's life permanently memorialized in his combat fatigues. The dominant identity being 'remembered', and that which Alan grew up with on a daily basis, was not that of a family man, nor is he remembered as an avuncular neighbourhood watchman, or a smiling community support, but rather, that of a quasi-militiaman. His mural renders his multi-facedness as a human being into a two dimensional single identity rendition; that of the guardian of a specific collective and cultural community narrative where aspirations to militarism, sacrifice and self-sacrifice are aspirational projections of individuals whose engagement in armed combat is related to violence undertaken in the name of criminality and sectarian killings, but which is glorified, by association, through the creation of hierarchical titles drawn from a British Army tradition.

Perhaps it is unsurprising, then, that his son Alan attached himself in a partnership of patronage to following the most powerful man on his estate with a view of both acquiring his own status and that of rising through the UDA's ranks to avenge his father's death. Alan unashamedly lived to recreate his father's reputation within the UDA and in so doing aimed to emulate a false memory projected by the painted persona of his father whom he considered to be Lt. Col. Bucky McCullough. However, before the end of the year he turned 21, Alan's body was found in a quarry with two bullets in his head. He had been executed by his father's former companions and shot dead for his connections to the renegade UDA faction. No mural was erected to the Young Soldier, but graffiti appeared on the Shankill on the day of his funeral justifying his murder.

Resilience

Rieff (2011, 28) notes that "History is not a menu. You can't have the solidarity that national myth helps form and sustain but not the self-absorption, or the pride but not the fear." This Janus-faced concept is applicable within loyalism and is manifest in the process of mural-making, impacting on how they are commissioned, created and maintained.

Sam Hinton and Lesley stand beside the two smaller images underneath *Resilience* which commemorate the two murals that were replaced. One of these registered the community's dissatisfaction with Sinn Fein's commitment to the Peace Process. The other, from 2007, celebrated the USA President Andrew Jackson's Ulster Scots heritage. Their time has now passed; they were not of significant importance on the LSCA's radar to retain, and the artist is unclear of the back story of by whom and why there were originally erected. 'Do you know Sam, Katy? He's been my minder on the estate.'

Cherry's *Resilience* mural is based on a quotation from and credits Tracie L Jackson of the Louisiana Justice Institute. With lettering over a cloudy sky, the mural reads:

'Stop calling me RESILIENT. Because every time you say, "Oh, they're resilient," that means you can do something else to me. I am not resilient'.

The plaque beneath the mural describes how it was chosen by the Lower Shankill Community Association as a quotation reflective of their 'struggle in attaining what is best for their community, at present and also, how it can shape their future'. A copy of the mural hangs in Ian McLaughlin's offices. It might also be suggested that the message being imparted by Jackson's quote is one of victimhood, a trope that is a large part of how some members of the PUL community chose to perceive and define themselves in an example of what Scott (1987) might considered to be a 'weapon of the weak'.

Both Lesley and Hinty provide different examples of resilience. Lesley has doggedly and successfully pursued a career as a freelance gallery and community artist in a climate where artists with less adaptability and flexibility in their practice have been unable to live by their art alone. She has sought publicly funded commissions, responded to invitations to tender and build a strong reputation as an artist. Incidentally, she is from a Loyalist background and within a mixed partnership – able to work safely in and representing the interests of a range of communities. 'Hinty', irrespective of all other roles he assumes, is an affable Jack the Lad with a twinkle in his eye and father of 'god knows how many now, Katy, more than anyone knows about'. He is named by Lister (2012) as being one of the 'hooded men' who swore Johnny Adair into the UDA in 1984 and remains connected to factions in the Ulster Political Research Group (UPRG), the political advisory body connected to the UDA leadership both within and outside the area.

The collective efforts by statutory services and community organizations to engage in programmes to reclaim the folk and community art on the Lower Shankill estate could be seen as a base of something of an unholy trinity of interdependence between themselves and artists alike. All of them acknowledge the need for change within the area and that social and economic regeneration, including that which comes through arts and tourism, can be aided by re-imaging paramilitary murals. But how that is progressed is problematic. The positives in replacing murals are many. Statutory service providers and arms' length bodies are able to fulfil their obligations under governmental and organizational policy directives. Community activists are able to clean up unwanted and obsolete murals, and by so doing, replace them with images that maintain their leadership, with and without paramilitarism being explicitly portrayed. Taxi drivers are able to service fares irrespective of the subject matter. New murals continue to assert internal and external messages of power and status within areas: they have the potential to generate income and ensure the activists are seen to facilitate and enable consultation with the community in the creation of the message. Finally, artists are able to increase their productivity and develop their practice by the creation of work that can be endorsed and or informed both by a receptive audience and by a grateful funding body with its own public relations machinery to spin the process.

On the other hand, the challenges facing all those with a vested interest in the murals' replacements are that the fragilities and limitations of each stakeholder needs to be mediated and managed sensitively so that, as they realize their desires, they are not seen to exert an overall authorial position that might compromise the needs of those others invested in the process. Given that the most powerful community activists are invariably still linked into paramilitary organizations and former armed groups, their negotiations are complex. In negotiating, they have to consider the views of those still wedded to those organizations as well as others within the community who wish to see a move away from their glorification. Consequently, the continuation of the life of the mural is itself the message, to paraphrase McLuhan's (1964) theory. Miller (2000) suggests three distinctive approaches to carrying out biographical research, 'realist' (based on grounded theory), 'neo-positivist' (based on the interpretation of structured interview techniques), and 'narrative' (the active construction emanating from the dialectic between interviewer and interviewee). I suggest that this model, when reapplied to the biographical within the culture of murals within working class Belfast, benefits from the addition of a fourth category: namely, that of the reflection of the local audience, not just resident, but also that of tourist and the funding and sponsoring agents. The mural's content and changes, in a number of instances, is superfluous to the structural ongoing changes and the recalibration of power that occurs over time with their perpetuation. The internal and external tourism aspect plays a key role in this reconfiguration.

Consequently, I propose that this 'reflective', distinct and essential fourth category be considered to be rooted in the dialogue between the self and others. It emerges over a period of time in those whose experiences have some level of connection and insight into trauma tourism. It provides the viewer with both an explicit and an indirect opportunity to engage in trans-generational recovery, allowing the 'insider' viewer to break a negative feedback narrative loop and restore the balance between the historical legacy and the present future. But equally, for those unprepared or ill-equipped for recovery, it can feed into the continuation of trans-generational trauma. Moreover, for the external 'viewer', the tourist (and those who sustain the tourist industry), it also can also provide insight into trauma voyeurism.

Memory entrepreneurs

In relation to the end of a life cycle for murals, McCormick and Jarman (2005) consider a schema comprising retirement, redundancy, recycling, redevelopment, reclamation, remonstration and restoration. The framework is valuable in as far as it recognizes the organic, dynamic nature of mural creation and the temporal nature of their existence. Furthermore, it provides a structure within which the community is able to own the shifting political sands in which it resides and operates irrespective of statutory responses to it. For the majority of tourists, the archaeology of murals on the Estate is not their concern – theirs is a more superficial and current flashbulb momentary interest. However, for those tourists with a more nuanced understanding of the historical and contemporary significance of the mural, the Lower Shankill Estate provides multiple examples of each of these typologies. The frequent turns in its residents' history indicate shifting political alliances and deposed paramilitary leaders, both of which have, at times, impacted greatly on the demographics of the area. What has remained constant is Bucky McCullough and the use of murals – both those left and those removed – to mark the territorial boundaries left in the wake of whatever local political turmoil has just played out.

Elizabeth Jellin (2004) proposes that agents of the state have a central role in establishing links between both history and memory. The notion of 'memory entrepreneurs' has been explored in relation to how selective and collective memory can be harnessed to agitate and reinforce meta-political narratives in other geographical areas (Zerubavel 1995; Misztal 2003; Olick et al. 2011). Within the context of West Belfast murals, providing a lens through which to consider the political traction of memory-making, it is useful to look not just at the role of the state, but also at the formal (and informal) alliances between funding agents (the state) and community activists (both pro- and anti-state). This chapter has not sought to propose a novel definition of collective memory. Since Halbswachs' 1925 framework was defined (Halbswach 1992), it remains wedded to the principle that both the content and process of memory-making can be shaped by and in collective social experiences. I do not seek to untangle the distinction between the imperative of history and the social construction of memory, which was Nora's undertaking (1989). Rather, my intention is to point to the symbiotic relationship between the artist, their sponsor and those they seek to serve that privileges how some community memories of historical truths and forensic facts become more equal than others through the creation and viewing of murals. The Estate's walls provide theatrical flats and backdrops to the dramas of its human trag-edies. Alan McCullough's descent into UDA disfavour was not considered worthy of recollection other than in passing as graffiti, but the legacy of his murderous father, Bucky McCullough, is rendered a single two-dimensional image whilst the collective united voice of victimhood and solidarity on the Estate is captured in multiple anonymous photographic images.

Conclusion

My interest remains focused on the choreography of mutually supporting and codependent structural and relational tensions between internal and external participants in the mural 'business'. On the one hand, there are 'internals': the mural artist, residents and sponsors (both funding agencies and community activists) who are committed to mural development for a range of reasons, including community cohesion and community relations. And on the other, there are the 'externals', who provide both a counter-balance and an overlap in terms of interpretation and commodification of the murals, in particular tourists and those driving an agenda for a trauma or political tourism. This latter group includes politicians, academics and some community activists. Within this, I am occupied with the negotiations around the creation, content and retention of both 'the contentious and the contested' and the 'do no harm' murals that create or subvert a collective sense of community memory which in turn is captured by tourists at a par-ticular point in time, thus providing a temporal tourist memory of space and place, which is often at odds with the nuances and actuality of changing dynamics within communities. Furthermore, I am mindful of the extent to which aesthetics, artistic integrity and creativity can be sacrificed as part of the trade-off as particular artists acquire favoured status within commu-nities for their compliance with community memory-making rather than those who bring alternative visions that might challenge those of the com-munity leadership or the funders' expectations.

Murals as folk-art forms advance a range of important debates in Northern Ireland in relation to identity, memorialization and to certain aspects of tourism that sit as comfortably in some quarters as they sit uncomfortably in others. The dim lighting of both arts funding and arts policy development impacts on the way in which such murals are developed and supported (or not), through the formal tourist industry. Skinner (2015) entertainingly and accurately points to Hansard recordings that indicate the political dichot-omy that elected representatives, strategists and policy makers find when debating the worth of promoting mural tourism. Given then, that the mu-rals' value as a tourist strategy is as contested as their content, is the solution then not to remember, or, as Elie Wiesel proposes, might this mean that "To forget would be the enemy's ultimate victory"?

To remember through murals, to revise the value of historical events and artistic endeavours through their messages and to see them as a gauge of communities' relationships with themselves or with the outside the world, are all issues that need to be at the forefront for those interested in pursuing the inclusion of mural visiting in any emerging tourism strategy. To that end, there are a number of potential proposals that might be thought through when appraising the potential of any such process. These considerations include muddling along in a 'do no harm' organic way, ignoring the destruction and recycling of murals without archiving them but providing tourists with that 'aphrodisiac of cordite' moment in terms of vicarious trauma. It could include building up the industry and craft of mural-making to maximize the cultural and economic potential of trauma tourism and, in so doing, aid government targets in terms of regeneration. It could be the imposing of a legislative stay on the making of contentious murals in a climate of building a more inclusive and less segregated society. Finally, public funds could be administered to create new mechanisms for community activists to work together to realize the artistic and economic potential of community art through non-contentious political murals. It is through this last option that the cultural and economic potential for murals can be collectively recognized and their benefits maximized, without disadvantaging those living in their shadow and exploiting their former traumas for the benefit of tourism.

Further up the Shankill Road, in an area still controlled by the paramilitary organization, the Ulster Volunteer Force (UVF) is a mural of the late David Irvine. The political party he led, the Progressive Unionist Party, remains the mouthpiece for that political body and a community group close to the party (The West Belfast Athletic and Cultural Society), who were key drivers in the removal and £50,000 fundraising to replace a UVF band mural with a mural of the war-artist William Conor. This was done specifically to broaden the area's appeal as a 'cultural corridor' for tourists. Close by, Irvine's mural is accompanied by a statesmanlike quotation (unattributed to its original author); the result is that the viewer recalibrates any view of Irvine away from that perspective which might focus on his role as a former paramilitary activist and prisoner arrested for the possession of commercial explosives when in a stolen car, to that of his later years as political leader and head of his party. So, perhaps, the answer then, is to revisit the Santayana quotation that accompanies Irvine's mural and to recognize that one option could be to rewrite this so that it reads: 'those who cannot remember the past are doomed to repaint it'.

References

Arts Council of Northern Ireland. 2013a. *Ambitions for the Arts: A Five Year Strategic Plan for the Arts in Northern Ireland 2013–2018*. Belfast, accessed March 8, 2016. http://www.artscouncil-ni.org/images/uploads/publications-documents/ambitions-for-the-arts-5-year-strategy.pdf.

————. 2013b. *Building Peace through the Arts: Reimagining Communities.* Brochure, accessed March 8, 2016.. http://www.artscouncil-ni.org/images/uploads/publications-documents/Re-Imaging_A5_8pp.pdf.

Brett, Rachel and Irma Specht. 2004. *Young Soldiers: Why They Choose to Fight.* London: Lynne Rienner.

Clarke, Laurie Beth. 2010. "Always Already Again: Tramua Tourism and the Politics of Memory Culture." *Encounters 1.* Department of Tourism and Transnational Studies, Dokkyo University, Japan, 65–74.

Feldman, Jackie. 2007. "Constructing a Shared Bible Land: Jewish Israeli Guiding Performances for Protestant Pilgrims." *American Ethnologist* 34 (2): 351–74.

Government of United Kingdom. 2014. *The Stormont House Agreement,* accessed March 8, 2016. https://www.gov.uk/government/uploads/system/uploads/attachment_data/file/390672/Stormont_House_Agreement.pdf.

Halbswachs, Maurice. 1992. *On Collective Memory.* Chicago: University of Chicago Press.

Jarman, Neil. 1992. "Troubled Images: The Iconography of Loyalism." *Critique of Anthropology* 12: 133–45.

————. 1993. "Intersecting Belfast." In *Landscape, politics and perspectives,* edited by Barbara Bender, 107–38. Oxford: Berg.

————. 1996a. "The Ambiguities of Peace: Republican and Loyalist Ceasefire Murals." *Causeway (Cultural Traditions Journal)* 3(1): 23–7.

————. 1996b. "Violent Men, Violent Land: Dramatizing the Troubles and the Landscape of Ulster." *Journal of Material Culture* 1 (1): 39–61.

————. 1998. "Painting Landscapes: The Place of Murals in the Symbolic Construction of Urban Space." In *Symbols in Northern Ireland,* edited by A. Buckley, 81–98. Belfast: Institute of Irish Studies, Queens' University.

Jellin, Elizabeth. 2004. *State Repression and the Labours of Memory.* Minneapolis, MN: University of Minnesota Press.

Lister, David and Hugh Jordan. 2004. *Mad Dog: The Rise and Fall of Johnny Adair and 'C Company'.* London: Random House.

McCormick, Jonathan and Neil Jarman. 2005. "Death of a Mural." *Journal of Material Culture* 10 (1): 49–71.

McLuhan, Marshall. 1964. *Understanding Media: The Extensions of Man.* New York: McGraw-Hill.

Miller, Robert Lee. 2000. *Researching Life Stories and Family Histories.* London: Sage Publications.

Misztal, Barabra A. 2003. *Theories of Social Remembering.* New York: McGraw-Hill.

Nora, Pierre. 1989. "Between Memory and History: Les Lieux de Memoire." *Representations* 26: 7–24. doi:10.2307/2928520.

Northern Ireland Executive Office. 2013. *Together Building a United Community.* Belfast: Office of the First Minister and Deputy First Minister, accessed March 8, 2016. https://www.executiveoffice-ni.gov.uk/sites/default/files/publications/ofmdfm_dev/together-building-a-united-community-strategy.pdf.

Northern Ireland Office. 1998. *The Belfast Agreement.* Government of the United Kingdom, accessed March 8, 2016. https://www.gov.uk/government/publications/the-belfast-agreement.

Olick, Jeffrey K., Vered Vinitzky-Seroussi and Daniel Levy, eds. 2011. *The Collective Memory Reader.* New York: Oxford University Press.

Ricouer, Paul. 2004. *Memory, History, Forgetting*. Chicago: University of Chicago Press.

Rieff, David. 2011. *Against Remembrance*. Melbourne: Melbourne University Press.

Rolson Bill. 2012. "Re-imaging: Mural Painting and the State in Northern Ireland." *International Journal of Cultural Studies* 15 (5): 447–66.

Scott, James. 1987. *Weapons of the Weak: Everyday Forms of Peasant Resistance*. New Haven, CT: Yale University Press.

Skinner, Jonathan. 2015. "Walking the Falls: Dark Tourism and the Significance of Movement on the Political Tour of West Belfast." *Tourist Studies* 1–17. doi: 10.1177/1468797615588427.

Wallace, Joanne. 2014. *Building Peace through the Arts: Re-imaging Communities Programme*. Belfast: Arts Council of Northern Ireland.

Zerubavel, Yael. 1995. *Recovered Roots: Collective Memory and the Making of Israeli National Tradition*. Chicago: University of Chicago Press.

Part VI

Future directions

16 Murals as a tool for action research

Rebecca Yeo

It was so good what we did together. All of us disabled people. We will never forget. We can't ever forget because we have proof, there it is what we did (Disabled asylum seeker speaking after completion of mural as part of research project, cited in Yeo and Bolton 2013).

Introduction

Previous chapters have considered research about murals. This final chapter considers murals as tools for research. The focus is on a lottery-funded project that I coordinated working with disabled people living in a wide variety of different circumstances in the UK (2013) and the project on which it was based, working with disabled people in Bolivia in 2007. In each place, people created murals depicting their key messages in the form of visual imagery. The murals served as a tool for bringing people together, eliciting information, promoting research findings and enabling a power shift, such that those traditionally conceived of as research 'subjects' have control and sense of ownership of the research output. This chapter focuses on the research design, rationale and impact of the work. For details of the research findings, the reader is referred to Yeo and Bolton (2013, 2007), from which the research citations are taken. Due to space limitations, only a small number of images are reproduced in this chapter. For more images, the reader is referred to the publications and the website of the UK project: www.disabilitymurals.org.uk.

The epistemological context of murals as research tools

This work should be seen in the context of the wider field of visual research methods. The use of such methods as theorized means of formal research only recently gained academic status with several publications since the start of the twenty-first century, including work by Sarah Pink (2012), Maggie O'Neill (2010), Patricia Leavy (2009), David Gauntlett (2007), Gillian Rose (2007) and Marcus Banks (2001). Even now, the use of such methods in research is often labelled as 'innovative', as if imagery is something new and radical. Yet, the use of maps, symbols and pictures stems from at least as long ago as cave painting. Images serve to express and communicate ideas in ways distinct from words. As Edward Hopper put it, 'if you could say it in words there would be no reason to paint' (cited by Leavy 2009, 220). Images can also serve to bring up new ideas. As Jung suggested, 'spending time with attention focused on creative activities gives us an opportunity to reach down into the ocean and bring up some significant truths' (cited by Gauntlett 2007, 79). In addition, the frequent inclusion of community art as a requirement of urban development suggests acceptance of art as a tool for building cohesive communities (see for example Lowe 2000; Congdon 2004; Kelly 1984). The core attributes of these functions of visual methods or art-based interventions relate closely to the rationale for the use of murals: providing an accessible means of communication, encouraging new insights and building awareness of individual and collective experience.

On a more theoretical level, the shift in the academic acceptance of visual methods may stem from epistemological developments. Positivist research paradigms, in which academic researchers are positioned as 'experts' in search of 'truth', may not easily equate with the use of imagery. There may be an easier fit with more recent constructivist paradigms in which the 'subjects' of research are positioned as 'active creators and shapers of the research process' (Banks 2001, 45). This is particularly relevant for work with marginalized people. Disabled academics such as Michael Oliver (1992) have argued that traditional research relationships actively reinforce positions of subjugation. The growth of rights-based agendas led to pressure to treat people as research partners rather than 'subjects' of investigation.

The study on which this chapter is based fits broadly within what Reason and Bradbury (2001, xxii) define as a 'family of approaches', including 'action research' with reflexive, participatory or emancipatory ambitions. The broad aim is not just increasing knowledge but also contributing to social change, or as Danieli and Woodhams (2005, 284) put it, bringing 'benefit to oppressed people'. More specifically, this study combines elements of action research and what Maggie O'Neill and Mark Webster describe as 'creative consultation' (2005). Such consultation 'engages with the imagination and prompts individuals and communities to move out of old, rigid ways of doing things and look for new solutions. It is fundamentally about change' (ibid). Before considering more specific rationale of the mural research design, it is necessary to understand the methodology in more depth.

The mural creation process

In the UK-based project, disabled people with specific lived experiences in common (such as asylum seekers, ex-service personnel, parents, people living in residential accommodation) worked together with artist Andrew Bolton to create a mural depicting their key messages. The murals were sited in public spaces in Bristol, London, Norwich and Frome, and Somerset (Figure 16.1).

Figure 16.1 Murals on display at the Houses of Parliament.
Source: Andrew Bolton and Rebecca Yeo.

Key elements of the research process deserve further consideration:

A. Preparation

Mural sites were sought with walls that were both accessible to those creating the murals and where many people would pass on a regular basis. Finding such sites can be difficult and time-consuming; however, the process of asking local people for advice serves an initial communication role, alerting the wider community to the research and furthering interest in the findings for a later stage. At the same time, disabled people with key experiences were found and invited to be involved.

B. Data collection

The images

The data-gathering process began with traditional focus groups and semi-structured interviews. People were then immediately invited to put their key messages into drawings, models or photographic images. As suggested by the citation from Jung above, it was found that the process of 'showing' rather than just 'telling' often results in new insights or clarity.

Some community art projects involve each person being given a separate 'part' of a 'whole' created by a professional artist. In contrast, in this project, people's ideas were combined, conveying the similarities and differences of lived experiences within a greater whole. In this way, the 'whole' becomes greater than the sum of the parts.

The facilitating artist created a design in close consultation with the group. Each mural was intended to encapsulate elements of everybody's images or ideas, while also ensuring a finished product with intellectual and aesthetic coherence. Sometimes, elements of several people's ideas were combined into a new image. If one person's image was felt to be distinct from others, or if it encapsulated others' ideas, then an individual's complete drawing was reproduced. The intention was to discuss and convey the commonalities and differences among people with some level of shared lived experiences.

More traditional semi-structured interviews were also carried out with policy makers and service providers. These were framed around the issues raised by the disabled people working on the murals.

The painting

The painting was done collaboratively with the research artist adapting the process to enable meaningful contributions according to different people's skills and preferences while also ensuring a professional finished product.

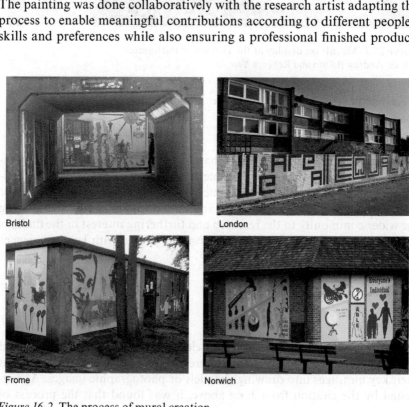

Bristol

London

Frome

Norwich

Figure 16.2 The process of mural creation.
Source: Andrew Bolton and Rebecca Yeo.

One person with a visual impairment painted onto sections of board cut to the shape she needed. Her sections were then attached to the larger mural, making a raised tactile edge. People were able to work on the sections they chose, at the level most accessible to their needs (Figure 16.2).

Communication and advocacy

Opening event

In each location, an official opening event was held. People involved in creating the murals were able to invite those whom they would most like to see the finished artwork and to understand its meaning. Audiences generally included: families, friends, service providers, local representatives as well as the general public. The events were a chance for people who are often labelled as recipients or beneficiaries, to control the agenda. The mural was a tool with which people could present themselves, their contribution to the community and their key messages to an attentive audience.

Exhibitions

The artwork was reproduced onto large screens, creating a portable exhibition to take the messages more directly to relevant people who may not see the murals in their original public setting. Venues included the Houses of Parliament, academic conferences, the TUC disabled workers conference and the Guardian newspaper. The research findings were also promoted through the use of short films, a website and social media. The more detailed findings were published by Leeds disability press: 'Real lives on the wall. Disabled people use public murals to convey the reality of their lives in the UK'. The research report combines text with reproductions of the visual images.

Before considering the impact of this use of murals in more detail, the rationale for these methods should be considered.

Rationale for using this methodology

The methodology is designed to privilege what Patricia Hill Collins terms the unique 'ways of knowing' (1990) associated with lived experience. Those involved in creating the murals had high levels of control of the final product, and thus of the manner in which their identities, perspectives and messages are promoted in a public space. Furthermore, the murals themselves were a physical means for marginalized people to claim a space in their communities.

The emphasis on accessibility serves in part to overcome problems associated with research which labels certain people as 'hard to reach', and which creates outputs exclusively in the form of reports that are neither accessible to, nor endorsed by, the research 'subjects' (O'Neill and Webster 2005). The mural creation process is intended to be accessible to those involved, and the final product is intended to report the key research findings in a publicly accessible manner, encouraging consideration of the existence and needs of the people who created it. The action research character of the methodology is reflected in the fact that communication and advocacy goals are integral to each stage of the process: locating mural sites, painting on the walls, mural opening events, films and exhibitions. The rationale can be further elaborated in terms of the impact on those involved in creating, as well as on those viewing the murals.

Impact of murals

The work can be considered to have two broad and overlapping objectives: (a) developing ideas; and (b) encouraging change.

Developing ideas

This work does not set out to gather 'facts', rather to exchange and develop ideas among all those involved in the research process. Indeed, the information conveyed by visual representation cannot be equated to 'facts' alone. As one person put it, each mural 'represents a lot of emotion and real lives … It's not just looking at it like, oh, there's a picture of someone. … It's the emotion behind it, not just what you can see'. This relates to the earlier citation from Hopper regarding the distinctiveness of imagery.

The development of ideas in this project may not be directly attributable to the mural, rather to the process of prolonged thinking, exchanging ideas and considering means of creative representation. Whatever the cause, ideas did develop quite radically during the creative process. One person first described her message as being about suicide; by the end, her focus was on the need to protect the rights of service users. People's ideas were influenced by each other and by their own internal processes. The creativity and social interaction in the process facilitated the development of ideas in terms of previous experiences, hopes for the future and a more general sense of identity. People learned of the commonalities and differences in each other's lives. An ex-serviceman explained how he had learned from people from different backgrounds and cultures, which had given him 'a feeling of solidarity … [I] feel part of a wider movement, national and international'. For him, the sense of solidarity led to a greater sense of possibility that was reflected in ideas and more practical change.

Individual and collective change

Social research is often related to aspirations for change. In some work, the intended change is expected to result from the research findings, whereas the action-research (Reason and Bradbury 2001) approach of this project has explicit aspirations that the process itself contributes to change. People involved in this work described multiple benefits from this project. One person contrasted their experiences with other research projects in which 'you give all this information but you don't get anything back'. The very tangible nature of the mural is a visible manifestation of what people perceived they were 'getting back'. In addition, there are many wider aspects of change, directly or indirectly attributable to the mural, all of which contribute to the commitment of time and energy necessary to complete the project.

At an individual level, the process of bringing people together to work on a collective goal is intended to encourage a sense of purpose and achievement on its completion. The visible progression of the mural, from a blank wall to an attractive artwork conveying people's messages to those in power, encouraged a sense of possibility. As O'Neill and Webster (2005, 20) put it, 'by engaging with the imagination people see there is another way of doing things and suddenly the impossible becomes possible'. The work had social impact for some of the individuals involved. The sense of isolation common to people living in marginalized positions was reduced by working with and getting to know people in similar situations. A mental health service user described how, 'through the mural I met lovely people ... it's like counselling'. Or, as a disabled asylum seeker explained at the mural opening event, 'I am happy right now ... I'm not feeling alone'. Such peer support is crucial in addressing isolation, but also in exchanging ideas and possible solutions. In addition, and not to be underestimated, is the importance of making the project a relaxed, enjoyable process. This may seem irrelevant to the serious business of academic research, but, according to David Gauntlett (2007), a major factor in the success of visual methods appears to be the extended time for informal reflection. He values the insights arising from casual conversation during periods of collective creativity, which he contrasts with the 'relatively formal contexts of an interview or focus group, where there is a tendency to artificial kind of talk' (2007, 97 building on the findings of Peter Dahlgren 1988). Gauntlett (2007) observes that relaxed interactions help the researcher to 'better understand people's identities and social experiences' (2007, 2). Furthermore, if people are giving up their time for this work, it is important that it feels enjoyable and worthwhile for them.

At a wider societal level, the public locations of the murals enabled those involved to claim a space in their communities through which to assert their existence and needs. It is important that the murals are finished to a professional standard in order that they are generally perceived as a positive contribution to the public space. The aim is for the murals to generate some level of collective ownership in the community. Echoing the contribution of murals to the heritage of a neighbourhood, as discussed in previous chapters, a passer-by explained that she would 'be very proud to show people when they come to town'. This collective pride is symbolic of the collective nature of the messages conveyed. A particular image within a mural may stem from a single person's idea, or may be an amalgamation of several people's ideas. In either case, the point is not whose idea it was, nor how prevalent it is, but that the issue exists within the community. The intention is that in this way, some responsibility for addressing the problems conveyed is taken from the individual to the wider community. As one passer-by explained, the mural 'makes me appreciate and feel sad about the place I live in at the same time. Great that the artwork is there, but terrible that people live like this'. Or as another passer-by put it, 'It has opened me up, made me think'. The mural encourages far greater consideration of the research messages than would be possible from a written report alone. According to an ex-serviceman, it works: 'I walk past that mural maybe four or five times a week. Every time I walk past, there's at least two or three, sometimes more, people stood in front of it, talking about it'. Some people were then motivated to take action. As one person put it, the knowledge that 'there are people being unfairly treated on my doorstep, has driven me to want to go out there and do something'.

Murals created with severely marginalized people, where little information is publicly available, serve a particularly important communication function. The deprivation and segregation described by disabled asylum seekers is rarely acknowledged by the wider population (Yeo 2015). Yet, the mural depicting the lived experiences of disabled asylum seekers stimulated passers-by to remark on unexpected commonalities. As one person put it, 'I didn't realize it was about disabled asylum seekers at first. Actually it's about much more than that. That fence is there for most of us, just to different degrees'. Or as another passer-by expressed, 'I can identify with all the different characters on there'. The work highlights the similarities between the lived experiences of the most marginalized and the wider population. Passers-by are not expected to understand other people's lives through looking at a mural; the intention is to be thought-provoking. One passer-by explained, 'Words cannot express my feelings. It blows your thoughts and feelings away. It will keep me thinking for ages'. The issue of interpretation of images for academic analysis and for advocacy purposes requires further consideration. The impact of the images will not be the same for each person who sees them. What is important is not a single understanding, but the contribution to public discourse. This relates to Michael Krausz's (2002) conception of 'multiplism'. In a similar vein to Fairclough regarding verbal language (1989), Krausz argues that the viewer's interpretation of an image is always influenced by their own experiences and perspectives and is therefore necessarily somewhat different from that of the artist/creator. The only feasible aim of imagery with regard to communication, like with verbal language, is to contribute to a dialogue. If installed in busy locations, murals can make this dialogue public in a manner unlikely to be achieved by a written report alone. The murals serve as an ongoing public reminder of the existence of those who created them, as well as of the messages conveyed. A County Councillor explained the importance for her:

> It is very important that those issues were brought up. I do not automatically think disabled access when I plan an event or consider how something will impact on people with learning difficulties or physical access problems. It does need to keep being brought to our notice.

The public nature of the murals serves as an advertisement for these issues. Through the murals, some of the most marginalized people gained the opportunity to address large numbers of people, including those in positions of power. The exhibition opening event at the Houses of Parliament in London was attended by members of both Houses, including the then Minister for Disabled People, Esther Mcvey MP. As one of the mural creators put it, 'It was one amazing day. I was very proud'. The experience gave people the strength to assert their rights: 'through the mural it has given me confidence and encouragement to know how to fight back'.

The nature of impact is notoriously difficult to measure (see for example Reeves 2002). Change in feelings or ideas is rarely measurable, nor is it the result of a single intervention. One person believed that the mural 'changed so much. It's magical. It's all to do with the mural. [...] Everyone's responding positively. It's had a huge impact. People are realizing that services don't fit. This project was the tipping point'. It is not the mural itself that changed things, but people's reaction to the mural which can be assumed to have been influenced by a number of different factors. The murals are considered to have contributed to a process of change as outlined above.

Limitations

Having outlined some of the many benefits of using murals as a research tool in terms of gathering information and contributing to social change, it is important to also acknowledge their limitations. Perhaps most obviously, visual imagery is not ideally suited to the involvement of people with visual impairments. Verbal or tactile elements can be included in projects, but this does not eliminate access barriers. Nonetheless, participatory modes of working using visual methods may still be more accessible than more traditional academic research in which the 'researched' have less control over the research outputs. A risk of using imagery is that the focus may be influenced by what can be visually conveyed. Marcus Banks (2001) believes that while it is 'relatively straightforward to create or select a visual image that illustrates a material object, it is much more difficult to create or select a visual image that illustrates an abstraction such as "society" or "kinship" or "unemployment"' (2001, 18). The complexity of an issue may be obscured if communication relies on imagery. Banks goes on to describe the 'dissonance between an individual's very real experience of – say – unemployment, and a photograph of the unemployed individual' (2001, 18). Such limitations can, however, also be applied to the more traditional academic reliance on words. The solution may be to combine imagery and words as appropriate to the concepts to be conveyed.

Conclusion

This action research methodology using murals is considered an effective means of research as well as a tool for social change. The value of murals as research tools may not, however, stem from anything intrinsic to the art, but from associated elements such as the facilitation of prolonged, reflective collaborative approach to data gathering; the sense of possibility and pride generated by creating something impressive for public display; and the equalizing of researcher-researched power relations in comparison with many more traditional research approaches. The work has particular value for use with marginalized people. As O'Neill and Webster put it, the process quite literally enables those involved to make their 'experiences visible' (2005). Whether or not the use of murals is appropriate to a study must depend on specific research goals. What is clear is that it would be beneficial to remove the 'innovative' label and bring visual methods, including murals, into the array of options conventionally at a researcher's disposal. Recognition of the value of such methods in research would bring academia in line with what has been commonly accepted in the fields of communication, psychology and community cohesion and has been used since at least the time of cave painting. It could enable research audiences to more easily 'see' what is meant.

References

Banks, Marcus. 2001. *Visual Methods in Social Research*. London: Sage.
Collins, Patricia Hill. 1990. *Black Feminist Thought: Knowledge, Consciousness, and the Politics of Empowerment*. Boston, MA: Unwin Hyman.
Congdon, Kristin G. 2004. *Community Art in Action*. Worcester, MA: Davis Publications.
Dahlgren, Kathleen. 1988. *Naive semantics for natural language understanding*. Dordrecht: Kluwer.
Danieli, Ardha and Carol Woodhams. 2005. "Emancipatory Research Methodology and Disability: A Critique." *International Journal of Social Research Methodology* 8 (4): 281–96.
Fairclough, Norman. 1989. *Language and Power*. Essex: Longman Group UK Ltd.
Gauntlett, David. 2007. *Creative Explorations: New Approaches to Identities and Audiences*. London: Routledge.
Kelly, Owen. 1984. *Community, Art, and the State: Storming the Citadels*. New York: Comedia Publishing Group in Association with Marion Boyars.
Krausz, Michael. 2002. *Is There A Single Right Interpretation?* Philadelphia, PA: Penn State University Press.

Leavy, Patricia. 2009. *Method Meets Art: Arts-Based Research Practice.* New York: The Guilford Press.

Lowe, Seana. 2000. Creating "Community Art for Community Development." *Journal of Contemporary Ethnography* 29: 357–86.

Oliver, Michael. 1992. "Changing the Social Relations of Research Production." *Disability, Handicap and Society* 7: 101–14.

O'Neill, Maggie. 2010. *Asylum, Migration and Community.* Bristol: The Policy Press.

O'Neill, Maggie and Mark Webster. 2005. "Creativity, Community and Change: Creative approaches to Community Consultation." *Rise up and Become...: A Toolkit to Put Learners at the Heart of RISE.* Leicester: NIACE.

O'Neill, Maggie and Phil Hubbard. 2010. "Asylum, Exclusion and the Social Role of Arts and Culture." *Moving Worlds: A Journal of Transcultural Writing. Asylum Accounts,* 12, http://www.movingworlds.net/volumes/12/asylum-accounts/.

Pink, Sarah. 2012. *Advances in Visual Methodology.* London: Sage.

Reason, Peter and Hilary Bradbury. 2001. *Handbook of Action Research.* London: Sage.

Reeves, Michelle. 2002. *Measuring the Economic and Social Impact of the Arts: A Review.* London: The Arts Council of England.

Rose, Gillian 2007. *Visual Methodologies. An Introduction to the Interpretation of Visual Materials.* 2nd ed. London: Sage.

Yeo, Rebecca. 2015. "'Disabled Asylum Seekers?...They Don't Really Exist' The Marginalisation of Disabled Asylum Seekers and Why it Matters." *Journal of Disability and the Global South.* Special edition: Disability, Asylum and Migration 2 (1): 523–550.

Yeo, Rebecca and Andrew Bolton. 2007. *'I Don't Have a Problem, the Problem is Theirs': The Lives and Aspirations of Bolivian Disabled People in Words and Pictures.* Leeds: The Disability Press.

———. 2013. *Real Lives on the Wall. Disabled People Use Public Murals to Convey the Reality of Their Lives in the UK.* Leeds: The Disability Press.

Index